FREE PRESS
PAPERBACKS

MEN

of

IDEAS

A SOCIOLOGIST'S VIEW

LEWIS A. COSER

A Free Press Paperback Classic
Published by Simon & Schuster

FREE PRESS PAPERBACKS
A Division of Simon & Schuster Inc.
1230 Avenue of the Americas
New York, NY 10020

First Free Press Paperbacks Edition 1997

FREE PRESS PAPERBACKS and colophon are trademarks
of Simon & Schuster Inc.

Manufactured in the United States of America

10 9 8 7 6 5 4 3 2 1

Library of Congress Cataloging-in-Publication Data

Coser, Lewis A., 1913–
    Men of ideas / Lewis A. Coser.—1st Free Press Paperbacks ed.
        p.   cm.
    Includes bibliographical references and index.
    1. Intellectuals.   I. Title.
    HM213.C628   1997   97-19975
    305.5'52—dc21   CIP

ISBN 0-684-83328-X

FOR HENRY JACOBY, COMPAGNON DE ROUTE

CONTENTS

Preface to the First Paperback Edition

IN OUR ERA THE PACE OF HISTORICAL CHANGE IS SWIFT indeed. Although this book was published only five years ago, extensive revision would be required to bring its last part, "The Intellectual in Contemporary America," up to date. During these few years there have occurred major events which have changed in significant ways not only the institutional setting in which American intellectuals work, but the character of the intellectual vocation itself.

First and foremost, the disastrous war in Viet-Nam into which the American people have been dragged by their government has led to an unprecedented movement of outrage among the majority of American intellectuals both inside and outside the academy. All previous wars in which America has been involved, though they invariably produced a cry of protest among a minority of dissenters, generally led to a strong affirmation of patriotic sentiment in both the universities and among unattached intellectuals. This is emphatically not the case now. Revulsion and disgust with the war in Viet-Nam is so widespread on the campuses and among intellectuals everywhere with but few exceptions, that it has led to the emergence of a new sense of solidarity among men of ideas. This solidarity was forged in the opposition against a government engaged in a cynical and manipulative effort to hide the true facts from the American people. American intellectuals awakened in consequence to the need of reaffirming one of their primary obligations: to speak truth to power.

The movement of protest against American involvement in Viet-Nam has assumed proportions unprecedented not only in America, in fact in all of modern Western history. It probably surpasses in intellectual consequence both the abolitionist movement and the French Dreyfusard campaign, and it certainly surpasses them in terms of numerical size. It is too early to say whether the alienation between intellectuals and the men of power which the war has brought in its wake will last for a long time, or whether it will subside once this horrible episode is brought to a close. In any case, there can be no doubt that any future sociology of American intellectuals will have to consider the Viet-Nam protests as one of the most profound watersheds in the history of American intellectuals.

Nor is the significance of the Viet-Nam events for American intellectuals exhausted by reference to the movements of protest that these events have evoked. Of almost equal importance, so it would seem to me, is the response of those intellectuals who lent their skills to the men in power in order to attempt to provide legitimation for the war. Whether their activities are judged to be a new instance of Benda's treason of the clerks or whether their case should be considered one in which intellectuals, hoping to manipulate men of power, end up by being manipulated in their turn, depends, at least in part, on one's political views and values. In any case, future historians and sociologists should find it rewarding to analyze the subtle and not so subtle ways in which some independent and autonomous men of ideas were transformed in recent years into pliable instruments of the men of power.

We are in the midst of a process of student revolt against the governance of the university and against the very structure and idea of the modern university which undoubtedly is in large part fueled by the anti-war protest, but has many other sources. Although it has aspects of a generational revolt, there is little sense in interpreting it, as Lewis Feuer and others recently have done, as yet another instance of the Oedipal struggle between tradition-bound fathers and rebellious sons. Generational struggles are as old as the hills and one can hardly explain a series of events clearly located in time and place by reference to perennial psychological themes. No variable can be accounted for by a constant. It will not do to analyze the student revolt simply in terms of the alleged motivations of the young. It will not do to evade the issues the students raise by focusing exclusive attention on the state of their minds rather than on the state of the university.

The *praxis* of student protest has helped to highlight deficiencies in the structure of the university as a seat of learning which have been only partly revealed by earlier critical analyses, some of which can be found in these pages. Inchoate, confused, simplistic and naive as many of the recent student demands have clearly been, they nevertheless have served in important ways to reveal the hidebound traditionalism, the unthinking adherence to routine solutions, the lack of capacity for innovative responses which have characterized many, indeed most, university administrations. To the extent that they have done this, the protesting students, perhaps often without intending it, have clearly led to the emergence of a new sense of self-consciousness, and a willingness to consider reform among many university administrators. In this respect the student protests have done a signal service to the life of the mind in America. By disturbing the peace and complacency that so often characterized academic routine in administration and faculty alike, the student movement has been a prime move on the road to intellectual innovation and renewal.

Yet the student protest has not been limited to proposals for the restructuring of the academy. It has also given rise to significant anti-intellectual tendencies which, if they were to prevail, would result in the destruction of the university as a seat of the intellect. Some of the recent demands for "relevance" voiced among student critics are couched in terms that suggest an extremely simplistic view of the world in which only that which has immediate and practical applications for the political business at hand has a place in the academy. Such a caricature of pragmatism is fundamentally alien to the free life of the mind, and it destroys the very purpose of the university. If the mind is chained to the immediate demands of the practicalities of the hour, it loses that autonomy without which it becomes a simple machine for "doing things." Paradoxically there is much in common between technocrats who have no use for free intellectuals and clamor for the production of ever more mental technicians, and supposedly radical students who cannot understand the needs of disinterested inquiry and clamor for the regimentation and politicizing of the intellect.

Universities have been a haven for intellectuals over the last few centuries to the extent that they allowed them to one degree or another to stand apart from the world of everyday affairs. They protected men of ideas from the insistent pressures of the market place and the political arena. If the boundaries that in the past separated the world of the university from the world at large are broken down, if the university can no longer provide a shield protecting its members, the life of the mind in America will be in mortal peril. A politicized university racked by youthful confrontation politics and adult backlash cannot provide the environment in which the intellect flowers.

These are some of the major issues that have come to the fore on the American intellectual scene since this book was written. There are many others, among them the relations between a new generation of black artists, intellectuals as well as pseudo-intellectuals, and their white counterparts. All of these issues ought to be investigated in depth, and one may confidently expect some serious studies of these topics in the near future. In the meantime, this book may perhaps suggest ways in which such studies may be undertaken. By providing some background detail about the relation of intellectuals to the social world in the past, it may help avoid that foreshortening of historical vision, that parochialism of the contemporary, to which many analysts of the present scene otherwise are likely to fall prey.

Lewis Coser

Stony Brook, N. Y.
Sept. 24, 1969

PREFACE TO THE ORIGINAL EDITION

> The *clerks* are all those whose activity essentially is not the pursuit of practical aims, all those who seek their joy in the practice of an art or a science or a metaphysical speculation, in short in the possession of nonmaterial advantages, and hence in a certain manner say: "My kingdom is not of this world."
>
> *Julien Benda*

> An intellectual person who was not intelligent would be, though not impossible, a rarity; but an intelligent person who is not intellectual we most of us flatter ourselves that we can find in the looking-glass.
>
> *H. W. Fowler*

FEW MODERN TERMS ARE AS IMPRECISE AS THE TERM "intellectual." Its very mention is likely to provoke debate about both meaning and evaluation. To many, it stands for qualities deeply distrusted and despised; to others, it connotes excellence aspired to though not often achieved. To some, intellectuals are impractical dreamers who interfere with the serious business of life; to others, they are the "antennae of the race." The very imprecision of the term, as well as the evaluative disagreements surrounding it, makes it mandatory to define the sense in which it will be used in this book. Here, as elsewhere, definitions, far from being neutral, have consequences.

Certain writers have tended to group under the term "intellectuals" everyone with a university education or all those, to quote Seymour M. Lipset, "who create, distribute, and apply *culture*, that is, the symbolic world of man, including art, science, and religion."[1] Such a wide definition, though it may have a number of practical advantages, will not be used here, as it obscures the distinctive characteristics of a numerically small yet qualitatively important category of symbol manipulators whose attributes are not to be found among the large number of persons engaged in the arts, the sciences, and religion.

Not all academic men are intellectuals, nor are all members of the professions; this fact is deplored by some and applauded by others. Intellect, as distinguished from the intelligence required in the arts and sciences, presumes a capacity for detachment from immediate experience, a moving beyond the pragmatic tasks of the moment, a commitment to comprehensive values transcending professional or occupational involvement. "Intellect," writes Richard Hofstadter, "is the critical, creative, and contemplative side of mind. Whereas intelligence seeks to grasp, manipulate, re-order, adjust, intellect examines, ponders, wonders, theorizes, criticizes, imagines."[2] Max Weber's famous distinction between men who live off politics and men who live for politics may serve us here. Intellectuals live for rather than off ideas.

While most men, in the professions as elsewhere, tend to be absorbed in the pursuit of concrete answers to concrete problems, intellectuals feel the need to go beyond the immediate concrete task and to penetrate a more general realm of meanings and values. They exhibit, to quote Edward Shils, "an unusual sensitivity to the sacred, an uncommon reflectiveness about the nature of their universe, and the rules which govern their society."[3]

Intellectuals exhibit in their activities a pronounced concern with the core values of society. They are the men who seek to provide moral standards and to maintain meaningful general symbols, who "elicit, guide, and form the expressive dispositions within a society."[4] In the tasks they perform, modern intellectuals are descendants of the priestly upholders of sacred tradition, but they are also and at the same time descendants of the biblical prophets, of those inspired madmen who preached in the wilderness far removed from the institutionalized pieties of court and synagogue, castigating the men of power for the wickedness of their ways. Intellectuals are men who never seem satisfied with things as they are, with appeals to custom and usage. They question the truth of the moment in terms of higher and wider truth; they counter appeals to factuality by invoking the "impractical ought." They consider themselves special custodians of abstract ideas like reason and justice and truth, jealous guardians of moral standards that are too often ignored in the market place and the houses of power.

Among the intellectuals' ancestors we may also reckon the

medieval court jester. The role of the jester, as Ralf Dahrendorf has argued,[5] was to play none of the expected roles. He had the extraordinary privilege of dispensing with adherence to the usual proprieties because he was outside the social hierarchy and was therefore also deprived of the privileges enjoyed by those within. His power was based on his freedom from the demeanor ordinarily required within the social hierarchy. He was among the lowly at the same time that he was permitted to criticize and even to ridicule the mighty. He might enunciate the most inconvenient truths without fear of reprisal; he might question what everybody accepted as fact provided that he did so under the guise of amusement —thereby denying or minimizing the seriousness of his attack. Yet, while he amused, he also upset the men of power. Although tolerated and even rewarded, he always faced an ambivalent reaction from those who were committed to serious business, for his wit and playfulness barely masked his critical thrust.

The modern intellectual is akin to the jester not only because he claims for himself the freedom of unfettered criticism but also because he exhibits what, for want of a better word, we may call "playfulness."[6] While earnest practitioners tend to focus on the tasks at hand, the intellectual delights in the play of the mind and relishes it for its own sake. Play, Johan Huizinga[7] suggested, is superfluous, it is disinterested, it is free. Not being "ordinary" life, it stands outside the routine satisfaction of immediate wants and appetites; it is not a means to an end but is satisfying in itself. The intellectual tends to shun those mental activities, so dear to the technician, that require the rigorous pursuit of prescribed means for the attainment of specified ends. He delights instead in the pleasures of sheer intellectual activity. Just as with the artist, the beauty of a set of formulas or a pattern of words may, for the intellectual, outweigh its practical application or immediate usefulness. Ideas, to him, have far more than mere instrumental value: they have terminal value. Intellectuals may not be more curious than other men, but theirs is what Veblen has aptly called *idle* curiosity.

Veblen did not equate "idle" with "unimportant" or "inconsequential" or suggest that intellectuals are mere playful gadflies. On the contrary, he would have agreed that they are usually committed men for whom the clash of ideas has overriding importance. Their very playfulness and lack of concern with the immediate business at hand is but another facet of their deep commitment to a comprehensive set of values. Intellectuals take ideas more seriously than do most other men, and this seriousness permits them to articulate interests and desires that may be only dimly sensed by nonintellectuals. They transform, in Karl Mannheim's phrase, conflicts of interests into conflicts of ideas,[8] and they increase a society's self-knowledge by making manifest its latent sources of discomfort and discontent.

Intellectuals are gatekeepers of ideas and fountainheads of ideologies, but, unlike medieval churchmen or modern political propagandists and zealots, they tend at the same time to cultivate a critical attitude; they tend to scrutinize the received ideas and assumptions of their times and *milieu*. They are those who "think otherwise," the disturbers of intellectual peace.

No doubt, individual intellectuals, as I shall show in this book, exhibit in varying degrees the characteristics sketched. Some may be more given to playfulness, others to earnest prophecy. My aim here is to describe typical concerns and orientations rather than individual blends. I am also aware that I may be charged with a tendency to idealize the collective portrait I have drawn. I can only assure the reader that, in describing and analyzing concrete cases in the body of this book, I have tried to depict the actors as faithfully as I can, warts and all.

Intellectuals, then, are not only puzzling but upsetting to the run of ordinary citizens. Yet, without them, modern culture is hardly conceivable. Were mental technicians and experts, their distant cousins, to pre-empt the field that intellectuals now occupy, modern culture would likely perish through ossification.[9] Without intellectuals to challenge the established routines and the traditions of the eternal yesterday—even while they maintain standards and articulate new demands—our culture would soon be a dead culture.

Men with intellectual dispositions have, no doubt, existed in all societies. Paul Radin has reminded us that even nonliterate cultures, from time immemorial, "contained individuals who were constrained by their individual temperaments and interests to occupy themselves with the basic problems of what we customarily term philosophy."[10] Yet I would contend that only the modern world has provided the institutional conditions for the emergence of a self-conscious group of intellectuals. More particularly and granting that the sophists and their descendants in the ancient world can be called distant ancestors of modern intellectals, I hold that intellectuals as a self-conscious congeries of men arose only in the seventeenth century. They are a modern phenomenon, and they came into their own with the beginning of modern history. What J. B. Bury wrote about the inception of modern history applies equally well to the emergence of modern intellectuals: "If we are to draw any useful lines of demarcation in the continuous flux of history we must neglect anticipations and announcements, and we need not scruple to say that, in the realm of knowledge and thought, modern history begins in the seventeenth century."[11]

It was only after the rigid edifice of medieval society broke down; after nominalism, the Reformation, and the Renaissance had fragmented the unified world view of the Church; after religious groups, secular powers, and political systems began to compete for the allegiance of individuals no longer tied to their traditional moorings; after new classes began to make their entry on a social scene previously dominated by upholders of feudal tradition that men of ideas began to find conditions favorable to the emergence of a self-conscious stratum of intellectuals with a peculiar ethos and sense of calling. No longer were men of letters reduced to expounding the one true doctrine or perishing as heretics. With the emerging multiplicity of power centers and reference groups, with the thawing of a frozen culture, there arose conflicts of ideas and hence the possibility of freedom, even though that freedom could at first be exercised only in the interstices of society. To be sure, from the Renaissance to the eighteenth century, intellectuals, lacking an independent public that they could address and that might support their efforts, were too often forced to attach themselves to powerful patrons as experts or scribes—just as today scribes serve illiterate Moslem merchants in transacting their business in the bazaars. But even so, the very multiplicity of competing patrons enabled the man of letters to choose among them. Wherever there exists the possibility of choice, there also exists a degree of freedom. But self-conscious intellectual groupings could blossom only with the decline of patronage and the emergence of a wider public for intellectual productions in the seventeenth and eighteenth centuries. It is to developments since that period that this book is limited.

One word about procedure: Fairly early in the planning of this work, I realized that it would require an unusually large measure of deliberate limitation. It became obvious that a comprehensive sociology of intellectuals would require a lifetime to write and would fill many volumes. As such was not my desire or intention I had to limit the subject matter severely. Only a very few of the multitude of intellectual currents that have agitated the modern world can be considered here. Temptations to treat many specific intellectual groupings—romanticism, for example, or Marxism had to be resisted. Similarly, it soon became apparent that, if the roles and careers of particular individuals were to be considered, the book would assume unmanageable proportions. Instead then of pursuing the chimera of comprehensiveness, this book limits itself to the discussion of certain general societal conditions and institutional settings that have favored or hampered the emergence and development of groups of self-conscious intellectuals in the Western world. Rather than discussing individual careers, it concentrates attention, except in a very few special cases, on groups of intellectuals. Even then, I have been selective rather than exhaustive. I shall discuss the Saint-Simonians but not the Fourierists, the Fabians but not the Owenites, the Jacobins but not the Girondins. My concern throughout is with certain groups of intellectuals who may be said to approximate "pure" sociological types, rather than with the many historical varieties of intellectual groupings and orientations. This book is to be read as an effort in historical sociology, not in historiography. The sociologist can never hope to rival the historian, who can invoke the rich texture and diversity of historical experience. He can only hope that, through the construction of certain generalized types, he will be able fruitfully to compare trends that transcend the domain of historical specificity. Such comparison is what, in a modest way, I have attempted in the pages that follow.

NOTES

1. Seymour M. Lipset, *Political Man* (New York: Doubleday & Company, Inc., 1960), p. 311.

2. Richard Hofstadter, *Anti-intellectualism in American Life* (New York: Alfred A. Knopf, Inc., 1963), p. 25. I have learned a great deal from this seminal book.

3. Edward Shils, "The Intellectuals and the Powers," *Comparative Studies in Society and History*, I (October, 1958), 5.

4. *Ibid.*, p. 6.

5. Ralf Dahrendorf, "Der Intellektuelle und die Gesellschaft," *Zeit*, 13 (March 29, 1963).

6. *Cf.* Hofstadter, *op. cit.*, especially pp. 30ff.

7. Johan Huizinga, *Homo Ludens* (Boston: Beacon Press, 1955), pp. 8–9.

8. Karl Mannheim, *Ideology and Utopia* (New York: Harcourt, Brace & World, Inc., 1936), p. 142.

9. See H. Stuart Hughes, "Is the Intellectual Obsolete?" *Commentary* (October, 1956).

10. Paul Radin, *Primitive Man as Philosopher* (New York: Dover Publications, Inc., 1957), p. xxi.

11. J. B. Bury, *The Idea of Progress* (New York: Dover Publications, Inc., 1955), p. 64.

Acknowledgments

This book would not, and could not, have been written without the active and almost daily participation of my wife, Rose Laub Coser, of Harvard Medical School and Northeastern University. I like to think of it as a joint production. My friends Irving Howe of Hunter College and Henry Jacoby of the Food and Agricultural Organization (Geneva, Switzerland) read earlier versions and made a number of exceedingly helpful comments. Mrs. Pauline Deacon of Brandeis University typed various drafts with her usual meticulous care. The administration of Brandeis University kindly provided financial help for typing expenses.

Shorter versions of several subchapters have appeared in *Arguments* (Paris), *Dissent* (New York), and *New Society* (London); they are reprinted here with the permission of the editors of those journals. A different version of Chapter 15 has previously appeared in *The Intellectuals*, edited by George B. de Huszar and published by The Free Press in 1960. Portions of Chapters 14 and 16 were presented to the American Sociological Society's annual meeting at Montreal in September, 1964.

I wish to express my gratitude for permission to quote from *Poems* by W. H. Auden, copyright 1934 (renewed 1961) by W. H. Auden, and from *Collected Poems* by Stephen Spender, copyright 1955 by Stephen Spender, both reprinted by permission of Random House, Inc., and Faber and Faber Ltd; from *Reflections of a Physicist* by Percy W. Bridgman, published by Philosophical Library, Inc.; from *Science and Common Sense* by James B. Conant, published by Yale University Press; from *An American Testament* by Joseph Freeman, published by Holt, Rinehart and Winston, Inc.; from *A Time to Dance and Other Poems* by C. Day Lewis, published by Jonathan Cape Limited; from "Mass Society and Its Culture" by Edward Shils, which originally appeared in the Spring, 1960, issue of *Daedalus*, Journal of the American Academy of Arts and Sciences, and which was subsequently included in *Culture for the Millions?*, edited by Norman Jacobs and published in 1961 by D. Van Nostrand Company, Inc.; and from the English translation of Adam Wazyk's "A Poem for Adults" published in the Spring, 1962, issue of *Dissent*. I wish also to thank Floyd Dell for permission to quote from his book *Love in Greenwich Village*.

L. A. C.

MEN of IDEAS

Part One

Settings for Intellectual Life

Chapter 1

INTRODUCTION

JUST AS ANIMAL SPECIES GROW ONLY IN ENVIRONMENTS conducive to their growth, so human types develop only if they encounter favorable institutional settings. There is no reason to believe that earlier centuries produced fewer persons capable of playing intellectual roles than have the last three, yet only in these last three centuries have intellectuals achieved a noticeable importance in culture. Actors or potential actors were available earlier, but the setting was missing, and only when actors and settings are present together can the play be enacted.

Two conditions seem essential for the intellectual vocation to become socially feasible and socially recognized. First, intellectuals need an audience, a circle of people to whom they can address themselves and who can bestow recognition. Such an audience will also, as a rule, provide economic rewards, but the prestige or esteem accorded to the intellectual by his public, his psychic income, may often be more important to him than the economic return.[1] Second, intellectuals require regular contact with their fellow intellectuals, for only through such communication can they evolve common standards of method and excellence, common norms to guide their conduct. Despite popular myth to the contrary, most intellectuals cannot produce their work in solitude but need the give and take of debate and discussion with their peers in order to develop their

ideas. Not all intellectuals are gregarious, but most of them need
to test their own ideas in exchange with those they deem their
equals.

The intellectuals' need for regular intercourse with their audience and for sustained commerce with their peers began to be met
in the seventeenth and eighteenth centuries, with the growth of peculiar institutions to meet that need.

In the following pages, I shall discuss in some detail eight institutional settings for intellectual activities: the salon and the coffeehouse; the scientific society and the monthly or quarterly review;
the literary market and the world of publishing; the political sect;
and, finally, Bohemia and the little magazine. No doubt, many
others could have been selected, and my choice is necessarily somewhat arbitrary. Yet I argue that these eight institutions share one
characteristic: Although used in varying degrees by different types
of intellectual, all have served as major incubators for the growth
of the intellectual vocation in the Western world. Finally, one other
institution, censorship, will be discussed as a prime example of negative institutional effects on the life of the intellect.

The salon, free from the rigid restrictions of courtly society,
afforded the previously insulated and isolated man of letters an
occasion to meet fellow writers and artists, as well as cultivated
admirers; the coffeehouse, that most democratic institution, allowed
the writer to meet the various layers of his public and of his fellows
on a footing of social equality. And both salon and coffeehouse
allowed men of letters to exchange ideas in an atmosphere free of
formal constraints. The coffeehouse in the age of Johnson and Boswell or the salon in the age of D'Alembert and Diderot became free
market places of ideas in which the norms of *laissez-faire* and
laissez-passer prevailed even before they could be applied to the
economic order.

Science as an ongoing social and moral enterprise can function
only if scientists receive rewards or incentives that sustain them in
their work. Darwin once phrased it well, "My love of natural science . . . has been much aided by the ambition to be esteemed by
my fellow naturalists." Or as Robert K. Merton has put it, "Recognition for originality becomes socially validated testimony that one
has successfully lived up to the most exacting requirements of one's
role as a scientist."[2] Hence the crucial importance of social institutions that help to organize the scientific enterprise and to ensure
that the scientist can present his findings to his public and receive

appropriate rewards. Such institutions are especially
cause the scientist is trained to be skeptical of his o~
of those of others as well. He must look to his peer
tion and does not allow himself to enjoy fully the i
tions of his work until other scientists have indic
of his findings.[3]

We are accustomed today to view the social system of science
as operating in relative isolation from the world of laymen, but it
was not always so. In particular, at the inception of the Scientific
Revolution in the seventeenth century, no clear-cut scientific roles
had yet been differentiated in society. Hardly one-third of the members of the Royal Society at the time it was chartered devoted
themselves mainly to science; the rest were interested amateurs. It
was an assembly of genuinely curious minds, fascinated by the new
experimental procedures but also by problems of practical utility.
It is a safe guess, indeed, that many if not most were less interested
in recondite speculation than in discovering a satisfactory way to
measure longitude. Be that as it may, the Royal Society, like similar
institutions in other countries, permitted British scientists for the
first time to assemble in a community of scholars, a community
moreover that was closely tied to a wider audience of interested
laymen ready to bestow recognition and to reward excellence. The
Royal Society helped to institutionalize and to legitimize the scientific enterprise and to impart to the scientific role a dignity and
status it had not previously possessed. The very structure of the
scientific societies in those early years helped to ensure that the
scientists of the period, far from being narrow specialists, would
be in fact wide-ranging intellectuals interested in all the major currents of ideas, from physics to theology, that stirred the times.

The salon, the coffeehouse, the Royal Society—whatever their
differences as institutions—made face-to-face contact possible between intellectuals and their peers and audiences. But such direct
contact is not always necessary. Communication through the printed
pages of a magazine or a review may well replace direct intercourse and fulfill essentially similar functions—especially in an age
in which the audience for serious intellectual productions has become too large for direct contact with more than a small fraction.
The great English reviews of the nineteenth century and the intellectuals associated with them made a deliberate effort to shape the
taste of the new middle-class audience, which eagerly turned to
them in search of standards for behavior and opinion, of guidance,

nd of enlightenment. In such independent reviews, groups of like-minded writers became focal points of intellectual controversy and moral debate. In the pages of these reviews, the great intellectual causes of nineteenth-century England, from philosophical radicalism to Darwinism, from electoral reform to the corn laws were debated, clarified, and popularized. We may doubt that Lord Keynes's dictum, "The ideas of economists and political philosophers, both when they are right and when they are wrong, are more powerful than is commonly understood. Indeed, the world is ruled by little else," truly applies to all periods of modern history, but it comes near to being true of Victorian England. Economists and political philosophers, although not they alone, found in the great English and Scottish reviews a major medium for the dissemination of their messages and their critical thoughts. In this sense, by linking writer and audience and ensuring their reciprocal influence, these reviews had effects similar to those of institutions that promoted direct contact in earlier and less complex social structures.

Perhaps even more important than these institutional settings, for the rise of independent intellectuals, was the emergence of a wide market for books in the eighteenth century and the concomitant emergence of bookseller and publisher as intermediaries between the author and the growing reading public. It was only in the eighteenth century that writing became a profession and that the writer was enabled to end his dependence upon a noble patron to become an autonomous man of letters. The rise of the middle class, the increasing literacy of that class, the rising status of the middle-class woman—all these factors encouraged a widening market for books. This market in turn made it possible, for the first time, for men of letters to live from the sales of their works. Booksellers and publishers began to assume key roles as intermediaries between public and author, and they often exploited their position in order to dominate the writer, even while they served him in his drive to conquer a share of the market. This ambivalence between publisher and author, which still continues to mark their relations, first emerged in the eighteenth century. Similarly, the pressures upon the writer to lower his standards in order to increase his sales also date from this period. Once the literary product becomes a commodity, it is subject to commercial considerations, and this situation creates a great deal of tension as well as temptation for the writer. The market makes him independent of the patron, but it threatens to enslave him to its own laws. The relations of the writer to the reading public and to the literary market, as well as his relations to the publisher, have assumed major importance for intellectuals ever since the eighteenth century.

Although the institutions discussed so far all had, in one way or another, some positive functions for intellectuals, it is naturally a mistake to believe that modern society always facilitates the intellectual's vocation. The discussion of political and moral censorship included here is meant to illustrate the ways in which particular social institutions are at times highly dysfunctional for the activities of intellectuals. Political as well as moral censorship is largely responsible for the alienation of intellectuals from their society, for the sense that they are so confined by the powers that be that only an alliance with others similarly afflicted may bring them the freedom from outside interference for which they crave. Censorship, perhaps more than any other single factor, has been responsible for the typical alliance of so many intellectuals with the forces of liberalism and radicalism.

Institutional settings are important not only as mediators of contact, direct or indirect, between intellectuals and their public, but they may also serve as means for certain types of intellectual to protect themselves and their friends from unwanted interference. In other words, such institutional settings may erect boundaries between groups of intellectuals and the world of laymen; they allow separation and differentiation and provide a shield from observation. The political sect, Bohemia, and the little magazine served such functions in times when the world of intellectuals had become much more differentiated than it had been in the eighteenth century.

It is sometimes assumed that those alienated from a particular society and its dominant values and concerns necessarily become isolated deviants and rebels pitting their vulnerable selves against oppressive society. This assumption is, of course, very far from the truth. To be sure, there are many cases of lonely rebellion, but, in general, rebellion like misery craves company. The rebellious tend to gather for mutual support and reinforcement, and the companionship of like-minded rebels sustains the alienated intellectual in his struggle. Hence the importance of radical political sects for the moral and emotional sustenance of intellectual deviants from the major assumptions of their times. The Saint-Simonians, whom I shall discuss in Chapter 9, were by no means the only such sect, although they were certainly the most colorful. Political sects often present rather bizarre features, but that should hardly be a surprise. The pain of separation and alienation from the surrounding society, the sense of loneliness, even when assuaged by companions, may often be so intense that it leads to styles of life and thought that appear more than a little insane to the settled denizens of the world. Yet the close involvement among members of such sects, the heightened sense of mission, the exalting sense of esoteric doctrine to remedy the ills of the world may also at times powerfully stimulate the creative imagination.

The technocratic elites that have today assumed such preponderance in political decision-making in large parts of the globe are, whether they know it or not, the descendants of the Children of Saint-Simon. And the two most powerful intellectual currents of the modern world, Marxism and psychoanalysis, were nursed within the confines of intellectual sects that, though not so pronouncedly esoteric and bizarre as the Saint-Simonian brotherhood, were equally intense in their intellectual commitments and even more productive of seminal ideas.

Although sectarian intellectuals usually exhibit a large measure of piety, Bohemian intellectuals tend to be endowed with more than usual degrees of playfulness. They tend to express their estrangement from genteel society with laughing contempt. Bohemians, like radicals, can hardly sustain their alienation without the support of likeminded fellows. Laughter also craves company, and Bohemia, the antithesis of respectable society, turns all convention upside down, and evolves its counterculture, its countersymbols, and its norms within a community of the uprooted. Flaubert called it "the fatherland of my breed." It certainly provided a congenial setting for some of the most creative men of the nineteenth and early twentieth centuries. It brought artists and writers together in their struggles with the *bourgeois* world, and its gradual disappearance may have contributed much to what Irving Howe diagnoses as "those feelings of loneliness one finds among so many American intellectuals, feelings of damp dispirited isolation which undercut the ideology of liberal optimism."[4] The death of Bohemia did not mean the death of critical and rebellious thought, as some who cling to the remnants of Bohemian life styles seem to believe. Rebellious intellectuals are likely to find other types of community in which to fortify themselves against the hostile world of the "squares"; it remains true that, while Bohemia lasted, it made a significant contribution to the literature, the criticism, and the speculative thought of the nineteenth and twentieth centuries.

Whereas the great English reviews of the last century in the main engaged in dialogue with a respectable and affluent audience of middle-class readers, there was another very different type of publication, addressed to a very much less respectable audience, that performed equally important functions on the cultural scene: the little magazine. It did not pretend to reach an inclusive public but attempted, on the contrary, to limit its appeal to an exclusive and highly differentiated audience. Its readership was found mainly in Bohemia, on its fringes, or among those part-time Bohemians who indulged in anti*bourgeois* antics between weekly employment in quite *bourgeois* enterprises. The little magazine, as its name implies, never achieved mass circulation; in fact, its editors would have been appalled at the very idea of becoming commercially successful. They self-consciously spoke for and to the intellectual and artistic *avant garde*. Their only tradition was, to use Harold Rosenberg's apt phrase, "the tradition of the new." They were the spearheads of modernity, of that vast renaissance in arts and letters that transformed the American, and to some extent the European, cultural scene within the comparatively short span of a few decades. A Rip Van Winkle who returned to the American literary scene in 1890, after a twenty years' absence, would have noted many changes, to be sure, but he would easily have recognized the main lineaments of the scene he had left. Had he returned in 1925 after an absence of the same length, however, he would have been utterly bewildered. The age of modernity ushered in by the excited and exciting programs, pronouncements, and appeals of 100 or so little magazines had, in the meantime, completely transformed the cultural scene and ripped up most of the familiar landmarks.

The little magazines and the relatively small coteries and cliques of innovating artists and writers associated with them served as spearheads of this revolutionary attack on the received ideas of the age. Though often splintered into rival sects and contending factions, their editors and writers were united in common opposition to genteel culture. And without this plethora of variegated, ephemeral, unorthodox, and uninhibited little magazines, the various strands of opposition would probably not have been able to articulate clearly their critical standards. We should remember this point

even as we witness how the victory has gone sour as the rebels of
yesterday have been assimilated into the cultural establishment of
today.

NOTES

1. Cf. Florian Znaniecki, *The Social Role of the Man of Knowledge*
(New York: Columbia University Press, 1940). Edward Shils's study of
Indian intellectuals, *The Intellectual Between Tradition and Modernity:
The Indian Situation* (The Hague: Mouton & Co., N. V., 1961), can be
read as an instructive case study of a situation in which the institutional
setting for intellectuals is not yet present.

2. Robert K. Merton, "Priorities in Scientific Discovery," *American
Sociological Review*, XXII (December, 1957), 640.

3. Norman W. Storer, "Science and the Creative Professions" (paper
read before the Eastern Sociological Society, 1962).

4. Irving Howe, "The Age of Conformity," *Partisan Review*, XXI
(January-February, 1954), 7-33.

Chapter 2

THE FRENCH
ROCOCO SALON

In the intimacy of the rococo salon and under
the stimulating guidance of brilliant women, there developed in
eighteenth-century France that common meeting ground for men
of letters and dilettantes that became, through criticism, support,
and encouragement, a major nursery of the "philosophical spirit."
Free from the restrictions of class precedence, preciosity, and
courtly manners, it served as an arbiter of taste and as a channel
for achieving recognition.

The salon has been called a "woman's kingdom." Women had
played central roles in the courts of the Italian Renaissance, the
immediate predecessors of the French salons, and had, of course,
been pivots of the French literary salons of the seventeenth century.
The famous Marquise de Rambouillet, whom we always envision
seated on her couch in the Blue Room of the Hôtel de Rambouillet
amid a select few literary personages, had been a kind of universal
judge of classical good taste.

In the seventeenth century, the French salon, like its Italian
model, was dominated by ladies of the high aristocracy. If com-
moners were admitted, it was on special sufferance. The salon was
at that time less formal in its style than official court society, but it
still exemplified an aristocratic way of life. By contrast, in the next
century, especially the latter half, the salon had lost its aristocratic

tone. It had become more informal, and it had opened its doors widely to all who had *esprit*. It slowly became dominated by women from the rising middle classes.

It was only in the eighteenth century that women who were not of the nobility really came into their own as key figures in literary and intellectual life. With rising standards of living, increased amenities, and lighter household burdens, women of the upper middle classes could begin to cultivate literary interests. Addison remarked about early eighteenth-century England: "There are some reasons why learning is more adapted to the female world than to the male. As in the first place, because they have more spare time on their hands, and lead a more sedentary life . . . There is another reason why those especially who are women of quality, should apply themselves to letters, namely because their husbands are generally strangers to them."[1]

In the first half of the century, the key French salons were still those run by the Marquise de Lambert and other members of the high aristocracy—though some were marginal members at that. Typical of this transitional period was Mme. de Tencin, an upstart lady of easy virtue from the provinces who, after successful intrigue and having made a large fortune, settled down to become one of the leading ladies of Parisian salon society, conferring upon herself the title of marquise. In the succeeding period, only the Marquise du Deffand still represented the aristocracy. Mlle. de Lespinasse, an illegitimate child who had come to Paris from the provinces as a companion to Mme. du Deffand; Mme. Geoffrin, the daughter of one of the Dauphin's grooms of the wardrobe, a glorified *valet de chambre*; and Mme. Necker, the *bourgeoise* daughter of a Swiss parson and the wife of a banker, were quite different social types from the women who had previously been the chief arbiters of salon society. They differed as much from the aristocratic ladies of the seventeenth-century salon as from the ordinary stolid, matronly housewives of the third estate. These brilliant hostesses fashioned the salon in their own image.

As for husbands, things may not have been quite so grim in France as Addison made them appear in England, but it remains that husbands—if husbands there were—played only minor supporting roles in most of the brilliant salons of the France of the *philosophes*. For example, Mme. Geoffrin, whose literary salon was, to quote Sainte-Beuve, "one of the institutions of the eight-

eenth century" had married, at the age of fourteen, a quite successful manufacturer of mirrors much older than herself and of rather
limited intelligence. When she opened her salon, he took care of all
the domestic details, assisted at all her receptions, but never took
part in the conversations. When, years later, a foreign visitor asked
the hostess what had become of the kind old man who had always
been seen, though not heard, at her receptions, she replied, "That
was my husband, monsieur, and he is dead."[2]

The Geoffrin case was extreme, but it is clear that the typical
French rococo literary salon always revolved around a brilliant
woman. In this respect, it derived from the Italian court with its
lady worship and its coterie of admiring courtiers. But the rococo
salon no longer catered to the nobility, and it no longer served the
same functions as its predecessors had. As Chauncey Tinker has
written, "Wit, intellect, and personality, rather than noble birth,
became the key to social success."[3] Early in the century, noble
women had become the key arbiters of taste; later, toward the middle of the century, *bourgeoise* women assumed such functions. The
salon thus became an equalizer of rank after having first served as
a kind of filter for sifting out those refined enough to be worthy of
the company of noble men and women of the world.

The salon was one of the great levelers in the age of *bourgeois*
ascendance. The men of letters were received on an equal plane
with the men of the world. No longer supernumeraries, whose
presence was reluctantly tolerated because they contributed amusement, they were allowed at the very center of the stage. "The only
great lords," wrote D'Alembert with pride, "whose intercourse the
men of letters ought to desire are those whom he can treat and
regard in all certainty as his equals and friends."[4] The aura of respect for men of noble birth that still prevailed in the first half of
the century had disappeared in the salons of Mlle. de Lespinasse,
Mme. Geoffrin, and Mme. Necker. There enlightened men of the
third estate and illustrious middle-class men of letters from abroad
—Walpole and Hume, Gibbon, Sterne, and Priestley—dominated the
proceedings.

The eighteenth-century salon was not merely a social gathering,
a scene of erotic banter, an exchange for literary and political
gossip, a center of intrigue—though it was all these things too. It
aimed at exerting a creative influence in the world of letters. It was
not mainly concerned with the finished literary product but at-

tempted rather to mold the world of letters as well as public opinion and to assist at the birth of new ideas. It was an informal academy for stimulating ideas by stimulating their authors.

The salon submitted new thought to the test of an informal literary jury consisting of older established men of letters and of their educated audience. It helped to introduce new literary talent, to vouch for authors, to establish reputations. In an age in which the fixed standards of classicism had fallen by the wayside, it aimed at establishing new standards by which authors could be judged. Much like a literary review, it attempted to sift the chaff from the wheat, bestowing recognition here and withdrawing it there, certifying the genuineness of intellectual products.

In an age in which the patronage of the court and of the high aristocracy was on the wane, the salon filled a gap: The great hostesses offered material aid to the faithful, fed them, even lodged them if need be (Marmontel stayed for years at Mme. Geoffrin's home, Morellet at Mme. Helvétius's), advertised new works, paid printers' bills (Mme. Geoffrin subscribed 200,000 livres to the *Encyclopédie*), and lauded the merits of their protégés to prospective patrons, publishers, and men of the theater. They procured pensions for them or managed to get them appointed to offices or to the French Academy. Mme. de Tencin obtained a chair in the Academy for Marivaux; Montesquieu's election was due to the efforts of Madame de Lambert; Marmontel owed his election to the assiduous campaigns of Mme. Geoffrin; and D'Alembert was indebted for his secretaryship of the Academy to Mme. du Deffand. The campaigns to ensure that the *philosophes* attained dominance in the Academy were hatched in the salons of Mme. Geoffrin and Mlle. de Lespinasse. Mme. Geoffrin created three "Immortals" in a single year.

But the salon's influence was not limited to the external aspects of literary life. It also helped to shape the literary style of the eighteenth century. Wrote Marmontel, "Those who desire to write with precision, energy and vigor may be content to associate with men only; but those who wish their style to be flexible and supple, to express affability and charm, will do well, I believe, to live with women."[5] And Diderot added, "Women accustom us to discuss with charm and clarity the driest and thorniest subject. We talk to them unceasingly; we wish them to listen; we are afraid of tiring or boring them; thence we develop a particular method of explaining ourselves easily, and this passes from conversation into style."[6]

The wit and grace of rococo style, its journalistic verve and epigrammatic vigor, but also its occasional shallowness and striving for easy effect—and its unceasing effort to be so clear as to be understood by an audience of educated dilettantes—all these qualities are intimately connected with the social *milieu* in which this literature was born. The salons were veritable incubators for the *esprit* that characterizes rococo literature—and that was so highly regarded by the great ladies who reigned in them. There authors could clarify their ideas by filtering them through the minds of peers and admirers; there they found occasions to test their worth in the liveliness of conversation and in continual exchange with significant others. The literature that emerged was eminently a literature of sociability, a literature of playfulness, liveliness, and sparkle—but also a literature that too often eschewed exploration of the deeply personal and the philosophically profound. Georg Simmel has remarked that it is considered tactless to display intimate traits, character, and mood in society because such display militates against that formal and playful *inter*action that is the very essence of sociability.[7] His remark helps us to understand why the style of most French eighteenth-century writers keeps close to the surface.

Authors had enjoyed the society of their fellows in taverns and taprooms in an earlier age, but the exclusively male fraternity of such gatherings had hardly been conducive to the development of the grace and refinement that characterize so much of rococo literature. Such qualities were better cultivated in the drawing room and in the presence of those cultivated ladies who were the new patrons, as well as the new critics, of the Age of Enlightenment.

"The salon," Tinker has written, "mediated between the author and the public. It aimed, like a true critic, to correct both the conceit of the author and the indifference of the world."[8] In an age in which a high proportion of the market for books could be found among the feminine reading public, the salon mediated in particular between the world of the feminine reader and the male writer. It allowed the intelligent woman to participate, even if only vicariously, in the trials and tribulations, the misery and grandeur of literary life. At the same time, it allowed the male author to gain encouragement, feminine support, and admiration. It drew authors from the seclusion of the study into the public limelight. Mme. Geoffrin was the first to "discover" the withdrawn D'Alembert, who lived in a hovel, and to introduce him to "society." Later

Mme. du Deffand launched him fully on his brilliant public career. Nor was this an isolated incident.

D'HOLBACH AND HELVETIUS

Although the *philosophes* ruled the roost at the salons, although the salons were favorite sanctuaries from which they could launch their forays against an insufficiently enlightened world, some writers chafed under the restrictions that inevitably accompanied salon life. Wrote Marmontel, an inveterate frequenter of salons: "The society of Mme. Geoffrin lacked one of the attractions which meant much to me: freedom of thought . . . She held our spirit as if on a leash."[9] Rebellion against the restraints imposed by the leading ladies of the salons, against the requirements of polite usage and decorous conduct, thus helps to account for the success of the two major salons dominated by men of letters rather than by women: those of the Baron d'Holbach and to a lesser extent of Helvétius. Marmontel certainly "appreciated the society of charming women," but he came to value even more highly the virile discussions at D'Holbach's dinner table: "D'Holbach's house, and later that of Helvétius, were the rendezvous of the society composed partly of the flower of Mme. Geoffrin's company, and partly of some men whom Mme. Geoffrin had found too daring and too risky to be allowed to her table. She esteemed the Baron d'Holbach, she loved Diderot, but on the sly, without compromising herself on their behalf. . . . We were no longer tied to apron strings as at Mme. Geoffrin's. But that liberty did not degenerate into license."[10]

Marmontel's friend, Morellet, left an excellent description of D'Holbach's salon: "The baron d'Holbach held two dinner parties per week, on Sundays and Thursdays, where—without prejudice to the other days of the week—ten, twelve, or even fifteen or twenty men of letters and men of the world or foreigners who loved and cultivated the things of the mind were wont to meet. There was plenty of simple but good food, excellent wine, excellent coffee; plenty of discussion and never a quarrel; the simple manners that are suited to intelligent and educated men, yet do not degenerate into ill-breeding; gaiety without folly and so much charm that although we arrived at two o'clock . . . nearly all of us often stayed there till seven or eight in the evening. That was the place to hear the freest, most animated, and most instructive conversation that ever was . . . There was hardly a bold and original idea in politics and religion that was not brought forward and discussed pro and con, nearly always with much subtlety and insight."[11]

Almost the same persons were wont to meet at the house of Helvétius, but conversation was said to be neither so free nor so systematic as at D'Holbach's, for "The mistress of the house broke up the society somewhat, by drawing to herself the men she liked best, and certainly not choosing the least interesting. Not that she liked philosophy more than Mme. d'Holbach; but the latter would sit in her corner and say nothing, or talk softly to some special friend, without hindering anybody; whereas Mme. Helvétius upset philosophical discussions badly with her sparkle, beauty and wit."[12] In other words, the gatherings at Helvétius's home still had too much the character of other salons.

Under the pressures of persecution, the menaces from Rome, the parliaments, bishops and archbishops, and Jesuits and Jansenists, the *philosophes* were drawn together in sect-like solidarity. The virile atmosphere at D'Holbach's offered more appropriate headquarters for embattled *philosophes* than the refined salons.

The patronage of literary women often led the writer to cultivate grace at the expense of seriousness and imagination. "He was compelled," observes Kingsley Martin, "to adjust his style according to the intellectual fashion; he had always to be alert to please his hostess, to write so that she could talk about his book without having read the part which cost the greatest effort and which would constitute its permanent value."[13] In the small world of the salons, where the same people met night after night at a few houses, it was of major importance not to be bored and not to bore, and wit therefore assumed a disproportionate importance among the literary virtues. Real differences of opinion, sharp clashes and conflicts of ideas would have ruffled the smooth plane of salon life, and there was always, therefore, the temptation to prefer the innocuous to the profound, the agreeable to the searching. When the exchange of ideas becomes a game, the genuinely creative intellectual may be shunned because he disturbs the rules—as Rousseau discovered. And the flattery, cliquishness, rivalries, and manipulation that salon society inevitably bred too often distracted the serious men of letters from the real work at hand.

The salons helped to democratize the life of the mind but also restricted it. The coffeehouses, to which we now turn, were almost completely unhampered by tradition, polite usage, and feminine restraints.

NOTES

1. Quoted in Ian Watt, *The Rise of the Novel* (Berkeley and Los Angeles: University of California Press, 1959), pp. 43–4.

2. Roger Picard, *Les salons littéraires et la société française* (New York: Brentano's, Inc., 1943), p. 203. I have profited much from this informative book. See also Jules Bertaut, *La vie littéraire au xviiième siècle* (Paris: Tallandier, 1954), and the chapter on the *philosophes* and the salons in Marius Roustan, *The Pioneers of the French Revolution* (Boston: Little, Brown & Co., 1926).

3. Chauncey Tinker, *The Salon and English Letters* (New York: The Macmillan Company, 1915), p. 25. I have borrowed freely from this seminal work.

4. Jean Le Rond d'Alembert, "Essai sur les hommes de lettres," *Oeuvres*, IV (Paris: Belin, 1822), 372.

5. Jean François Marmontel, *Mémoires*, I (Paris: Firmin-Didot, 1891), 312.

6. Quoted in Kingsley Martin, *The Rise of French Liberal Thought* (New York: New York University Press, 1954), p. 105. Martin's chapter on the salon is outstanding.

7. Kurt H. Wolff, ed., *The Sociology of Georg Simmel* (New York: The Free Press, 1950), pp. 40ff.

8. Tinker, *op. cit.*, p. 31.

9. Marmontel, *op. cit.*, p. 329.

10. *Ibid.*, pp. 312, 314–5.

11. Abbé Morellet, *Mémoires (Inédites)* (Paris: Baudouin, 1823), pp. 133–4.

12. *Ibid.*, p. 141.

13. Martin, *op. cit.*, p. 105.

Chapter 3

COFFEEHOUSES IN
EIGHTEENTH-CENTURY
LONDON

THE ROCOCO SALON HELPED TO ELIMINATE THE aristocratic monopoly on culture and patronage and permitted the lowly born man of letters to communicate on an equal footing with the noble-born. It developed a common standard for the rating of wit and intelligence. It thus contributed to the breakdown of barriers set up by inherited privilege and substituted universalistic criteria of intellectual achievement. Yet the salon, depending as it did on the initiative of a gracious lady who imposed her taste, even though based on new standards, was still far from being democratic in its criteria of admission. Only those who lived up to her standards gained access to the salon's advantages. A truly free meeting place was first provided by the coffeehouse, an institution that is roughly contemporary. There standing rested uniquely on wit and intelligence without any consideration of rank, manners, or morals.

To be admitted to a salon depended on introductions and hence on the prior approval of at least some social gatekeepers. None was required for admission to coffeehouse society. The coffeehouse was free from the control of female guardians of the proprieties and was open to all, regardless of belief, creed, or station. On entering, a man paid a penny at the bar, agreed to observe certain minimal standards of conduct, and was then free to participate as an equal

in debate, discussion, and social intercourse. He was free to take
any vacant seat and to engage those around him in conversation. If
unable to read, he could hear the news read out loud by one of the
company, or he could listen to poets, critics, playwrights, and
novelists reading from their works and being criticized by peers
and ordinary guests alike.[1] There, in Macaulay's words, "earls in
stars and garters, clergymen in cassocks, pert Templars, sheepish
lads from Universities, translators and index makers in ragged
coats"[2] could all meet on equal social footing. A contemporary
pamphlet describes this scene with considerable sociological sophistication: "As you have a hodge-podge of Drinks, such too is your
Company, for each man seems a Leveller, and ranks and files himself as he lists, without regard to degrees or order; so that oft you
may see a silly *Fop*, and a worshipful *Justice*, a priping *Rock*,
and a grace *Citizen*, a worthy *Lawyer*, and an errant pickpocket,
a Reverend *Nonconformist*, and a Canting *Mountebank*; all blended
together, to compose an *Oglio* of Impertinence."[3] Nor were coffeehouse owners unmindful of the democratizing functions of their
establishments. Regulations, printed on large sheets of paper and
posted on the walls, stipulated: "First, gentry, tradesmen, all are
welcome hither, and may without affront sit down together: Pre-
eminence of place none here should mind, but take the next fit seat
that he can find: nor need any, if finer persons come, rise up for
to assign to them his room . . ."[4]

The coffeehouse thus leveled rank, but it led at the same time
to new forms of integration. It helped to replace a solidarity based
on common styles of life or common descent by one based on like
opinion. A common opinion cannot be developed before people
have an occasion to discuss with one another, before they have
been drawn from the isolation of lonely thought into a public world
in which individual opinion can be sharpened and tested in discussion with others. The coffeehouse helped to crystallize a common
opinion from a multitude of individual opinions and to give it form
and stability. What the newspaper had not yet been able to accomplish was achieved to a large degree by the coffeehouse.[5]

"Each Coffee-house is filled," says Shadwell in the prologue to
his play, *The Woman-Captain*, "with subtle Folk, who wisely talk,
and politickly smoke."[6] Individuals learned in contact with others
to value their own opinions, and they also learned to be guided by
standards that slowly emerged from reciprocal interaction and discussion. Heteronomous standards of tradition were thus replaced by

autonomously evolved standards of mutuality.[7] Until the days of the coffeehouse, standards had been formed by a noble or religious elite. Outside elite society, men might give much thought to particular problems or issues, but, as there was little chance for ordinary men to gather, individual opinion could not cohere into group opinion. In the coffeehouses, individual opinion could be tested, discarded, changed, disseminated, so that, at the end of the filtering process, something like cohesive group opinion would emerge. As today we may know a man by the paper he reads or the political organization to which he belongs, so it became possible, once the coffeehouse had achieved its impact, to identify him by the coffeehouse he frequented.

In the coffeehouses, men developed an interest in their fellows' habits of thought as well as in their manners; they cultivated, as Harold Routh has said, "a gift for investigating other people's prejudices and partialities, and they realized the pleasure of winning their way into the intricacies of another man's mind."[8] If men were to enjoy daily intercourse across the cleavages of birth and rank and station, they had to respect one another's opinions and to cultivate the art of listening. Coffeehouse society thus bred a new respect and tolerance for the ideas of others; it blunted the edge of diversity by cultivation of sociability and tolerance. Men who might have been despised and shunned in an earlier age because they proved eccentrically unwilling to bend to the standards of tradition were now heard with attention and respect and were greeted as potential contributors to a common pool of opinion. Coffeehouse society was thus peculiarly apt to encourage sociability as well as tolerance.

It stands to reason that, in a group in which conversation was so central an activity, those who excelled in the manipulation of words—intellectuals—assumed a pre-eminent role. That was indeed the case. Dryden dominated the company at Will's Coffeehouse for a generation, presided at its debates as "the Oracle," and set a standard of literary appreciation that spread from Will's to the world of letters. At Button's in a later day, Pope, Steele, and Addison led the company. Steele's and Addison's successful attempts to create a new code of practical middle-class morality and a middle-class aesthetics through *The Tatler*, *The Spectator*, and *The Guardian* were anchored in coffeehouses. The editors of these papers drew many of their most brilliant pages from scenes they had observed in the coffeehouses or from conversations they had shared there.

It was not for nothing that Addison spent six or seven hours at Button's every day. Londoners dined early in the eighteenth century, so that men began to gather soon after six at the coffeehouses. There news and gossip were received and discussed, and the pulse of the groups could be taken and welded into coherent opinion. Readers and writers could discuss freely and without inhibition the latest contributions to the journals. The writers tested ideas and experimented with them; the readers felt that, through discussion with editors and writers, they could, even if only to a slight degree, influence those journals that formed public opinion.

Although the coffeehouse assisted in the preparatory stages of literary production, its role was not thus limited. The coffeehouse also provided sustained criticism of the finished product. At the coffeehouses, clients could read all the current pamphlets fresh from the printers, as well as all the daily or occasional papers, for a very moderate subscription. Conversation would quite naturally revolve to a large extent around the comments recently made by authors or critics. And, as authors participated actively in these conversations, they were likely to put to good use criticisms of their previous contributions. Oral and written communication thus naturally complemented each other.

Until the Restoration, writers and readers had had hardly a chance to get together. Now they became engaged in dialogue, and their mutual influence was considerable. Most earlier writers had only rarely left their libraries, and their styles, nurtured on classical standards, had tended to be ponderous or precious; now writers developed an ear for conversational English. The bookish phraseology of an earlier age gave way to an easy colloquial style. And, to the extent that the writer's style changed through contact with the reader, he also increased his influence on the reader. The middle-class audience grew rapidly, and, as its taste began to be shaped, as well as reflected, by authors—who had become peculiarly concerned with an audience with which they literally rubbed shoulders in the coffeehouses—the social distance between author and public decreased.

The coffeehouse as a clearing house of ideas encouraged an invigorating dialogue between the man of letters and his public. There Defoe and Swift, Fielding and Goldsmith made contact with the ideas of their time and learned what their audience's interests were. There the writer was afforded a chance to put his stamp upon half-formulated ideas that had previously floated vaguely in the air. Addison's famous letterbox at Button's, designed in the form of a lion's head, symbolized the new relationship between author and public. Addison wrote about it, "This head is open to a wide and voracious mouth, which shall take in such letters and papers as are conveyed to me by my correspondents, it being my resolution to have a particular regard to all such matters as come to my hands through the mouth of the Lion . . . Whatever the Lion swallows I shall digest it for the use of the public."[9]

All coffeehouses were scenes of mixing. Nevertheless particular coffeehouses were preferred meeting places for particular groups. Whigs would repair to Button's or St. James's, while Tories would frequent White's Chocolate House. Particular coffeehouses specialized in clienteles interested in the arts, foreign news, domestic news, scientific learning, and the like. While coffeehouses served as unprecedented levelers, disrupting the former structures of rank and status distinctions, they also helped to redraw distinctions on another level. They served different clienteles, and conversation was likely to vary in different places. In the coffeehouses near the Temple, legal matters naturally formed the principal subject of discussion, although the latest play often took precedence in discussion over the latest legal scandal. At North's, patrons talked mainly of elections, rotten boroughs, and political deals. At Child's and The Chapter, talk was mainly of tithes, rectories, and lectureships, for there university men and country clergymen visiting London attempted to learn what was going on in the world of letters. In other coffeehouses, booksellers and publishers were wont to congregate, and literary hacks, critics, and Grub Street journalists would hang about in search of employment. In some coffeehouses, political feelings ran high; in others, one was likely to learn more about the prices of pepper and indigo than about politics or literature. In the early part of the eighteenth century, there were about 2000 coffeehouses in London, and every profession, trade, and party had its favorite. Yet in most of these establishments, ordinary men, nonspecialists, and nonprofessionals would gather around the habitués and absorb through discussion with them some of their specialized knowledge and interests.

As the century wore on, however, tendencies toward exclusion slowly began to take the lead over originally inclusive trends. Within many of these coffeehouses, members began to develop informal "clubs" in which like-minded men united in defense of the Hanoverian succession, of deism, of the ancients against the moderns, and of many other political, philosophical, or economic ideas. The coffeehouses had started to draw men together; as they developed, they again drew men apart. But the new divisions were on lines of achievement and interest rather than of rank.

The custom developed that a group of men, not necessarily close friends but having common tastes and interests, would meet regularly and dine together in a tavern or coffeehouse to discuss the events of the day from a common point of view. The many literary "clubs" founded by Dr. Johnson were typical of this development. What accounts for the trend, at least insofar as intellectuals are concerned, was the fact that they had gradually gained a pride of craft, a sense of their pre-eminent dignity and importance, and were wont to discuss intellectual matters among themselves. As the profession of letters gradually emerged as a specialized and separate craft with its own secrets, its own gossip, its own codes, it was natural that men of letters attempted to separate themselves from those with other interests and concerns. As writing became a more specialized and self-conscious activity, subject to stricter canons of craft and technique, it was no longer sufficient for the writer to talk to a mixed audience of professionals and laymen; he sought the company of his peers. And so, in the age of Johnson, the informal gathering of a stable coterie of friends and peers, the "club," began to displace the free-for-all of the coffeehouses of the age of Addison and Steele. The writer and his audience again grew apart. This division was symbolized by a growing ecological separation: While the public would congregate in the main rooms of a tavern or coffeehouse, the writers would gather in an exclusive club in one of the back rooms and would symbolically close the door to the outside world. From then on, communication between author and public was no longer immediate and personal; it was increasingly mediated through monthly magazines and quarterly reviews, which began their ascendancy at roughly the same time as the decline of the coffeehouse.

The age of the coffeehouse was short in England—it lasted longer on the Continent—but it marked the emergence of a literature closer to the realities of daily life. Through the vivifying contact between writer and audience that it brought about, the coffeehouse helped to transform literary style, as well as subject matter. It helped to draw the author from the isolation of the study into the world of ordinary men and women. It allowed intellectuals

to perform one of their most important tasks: to contri'
formation of public opinion.

NOTES

1. *Cf.* Aytoun Ellis, *The Penny Universities* (London: Secker & Warburg, Ltd., 1956), p. xv and *passim*. This book is the best history of British coffeehouses.
2. Quoted in *ibid.*, p. xv.
3. Quoted in Robert J. Allen, *The Clubs of Augustan London* (Cambridge, Mass.: Harvard University Press, 1933), p. 14.
4. Quoted in John Timbs, *Clubs and Club Life in London* (London: John Camden Hotten, 1872), p. 272. For further details, see Ralph Nevill, *London Clubs* (London: Chatto & Windus, Ltd., 1911).
5. *Cf.* Alexandre Beljame, *Men of Letters and the English Public in the Eighteenth Century* (London: Routledge & Kegan Paul, Ltd., 1948), pp. 163–4.
6. Quoted in *ibid.*, p. 163.
7. On the distinction between autonomy and heteronomy of moral norms, *cf.* Jean Piaget, *The Moral Judgment of the Child* (New York: The Free Press, 1948).
8. Harold Routh, "Steele and Addison," *Cambridge History of English Literature*, IX (Cambridge: Cambridge University Press, 1912), 26–65, especially 31–2. I have borrowed freely from this important treatment of the influence of the coffeehouses.
9. Quoted in Ellis, *op. cit.*, p. 173.

Chapter 4

THE ROYAL SOCIETY
AND THE RISE OF
MODERN SCIENCE[1]

THE SPREAD OF SCIENTIFIC ENDEAVORS AND THE
enhanced cultivation of the natural sciences in the seventeenth century owe as much to sociological factors as do the parallel rise and
enhancement of letters. As salons, coffeehouses, and clubs drew
together literary practitioners and their audience and raised the
status of authorship, so the scientific societies of the seventeenth
century, of which the Royal Society was the most eminent, served
to narrow the distance between scientists and educated laymen, to
legitimize scientific pursuits, and to further the institutionalization
of science as a highly valued component of the social order. They
were the most important matrices for the emergence of a self-
conscious scientific vocation.

Few knowledgeable men today are likely to view the history of
modern science as that of a series of geniuses making discoveries
in isolation. It is by now generally recognized that the scientific
enterprise developed within a scientific community and within an
institutionalized setting. But the nonspecialist may be surprised to
learn that, at the origin of modern science, one finds gatherings of
men impelled by a vital curiosity about the facts of nature but, for
the most part, not scientists themselves. Dilettanti and amateurs,
rather than specialists and experts, developed the ground on which
was to grow the more austerely formalized science of a later age.

Among the ninety-six first Fellows of the Royal Society when it was chartered in 1662, there were fourteen noblemen, barons, and knights; eighteen esquires; eighteen physicians; five doctors of divinity and two bishops; and a goodly number of merchants and businessmen. Hardly one-third of them could truly be called "men of science." It was an association not primarily of scholars but of amateurs interested in experimental science and curious about the new vistas that science and discovery had lately opened to the learned and laymen alike. Bishop Sprat, the first historian of the Society, proudly wrote, "Men did generally think no man was fit to meddle in matters of consequence but he that had bred himself up in a long course of discipline for that purpose . . . Experience . . . tells us greater things are produced by free way than the formal." "We find noble rarities to be every day given in," writes Sprat elsewhere, "not only by the hands of the learned, but from the shops of mechanics, voyages of merchants, ploughs of husbandmen, gardens of gentlemen." It was doubtless recognition that scientific amateurs were only partly dispensable from the regular cares of their occupational pursuits that led the Society to require, in Sprat's words, "not the whole time of any of their members, except only of their curators. From the rest they expect no more but what their business, nay, even their recreation can spare." In other words, in order to maximize the chances of attracting gifted dilettanti, the Society made sure that those for whom science was but an avocation were not to be rebuffed by too stringent demands on their time.

The origins of the Society go back to 1645, when a number of curious young men formed a kind of luncheon club at one of the London taverns, agreeing to meet once a month to discuss and experiment together. One of its members, Robert Boyle, referred to it in his letters as the "invisible college," and it is known by that name to this day. The original members, about ten in number, were all educated men, but they were for the most part clergymen, linguists, and physicians, rather than professional scientists. When they came together to study "Physick, Anatomy, Navigation, Staticks, Mechanicks, and Natural Experiment," they were impelled by natural curiosity or utilitarian considerations more than by professional concerns. They took interest in Galileo's discoveries with his newly devised telescope and in the novel anatomical and physiological fields opened up by Vesalius and later by William Harvey's discovery of the circulation of the blood, but they also were interested in magnetic and sympathetic cures, in tools and instruments that might be beneficial in navigation and warfare, and in news from abroad about freaks of nature or the customs of strange peoples.

The membership of the group increased in the course of time, but its composition hardly changed. After the group moved to Oxford because of the vicissitudes of the Civil War, it included perhaps a greater number of university-attached professional scientists, but upon its return to London in 1660 it again opened its doors wide to those whom Sprat described as "gentlemen, free and unconfined . . . who by the freedom of their education, the plenty of their estates and the usual generosity of noble blood, may be well supposed to be most averse from sordid considerations."

The men, gathered together in the various informal groups that preceded the Royal Society and then in the more formal setting of the Society itself, were impelled by pervasive curiosity about the facts of nature. No longer satisfied with the certainties of the churchmen and scholastic philosophers, they endeavored to wrest her secrets from nature by experiments and observation rather than by deductive reasoning. They tried to arrive at knowledge through debate and confrontation of evidence rather than through reliance on authoritative writers. They saw themselves, in Bishop Sprat's words, as the spokesmen of a "learned and inquisitive age," endeavoring "to separate the knowledge of Nature from the colours of Rhetorick, the devices of Fancy, or the delightful deceit of Fables."

The determinants of this new attitude were various. No doubt, as Robert K. Merton has persuasively argued, the Puritan ethic served as a major force to enhance the cultivation of science. The study of nature, Puritans felt, was both to the greater glory of God and the good of man. It permitted fuller appreciation of the splendor of His works, and it also allowed contributions to the welfare of man by making possible the domination of nature through technological invention.

Not all those engaged in the new cultivation of the sciences were Puritans, of course. For some, their newly found inquisitiveness and curiosity were rooted simply in a quest for certainty among the facts of nature to replace the dogmatic sources that had dried up. For others, and among them were scientists as well as amateurs, frankly utilitarian considerations were in the forefront. With the bourgeoning of economic enterprise, especially in transport and navigation, persistent pressures for the solution of practical problems in those areas made themselves felt. Advanced navigational aids were of major importance in an age that saw the rapid expansion of foreign commerce; astronomy was of central practical value in finding the longitude; determination of the times of the tides was imperative for navigation.

A contemporary ballad captures well the spirit of "that choice company of Witts and Philosophers who meet on Wednesday weekly att Gresham College [the immediate predecessor of the Royal Society]." It illustrates in particular the close connection between scientific and utilitarian pursuits that was the mark of the early years of the Royal Society:

> Our Merchants on th' Exchange does plott
> T' increase the Kingdom's wealth by trade.
> Att Gresham College a learned Knott
> Unparalle'd designes have laid
> To make themselves a Corporation
> And knowe all things by Demonstration . . .
> Oxford and Cambridge are our laughter;
> Their learning is but Pedantry.
> These new Collegiates doe assure us
> Aristotle's an Asse to Epicurus.
> By demonstrative Philosophie
> They plainly prove all things are bodyes,
> and those that talk of Qualitie
> They count them all to be meer Noddyes.
> Nature in all her works they trace
> And make her as playne as nose in face . . .
> These men take nothing upon trust
> Therefor in Counsell sate many howres
> About fileing Iron into Dust
> T' experiment the Loadstone's powers; . . .
> A second has describ'd att full
> The Philosophie of making Cloath;
> tells you what grasse does make coarse wooll
> and whatt it is that breeds the Moth.
> Great learning is i' th' Art of Cloathing
> Though vulgar people thinke it nothing . . .
> The College will the whole world measure
> Which most impossible conclude,
> and Navigation make a pleasure,
> By fynding out the Longitude . . .

London merchants, whether members of the Society or only well-wishers, naturally exerted pressure for consideration of topics that had practical significance for them. The King and the court also pressed for the solution of problems, whether in military technology or in commerce and industry, that might be beneficial to the nation. Utilitarian considerations were thus of coequal importance with those stemming from concern with pure science. As Dorothy Stimson has written, "By virtue of their official position and their location in the City, these Gresham professors [the predecessors of the fellows of the Royal Society] were in close association with the sea captains, the shipbuilders and the administrative officials of the English Navy. Their learning was not just for the lecture halls but had practical value as well . . . These Gresham professors did not scorn association with so-called practical men; they were willing to work on practical problems themselves. They not only cooperated with other men of like mind, but they sought their help and used their experience as a basis for their own theories which they again put to the test of practical use."[2]

It is this utilitarian seeking that, together with the new Puritan ethos, helped to legitimize scientific concerns in the minds of the educated, whether gentry, city merchants, or the court. Science, so they must have felt, paid off. It was in tune with the inner-worldly concerns of an activist society in rapid expansion. When practical men of affairs felt honored by invitations to become Fellows of the Society or to help its work by providing instruments or space for experiments, the distance between science and the world of everyday affairs decreased.

The very fact that nonscientists and interested amateurs were allowed to serve as equals in the affairs of the Society was a powerful means for legitimizing and institutionalizing science. The scientist was no longer viewed as a man of esoteric and disturbing, perhaps threatening, knowledge but as a man distinct from the common run of the educated by a greater specialization of his knowledge. Qualitative distinctions between men of science and other citizens gave way to quantitative assessments of relative amounts of knowledge. The new scientists did not pore over recondite treatises in incomprehensible languages but proceeded by demonstrations and experiments understandable to educated laymen. Wrote Sprat about the weekly meetings of the Oxford Philosophical Society, "Their proceedings were rather by action than discourse; chiefly attending some particular trials in Chemistry or Mechanicks; they had no rules nor method fixed. Their intention was more to communicate to each other their discoveries . . . than united, constant and regular disquisitions."

While laymen felt like outsiders in the disputes of the learned classicists, while Renaissance humanists had debated mainly by methods and in forms far removed from the experience of all but a very few courtly patrons, the new men of science were close to their audience of interested laymen. No doubt this audience could not follow complicated astronomical calculations or mathematical theorems, but it could observe the ingenious experiments with Boyle's air pump, the new microscopes and telescopes, lenses, and boilers. Amateurs as well as specialists were interested when, for example, "on November 1st, 1677 there were produced a great many exceedingly small and thin pipes of various sizes, some ten times, others a tenth as big as a hair, to test Leeuwenhoek's experiments." When no micro-organisms were found, it was decided to acquire a better microscope. At the next meeting, a better microscope was available, yet the small animals were not seen. But on December 6, 1677, they were seen.[3]

The effort to draw laymen as well as specialists into the labors of the Society is perhaps best illustrated by the fact that, at every meeting of the Society, the curator, Robert Hooke, exhibited experiments not only for their intrinsic interest but to put the spectators on the right way to investigation and to teach them how to draw legitimate conclusions from their own observations. These experiments, as well as the debates that followed them, initiated laymen into the modes of inductive reasoning, controlled observation, and empirical testing. They allowed him gradually to free himself from reliance on received opinion and instilled in him habits of skeptical scrutiny of presented evidence. The Society thus powerfully influenced the mental habits of the age even as it contributed to the development of its technological equipment.

At a later time, the paths of the scientist and the amateur were to diverge again. The fact that scientific institutions became differentiated reopened the gulf between scientific knowledge and that of the educated layman that the seventeenth and eighteenth centuries had attempted to close. It remains true, however, that the enhanced cultivation of science in the seventeenth century, although ultimately rooted in religious interests as well as utilitarian considerations, owes much to the reception of science afforded by the association of amateurs with scientists in the Royal Society and its predecessors. By drawing together men from different stations and positions and associating them in a common enterprise, the Royal Society contributed forcibly to the legitimation of scientific research in the minds of the cultivated. By providing a common language and common criteria by which persons variously located in the social structure could converse about common concerns, the Royal Society and similar scientific societies in Italy, France, and Germany helped considerably to mold the ethos of scientific and technological domination over nature that has pervaded the Western world ever since. For science to gain the autonomy and power it has since achieved, it had first to steep itself in the everyday concerns of man, to establish contact with ordinary men of affairs, to give up exclusive preoccupation with esoteric arcana. And in this respect the Royal Society was a powerful force. At a time when the English universities, with the significant exception of medical schools, shielded themselves from the *vulgus profanum* by an almost exclusive emphasis on dead learning and the transmission of accepted knowledge, the invention of a new social institution, the scientific society, made it possible to incorporate into the fabric of the social order that new type of experimental knowledge on which the further course of the West's peculiar orientation to the world was thenceforth to be based.

An essential component of the growth potential of an occupation or activity in a given society is the relative prestige accorded its practitioners. Only professions that enjoy prestige are likely to gain the degree of support and deference necessary for systematic growth and enhancement. A minimum of prestige is essential if the occupation is to recruit qualified practitioners and to ensure receptivity for the results of their labors. As long as science was given a low rank in the social evaluation of intellectual pursuits, it could exist only in the interstices of society, as a by-product of other types of activity, or within the private workshops of isolated scholars.

The importance of prestige explains why the charter that Charles II granted to the Royal Society in 1662 is of symbolic significance. It opened with this statement: "We have long and fully resolved with ourselves to extend not only the boundaries of Empire but also the very arts and sciences. Therefore we look with favor upon all forms of learning, but with particular grace we encourage philosophical studies, especially those which by actual experiments attempt either to shape out a new philosophy or to perfect the old. In order therefore that such studies . . . shine conspicuously among our people and that at length the whole world of letters may always recognize us not only as the Defender of the

Faith, but also as the universal lover and patron of every kind of truth . . . we have ordained . . . there shall be a society . . . which shall be called . . . the Royal Society." The King gave his stamp of approval and recognition to scientific activities even to the extent of putting them on the same plane as religious activities. The status of scientific practitioners was thus located near the very apex of the status hierarchy, where once men of the cloth alone had represented the claims of intellect. Since then, science has not been dislodged from its eminent position in Western societies.

The belief in the value of scientific pursuits depends, as we have seen, on the existence of appropriate cultural conditions. In addition to the requisite social support that makes it possible to recruit persons for systematic careers in the sciences, another important precondition for the growth of science is the development of a corporate consciousness among scientists themselves. Such self-consciousness was enhanced by the recognition given scientific endeavors in seventeenth-century British society, and it was further increased by the opportunity the Royal Society afforded scientists to establish contact with one another both in Britain and abroad.

The Royal Society served as a central link in a chain of communication that brought scientists from all over the Western world into contact. It instilled in individual scientists a sense of membership in a community of like-minded men interested in similar problems. It drew the man of science from the isolation of private laboratories and libraries into the public world, where he encountered others similarly devoted to their calling. "The fame of the Society," wrote Henry Oldenburg, one of its first secretaries, in 1668, "riseth very high abroad; and makes strangers flock hither in troops; insomuch that since this March I have had no less than two dozen travellers addressed to me." *Philosophical Transactions*, issued by Oldenburg on behalf of the Society, soon became the central medium for the transmission of scientific news and the major battleground of scientific opinion. It served to link all scientific efforts, both in England and abroad, and became the agency through which issues like the priority of discoveries were to be adjudicated. It served not only to develop a communication network but, like the Royal Society itself, also to lay the foundations for the gradual emergence of a specific scientific ethos. In both capacities, it helped to create conditions for the growth of a scientific culture and served to integrate individual scientists in the common enterprise of the scientific community.

By bridging the gap between scientists and laymen, by helping to legitimize scientific pursuits, by securing recognition of science by the men of power, by raising the status of scientists and thus allowing regular recruitment to scientific careers, by increasing communication and co-operation among scientists, by drawing them out of their private isolation into a public world—in all these and many other ways, the Royal Society provided an institutional setting without which modern science in England would, to say the least, have faced a more arduous journey. Without that matrix, the rapid and continuous flowering of modern science could hardly have been imagined.

NOTES

1. This chapter is based mainly on two excellent studies: Martha Ornstein, *The Role of Scientific Societies in the Seventeenth Century* (Chicago: University of Chicago Press, 1938); and Dorothy Stimson, *Scientists and Amateurs, A History of the Royal Society* (New York: Abelard-Schuman Limited, 1948). I have also profited greatly from Robert K. Merton's writings on seventeenth-century science, in particular his "Puritanism, Pietism and Science" and "Science and Economy of 17th Century England," *Social Theory and Social Structure* (new ed.; New York: The Free Press, 1957), pp. 574–627; and his *Science, Technology and Society in 17th Century England* (Osiris Monographs [Bruges: St. Catherine Press, 1938]). Bishop Sprat's *The History of the Royal Society*, first published in 1667 and recently reissued (Jackson Cope and Harold W. Jones, eds., Washington University Studies [St. Louis: 1958]), is a most delightful contemporary account that has helped me much.

2. Stimson, *op. cit.*, pp. 29–30.
3. Ornstein, *op. cit.*, p. 115.

Chapter 5

THE PROFESSION OF LETTERS
IN EIGHTEENTH-CENTURY
ENGLAND

Not before the middle of the eighteenth century did writing begin to be looked upon as a profession. In England, the phrase "an author by profession" came into frequent use at that time.[1] To be sure, men had devoted themselves to the craft of writing at earlier times. But the emergence of professional writers, that is, of men earning their livelihoods from writing, depended on a relatively wide reading public—and such a public was not available until the eighteenth century. The man of letters must rely on the patronage of the rich and powerful as long as intellectual products, though appreciated by connoisseurs, cannot be sold on a relatively wide scale.

An enlarged market for books was a socially necessary precondition for the emergence of professional men of letters, but it was not the only precondition. Once books have become a commodity, there must be men to do the marketing. Those who market books therefore assume major importance in intellectual life. From the eighteenth century on, publishers and booksellers became major arbiters of intellectual life. As the noble patron and the governmental stipend receded in importance, the plebeian bookseller and publisher became the transmission belt in the world of ideas. Furthermore, as readers do not necessarily buy books but may only borrow them, lending libraries also became important intermediaries between an author and his public.

Not all intellectuals were men of letters; scientific and academic intellectuals depended more on institutions other than the three mentioned here. This chapter will, however, be limited to literary men, for it is their social position that changed most significantly in the eighteenth century.

Among the writers, there were a great number of hacks and scribblers. The widening reading public encouraged the emergence of a new breed of highly unintellectual hack writers, but it also allowed men like Alexander Pope or Dr. Johnson to cultivate life styles appropriate to their intellectual calling. Intellectuals were certainly not the only ones—in fact, they were a minority—who profited from the new reading public, the publishing industry, and the libraries. But without these institutions, the intellectual writers of the time could not have flourished as they did.

THE WIDENING READING PUBLIC

There were three related social changes that account for the growth of the reading public in the eighteenth century: the increase in the number and the specific weight of the middle class, the rising standards of education in the middle class, and the changed social role of the middle-class woman.

The social ascent of the middle class brought the emergence of new strata with enough leisure and education to develop a taste for reading books. In the preceding century, this taste was limited to a relatively small elite. In the seventeenth century, the bulk of the middle class, if they read at all, read mainly religious tracts and political broadsheets. Only in the eighteenth century did the growing middle classes broaden their concerns and evince wider interest in other types of literature. Furthermore, while in preceding centuries the audience for literature was almost exclusively male, the eighteenth century saw the emergence of women as major consumers of literature. This change must in turn be accounted for by a marked change in the role of middle-class women who, at that time, gained leisure as they were relieved of the habitual drudgery of household routines.

The new middle class of merchants, tradesmen, shopkeepers, and clerical workers turned to reading in its desire for self-improvement. In its urge to rival the upper classes in sophistication and knowledge, it turned to newspapers, periodicals, magazines, and books—especially novels. Reading became an activity indulged in and approved by those who had already achieved social status and by those who saw in it an instrument to achieve the higher status to which they aspired.

Although the absolute number of readers greatly increased in comparison to earlier periods, it remained relatively small. But the very limitation of reading to one segment of the population narrowed the gap between the literate middle class and the elite, while widening that between the literate and their inferiors. Reading thus helped to enhance middle-class status. There was less than one newspaper buyer per 100 persons weekly in 1704, and, although the newspaper-buying public tripled in the first fifty years of the century, it still remained a small part of the total population. Even if Addison's claim in *The Spectator* that twenty readers read each copy is accepted, the total is still only half a million readers—about one in eleven—in the total population. The fact remains, however, that the reading public, while still small compared to the next century, was growing very rapidly.

The increase in the number of printing houses and the increasing sales of books serve as indications of the increase in readership. There were sixty London printing houses at the Restoration, seventy-five by 1724, and between 150 and 200 by 1757. *Paradise Lost* sold only 1300 copies in two years, but, in the eighteenth century, novels and histories began to be published in large editions. Five editions of *Pamela* were sold in a single year, 6500 copies of *Joseph Andrews* in thirteen months, the same number of *Sir Charles Grandison* in a few months. After the middle of the century, political books like Price's *Observations on the Nature of Civil Liberty* and Paine's *Rights of Men* also sold more than 50,000 copies each within a few weeks. Although at the beginning of the century the total annual output of new books was only 100, it had jumped to nearly 400 at the century's end.

Two additional factors, closely tied to the class structure, account for the persistent limitation of the book-reading audience to the middle and upper classes: the limited literacy of the population and the high prices of books. Many small farmers and the great majority of the country poor could not read at all. In the towns, most of those below middle-class status attained at best a kind of semiliteracy. As late as 1788, about one-quarter of the parishes of

England had no schools at all. In the towns, certain special categories among the lower orders—like domestic servants and apprentices—that had some measure of leisure time, attained fairly high levels of literacy and furnished many avid readers, especially of novels, but such other categories as laborers, sailors, and soldiers were still illiterate.

The high costs of books were an additional restraint on the growth of the reading public. At the time when a laborer's wage was about ten shillings a week and when a pound a week was considered a decent weekly wage for a skilled artisan or small shopkeeper, original editions usually sold for about five or six shillings. As roughly half the total population lived near the subsistence level, it could not be expected that many book buyers would come from these strata—even had they been literate. And even though successful novels gradually came to be published in two or more small volumes at three shillings each, whereas folios for the libraries of the well-to-do would cost a guinea or more, these prices were still within the reach only of the traditional elites and of the fortunate few who had risen from lower-class or lower middle-class positions into the expanding strata of wealthy shopkeepers, independent tradesmen, and higher clerical employees. A set of *Tom Jones* or *Clarissa*, even in relatively cheap and many-volumed editions, would cost a laborer or a skilled worker one or two weeks' wages.

The exclusion of the lower classes from the book market made reading a "distinguished" activity. Reading served many purposes, of course. But it was also a badge of high status, marking off the cultivated few from the illiterate majority.

Among the middle-class readers, women outnumbered men.[2] While the middle-class man was involved in business and trade, the middle-class woman managed the sphere of consumption. To her fell the duty of evolving styles of conduct appropriate to the new status her family had achieved. She was helped in this task by the leads provided by the new middle-class literature.

Middle-class women were no longer so closely tied to the household as they previously had been. Spinning and weaving and the making of bread and beer, soap and candles had long pre-empted the time of the middle-class woman. But in eighteenth-century London and, to a lesser extent, elsewhere, servants were plentiful and inexpensive, and many of the household staples previously produced at home were easily available through commercial channels.

With the rising standard of living and especially with the increased amenities that became available for the middle-class home in the eighteenth century, reading became a favored leisure activity. Living quarters before the seventeenth century had typically been overcrowded and lacking in privacy; they were usually dark, for taxes on windows encouraged as few windows as possible. And candlelight even at night was considered a luxury.[3] In the eighteenth century, in contrast, the middle-class home became more spacious, afforded greater privacy, and generally permitted a certain *bourgeois* comfort. In the middle class, both women and men no longer found it necessary to spend most of their leisure time outside the home at taverns and coffeehouses or at plays, operas, and the like. They could relax with books in reasonable comfort at home. Middle-class men, involved in the arduous struggle to make their livings, absorbed in daily economic routines, and still drawn to exclusively male activities like sports or drinking, availed themselves much less of the opportunity to enjoy the quiet relaxation of reading than did women.

Naturally, certain types of literature—political or learned treatises, for example—were still read mainly by men. But religious books, books on manners and morals, and above all novels were read mostly by women.

Women read Richardson and Fielding, Smollett and Goldsmith not only for amusement but also for moral guidance. These novels, like the middle-class periodicals from *The Tatler* and *The Spectator* to their hundreds of later imitators, served the moral education of the middle class. They helped to provide standards of behavior and guides to conduct; they instructed even as they amused; they set the tone and furnished the moral climate for a middle class resolutely bent on economic ascent in an increasingly individualistic age, in which the dour Puritan standards of an earlier age no longer seemed appropriate but in which stern moral conduct was still a badge of respectability. After the days of Addison and Steele, the literary man was regarded not only as an entertainer, but also as a taste-maker and moral guide.

BOOKSELLERS AND AUTHORS

The expanding public was the decisive factor in the development of literature as a profession, but the relation of the author to this public was only indirect; hence the essential role of booksellers as intermediaries. The bookseller replaced the patron as a source of support, but, although he made it possible for the author to attain freedom from patronage, he brought about new types of dependence. As early as 1725, Defoe noted, "Writing . . . is become a very considerable Branch of English Commerce. The Booksellers are the Master Manufacturers or Employers. The several Writers, Authors, Copyers, Sub-Writers and all other operators with Pen and Ink are the workmen employed by the said Master-Manufacturers."

Defoe's picture is somewhat exaggerated, of course. Although many hacks were in fact not much more than the hirelings of booksellers, this statement is by no means true of the major authors of the day. Far from being mere employees of the booksellers, they achieved considerable independence by striking shrewd bargains with them and by thus gradually acquiring secure economic standings and becoming autonomous men of letters. Nevertheless, Defoe put his finger on the fact that bookselling had become a major branch of commerce and that intellectual products had become a commodity. Like any other commodity, books depended for their sale on the conditions of the market, as well as on the booksellers' ingenuity and enterprise in marketing them.

Booksellers began to experiment with new devices to expand their markets and to build their audiences. Subscriptions, for example, were introduced as a method of selling books by Dryden's enterprising publisher, Jacob Tonson, and were soon widely adopted. Tonson reasoned that, given the smallness of the reading public, it would be hazardous to publish without some guarantees of reasonable sales. He therefore adopted a method by which books were subscribed in advance of publication. Dryden's verse translation of the works of Vergil was published in this manner. There were two series of subscribers. The first paid five guineas and received specially engraved copies suitable for the private studies of the well-to-do. The second received simpler volumes—but paid only two guineas. The publisher thus took advantage of the growing differentiation in the market for books and attained more readers than he would otherwise have reached.

The venture paid off handsomely, and Dryden received approximately £1400—that is, about as much as he had received earlier for fourteen successful plays. After that, Dryden was well paid, receiving, for example, a total of £250 for his *Fables*. Pope was even more successful than Dryden. His translations of the *Iliad* and the

Odyssey, published through subscriptions, brought him a fortune of about £9000 and enabled him to live comfortably in a country house in the neighborhood of London. He could write with pride:

> But (thanks to Homer) since I live and thrive,
> Indebted to no Prince or Peer alive.

Later in the century, Johnson, Goldsmith, and others also managed to achieve financial independence, partly through royalties and partly through subscriptions. Johnson, after years of poverty, received a total of £400 for his *Lives of the English Poets.* One understands why he observed to a friend, "Sir, I have always said the booksellers were a generous set of fellows." But many fared less well and had less warm feelings for the booksellers. To begin with, the new subscription system involved humiliations not too dissimilar from those involved in the patronage system. Many a major author was forced to go from house to house to sell subscriptions for his books. Furthermore, any writer in whom booksellers did not immediately discern the qualities necessary for commercial success was forced, at least for a time, to make a living as a general hack. The eighteenth century was indeed the first in which it was possible for an author to become independent of the patron, but it also saw the birth of Grub Street. The denizens of Grub Street abridged, translated, compiled, and wrote treatises on any subject that would sell; they were drudges of the pen who, as a contemporary author remarked, lived in such circumstances that "there is no difference between the Writer in his Garret and the Slave in the Mines."[4] To be sure, a majority of the Grub Street hacks simply had no talent and would have had no chance to become independent men of letters under any conditions. But Grub Street consisted not only of the dregs of the writing profession; many major writers also served long sentences there before achieving due recognition. Some of them became the victims of a system in which the bookseller wielded a very heavy hand over the author.

When many authors aspire to write for what is still a relatively small market, the bookseller has many an occasion to exploit them and the public alike. Grub Street in the time of Pope was described by Roger North: "It is wretched to consider what pickpocket work with the help of the press these demi-book-sellers make; they crack their brains to find out selling subjects, and keep hirelings in garrets, on hard meat, to write and correct by the great; so puff up an octavo to a sufficient thickness, and there is six shillings current for an hour and a half's reading and perhaps never to be read or looked upon after."[5]

The booksellers had so powerful a grip on unknown writers that the latter had simply to accept what was offered them. Johnson, before he attained fame, we are told, would have taken even less than ten guineas for his *London*. No wonder, then, that the great publishing houses founded in the eighteenth century soon made publishing into "big business." Henry Lintot, Pope's publisher, left £45,000 to his daughter at his death in 1758. A number of other publishers left similar or even greater sums.

After he had achieved some recognition or some independent income, an author could drive a fair bargain. Hume, having a private income, received £50 for the first edition of the *Treatise of Human Nature*—which did not sell at all. But Goldsmith was paid only sixty guineas for the very successful *Vicar of Wakefield* at a time when he was not yet well known.

As the century grew older and the market increased, "best selling" authors received very substantial sums for their books, through either subscriptions or straight sales. Between 1754 and 1760, Hume received the sum of £3400 for his *History*, and Robertson was paid £4500 for his *Charles V*. In 1726, Swift's *Gulliver's Travels* netted him only £200, but Fielding later received £700 for *Tom Jones* and £1000 for *Amelia*. Toward the end of the century, even fairly mediocre novelists could make fairly comfortable livings.

CIRCULATING LIBRARIES

The growth of circulating libraries aided the expansion of literature. At a time when the prices of books were very high in relation to the purchasing power of the great majority of the population, circulating libraries were an important social invention. They furnished those who had acquired a taste for reading with access to books otherwise out of their reach. They helped to reduce the gap between interest in reading and purchasing power.

The first circulating library was opened in London in 1740. Rivals quickly sprang up in London and in the provinces as well. By the end of the century, about 1000 libraries dotted the country. Their rapid success testifies to the growing interest in reading.

Given the relatively modest subscription fee—fifteen or twenty shillings a year entitled the member to borrow any books or magazines available—libraries appealed to members of the middle classes and to the literate among the lower classes. They usually specialized in novels and catered mainly to a female public. A governess or, more rarely, a domestic servant who could not afford to buy books could manage to pay the subscription.

Furthermore, borrowing books allowed prospective buyers to preview them before deciding on purchases. Contrary to the initial fear of the booksellers, who had perceived libraries as competitors, libraries enhanced sales rather than restricting them. "I have been informed," wrote James Lackington, a successful bookseller, in his *Memoirs*, "that when circulating libraries were first opened, the booksellers were much alarmed, and their rapid increase, added to their fears, had led them to think that the sale of books would be much diminished by libraries. But experience had proved that the sale of books, so far from being diminished by them, has been greatly promoted, as from those repositories many thousand families have been cheaply supplied with books, by which the taste of reading has become much more general, and thousands of books are purchased every year, by such as have borrowed them at those libraries, and after reading, approving of them, became purchasers."[6] "Circulating libraries," said Lackington in a later part of the *Memoirs*, "have also greatly contributed toward the amusement and cultivation of the sex; by far the greatest part of ladies now have a taste for books . . . Ladies now in general read, not only novels . . . but they also read the best books in the English language, and many read the best authors in various languages . . ."[7]

Circulating libraries, then, along with the various book-buying and book-discussion clubs that were organized by cultivated upper middle-class women at mid-century, helped considerably to widen the audience for books. The growth of the book market, to which they contributed both directly and indirectly, enabled publishers in turn to pay authors better.

THE COMMERCIALIZATION OF LITERATURE

The publisher, who exploited the opportunities inherent in the rising demand for books, was a major aid to the writer in his struggle to attain independence from the servitude of the patronage system. Nevertheless, relations between writers and booksellers remained tense and ambiguous throughout the century. One writer might at times express his feeling of gratitude for the services rendered by the booksellers in spreading his work, while indulging at other times in bitter denunciations of the commercialization of writing, for which the booksellers were allegedly responsible. Oliver Goldsmith provides a case in point.

The author of *The Vicar of Wakefield*, that man of letters extraordinary, author of countless translations and compilations, contributor to many periodicals, novelist, and social critic, on some occasions expressed his gratitude to public and publishers and at others criticized them with a biting tongue. "At present," he could write, "the few poets of England no longer depend on the Great for subsistence, they have now no other patrons but the public, and the public, collectively considered, is a good and generous master . . . Every polite member of the community, by buying what a man of letters writes, contributes to reward him. The ridicule therefore of living in a garret, might have been wit in the last age, but continues such no longer, because no longer true. A writer of real merit now may easily be rich. . . ."[8] "I look to the booksellers," he also wrote, "for support; they are my best friends, and I am not inclined to forsake them for others."[9] But elsewhere Goldsmith suggested that "the man who, under the protection of the Great, might have done honor to humanity, when only patronized by the bookseller, becomes a thing little superior to the fellow who works at the press."[10] The same Goldsmith who had praised the booksellers could also write, "The author, when unpatronized by the Great, has naturally recourse to the bookseller. There cannot perhaps be imagined a combination more prejudicial to taste than this. It is of the interest of the one to allow as little for writing, and of the other to write as much as possible."[11]

Writers and publishers were often natural allies, each depending on the other in the effort to explore the possibilities of an expanding market. But theirs was, at best, a kind of antagonistic co-operation. The writer often found that, although he might owe some of his independence to the efforts of his publisher, he was also bound to him by ties nearly as restricting as those of patronage. The bookseller was an intermediary, and as such he suffered from the hostilities that have afflicted the man in the middle in many social orders. When the writer complained of the patron, he could place the blame on a concrete person with whom he had direct contact. The matter was different in the case of the bookseller, who could shift the blame on to the state of the market and the anonymous forces that governed it. The bookseller sought to represent himself as an interpreter of market trends rather than as the originator of aesthetic judgments. But this very strategy too often resulted in heightening the wrath of his authors. It was often difficult for them to blame the faceless public, but they could easily attack the concrete middle man.

The publisher and the author had a common interest in expanding the audience for books, yet the author was often appalled at the ways in which the publisher attempted to advertise and peddle his wares. He also resented the debasement of taste in the more sensational works that enterprising or unscrupulous publishers began to pour onto the market. It is since that period that one discerns the operation of a cruel dialectic that is still at work: Publishers help to expand the market for books; they exploit all the commercial possibilities involved in a growing reading public; but, in the process, they cater to a public less sophisticated in its taste and thereby put pressure on the writer to conform to majority taste. The very democratization of the reading audience endangers quality. Earlier writers, addressing a restricted audience, could much better afford to adhere to established canons of taste. Ever since the late eighteenth century, however, the insistent query of authors has gone unanswered: For whom does one write?

The tastes of the shopkeepers, apprentices, housewives, and clerks who were a sizable part of the new audience were clearly different from those of wealthy squires, city merchants, and the gentry. Their cultural backgrounds were more primitive and their tastes cruder. How, then, was a writer to reach a wide audience without debasing his standards? If he addressed himself only to the cultural elite, he cut himself off from a major share of the market and restricted his influence. Such a self-denying ordinance was likely to lead to isolation from the major popular trends. But if he sought to reach a larger public and to help cultivate and elevate its tastes, to become a preceptor for the new middle classes, he encountered the need to entertain even as he instructed. Although an author might endeavor to improve the ideas and opinions of his audience, he was still under the obligation to reflect them. Who is to judge the merits of a writer, Johnson, Goldsmith, and many of their contemporaries asked, when success among a broad reading public devoid of secure standards can no longer be the guide? "He that endeavours after fame by writing," says Johnson, "solicits the regard of a multitude fluctuating in pleasures, or immersed in business, without time for intellectual amusements; he appeals to judges, prepossessed by passions, or corrupted by prejudices, which preclude their approbation of any new performance. Some are too indolent to read anything, till its reputation is established; others too envious to promote that fame which gives them pain by its increase."[12]

These qualms and queries were to be voiced with increasing frequency in the next century, when the writers would face a mass audience of vastly greater proportions than those of the eighteenth century would have dared envisage. At this point, it is enough to record the fact that, with an expanding audience and a perfected machinery for the making and distributing of books, the eighteenth-century writer had at least achieved the possibility of obtaining independence from the ties of patronage. There was at last a profession of letters recognized by all, accorded a measure of prestige and esteem, and assuring its successful practitioners dignified livelihoods. It is true that the new profession was faced with problems unknown in the age of aristocratic patronage. But it had in any case attained dignity and autonomy, and it inspired fierce pride in its practitioners.

It might be well to close with the testimony of Dr. Johnson. Boswell records the following conversation between Johnson and his friends Watson and Boswell: "Now learning is itself a trade. A man goes to a bookseller and gets what he can. We have done with patronage. In the infancy of learning, we find some great man praised for it. This diffused it among others. When it becomes general, an author leaves the great, and applies to the multitudes." *Boswell*: "It is a shame that authors are not now better patronized." *Johnson*: "No, Sir. If learning cannot support a man, if he must sit with his hands across till somebody feeds him, it is as to him a bad thing, and it is better as it is. With patronage, what flattery! What falsehood! While a man is in equilibrio, he throws truth among the multitude, and lets them take it as they please: in patronage, he must say what pleases his patron, and it is an equal chance whether that be truth or falsehood." *Watson*: "But is it not the case now, that instead of flattering one person, we flatter the age?" *Johnson*: "No, Sir. The world always lets a man tell what he thinks his own way."[13]

NOTES

1. A. S. Collins, *The Profession of Letters* (London: Routledge & Kegan Paul, Ltd., 1928), p. 21. I have relied heavily on this as well as on Mr. Collins's other work in this field, *Authorship in the Days of Johnson* (London: Robert Holden and Company, 1927). Alexandre Beljame's

classic *Men of Letters and the English Public in the Eighteenth Century* (London: Routledge & Kegan Paul, Ltd., 1948) has been of very great help to me. Of more recent studies, I have profited enormously from Ian Watt's fine *The Rise of the Novel* (Berkeley and Los Angeles: University of California Press, 1962); and from Leo Lowenthal's fine "The Debate over Art and Popular Culture: English Eighteenth Century as a Case Study," *Literature, Popular Culture and Society* (Englewood Cliffs, N. J.: Prentice-Hall, Inc., 1961). Other books from which I have learned much include Richard D. Altick, *The English Common Reader* (Chicago: University of Chicago Press, 1957); Raymond Williams, *The Long Revolution* (London: Chatto & Windus, Ltd., 1961); and Louis Dudek, *Literature and the Press* (Toronto: Ryerson Press, 1960).

2. On the new role of women, see Watt, *op. cit.*, especially Chapter II.

3. *Cf.* Lewis Mumford, *The Culture of Cities* (New York: Harcourt, Brace & World, Inc., 1938), especially pp. 39ff.

4. Quoted in Collins, *Authorship*, p. 25.

5. Quoted in *ibid.*, pp. 25–6.

6. James Lackington, *Memoirs of the Forty-Five years of the Life of James Lackington, Written by Himself* (London: 1803), p. 255. As quoted in Collins, *Authorship*, pp. 245–6.

7. *Ibid.*, p. 259. As quoted in Lowenthal, *op. cit.*, p. 58.

8. Oliver Goldsmith, *The Citizen of the World*, Letter 84 (London: J. M. Dent & Sons, Ltd., Publishers, 1934).

9. Quoted in Beljame, *op. cit.*, p. 384.

10. Quoted in Lowenthal, *op. cit.*, p. 75.

11. Quoted in *ibid.*, pp. 61–2.

12. Quoted in *ibid.*, p. 76.

13. Quoted in Beljame, *op. cit.*, p. 386.

Chapter 6

THE COMMERCIALIZATION OF WRITING: FOUR CASES FROM NINETEENTH-CENTURY ENGLAND

THE EIGHTEENTH-CENTURY INCREASE IN THE READING public and the expansion in the production of books provided but feeble intimations of things to come. The next century saw the development of a mass market for books, the first time in the history of mankind that the bulk of a nation's population had attained literacy. While the previous century had witnessed the gradual emergence of professional men of letters depending for their livelihoods on the sale of their literary products on an open market, the nineteenth century was the first in which bookselling became a mass-production industry catering to a mass public.

The population of England had been about seven million in 1750, a century later it had reached nearly twenty-one million, and by 1901 it had grown to thirty-seven million. During the same period, literacy spread rapidly. In 1839, not quite 60% of marriage partners were able to sign their names in the marriage register. By 1873, this figure had risen to nearly 78%, and twenty years later all but 5% of the registrants were able to sign their names.[1] There is, of course, a difference between the ability to sign one's name and the capacity to read a book. Nevertheless, these figures are indicative of the general trend. Even though there were still quite a number of functional illiterates in the British population at the end of the nineteenth century, the majority of British adults had by then mastered the technique of reading. This fact is clear from the history of British education, which shows a gradual rise of educational facilities from the beginning of the century. In the last quarter of the century, universal elementary education was finally introduced.

The annual numbers of new books published tell the same story. They rose from 580 in the 1820s to more than 2600 by mid-century to 6000 in 1901. The prices of books declined: The average price of a book was around twelve shillings in 1828 and around seven shillings in 1853. After 1850, "shilling novels" especially catering to lower-class taste began to be mass-produced, and various cheap reprint collections of the standard English poets became available at three shillings each. Scott's *Waverly* novels, which had originally cost £34/10 for the set, were reprinted for large sale at £12 a set or five shillings a volume. Cheap reprint series like the Parlour Library and the Railway Library were now available in all the bookstalls and at railroad stations. Furthermore, the most successful contemporary novels appeared in serialized form in such publications as Dickens's *Household Words* or his *All the Year Around*. The former had sold some 40,000 copies a week; its successor sold 300,000 a week in the 1860s.[2] While the old circulating libraries with their annual subscription rates of around a guinea had effectively limited their services to those with money to spare, free public libraries spread rapidly after an Act of Parliament in 1850 empowered town councils to establish them. By 1889, England had 180 such free public libraries, and by 1911 the public-library service was available to 62.5% of the population.

The circulation of daily newspapers trebled between 1855 and 1860. It doubled again between 1860 and 1870. The *Daily Telegraph* had a circulation of 141,000 by 1860; by 1896, when it was still the leading paper, its circulation was 300,000. And in 1900, Northcliffe's new *Daily Mail* had reached a circulation of almost a million.

These few figures suggest the immense change in the literary situation that occurred in the nineteenth century. The market for literary works had suddenly expanded from a very limited part of the population to the vast bulk of it. Not, of course, that any and all literary products would now find a mass market. But such a market was, for the first time, potentially available. There were, of course, as there are today, enormous differences between elite and mass tastes, but the phenomenal rise in literacy had made it possible to reach audiences that were totally beyond the authors of any previous age. Multitudes of people who had been, as it were, submerged, unable to participate in any way in the fund of knowledge conveyed by the printed page, were suddenly enabled to reach out, if they so desired, for whatever cultural goods were available.

But as the public so vastly increased it also became vastly more differentiated. The uneasy questions that had already arisen at the end of the eighteenth century—For whom does one write? What is the public? What are standards?—were now heard more insistently and more frequently. Robert Southey's often quoted "The Public and Transsubstantiation I hold to be the two greatest mysteries in or out of nature" could hardly have been uttered by a Dryden or a Richardson—they were able to know their publics.

In consequence, the nineteenth-century author had choices unavailable to his predecessors. He could deliberately refuse to write for a mass public, restricting his readers to a circle of devotees. (One thinks here of Coleridge's proposal for a clerisy, a new class that, "in its primary acceptation, and original intention, comprehended the learned of all denominations; the sages and professor of . . . all the so-called liberal arts and sciences.") He could "write down" to the masses and provide them with entertainment devoid of artistic merit. Or he could make efforts to reach a mass audience while still clinging to certain artistic standards.

In the following "case studies," I shall limit myself to the discussion of a few representatives of the third type. The second type clearly does not interest us here—for these purveyors of mass entertainments can hardly be called "intellectuals" even in a very broad sense. I shall not discuss the first type because it belongs in the main to an earlier time, preferring withdrawal from the mass market to immersion in it. This type was relatively untouched by the new pressures and tensions attending the lives and works of literary men who attempted to maintain the integrity of their creations while at the same time trying to accommodate themselves to the commercialization of literature naturally entailed in the new mass media. Of the four writers to be discussed—Walter Scott, William Thackeray, Charles Dickens, and George Eliot—the first three, while clinging to artistic standards, succumbed in varying degrees to the new commercial pressures. George Eliot triumphantly resisted them all.

WALTER SCOTT

Macaulay once described Walter Scott in a letter as "Perpetually sacrificing the perfection of his compositions, and the durability of his fame, to his eagerness for money; writing with the slovenly haste of Dryden, in order to satisfy wants which were not, like those of Dryden, caused by circumstances beyond his control, but were produced by his extravagant waste or rapacious speculations . . ."[3] This harsh judgment may have been based, in part, on Macaulay's Whig distaste for an eminent Tory, yet we find it repeated, though in somewhat tempered form, among modern critics. T. F. Henderson, for example, writes in *The Cambridge History of English Literature*,[4] "Great as was the actual achievement of Scott, it has reasonably been doubted whether he made the most of his extraordinary endowments. It was hardly contributory to this that, though by no means a poor man, he set himself with desperate eagerness to enrich himself by literature. While he had a deep enthusiasm for the literary vocation . . . yet, his social aspirations seem to have been stronger than his literary ambitions." Of Scott's style, he adds, "Rapidity of production was one of his special gifts . . . but it was not incumbent on him to omit careful revision of his first draft."

Most modern critics seem to agree that Scott's work had an enormous influence, that it opened entirely new vistas to the European novel, but that it was also deeply flawed. There seems to be further agreement that Scott's carelessness in composition and construction, his many contradictions in detail, his heavy style, and his clumsiness stemmed to a large extent from his desire to produce books in large quantities that would bring him high returns. The last minstrel became the first best seller.[5] Scott's case is among the early examples of a writer who becomes the victim of his own commercial aspirations.

Scott was phenomenally successful. He attracted a very large audience even before he turned to the novels on which his fame ultimately rests. And when he started his *Waverly* series, "it was by gathering a popular audience such as no novelist had had before that [he] made the novel respectable."[6]

Scott's poem, *The Lay of the Last Minstrel*, was the first English poem to become a best seller in the modern sense of the word, selling 44,000 copies before it appeared in the *Collected Edition* of

Scott's works.[7] *The Lady of the Lake* had similar phenomenal sales, 25,000 copies being distributed within eight months and another edition of 3000 in the press.[8] The *Waverly* novels had even larger sales and netted Scott a fortune. A later work, *Life of Napoleon Bonaparte*, was the first biography to sell as well as popular fiction. Its two editions brought him £18,000.

Nor was writing novels and poetry Scott's only source of income. He edited many works for the press, contributed often to reviews and magazines, received £1300 a year as a clerk of sessions in Edinburgh, and was involved in the running of a publishing and printing house.

"I love to have the press thumping, clattering and banging in my ear," wrote Scott in his *Journal*. "It creates the necessity which always makes me work best."[9] This comment indicates the extent to which Scott's creative process was tied to the demands of the market. It also shows to what degree Scott was involved in, and aware of, the commercial aspects of his writing. And it suggests why Scott involved himself directly in the world of printing and publishing although he was not, like Richardson, a printer by trade. Far from being content to deliver a manuscript to a publisher after striking the requisite bargain, he sought direct contact with the commercial side of publishing. Fairly early in his career, while involved in many other activities, both literary and nonliterary, Scott acquired the controlling interest in a publishing house.

The reasons for this venture were complex. Scott held a grudge against the major Edinburgh publishing firm of Archibald Constable. He wanted to help his friends John and James Ballantyne to establish themselves in the Edinburgh publishing and printing business, and he was fascinated by the world of commercial book production and relished the opportunity to market his own books as well as those of others.

Scott and his two friends, the Ballantynes, founded the publishing firm of John Ballantyne & Company in Edinburgh in 1805. From then till the end of his life, Scott remained in the publishing business. He put up the capital for his half-share of the enterprise, but there is reason to believe that he also furnished the capital for the shares of the two brothers.[10] He invested at least £9000 in the firm between 1805 and the end of 1810.[11] For a time, the venture was quite successful, mainly because of the sales of Scott's own works. Yet there were continual difficulties, and Scott was repeatedly asked to provide funds at a moment's notice to avert a crisis.

On the other hand, Scott also from time to time borrowed from the firm in order to buy land for his country estate. In any case, his private finances were inextricably involved with the fortunes of the publishing business.

The Ballantyne venture proved unsuccessful in the long run. Finally, in May, 1813, John Ballantyne & Company had to be liquidated as a publishing house. Its assets were bought by its competitor, Archibald Constable, once owner of a small bookshop, who had become the leading Scottish publisher. But this failure did not end Scott's romance with printing and the book trade. Although Constable was now his publisher, a new printing house, James Ballantyne & Company, set up by Scott, continued to print his books. And Scott provided almost all the capital for the new firm.[12] For years, Scott's very substantial profits from his books went into extravagant purchases of land and additional buildings for his country estate, Abbotsford, or into the Ballantyne firm. Never very well versed in finance, Scott failed to keep close track of his income and expenses. The income was very large indeed, but his sinking so much money into Abbotsford meant that his cash position was never very good, even in the years of prosperity. Between 1816 and 1821, he had been forced to borrow money by means of bills drawn by Ballantyne on Constable and then discounted by the banks. Suddenly, late in 1825, after a year of wild speculation, the bankers began to refuse to extend further credit, and a financial crisis ensued. First Hurst and Robinson, Constable's London connection, went bankrupt for £300,000. Constable soon followed for £250,000, and Ballantyne owed Constable and the banks £117,000. The ensuing failure of the firm made public for the first time the fact that Scott owned it. Early in 1826, Scott realized the extent of the catastrophe: "Constable has failed," he exclaimed, "and I am ruined *du fond au comble*."[13]

Scott could have induced the Ballantyne firm to declare itself insolvent, come to some agreement with the creditors, and begun afresh. He refused this way out, however, for he considered it dishonorable. He decided to pay every penny of his debts. With the agreement of the firm's creditors, a trust was set up, under the terms of which Scott undertook to repay his debts from the proceeds of his future literary work. These debts amounted to nearly £120,000, apart from a mortgage on his Abbotsford estate. At the time of his death six years later, Scott still owed £22,000 plus interest. He was fifty-five when the catastrophe occurred, and he spent the rest of his life trying to clear his name.

Scott's obsession with money had many precapitalistic features. He was not concerned simply with gaining a fortune, as many a *bourgeois* writer was later to be. Money was to him a means for acquiring more and more land and for adding more and more wings to his country house. Scott's major ambition was to found an independent branch of the "clan Scott" and to symbolize it in the splendors of his estate. His involvement in printing and publishing and the turning of his immense talent to commercial uses were, in a way, an attempt to utilize the new means of capitalistic production for the market in the service of a feudal ideal. The desire to become laird of Abbotsford fired Scott's energies and involved him in publishing ventures, speculations, and commercial exploitation. Although he plunged into business, however, Scott had none of the characteristics of the rational and prudent businessman. He was generous, trustful, improvident, and indifferent to the details of commercial transactions. "The combination," says Hesketh Pearson, "resulted in catastrophe."[14]

Yet Scott was also genuinely devoted to literature. He was probably quite sincere when he told his son-in-law, "I never knew the day that I would have given up literature for ten times my late income."[15] Nevertheless, he would have served literature better had he served commerce less well.

The story of Scott's life in his last few years, when he was driven to exhaust himself at the writing table in order to clear his name and reputation, reads like a tragic coda to his literary career. He was now truly the slave of the market, flogging himself on to produce more and more in order to satisfy his creditors. The book market, which had seemed to offer so many opportunities for realizing his dreams of feudal grandeur, had now become a cruel slave master.

WILLIAM M. THACKERAY

Until his early twenties, Thackeray was a young gentleman who could look forward to living on the substantial fortune that his father had bequeathed to him. Then suddenly the estate was lost in the failure of several great Indian agency-houses in which it had been involved, and Thackeray found himself a poor man. He spent much of his life in efforts to recoup his fortune, and his literary activity was in the main devoted to this end. There are few writers, one surmises, to whom money is as important as it was to Thackeray, perhaps few also who have been as much guided in their literary labors by the quest for it.

Thackeray started his literary career as a London journalist. Journalism in the 1830s was not yet considered a respectable calling for a gentleman. "Magazine work is below street sweeping as a trade," Carlyle wrote in 1831.[16] And Thackeray himself wrote later, "a literary man . . . ranks below that class of gentry composed of the apothecary, the attorney, the wine-merchant, whose positions, in country towns at least, are so equivocal."[17] But Thackeray's needs were so pressing that he could not afford to be squeamish. For the first ten years of his writing career, he was a columnist, first for *Fraser's Magazine* and later for *Punch*, in order to make a living. It is interesting to note that he used a pen name in those years, perhaps so as not to endanger his social standing among his friends. His pay was poor; *Fraser's* at first paid him £10 a sheet (sixteen magazine pages), later raising him to twelve guineas a sheet. After a few years, however, Thackeray became one of the most renowned free-lance journalists in London, contributing to a dozen magazines and newspapers. Most of the work of this period was dashed off quickly under the pressures of deadlines. He wrote enormously, enough in fact to fill several volumes each year. But in all those years, says his biographer, Gordon N. Ray, "he anxiously desired a success which continually evaded his grasp."[18] He tried his best, wrote Thackeray himself, to "chasten and otherwise popularize" his style. "I can suit the magazines," he wrote, "but I can't hit the public, be hanged to them." He was forever asking himself, "How are we to take this great stupid public by the ears?" Later he told friends that he had "fought fiercely" for popularity, but all seemed in vain, though matters improved considerably after he joined *Punch*.[19] He then earned about £800 a year, and *Punch* paid "more than double what I get anywhere else."

Success finally came with the publication of *Vanity Fair*. Thackeray could at last afford to abandon journalism—except for his work on *Punch*, where the high pay kept him writing a while longer. But he was still as haunted by the quest for money as he had been in his impecunious days as a journalist. *Vanity Fair*, first published in monthly numbers and then issued as a book, netted him £2000. He became a popular favorite,[20] but he had to start on a new novel immediately to stay among the front-runners.

Even before finishing *Vanity Fair*, he signed a contract for his next novel, *Pendennis*, which was to bring him "£1000 a year."

This book was also to appear in serial form, and Thackeray wrote each installment a few days before it appeared. Although he was no longer a journalist, he produced novels under the pressures of deadlines similar to those he had had to meet in his younger years. The monthly parts of *Vanity Fair* and *Pendennis* were dashed off a few days before they were published, the printer's boy often waiting for the author to finish the sheets before carrying them off to the press.[21]

Thackeray soon came to move in the highest social circles; he became one of the most admired authors of Victorian England. But still he felt impelled to write hurriedly and to write for popular success. "If I could get a place and rest," he confessed, "I think I could do something better than I have done, and leave a good and lasting book behind me."[22] But he was never to have that rest until it was too late and his creativity already exhausted.

In further efforts to augment his income, Thackeray began to lecture, first in England, then in America. He appears never to have enjoyed this work as Dickens did. But he found it "the easiest and most profitable business."[23] He wrote that "my conscience revolts at the quackery,"[24] but still he went on. He hated this "ambulatory quack business," but his first American tour, for example, netted him £2500, which was invested in 8% railway bonds that brought him about £200 a year. His second American tour netted £3000.

In 1853, he wrote to his mother, "I have signed and sealed with Bradbury and Evans for a new book in 24 numbers like *Pendennis* —Price £3600 plus £500 from Harper and Tauchnitz. It's coining money isn't it?"[25] Thackeray felt by no means confident that he could bring the book off, for he felt played out—but publish he must. "I am about a new story," he writes, "but don't know as yet whether it will be any good. It seems to me I am too old for story-telling: but I want money and shall get 20,000 dollars for it."[26] The book was written in fits of depression and under the constant prodding of the need for money. "I sleep like a monk," writes its author, "with a death's head in my room. 'Come', says the cheerful monitor, 'rouse yourself. Finish *Newcomes*. Get a few thousand pounds more, my man, for those daughters of yours. For your time is short. . . . Get 200 a year apiece for your girls and their poor mother, and then come to me!' So be it . . ."[27] "But I can't but see it as a repetition of past performances," he also writes, "and think that vein is pretty nigh worked out in me. Never mind: this is not written for glory but for quite as good an object, namely money."[28]

Marx's description of alienation strikes one as peculiarly relevant to Thackeray's work in his later period. "His work is not voluntary but imposed, *forced labor*. It is not the satisfaction of a need, but only a means for satisfying other needs. . . . It is not his work but work for someone else . . . in work he does not belong to himself but to another person . . . The work is *external* to the worker . . . it is not a part of his nature . . . consequently he does not fulfill himself in his work but denies himself, has a feeling of misery, not of wellbeing, does not develop freely a physical and mental energy, but is physically exhausted and mentally debased."[29] Thackeray, using the novel mechanisms of market production of literary wares, finally became, like Marx's worker, a mere cog in the machinery of production.

Newcomes was another success. Thackeray now set out on another lecture tour, reading his *The Four Georges*; this tour earned him more than £5000, but he finally gave up lecturing, "I am sick of letting myself out for hire."[30] He accepted the editorship of *Cornhill* Magazine, from which he received almost £600 a month. But his creativity was clearly declining. "I sit for hours before my paper," he confessed, "not doing my book, but incapable of anything else, and thinking upon that subject always, waking with it, walking about with it, and going to bed with it. Oh, the struggles and bothers—oh the throbs and pains about this trumpery!"[31] Ill health bothered him, but he went on with dogged determination to finish another and yet another mediocre work. "I can repeat old things in a pleasant way," he told a friend, "but I have nothing fresh to say."[32]

In the last three years of his life, Thackeray was guaranteed an income of £7000 a year (up to that date, he had earned about £32,000 in all). After his death, his estate amounted to considerably more than the £18,000 at which Thackeray had valued it. He had finally recouped the fortune he had lost as a youth. But at what price?

It is always hazardous to conjecture that an author would have produced superior work had circumstances been more favorable. But in Thackeray's case, such a judgment is inescapable. Had not the terror of failure driven him like the furies, had he not lived in an age in which the commercialization of literature offered ever new temptations to one willing to be tempted, he would have written much less, and his work would have revealed fewer flaws. *Vanity Fair* and *Pendennis*, at least, will always be considered splendid examples of the English novel, but his work was nevertheless deeply flawed, if only by the compromises he made in order not to infringe the Victorian standards of propriety, in order not to offend his readers. Thackeray was not himself a prudish man. On the contrary, he loved to tell salacious stories and crude jokes in the company of his cronies. But his novels live up to the most exacting standards of middle-class morality—and lose thereby. For example, as Gordon Ray remarks, in the real world, "A young man in Pen's situation [in *Pendennis*] would in all probability have made Fanny his mistress. But as a character in a novel, by seducing Fanny, Pen would have become a villain, and since he is Thackeray's hero . . . this is impossible. Hence nothing happens . . . The incongruity is so marked, the anti-climax so extreme, that this episode has become a *locus classicus* of Victorian reticence."[33] Thackeray often complained that "Society will not tolerate the Natural in our Art"— but he always finally accepted society's dictates, for going against them would have endangered success. While an editor of *Cornhill*, he declined a short story by Trollope because it alluded "to a man with illegitimate children, and to the existence of a woman not as pure as she should be."[34] In almost all his writings, Thackeray adapted his manner to the public taste. Louis Dudek is right when he remarks, " 'What the people like is sentiment,' he had observed during one of his lecture tours; and this view could only lead to a willingness to gratify the public, when success meant so much."[35]

Thackeray confessed in one of his letters, "I don't care . . . for my art enough."[36] Most of later literary criticism concurs in this judgment. It was, perhaps, Thackeray's personal failing, but his incessant pursuit of the bitch goddess success was one of the major, perhaps the dominant, response to an age in which literary pursuits had become commercialized. It was possible to resist the lures of mass success, as some eminent Victorians did. Thackeray, however, was unable to do so.

CHARLES DICKENS

The private furies that drove Charles Dickens in his quest for public success and in his frantic efforts to accumulate ever larger sums of money through his writing and public speaking are of concern to us in only a peripheral way. The center of interest here is less his private motives than the social framework that allowed such dreams to be realized. No doubt, the deep traumata of Dickens's youth—his father's incarceration in a debtors' prison, his own abrupt removal from school soon after his twelfth birthday and his forced labor in a dingy blacking warehouse for six shillings a week, the grinding poverty of his early years—all these factors and many more account for much of Dickens's concern with money and success in his later years. But the fact is that, only in an age in which publishing had come of age, in which the products of the printing presses reached practically the whole of the British population, could a writer acquire a fortune.

Undoubtedly, Dickens's capacity to transcend class barriers among his readers made him the leading Victorian best seller. Perhaps no other novelist in the English language ever equaled Dickens in this respect. He was read by the upper and by the middle classes, but he also had an immense following in the lower strata of society. After *Pickwick Papers*, he commanded an audience that had no equal in England. "Judges on the bench and boys in the street," wrote his biographer and friend Foster *à propos* the reception of the *Papers*, "gravity and folly, the young and the old, those who were entering life and those who were quitting it, alike found it to be irresistible."[37] No wonder that his publishers, who had originally sought out the unknown young man to do a piece of hackwork, paid him an extra sum of £2000 above the meager amount they had originally contracted to pay him. They had made about £14,000 on this work alone.[38]

This early success was to be repeated over and over again. It would be tedious to enumerate here the sales figures for his novels and the sums he received for them. Suffice it to say that, when he died, his estate amounted to £93,000, all of it earned through writing, editing, and lecturing.[39] (His earnings over the years were, of course, much greater. Dickens lived on a lavish scale, and he had to support his own large family, as well as a number of relatives.)

After publication of *Pickwick Papers*, Dickens always had a sizable bank account. Certainly after the writing of *Dombey and Son*, when he was not yet forty years old, Dickens was economically secure. What, then, accounts for the fact that his letters, earlier and later, contain almost obsessive references to profits and sales?

"The *Haunted Man* has sold at this minute (being published this morning) 18,000!!!" "My clear profit—my own, after all deductions and expenses—has been more than a thousand guineas a month." "I am going on (between ourselves) at a *clear profit* of £1300 per week."[40]

Such references abound. Yet, in contrast to Thackeray, Dickens was hardly moved by the lure of gain in itself.

For Dickens, money was a means rather than an end. Perhaps monetary returns were symbolic of what he craved most: the love of his audience. The sales of his books, the success of his lectures and of his magazines, supplied him with continued assurance that he was loved. It was the visible embodiment of the favors, the adoration, of his audience.

While Thackeray consciously trimmed his work to current winds of doctrine, Dickens strove to preserve his artistic integrity. He was very much concerned with the dignity of the writer's calling. He exhibited a high seriousness lacking in Thackeray. He saw himself as a reformer, as well as an observer, of manners and morals. Yet his striving for success did impair his work.

In the first place, Dickens wrote too much. He had an almost demoniacal energy. But even a man of such exuberant powers could not always sustain the pace at which he drove himself. There were times when he was writing two novels at the same time, others when he simultaneously wrote Christmas stories, worked on one novel or another, and edited his magazine *Household Words*. These pressures could not but lower the quality of the writing. Furthermore, almost all his work was first produced in numbers or in serial form. This mode of production, most closely resembling journalism, had the advantage of allowing the writer to gauge the public's response almost immediately, rather than only upon completion of a work. Dickens would produce only two or three numbers ahead of that on press, so that he could take the public's reaction to earlier numbers into account while working on later chapters. This mode of publication was to Dickens a means of increasing his closeness to the public, but it also forced him to produce hastily and under the influence of moods momentarily induced by his readers' reactions. "You can rely on my knowledge of the audience," Dickens wrote to Bulwer Lytton.[41] His knowledge of his audience indeed enabled him never to lose touch, but this very closeness to the public pulse also forced him to adopt a style and a manner of construction that often left much to be desired. In his work, there is little of the carefully devised structure that one encounters in the work of George Eliot, for example.

Dickens was a crusading reformer at heart. But his desire to remain in touch with his beloved public also seems to have prevented him in most of his work from making a radical critique of Victorian society. He wanted to be ahead of his readers—but not too much. His editing of the phenomenally successful *Household Words* suggests this attitude. Each number contained material attributable to the reformer's zeal, yet "among the six to nine items filling its twenty-four pages, there were never more than two or three devoted to reform causes; usually there was only one."[42] Dickens provided amusement above all and did not allow reform to interfere with the main appeal of his magazine. No wonder that Lord Northcliffe, the father of yellow journalism, was later to pay Dickens the dubious compliment of calling him the greatest editor either of his own or any other age.[43]

Had Dickens lived a century earlier, his most characteristic problem—that of never losing touch with his public—would not have arisen. The public, in his day, was a mass public, no longer the fairly restricted middle-class audience of Richardson or Goldsmith. Those writers still had opportunities to encounter their public directly in London coffeehouses, in stage coaches, or at the homes of friends and well-wishers. There were no such opportunities in Dickens's age, yet he was possessed by an overriding urge to commune with his readers. Hence his eagerness to bend to his wishes such new media as serials, numbers, popular magazines. Hence also that climactic involvement with his audience through public readings during the last ten years of his life.

At these readings throughout the length and breadth of England, as well as on extended American tours, the crowd was enthusiastic, the theaters and lecture halls overflowed, and Dickens's appearances occasionally threatened to lead to public riots. A consummate actor, Dickens could make his audience weep in sorrow, gasp in fright, or recoil in horror as he read from his work. He gave no less than 423 paid readings, for which he was paid more than £100 each.[44]

But this financial success was not the only reason public readings appealed to Dickens. He seems to have derived from these occasions and from the ensuing popular applause as much psychic satisfaction as did his public. He achieved an ecstatic communion with his listeners. The power to make them weep and cry, the ability to play upon their sensibilities at will seems to have given Dickens almost orgasmic pleasure. He was often totally exhausted by a public appearance, near collapse after having spent all his energies to reach the climax, yet in his last years he began to neglect his writing for more tours, more revivifying contract with his audience. He defied the advice of friends and medical men, giving still more readings, tasting again and again his power to make people laugh or cry.

In the final analysis, then, it was not perhaps Dickens's quest for money that most deeply influenced his work, although it played its part, but his ever renewed quest for public adulation. Living in an age in which everyone was a potential reader and in which it was clearly no longer possible to establish personal contact with even a small fraction of the public, Dickens, urged on by his insatiable desire for applause, nevertheless tried, desperately and anxiously. He knew more of his public than perhaps any other author in his time. But he finally consumed himself in what was bound to be an illusory quest.

GEORGE ELIOT

The mere existence of a market for books and other literary productions tempts writers to depart from the canons of their craft. Although many have found it hard to resist the temptation, it can be resisted nevertheless, as the life and work of George Eliot testify.

"Poor Dickens' latter years," wrote George Eliot in a letter, "wear a melancholy aspect, do they not?—in the feverish pursuit of loud effects and money."[45] George Eliot's own literary life was guided by different standards. Not that she disliked money—"We are not greedy," she wrote, "though we are far from being indifferent to money . . ."[46] Elsewhere she noted, "I prize the money fruit of my labour very highly as the means of saving us dependence or the degradation of writing when we are no longer able to write well or to write what we have not written before."[47] George Eliot was aware of the importance of commercial success, but she never compromised her artistic standards in order to gain it.

In an age in which serial publication was thought to be the main avenue to wide circulation and high returns, she refused to resort to it—except in one case. She felt that the demands on her time, the need to publish, as it were, under the pressures of deadlines, would be detrimental to her work and to her artistic integrity. "Unless she sees her book nearly completed," writes her companion, George Henry Lewes, "and such as she considers worthy of publication, she objects to begin printing it."[48] And even the one case in which she departed from this standard, the agreement to publish *Romola* in *Cornhill*, reveals her amazing capacity to resist pecuniary considerations in her work. The story is worth retelling.

The publisher George Smith offered her the unprecedented sum of £10,000 for *Romola*, stipulating that the book was to be of such a length that it would "extend through sixteen numbers of the magazine." When the book was almost completed and publication about to start, George Eliot told the publisher that she could not in good conscience divide it into sixteen parts and that it would have to be published in twelve. Smith could not agree to this request, for it would have made each installment too costly. So George Eliot agreed to be paid only £7500, rather than allow artistic damage to the novel. Smith later wrote, "George Eliot was immovable and threw away £2500 on what many people would think a literary caprice, but what she regarded as an act of loyalty to her canons of art."[49]

Lewes and she lived in considerable financial difficulties in the first struggling years of their union. They certainly needed every extra pound either one could add to their income. Although Lewes, quite in tune with the literary *mores* of the time, was often tempted to engage in a variety of commercial projects, George Eliot refused to do so. A writer who had begun her career with translations of Strauss and Feuerbach, as well as of Spinoza, all of which were evidently labors of love rather than commercial enterprises, she adhered to her severe early standards throughout her career. After the publication of *Adam Bede*, however, financial independence was assured. George Eliot's books commanded major attention, and she received a very substantial literary income. *The Mill on the Floss* brought her more than £4000, *Felix Holt* £5000. *Middlemarch* sold 33,000 copies in a few years and netted her nearly £9000. *Daniel Deronda* brought over £9000.[50] All told, her literary income over the years amounted to some £45,000—a very sizable fortune. The money, carefully invested, brought a regular and stable income. Yet, had she employed methods of publication like those Dickens or Thackeray resorted to, she could have increased this fortune tenfold.

George Eliot felt strongly that a work of art was an organic growth. When she started a new book, she became completely absorbed in it, convinced that once it had begun to take shape in her mind, it would impose its own rhythms and demands on her. After finishing *Middlemarch*, she wrote, ". . . I have finished my book and am thoroughly at peace about it—not because I am convinced of its perfection, but because I have lived to give out what it was in me to give . . . When a subject has begun to grow in me I suffer terribly until it has wrought itself out—become a complete organism; and then it seems to take wing and go away from me. That thing is not to be done again—that life has been lived."[51] Given such a high conception of the writer's craft, it is understandable why George Eliot had "the strongest objection to cutting up my work into little bits; and there is no motive to it on my part, since I have a large public already . . . if I could gain more by splitting my writing into small parts, I would not do it, because the effect would be injurious as a matter of art."[52]

Not only serial publication and its injurious effects on literary integrity appalled George Eliot. She also strongly believed that one should write only when one had something important to say. Complaints about the tendency of contemporary writers to write too much frequently recur in her letters. "I have the conviction," she wrote, "that excessive literary production is a social offence."[53] Elsewhere she added, "Every one who contributes to the 'too much' of literature is doing grave social injury. And that thought naturally makes one anxious."[54]

George Eliot's letters show that this woman, who had lost her religious faith early in life, considered writing a kind of priesthood, one that imposed the most exacting standards on its practitioners. She loved her public and was deeply concerned with its reactions to her books, but she would have considered it an insult to that public to stoop to conscious efforts to please or to placate it. This attitude accounts for the magnificent integrity of her production. She stated her credo when she wrote, ". . . while I am unable to write a sentence for the sake of pleasing other people, I should be unable to write at all without strong proofs that I had touched them."[55] And she restated it shortly afterward in a letter to her publisher: "Still it is a comfort to me to read any criticism which recognizes the high responsibilities of literature that undertakes to represent life. The ordinary tone about art is, that the artist may do what he will, provided he pleases the public."[56]

George Eliot's career proves the untenability of overly deterministic interpretations of the situation of writers in a commercial age. Such an age may indeed lower the quality of the artistic offerings of many writers who are willing to compromise, but it does not necessarily do so. The temptation can be resisted, and it can be resisted without turning one's back on the public and without exclusive reliance on the approval of an esoteric coterie. George Eliot was one of the most widely read authors in her lifetime. She commanded an enthusiastic audience not only in England but also in America and on the Continent, yet her works grew organically from her own preoccupations, her own travail, her own struggles to achieve perfection. That is why she achieved a depth of moral and aesthetic seriousness that went, as a modern critic, Walter Allen, has noted, beyond anything the early Victorians proposed. Dickens and Thackeray "saw themselves sometimes as preachers and reformers, always as public entertainers."[57] George Eliot's conception of her art was much nearer to that of Flaubert in its exacting demands upon the writer. She lacked the surface graces of a Thackeray, but she gave a much richer and fuller picture of human behavior, for hers was a fuller response to life. While Thackeray was a man defeated by life, her life was a triumph.

NOTES

1. These data are quoted from Raymond Williams, *The Long Revolution* (London: Chatto & Windus, Ltd., 1961), p. 166. I have used Mr. Williams's data throughout the first few pages of this chapter.

2. Edgar Johnson, *Charles Dickens, His Tragedy and Triumph* (New York: Simon and Schuster, Inc., 1952), pp. 946–7.

3. G. E. Trevelyan, ed., *Life and Letters of Lord Macaulay* (New York: Harper & Row, Publishers, 1870). Letter to Napier, June 26, 1838.

4. *Cambridge History of English Literature*, XII (New York: G. P. Putnam's Sons, 1916), 30–1.

5. I borrow this phrase from Harry Levin, *The Gates of Horn* (New York: Oxford University Press, Inc., 1963).

6. Walter Allen, *The English Novel* (Everyman ed.; New York: E. P. Dutton & Co., 1954), p. 135.

7. Hesketh Pearson, *Walter Scott* (London: Methuen & Co., Ltd., 1954), p. 64.

8. *Ibid.*, p. 89.

9. David Douglas, ed., *The Journal of Sir Walter Scott*, I (New York: Harper & Row, Publishers, 1890), p. 122.

10. Pearson, *op. cit.*, p. 87.

11. *Ibid.*, p. 97.

12. *Ibid.*, and Stephen Gwynn, *The Life of Sir Walter Scott* (Boston: Little, Brown & Co., 1930), Chapter X.

13. Pearson, *op. cit.*, p. 226.

14. *Ibid.*, p. 222.

15. *Ibid.*, p. 231.

16. Quoted in Gordon N. Ray, *Thackeray: The Uses of Adversity* (New York: McGraw-Hill Book Co., Inc., 1955), p. 194. I have used

this volume and the second volume of Mr. Ray's monumental biography as my major sources.

17. *Ibid.*, p. 195.

18. *Ibid.*, p. 346.

19. *Ibid.*, p. 347.

20. *Ibid.*, p. 428.

21. Ray, *Thackeray: The Age of Wisdom* (New York: McGraw-Hill Book Co., Inc., 1958), pp. 175–6.

22. *Ibid.*, p. 132.

23. *Ibid.*, p. 168.

24. *Ibid.*, p. 169.

25. *Ibid.*, p. 222.

26. Ray, ed., *The Letters and Private Papers of William Makepeace Thackeray*, III (Cambridge, Mass.: Harvard University Press, 1945–1946), 293–4.

27. *Ibid.*, p. 359.

28. *Ibid.*

29. *Economic and Philosophical Manuscripts*, quoted in Thomas Bottomore and Maximilian Rubel, eds., *Karl Marx, Selected Writings* (London: C. A. Watts & Co., Ltd., 1956), pp. 169–70.

30. Ray, ed., *Letters*, IV, 60.

31. Ray, *Wisdom*, p. 364.

32. *Ibid.*, p. 371.

33. *Ibid.*, p. 125.

34. *Ibid.*, p. 310.

35. Louis Dudek, *Literature and the Press* (Toronto: Ryerson Press, 1960), p. 203.

36. Ray, *Letters*, III, 13.

37. Johnson, *op. cit.*, p. 155. I have relied on this fine biography throughout.

38. *Ibid.*, p. 205.

39. *Ibid.*, p. 1146.

40. Quoted in Dudek, *op. cit.*, pp. 167–8. Mr. Dudek's study of Dickens in this book was most helpful to me.

41. Johnson, *op. cit.*, p. 176.

42. *Ibid.*, p. 717.

43. *Ibid.*

44. *Ibid.*, pp. 1145–6.

45. Gordon S. Haight, ed., *The George Eliot Letters*, VI (7 vols.; New Haven: Yale University Press, 1954–1955), 23.

46. *Ibid.*, p. 303.

47. *Ibid.*, III, 396.

48. *Ibid.*, IV, 18.

49. Anne Fremantle, *George Eliot* (London: Gerald Duckworth & Co., Ltd., 1933), pp. 108–9; and Haight, *op. cit.*, IV, 34.

50. On her literary earnings, see Haight, *op. cit.*, VII, 358ff.
51. *Ibid.*, V, 324.
52. *Ibid.*, VI, 179.
53. *Ibid.*, V, 185.
54. *Ibid.*, 212.
55. *Ibid.*, III, 393.
56. *Ibid.*, 394.
57. Allen, *op. cit.*, pp. 254–5.

Chapter 7

BRITISH NINETEENTH-CENTURY REVIEWS

FROM THE EARLY NINETEENTH CENTURY ON, THE independent review, published by a group of like-minded writers, served as a major influence on intellectual life in England. In an age of rapidly increasing readership, which called forth a flood of publications of various sorts, pressures arose for the emergence of institutions that would serve to establish standards and to guide tastes and would at the same time help to clarify public opinion by the formulation of political doctrine. As ideas could no longer be debated with ease in direct contact between writer and public, the need for intermediaries arose. As the patron with his individual taste was displaced by a wider audience and then as the relatively small reading group that had frequented the coffeehouses grew from year to year, institutions arose to clarify taste and to transform clashes of interests into conflicts of well formulated sets of ideas. The nineteenth-century reviews and the intellectuals associated with them helped to fashion the ideological, political, and aesthetic preferences of the new middle-class audience. Such reviews either reflected fairly broad spectra of opinions, representing general political tendencies, or they were mouthpieces for specific doctrines and ideas.

After the early eighteenth century, authors gradually reached the point where they could address a large body of readers who were sufficiently cultivated to welcome and purchase a variety of literary productions.[1] To be sure, the reading public was still most restricted by modern standards—Edmund Burke estimated it at 80,000 out of a population of roughly six million in the 1790s—so that Dr. Johnson's assertion that England had become "a nation of readers" must be taken with a grain of salt.[2] Nevertheless, the reading public, as we have seen, grew rapidly throughout the eighteenth century, and this growth accelerated in the early parts of the succeeding century.

During the eighteenth century, essay serials, magazines, monthlies, and reviews multiplied. The publishers of various types of periodical gradually attracted the leading poets, essayists, and critics, so that "a roster of names prominent in periodical literature is very nearly an outline of the literary history of the eighteenth and nineteenth century."[3] By 1800, a total of 264 periodic publications was being printed in England. But many of them were published by booksellers and publishers who also published books and therefore had a major interest in having their books "puffed" by authors writing in their subsidized publications. Much of what went by the name of "reviewing" in the eighteenth and early nineteenth centuries was but thinly disguised advertisement for the wares of publishers. *The Westminster Review* described this practice in 1828, in terms that sound familiar to modern readers: "A publisher in a large way can put in or divert from the pockets of any newspaper proprietor many hundred pounds a year . . . Here is the secret of laudatory critiques, of favourable quotations, of sly allusions and grossly eulogistic paragraphs . . . A tacit contract subsists between one trade and the other; the one to pay, the other to praise. Criticism . . . has thus become one of the disguises in which the monster Puff stalks abroad seeking whom he may gull."[4]

Nor was it the pressure of advertisers and booksellers alone that adversely influenced the growing periodical literature. James Mill had already pointed out in an earlier issue of *The Westminster Review* that a periodical "cannot, like books, wait for success, but must succeed immediately, or not at all, and is hence almost certain to profess and inculcate the opinions already held by the public to which it addresses itself, instead of attempting to rectify or improve those opinions."[5] The periodical was thus likely to lose its independence either through the undue influence of publishers and advertisers or through the exigencies of a market situation that encouraged adaptation to public opinion rather than shaping of it.

And yet an ever-increasing reading public, no longer enjoying close association with men of letters, groped for criteria by which to assess the intellectual production of the age. The great independent quarterlies of the early nineteenth century, *The Edinburgh Review*, *The Quarterly Review*, and *The Westminster Review*, performed this role in England. In other countries, similar reviews served the same functions in roughly the same period, thus attesting to the broad similarity of conditions in the more developed Western nations. Later in the nineteenth century, other British reviews displaced the earlier initiators of independent reviewing.

The discussion that follows of the early *Edinburgh* and *Westminster Reviews* does not imply invidious comparisons with other reviews but only reflects the need to limit this exposition to a few concrete illustrations. They were chosen mainly because they represent the two major varieties of modern reviews: the first, the broad review of opinion and the second, the more narrow mouthpiece for a particular set of doctrines.

The great nineteenth-century reviews flourished because they met a need, but they were born out of the desire of small groups of writers to find tribunes from which they could express their independent ideas. Authors and editors of these reviews were wont to quarrel with one another, and there were constant shifts in editorial policy, resignations, secessions, and the creation of rival organs. Nevertheless these reviews could not have come into being except for the close collaboration of groups of men united in the advocacy of common sets of principles and beliefs, whether narrowly or widely conceived. Such collaboration is attested by the fact that these reviews did not publish signed articles but intensified the impact of their messages by using the majestic "We." They were truly the results of concerted thinking rather than of unaided individual efforts. Who, then, founded these reviews?

The founders were mostly younger men, whose capacities for innovation had not yet been deadened by routine participation in the traditional groves of intellectual life. The founders of *The Edinburgh Review* were all young men when the review was born in 1802: Sidney Smith, the father of the review, was thirty-one; Francis Jeffrey, the editor, twenty-nine; Broughan and Horner, its most active early contributors, twenty-four.[6] They belonged to the same generation and had been shaped and influenced by roughly the same set of historical events. Three of them also shared the same profession: the law. All of them were highly educated but poor, all discontented to one degree or another with the intellectual life of Edinburgh as well as with the professional careers open to them. The Edinburgh bar was dominated by the Tories, and the prospects for young Whig lawyers were quite bleak. As these young Whigs chafed under the manifold frustrations of Edinburgh professional, political, and intellectual life, they first conceived the idea of founding a review as a means of overcoming the lack of excitement in staid Tory society, a means to hit back at oppressive Tory dominance, and perhaps also as a means of personal advancement.

The *Westminster Review* was founded two decades after *The Edinburgh Review* on the initiative and with the backing of the aged Jeremy Bentham. It was to serve as a platform for the exposition of the Benthamite panacea—"the greatest happiness of the greatest number." But neither Bentham nor his faithful propagandist James Mill was in fact the moving spirit of the enterprise. This task fell to men of a younger generation. John Bowring, a city merchant and linguist, was thirty-two when he assumed the editorship. But the most active group of the early *Westminster Review* collaborators belonged to an even younger generation. This handful of very young men, led by James Mill's son, John Stuart Mill, then only seventeen years old, and calling themselves the Utilitarian Society, functioned as a sort of ginger group, prodding their more cautious elders into combat for the principles of pure Utilitarianism. The Utilitarian Society, writes its founder, was "to be composed of young men agreeing in fundamental principles—acknowledging Utility as their standard in ethics and politics . . . and meeting once a fortnight to read essays and discuss questions conformably to the premises thus agreed on."[7] It never had more than ten members, but it was composed of an elite of young intellectuals who had arrived at a common outlook after exhaustive and exhausting discussions. At first in Bentham's house, later in the city banking house of one of its members, George Grote, the group would meet to discuss James Mill's *Elements*, Ricardo's *Principles* and various manuals of political economy and logic. In 1825, the young propagandists invaded a co-operative society composed of disciples of Robert Owen, against whom they defended the principles of Utility in debates lasting five or six consecutive weeks, and thus established themselves in the public limelight. The little band of John Stuart Mill and his friends completed their philosophical education in common bouts with intellectual adversaries and thus readied themselves for active participation in the intellectual battles of the day.

Although the founders of *The Edinburgh* and *The Westminster Reviews* were mainly young men consciously bent on breaking with tradition, they were not without an intellectual inheritance. The young Utilitarians were in almost continuous contact with the earlier generation of Benthamites and with Bentham himself. John Stuart Mill's thought was still almost completely under the shadow of his father, and such older adherents to the Benthamite dispensation as Francis Place (a Charing Cross tailor and political reformer) and Joseph Hume (one of the early exponents of Benthamism in Parliament) exercised a stimulating, as well as a restraining, influence on the Young Turks of Utilitarianism. Even though they saw themselves as innovators, they were conscious of tradition. *The Edinburgh Review* collaborators, although not so directly tied to a specific philosophical tradition, also saw themselves as continuing a broad ideological orientation. They were closely linked to the Scottish "renaissance" of the preceding century. Several of the young men who founded *The Edinburgh Review* had known Adam Smith and William Robertson, Robert Burns and David Hume. They considered themselves the self-conscious perpetuators of Scottish eighteenth-century liberalism at a time when Scotland was dominated by the Tory cohorts of Henry Dundas, who, through skillful use of patronage power, had become the "manager" of Scotland. Most of them had listened to Dugald Stuart, Professor of Moral Philosophy at the University of Edinburgh, whose Whiggism provided them with a common intellectual framework and further linked them to the intellectual heritage of the Scottish enlightenment.

Around the turn of the century, most of the men who were to be associated with the new *Review* were members of the Academy of Physics and the Speculative Society, where young intellectuals in and around Edinburgh University discussed legal reform, literary subjects, and "the investigation of nature, the laws by which her phenomena are regulated, and the history of opinions concerning these laws."[8] The contributors to *The Edinburgh Review*, like the young Utilitarians of a later day, thus had occasion to meet in close personal and intellectual contact prior to the founding of their review and at the same time to renew their ties with elders who embodied the tradition they hoped to preserve in the very effort of renewing it. They had ascertained their respective opinions, de-

bated their points of agreement and difference, slowly formed a
common outlook through common intercourse in an otherwise
hostile intellectual atmosphere.

There is no better gauge of a magazine's impact than the response of its audience. The immediate success of *The Edinburgh
Review*, a success that seems to have been something of a surprise
to its founders, testifies to the fact that readers had, so to speak,
been waiting for it. Perhaps the background of frustration that had
marked its young authors in Edinburgh mirrored the more general
frustrations of a rising middle-class reading public suffering from
Tory domination in the world of ideas and politics all over the
country. Be that as it may, the fact is that the new middle-class
public responded with immediate sympathy to the first issue of the
Review. It apparently felt that this review attacked its problems,
talked its language, shared its own preoccupations, and was untrammeled by commercial servitude. Within a year, the first issue of
The Edinburgh Review had sold over 2000 copies. Succeeding issues
sold 5000 copies each. In a period of twelve years, the circulation
went up to a phenomenal 13,000 copies—at a time when *The Times*
printed only 8000 copies daily. Editor Jeffrey calculated that each
copy of the *Review* was read by about three readers, many borrowing it from friends or reading it in libraries. Because the price
—five and later six shillings—was such that only people who were
fairly well off could buy it and because its literary and cultural
level was quite high, it seems likely that the *Review* was read by
practically everybody among the well-to-do who had the leisure
and cultivation to read at all.

The Review's independence of judgment was one of the reasons
for its success. Although earlier reviews had upon occasion published severely critical pieces, *The Edinburgh Review* was the first
to pay sustained attention to critical standards. From its inception,
it gave notice that it would not hesitate to attack even established
reputations. Half the review articles in the first issue were adversely
critical pieces. They were written with wit and incisiveness and
contrasted most favorably with the tepid style readers had been
accustomed to in other periodicals.

Consistent political orientation even more than style and manner
of presentation distinguished the *Review*. It fought persistently for
a number of the central issues—Catholic emancipation, Parliamentary reform, free trade, abolitionism, legal reform—that agitated
Whig circles. It formulated the arguments and marshalled the facts

that Whig men of letters and Whig politicians in Parliament would use in their debates, thus serving to broaden the appeal of liberal ideas. It preached the gospel according to Adam Smith and Malthus, fought against Tory abuses, and so reformulated the tradition of the eighteenth-century Enlightenment as to make it serviceable for the early nineteenth century. The *Review* supplemented the private library of the Whig squire, the city merchant, or the country parson by critically sifting new books and establishing literary models, beside helping to form political opinion on the great issues of the day. Walter Bagehot put it well when he wrote, "The modern man must be told what to think shortly, no doubt, but he *must* be told . . . *The Edinburgh Review*, which began the system, may be said to be, in this country, the commencement on large topics of suitable views for sensible persons."[9]

The *Review*'s readers were far from a passive audience before omniscient writers. They sent critical letters, debated particular contributions, or sent contributions of their own. The editors and authors answered a great number of them and carried on a vast correspondence that further helped to bind the *Review* and its readers. In these ways "it met," to quote its historian John Clive, "the needs of a new public anxious for enlightenment and moral guidance; . . . perhaps its most important service was to instill in its readers respect for the power of their opinions, in other words, to exalt the *idea* of public opinion in the eyes of the public."[10]

While *The Edinburgh Review* thus served as an important influence on the reading public, it had an equally large influence on its contributors. It helped to draw together a galaxy of authors in addition to the small group of its founders. William Hazlitt, Thomas Carlyle, Macaulay, Malthus, and many less well known authors, though by no means always in agreement with everything said in the *Review* and not always faithful to it, developed a special kind of kinship with it. Although authors no longer necessarily had that close personal contact with one another that had characterized the coffeehouse, they grouped themselves around the *Review*, sharing in a common universe of ideas. For many, the *Review* provided not only intellectual contact but also the setting for personal meetings. The editorial office became a kind of informal forum where writers would meet one another, the editor, or, upon occasion, a reader.

The *Review* not only served to magnify the influence of writers upon their audience, it also increased their professional status and contributed to the professionalization of authorship. Its predecessors had paid their contributors wretchedly, so that most writers were either wealthy amateurs who did not have to live off their writings or Grub Street hacks. *The Edinburgh Review* paid unprecedented rates. Each writer was initially paid ten guineas a sheet as a minimum, and this figure was soon raised to sixteen guineas. As most articles brought more than the minimum, the average rate per sheet came to between twenty and twenty-five guineas—a quite considerable sum in an age when textile workers earned two shillings a day. The editor received fifty guineas an issue, in addition to what he earned for his own contributions. Furthermore, *The Edinburgh Review* established the principle, later adopted by its competitors, that every author was bound to accept payment. There was no longer to be a class distinction between those who disdained to be paid for their contributions on social grounds and those who had to earn their livings by writing. All were to be on the same footing, and the eighteenth-century distinction between Grub Street hacks and gentlemen of leisure disappeared.[11] Reviewing became a profession that attracted the very elite of writers. *The Edinburgh Review* thus contributed to the raising of the standards of authorship as significantly as it contributed to the raising of the standards of cultivation and political sophistication among its readers.

In the early 1820s, the Whigs had *The Edinburgh Review* and the Tories *The Quarterly Review*, which, except for its politics, resembled *The Edinburgh Review* in most respects. In 1824, *The Westminster Review* joined the company, representing Benthamism, the third major intellectual tendency in the Britain of the day. But although it followed its predecessors broadly in its mode of presentation, it also differed significantly from them. Where the earlier reviews reflected fairly broad spectra of opinion, *The Westminster Review* was founded explicitly as the organ of the Benthamites. From its inception, it had a much more specific program than that of the Edinburgh Whigs. While the latter had often been fresh and provocative, they had never been particularly radical; *The Westminster Review* was, by contrast, militant and dogmatically committed to the radical verities. In the very first issue, James Mill directed a merciless attack on *The Edinburgh Review*, accusing it of lack of principle and denouncing its habit of cleverly dodging major issues to gain the favor of all. *The Edinburgh Review*, he asserted, had no more concern for the interests of the common people than had the Tories of *The Quarterly Review*. *The West-minster Review* stood for radical reform, for middle-class ascend-ancy, for the application of the principle of greatest happiness to all aspects of British political, legal, and social life. With zestful irreverence, it attacked religious prejudices and intolerance of Catho-lics as well as of Deists, national prejudices and infringements upon the principle of democracy, conservative prejudices and the Burkean glorification of chivalry. "They scandalized," wrote Elie Halévy, "and set out to scandalize opinion by the affectation of their intransigence, and by the ostentation of their orthodoxy. They made it their mission to denounce all the 'vague generalities' which led moralists and politicians astray before the appearance of the Utilitarian philosophy."[12] They showed with relentless and doc-trinaire logic that only true believers in the principles of utility had access to the truth and that its adversaries could only be either "sentimentalists" or "idiots." *The Westminster Review* writers tended to substitute *a priori* reasoning for the inductive method, believing as they did that one could deduce the principles of gov-ernment from a few self-evident propositions about human nature. They were often insufferably dogmatic, merciless, and bitter in their onslaughts, but they did succeed in leaving an undeniable impress on British nineteenth-century opinion. If for no other reason, beyond the peculiarities of their doctrine, in their zeal for reform, in their advocacy of middle-class democracy, they were spokesmen for the more radical among the middle class and for all reformers.

Both *The Edinburgh Review* and *The Quarterly Review* were exponents of sets of political ideas, but *The Westminster Review* in its Benthamite phase—it was to change its politics in later years—advocated Benthamism as a kind of sovereign cure for all the ills of mankind. The *Review* was thus the organ of a specific school of political and philosophical thought unlike the other reviews, which served as broad platforms for sets of general principles. If it lacked the broadness of *The Edinburgh Review* and the latter's comparative tolerance, it made up for the lack by a consistent if somewhat monomaniacal devotion to propagation of Benthamite ideas. It never reached as wide a circle of readers—the first issue sold 2000 copies in its first edition and another 1000 in a second, but later second editions never proved feasible—as did *The Edin-burgh Review*, which sold roughly six times more copies, but its

influence on the core of Benthamite believers and on an outer fringe
of sympathizers was profound. It was the organ of a faction and
its most articulate propagandizer. It aimed to persuade rather than
to interest, to convert rather than to divert. Its missionary zeal
might annoy the indifferent, but it fired the energies of believers.

The *Westminster Review*, the organ of a sect, did not remain
free of the ailments peculiar to all sects: splits and secessions. Even
at its inception, the older Benthamites had fought among themselves, and the young Utilitarians around John Stuart Mill had in
their turn never succeeded in making the *Review* conform to their
desires. Nevertheless, initial success had temporarily led to a patching
of differences so that the *Review* appeared to outsiders as the
organ of a united group. But by 1828, when circulation had fallen
considerably and the *Review* had experienced severe financial trouble, key contributors revolted against Bowring's editorship, and the
Mill group finally withdrew completely. The *Review* then became
a comparatively uninteresting repository of Benthamite orthodoxy.
Finally, in the middle Thirties, when even John Stuart Mill no
longer could bring himself fully to accept orthodox Benthamite
doctrine, the Benthamite party disappeared, and *The Westminster
Review* became a general liberal organ. But in its early days it had
been a most potent stimulant for the ideas of radical social, judicial,
and electoral reforms that marked the century. The little band of
intellectual enthusiasts that had initially gathered round it had labored mightily to change public opinion in favor of reforms.
Without those efforts, such reforms—from repeal of the corn laws
to the broadening of the franchise—could never have been entered
upon the statute books of Britain. The impact of *The Westminster
Review* was less widespread but not necessarily less profound than
that of *The Edinburgh Review*. Although this organ of a sect
finally succumbed to its very sectarianism, it nevertheless, in the
relatively short period of its existence as a Benthamite organ, had a
profound effect on British intellectual and political life.

Intellectuals gathered around reviews like *The Edinburgh* and
The Westminster Reviews were thenceforward to use them as potent means of molding public opinion and taste. It is impossible
to write about nineteenth- or early twentieth-century intellectual
and political life without giving such reviews sustained consideration. They had become one of the central institutions of intellectual
life.

NOTES

1. *Cf.* Alexandre Beljame, *Men of Letters and the English Public in the Eighteenth Century* (London: Routledge & Kegan Paul, Ltd., 1948), *passim.* See also A. S. Collins, *Authorship in the Days of Johnson* (London: Robert Holden and Company, 1927); and Collins, *The Profession of Letters* (London: Routledge & Kegan Paul, Ltd., 1928).

2. Collins, *Profession*, p. 28.

3. Walter Graham, *English Literary Periodicals* (New York: Thomas Nelson & Sons, 1930), p. 15. This book is the standard work on British literary periodicals.

4. Quoted in George L. Nesbitt, *Benthamite Reviewing* (New York: Columbia University Press, 1934), p. 120. I have drawn heavily on this excellent history of *The Westminster Review*'s early years.

5. John Stuart Mill, *Autobiography* (New York: Columbia University Press, 1924), p. 65.

6. For details on *The Edinburgh Review*, I have relied heavily on John Clive, *Scotch Reviewers* (Cambridge, Mass.: Harvard University Press, 1957).

7. Mill, *op. cit.*, p. 56.

8. Quoted in Clive, *op. cit.*, p. 21.

9. Walter Bagehot, "The First Edinburgh Reviewers," Forrest Morgan, ed., *Works*, I (Hartford, Conn.: The Travelers Insurance Co., 1891), 7.

10. Clive, *op. cit.*, p. 184.

11. *Ibid.*, pp. 33–4.

12. Elie Halévy, *The Growth of Philosophical Radicalism* (New ed.; Boston: Beacon Press, 1955), p. 484. This fine book is the standard work on Benthamism.

Chapter 8

CENSORSHIP

CENSORSHIP IS MUCH OLDER THAN THE PRINTED WORD. But ever since the printing press made possible a wide diffusion of ideas, censorship has come fully into its own. Whatever the political constellation or form of government, no matter what the historical period, censorship has functioned everywhere as an important mechanism of social control. The powers have attempted everywhere to restrict the spread of ideas that they have deemed contrary to their own interests or to the good of the citizenry.

The fact that the censor erects barriers between writers and their audience, thus inhibiting the direct play of influence between them, makes him a most significant, though often neglected, determining force in intellectual life. The censor attempts to build a protecting wall between the reader and the potentially dangerous writer. What is intended as a solid wall turns out, in a great many cases, of course, to be only a semiporous partition, but it is true nevertheless that, to one degree or another, censorship succeeds in impeding the "natural" flow of ideas. It is therefore everywhere an obstacle to free intellectual life.

Types and degrees of censorship have varied widely in the modern world. Certain governments in certain periods have been quite indifferent to the possible moral corruption of their citizens, while being profoundly concerned with their possible contamination by unconventional political ideas. At other times, accepted religious dogma has been the main object of solicitude, and censorship has attempted to prevent the spread of ideas deemed heretical or blasphemous. At still other times, political, as well as social and religious, ideas have been rather scrupulously protected from censorial interference, while unconventional discussions of sexual matters have been repressed and labeled "obscene."

POLITICAL CENSORSHIP: PRE-REVOLUTIONARY FRANCE

Censorship cannot be understood outside its social context. Like other types of legal control, it can operate successfully only to the extent that at least a significant portion of the population and of the law-enforcement officers accept it and agree to its implementation. In other words, in the modern world, public opinion—except in totalitarian societies—is in fact more powerful than censorship. If it refuses endorsement of the censors' activities, they become ineffective. The case of pre-Revolutionary France is instructive in this respect.[1]

In eighteenth-century France, the main effect of forbidding the sale or publication of "undesirable" books was to increase their prices, for interested readers continued to avail themselves of costly illegal publications. To be sure, these higher prices restricted the sale of forbidden books to the moneyed elite and limited the influence of "subversive" ideas primarily to the nobility and the middle classes. But it was among these classes that a public opinion hostile to censorship first crystallized under the influence of the very writers whom the censors had attempted to repress. Large proportions of these classes were strongly motivated to buy *enlightened* literature by any means, even though the cost in monetary terms and in risk might be high.

The statutes governing censorship were exceedingly severe: An edict of April, 1757, announced the death penalty for authors and printers of unauthorized books; in 1767, the parliament passed a decree forbidding anyone to write on religious questions; a decree of 1774 obligated printers to obtain permission before printing a book and again after having printed it; in 1787, a decree was published permitting the surveillance of the sale of books in such previously privileged places as royal and princely mansions, to which the police had had no access till then. The list of such measures could be extended at will. From year to year, the number of policemen and spies employed to enforce this repression increased. They seemed to be everywhere—in streets, at fairs, in cafés, at dances. Informers were given large rewards for denouncing illegal publications. The number of authorized printers and booksellers was restricted in order to make surveillance easier. The list of books publicly burned on the grand staircase of the *Palais* at Paris is very long indeed. Many authors—Diderot, Morellet, and Marmontel among others—were imprisoned in the Bastille or at Vincennes. And while writers were usually given fairly short sentences, printers, booksellers, and readers of banned books were often handled with utmost severity. In 1768, an apprentice pharmacist who had bought a copy of *Le christianisme dévoilé* was condemned to nine years at forced labor, the man who had sold him the book received a five-year sentence at forced labor, and the bookseller's wife was condemned to imprisonment.

Yet despite this impressive display of repressive measures, unauthorized books were sold everywhere. Printers, librarians, booksellers, might not have been activated by libertarian motives, for the lure of commercial advantage and monetary gain would have been quite sufficient. A forbidden book immediately increased in price and whetted the appetite of an avid public. Forbidden books often sold many more copies than did the authorized ones. Illegal printing presses mushroomed in Paris and in the provinces. The presses of London, Amsterdam, Geneva, and Germany printed Voltaire and Rousseau, Holbach and Morelly, and hundreds of forbidden editions were printed abroad each year. These books poured into France on ships anchoring in Bordeaux, Le Havre, and Boulogne or crossed the Dutch border in private vehicles and especially in the carriages of the aristocracy, which were not checked. It was not only profitable but fashionable to help in the diffusion of forbidden books.

Noble lords sometimes provided asylum for persecuted authors in their provincial domains. After the revocation of the printing privilege for the *Encyclopédie*, the all-powerful minister Malesherbes himself arranged for the editors' manuscripts and documents to be hidden in his own house. The same Malesherbes tried to protect such books as *Emile* and *La Nouvelle Héloïse*. He initiated the practice of acting with great severity in the granting of official permissions to print, while at the same time giving tacit permissions, which, though not legally binding, sufficed in most cases to protect writer and printer. And soon the censors themselves could not longer be relied upon. Ostracized and ridiculed, they lost their sense of mission, their pride in their work. And as the name of "censor" became an insult, the profession attracted only the most mediocre—who could often be easily fooled—or people who were only too willing to assist the persecuted writers through various kinds of complacency. Sometimes the censors themselves praised in the most flattering terms the very books they forbade.

Yet exorbitant prices limited the sale of forbidden books. Censorship, which manifestly was set up to impede the flow of "enlightened" ideals in *all* classes, although it did not succeed in that aim, did serve to restrict this flow to the elite and middle social strata. The discrepancy between the official censorship regulations and their real impact was almost grotesque. There was little relation between *le pays réel* and *le pays légal*.

Given the limited audience, the sale of forbidden books was impressive. Voltaire's *Candide* went through forty-three editions before the Revolution; *La Nouvelle Héloïse* appeared in seventy editions, both pirated and authentic, before 1800. Most of Voltaire's better known works had about thirty editions before the Revolution. The *Encyclopédie* had 4000 subscribers in 1753; later two new editions appeared in France, and two pirated editions were printed in Italy and Switzerland. Considering that an edition might run anywhere between 500 and 4000 copies, in an age in which literacy was still severely limited and prices were high, these figures are impressive indeed. The forbidden books of the eighteenth century had a wider circulation and sale than the authorized books of the preceding century. What is more, in the same period and addressing the same potential readers, forbidden books often sold much better than even conventional "best sellers." Fénelon's *Télémaque*, the most widely read book apart from the works of the *philosophes*, had sixty-three editions from 1699 to 1789; that is, it attained in ninety years only the same number of editions that *La Nouvelle Héloïse* had reached in forty.

We may conclude from this rapid survey that censorship is ineffectual unless it can rely on fairly strong support from public opinion. Corrosive criticism by the *philosophes* had helped to undermine the system of values and the customs on which the *ancien régime* had relied to maintain itself. The middle class turned progressively from its initial attempt to climb the ladder of success in the old society to a system of ideas and values that opposed that society. To the extent that public opinion moved away from support of the power-holders of the *ancien régime* censorship became ever more difficult to enforce. And as the nobles themselves, whose interests might have predisposed them to support the regime, mocked and ridiculed its votaries and institutions, censorship became a farce.

When the very men who are supposed to uphold the law flout it more or less openly, the law becomes unenforceable. Social control must break down when the agents of control can no longer be relied upon. At that point, the passing of new laws is ineffectual. Indeed, the more severe the penalties, the more lax their application. Officials who would be prepared to hand out relatively weak penalties tend to overlook offenses involving very severe sanctions. When antiquated English laws in the early nineteenth century continued to prescribe hanging for theft and similar offenses, juries simply became reluctant to punish such offenders at all. When French eighteenth-century law prescribed imprisonment for writing books ridiculing the Church or the fads and foibles of the court, magistrates became more reluctant to apprehend, let alone to sentence, culprits. The very severity of the law thus led to its impotence.

Yet it would be superficial to maintain that eighteenth-century French history records the simple victory of pen over sword. In the first place, the censors, by forcing increases in the prices of books, indirectly decreased their circulation. The growing literacy in the population was thus at least partly neutralized by the fact that forbidden books were too expensive. The high prices of books that censorship brought about did not unduly perturb the upper and middle classes. In fact, they may even have welcomed them, for they had no interest in allowing their inferiors access to the ideas they themselves espoused. Tsarist censors used to permit the printing of such bulky and expensive books as *Das Kapital*, while prohibiting the publication of pamphlets and short works that might penetrate more easily into the lower orders. French prerevolutionary censors had no such intentions, but their policies had similar effects.

To the extent that its direct efforts achieved some success and to the extent that it succeeded unwittingly in raising the prices of books, censorship reduced the public of the *philosophes*. Their actual audience fell short of their potential audience.

The impact of censorship on the authors of censored books is perhaps even more profound. An author's sense of status is powerfully enhanced by a favorable response from his public. Florian Znaniecki has put the matter well: "Every social role presupposes that between the individual performing the role . . . and a larger or smaller set of people who participate in his performance . . . there is a common bond constituted by a complex of values which all of them appreciate positively."[2] A person cannot perform his role without a sustaining social circle; a writer cannot write without an audience. It follows that whatever restricts and restrains the audience impairs the work of the writer and renders his role more difficult. Not that the eighteenth-century writers completely lacked for an audience—but they nevertheless chafed under a censorship that artificially restricted it. The very capriciousness of the censorship, which allowed a certain leeway to the writer, may in fact have angered him all the more. The sense that he forever depended on the arbitrary actions of obscure officials, never able to say beforehand what would be allowed or disallowed, may actually have exacerbated the author's anger and rage.

Most of the *philosophes* were by no means revolutionaries. Most were, in fact, only too willing to support an enlightened monarchy, but the continued petty annoyances put in their paths; the snubs and insults they had to suffer; all the thousand and one hurts to their pride, their sense of mission, and their sense of personal rectitude that they had to endure combined to drive them ever further from the *ancien régime*. The very censorship instituted to maintain loyalty to the regime undermined the loyalty of its intellectuals. And the intellectuals in turn conveyed their alienation to their readers. The bitterness of the author was communicated to the reader, and its impact was probably enhanced by the fact that the book had been procured under difficult circumstances and at a financial sacrifice. That in which one invests much is likely to have a more powerful meaning than what requires little effort.

Censorship became an unintentional but powerful agency of alienation. There were many other abuses and oppressions that called forth the wrath of the *philosophes*, but censorship concerned them directly, touched upon the very mainsprings of their social position. And it concerned their economic position as well. Even though they may have rejoiced at the great number of clandestine editions that appeared despite the censors, they must also have reflected bitterly upon the fact that they received no royalties from most of them. Censorship robbed them of part of their audience and of a major portion of their literary property. While the *bourgeois* may have been most deeply moved by those restrictions on the free flow of goods that prevented them from reaching their markets, the intellectual was most angered by those barriers to the commerce of ideas that prevented him from reaching his full potential audience and from realizing a fair return for his work.

Censorship contributed its share to that divorce of the intellectual from the reigning assumptions of the dominant strata that has marked modern history. What is more, the conflict with the censors gave authors a collective cause, a banner around which to rally. It made for the strengthening of a collective consciousness, for awareness of a community of real and ideal interests transcending the manifold differences that otherwise divided intellectuals. Furthermore, the very conflict that mobilized the energies of the intellectuals also motivated them to find allies in wider strata of the population. They tied themselves to the interests of those *bourgeois* readers whose struggles against the *ancien régime* may have been motivated initially by quite different motives but who, under the influence of the *philosophes*, increasingly identified their own cause with the cause of freedom that inspired the intellectuals. Censorship had the unanticipated consequence of initiating the modern alliance between the cause of freedom and that of the intellect.

MORAL CENSORSHIP: THE VICTORIAN ERA IN AMERICA

Each society suppresses those activities that it judges to be peculiarly damaging to its dominant interests and concerns. This observation is true in the sphere of politics and religion, but it applies especially to sexual matters.[3] What is considered obscene or lascivious varies a great deal with time and place, and such evaluation must be understood in terms of dominant preoccupation and dominant interests. English literature was as free-spoken as any other from the days of Chaucer to those of Smollett. Only from the last years of the eighteenth century until today (or should one say just yesterday?) have England and the United States indulged in the suppression of writings deemed obscene. In fact it was only in the second half of the nineteenth century that censorship of "obscenity" assumed any major proportions in those two countries.

As long as the bulk of the population was either illiterate or
excluded from the book market for financial reasons, as long as an
educated and cultivated elite held a near monopoly of power and
was able to control the flow of ideas, very little was heard of laws
to suppress obscenity. Only as the masses began to make their entry
into the arena of history, as the monopoly of power and education
slipped from the hands of the elite, did censorship laws for obscenity assume any serious importance.

In England, the Obscene Publications Act, on which most of
the subsequent censorship of sexual writing has been based, was
passed in 1857, only a few years before passage of the Compulsory
Education Act in 1870. The connection between the growing literacy of the people and the interest in preventing publication of anything considered detrimental to sexual morals was hardly accidental.
This kind of censorship entered the scene only after the Industrial
Revolution. The lax and often licentious upper classes of the eighteenth century were not interested in suppressing obscenity in
literature. Their own standards were permissive, and they evidently
believed the lower classes were sufficiently protected by traditional
religious controls and lack of access to secular literature. To be
sure, Puritanism and the relatively strait-laced moral standards of
the middle—as distinct from the upper—classes were powerful influences against the freedom in matters of sexual morality that had
characterized Merrie England in the aristocratic age. Yet it is not
without significance that the Bible, which was, of course, the very
dearest of all books to the Puritans, was read with unalloyed devotion in the eighteenth century and that it was only in the subsequent
century that Noah Webster felt it necessary to edit an expurgated
edition because, he said, "Many passages are expressed in language
which decency forbids to be repeated in families and on the pulpit."

Once the lower classes had been freed from religious and traditional restraints, management of them became a key problem. With
the Industrial Revolution and the growth of an urban mass of laborers, the ruling strata faced unprecedented problems of control. Even
though the open political rebelliousness of the lower strata had
been crushed or dissipated by the end of the Age of the Chartists,
subtler forms of disaffection from reigning patterns of conduct
still threatened the established order. Industrial society demanded a
relatively high standard of literacy for the masses, and mass literacy
meant that it was no longer possible to shield them from the impact

of novel ideas—especially as cheap editions and cheap magazines had become easily available to the common reader.

Industrial society demanded of its workers methodical and disciplined work habits. It demanded that workers accept the "Puritan ethos" and its accompanying morality of postponed gratification. Unsupervised sexual relations, to the extent that they endanger the central role of the family in the channeling and domestication of sexual drives, hamper the required discipline of the work force. Free love not only creates fortuitous associations that, by their very nature, are not subject to control; it may also foster a spontaneity in human relationships and human personality that is incompatible with the discipline demanded from the lower classes. Whether or not so-called "obscene" literature in fact stimulates sexual appetites and loosens the ties of repression in the individual need not concern us here; the fact is that the powers that be in the Victorian Age believed that it did. Nor need we assume that the connections among sexual repression, political domination, and industrial discipline were at all times consciously recognized by those who instituted and supported censorship in sexual matters. The fact that censorship came to the fore not in the Puritan Age but only after the Industrial Revolution had led to the emergence of large urban masses is enough to indicate that it was latently connected with the need for novel forms of social control.

Furthermore, one need not rely on theoretical considerations alone. The manner in which censorship was practiced supports the view that suppression of obscenity and of subversion often go hand in hand. When, in 1818, the radical bookseller Richard Carlile brought out an edition of Paine's *Age of Reason*, prosecution was started by the Society for the Suppression of Vice. In a later age, the works of Lenin and Trotsky were seized as "obscenity" in America. Walt Whitman's *Leaves of Grass* was banned not only because of the author's frankness in matters of sex but also because his whole libertarian credo appalled the upholders of the genteel tradition. And later still the condemnation of Sinclair Lewis's *Elmer Gantry* can hardly have been caused by fear that it would stimulate lascivious thought. It came because the seduction of its religious hero cast doubt upon the uprightness of the upholders of tradition.

As long as the traditional forms of repression, whether religious or secular, sufficed and as long as the masses had no access to books or magazines, sexual censorship remained at most a peripheral matter. Only when the new modes of industrial and urban life had irrevocably damaged the traditional fabric did censorship in this area assume major proportions. Censorship was one of the by-products of the period of industrial take-off. In America, some states had attempted to strengthen the common law against "obscene libel" in the early parts of the nineteenth century, but federal legislation was not propounded until the first major upsurge of industrialism and urbanism, that is, in the 1860s. In 1865, the transmission of obscene books and pictures by mail was prohibited by federal legislation, and, in 1872, an amending act to strengthen previous legislation was pushed through Congress under the impetus of Anthony Comstock and his YMCA vigilante committee, later known as the New York Society for the Suppression of Vice. (It is interesting to note that the American Society postdated its British namesake by seven decades, that is, roughly the same number of years that separate the beginning of the industrial take-offs in England and in the United States.) This statute, with a companion law passed two years later, made it illegal to ship obscene literature in interstate commerce and has been the main legal basis of censorship in the United States ever since.

In New York, Comstock's Society was given the power of search and seizure and gradually built itself into a semipublic national censor of literature deemed obscene. The Boston Watch and Ward Society soon followed it, and until World War I similar societies sprang up all over the United States to supplement with private vigilante action official efforts on the state, city, or federal levels.

When the Comstock laws were adopted, they contained the words "lewd," "lascivious," "indecent," and "obscene." Such words may naturally be interpreted in very different ways, depending on the temper of the age and the interpretations of the judges. Conservative judges tended to give them very narrow definitions and thus condemned books that seem to the modern mind inoffensive indeed. Walt Whitman and Emile Zola, G. B. Shaw and Guy de Maupassant, Theodore Dreiser and H. G. Wells, Upton Sinclair and Sherwood Anderson at one time or another fell afoul of the censors. In 1892, M. A. Warren, the author of *Almost Fourteen*, a book of sexual instructions for adolescents, was forced to resign his headmastership after his book had been condemned as obscene. And even as late as 1929, threescore books, among them works by Sinclair Lewis, Ernest Hemingway, Bertrand Russell, and Warwick Deeping, were condemned in Boston under a most restricted definition of such key terms as "obscene."

Yet change in public opinion on sexual matters was rapid indeed in the first quarter of the twentieth century. In 1907, Dr. C. W. Malchow, President of the Physicians and Surgeons Club of Minneapolis, was sent to jail for selling through the mails his book, *The Sexual Life*. Despite the fact that the work had been praised by educational and medical journals and was strongly recommended by a meeting of Methodist ministers, President Theodore Roosevelt, when asked for a pardon by members of Congress, only expressed regret that it was not in his power to lengthen the sentence. When the twentieth century was young, only isolated voices protested against the philistine standards predominant among the judiciary enforcing nineteenth-century laws. Public opinion was still dominated by Victorian morality. Yet, only a few years later, standards had changed considerably. When Comstock died in 1915, he, who had held for most of his life the power of life and death over much of the literature of the United States, was already a figure of fun for the younger generation.

It is customary to attribute the change in sexual standards that blossomed after the return of the young servicemen from Europe in 1918 to a shift in the climate of ideas. Many ideas and practices that had been viewed as wicked and evil were soon to be regarded as wholesome and "natural." Dr. Kinsey and his associates have amply documented the radical revolution in sexual habits that occurred in the United States around that time. But it would be superficial to attribute all this reawakening simply to a shift in ideas or in cultural standards. Certainly the acceptance of Freud in the Twenties, to cite only one example, was of considerable importance. Yet we must ask why Freud was so enthusiastically received? Underlying these shifts there were rapid changes in the social structure of the United States.

Censorship had had its heyday in the periods of industrial take-off both here and in England. It was essentially an effort to maintain traditional sexual morality in the face of a rising new industrial social structure. It was an effort forcibly to inculcate in the emergent new class of laborers a stern morality of duty and discipline. But by the 1920s the new industrial civilization that had matured in the Victorian Age had fully come into its own. In America especially, the small town and the agricultural hinterland declined in specific weight. Life in the modern city, in the immigrant slums as well as on the Gold Coasts of the *nouveaux riches*, was no longer susceptible to old-time controls. The mobile men who lived in the anonymity of the city began to develop new standards of morality. And these standards, while reflecting the emancipation from traditional controls embodied in the city's life styles, no longer represented the Victorian morality embodied in the censorship laws. Laws that had been evolved in order to hold in check the tide of moral dissolution brought about by the Industrial Revolution in its take-off period were no longer able to control the new morality of the mature urban civilization.

The old morality did not suddenly disappear. Some of the most vicious attempts at suppression of books date precisely from the 1920s. Yet slowly the standards of the judiciary began to shift, in tune with the changed standards of public morality. The law followed the mores. The course drifted away from the Cockburn standards ("the test of obscenity is this, whether the tendency of the matter charged as obscenity is to deprave and corrupt those whose minds are open to such immoral influences and into whose hands a publication of this sort may fall"). In 1923, Judge Learned Hand handed down an opinion in which he wrote, "I hope it is not improper for me to say that the rule as laid down, however consonant it may be with mid-Victorian morals, does not seem to me to answer to the understanding and morality of the present time, as conveyed by the words 'obscene, lewd, or lascivious.' I question whether in the end men will regard that as obscene which is honestly relevant to the adequate expression of innocent ideas, and whether they will not believe that truth and beauty are too precious to society at large to be mutilated in the interests of those most likely to pervert them to base uses."[4]

When, in 1933, Judge Woolsey exonerated James Joyce's *Ulysses*, which had been banned previously, he wrote, "Whether a particular book would tend to excite such [impure and libidinous] impulses and thoughts must be tested by the Court's opinion as to its effect on a person with average sex instincts. It is only with the normal person that the law is concerned." He discarded the old English rule of "isolated passage" obscenity and declared that a book should be judged on its total effect. *Ulysses*, he ruled, despite isolated obscene passages, was not a book written "to promote lust or portray filth for its own sake." Ever since this ruling, censorship has encountered a series of humiliating defeats in the federal courts. The recent decisions freeing Henry Miller's *Tropic of Cancer* and

D. H. Lawrence's *Lady Chatterley's Lover* from the censors' bans came as the climax to a long series of cases in which the still extant law was gradually reinterpreted almost to the point of innocuousness.

Not that censorship of "obscenity" is dead in the United States. In fact, as the publishers of *Tropic of Cancer* learned to their shock, even though federal standards have been relaxed, city ordinances, state courts, and police rulings are almost equally effective in suppressing books. To this day, Edmund Wilson's *Memoirs of Hecate County* cannot be bought in the State of New York, and a multitude of local regulations and state laws forbid the sale or circulation of an impressively long list of major works of world literature. Nevertheless, after the first Kinsey Report, a national best-seller impressively documenting the drastic changes that have taken place in sexual practices over a half-century, the battle of the censors to prevent the spread of ideas about sex was bound to fail. When there are so few "pure" minds to protect, the very enterprise of protection is bound to appear ridiculous and quixotic.

The economic effects of censorship for obscenity were as drastic as they had been in the case of political or religious censorship. The forbidden books rose in price—but in most cases the authors derived no benefit. The case of *Ulysses* is instructive. When it first appeared in serial form in *The Little Review*, the Court ruled that it contravened American law and fined the editor of *The Little Review* $100. Five hundred copies of the complete work, published in Paris in 1922, were burned by the American Post Office Department. As a consequence, it became impossible to copyright the work, and pirated and bowdlerized editions were issued to meet the demand. It is estimated that some 30,000 copies were sold clandestinely in the United States and elsewhere before the ban was finally raised in 1934. From these sales, the author naturally received no royalties whatsoever. The case of *Lady Chatterley's Lover* is similar.

It would be absurd to attribute the alienation of many *avant garde* authors of the nineteenth and twentieth centuries solely to the battle with the censors, yet one may well maintain that these battles contributed in no mean measure to such alienation. To these authors, the censor came to be the very symbol of the philistinism, hypocrisy, and meanness of *bourgeois* society. "Comstockery" became the incarnation of the perverted morality of the dominant middle classes. Many an author who was initially apolitical was drawn to the political left in the United States because the left was in the forefront of the battle against censorship. The close alliance of *avant garde* art with *avant garde* political and social radicalism can be accounted for, at least in part, by the fact that they came to be merged in the mind of many as a single battle for freedom against all repression, be it sexual or political.

Sexual censorship had a measure of success during the period in which it was in tune with the dominant morality and the public opinion of the dominant strata in society. It helped to deepen a repression conducive to tightening the hold of the ruling strata over the newly emerging lower classes. Yet, once the new urban civilization had fully emerged and had evolved its own life styles and mores, censorship became increasingly inoperative. When sexual practices were freed from traditional inhibitions, it became ever more obvious that a literature reflecting these practices could no longer be suppressed. The smalltown mind of the provincial backwoodsman, though still powerful in the backwaters, proved incapable of withstanding the mainstream of national ideas.

The French political censorship in the years immediately preceding the Revolution was ineffective because neither the educated public nor the censors themselves believed any longer in the standards it was supposed to uphold. Similarly, sexual censorship collapsed in the United States around the middle of the twentieth century—at least on a national scale—because neither the public nor the judges any longer shared the values it was supposed to support. The morality of the industrial city had eroded the standards of repressive gentility.

But in both cases, censorship, while it lasted, was one of the major agents causing the alienation of intellectuals. It contributed its share to that divorce of the intellectual from the reigning assumptions of the dominant strata that has marked modern history. The very conflict with the censors gave authors a collective cause around which to rally. As political censorship in eighteenth-century France had helped to forge an alliance between those who stood for economic and political freedom, between those who wished for *laissez-faire* in economic affairs and those who wished to institute a free market place of ideas, so, in the twentieth century, the battle of authors against the censorship of sexual expression aligned them with liberal or radical critics of the *status quo*. Here again the censors inadvertently helped to bring about an alliance of otherwise quite diverse interests. Censorship heightened self-consciousness and the sense of mission among the intellectual community. His conflict with the censors clarified for the intellectual the direction of his material as well as of his ideal interests.

NOTES

1. In this discussion of French prerevolutionary censorship, I have relied mainly on Daniel Mornet's classic *Les origines intellectuelles de la révolution française* (4th ed.; Paris: Armand Colin, 1947). Cf. J. P. Berlin, *Le commerce des livres prohibés à Paris de 1750 à 1789* (Paris: Belin, 1913).

2. Florian Znaniecki, *The Social Role of the Man of Knowledge* (New York: Columbia University Press, 1940), p. 13.

3. This section is based mainly on the following books: Alec Craig, *The Banned Books of England* (London: George Allen & Unwin, Ltd., 1937); Craig, *Above All Liberties* (London: George Allen & Unwin, Ltd., 1942); Morris L. Ernst and William Seagle, *To the Pure* (New York: The Viking Press, Inc., 1928); and Paul Blanshard, *The Right to Read* (Boston: Beacon Press, 1955). On Comstock, cf. Heywood Broun and Margaret Leech, *Anthony Comstock* (New York: Liveright Publishing Corp., 1927). Walter M. Daniels, ed., *The Censorship of Books* (New York: H. W. Wilson Co., 1954), contains a valuable bibliography.

4. Quoted in Craig, *Banned Books*, p. 116.

Chapter 9

THE POLITICAL SECT:
THE SAINT-SIMONIANS[1]

THE SAINT-SIMONIAN SECT, IN ITS RELATIVELY BRIEF history, presents almost all the stages of the typical history of political sects. In fact, some of its features appeared in such heightened forms that they seem almost caricatures. The abnormal may serve to illuminate the normal.

Political sects have played a major role in the life of many intellectuals since the early nineteenth century. They have been important nurseries for modern ideologies and have provided natural habitats for ideologists. In such sects, otherwise isolated and alienated intellectuals have found—though often for relatively short periods only—sustaining fellowships of like-minded men, the fraternity for which they yearn, a fraternity denied to them in the society at large. Devoted to a doctrine radically at variance with the prevailing climate of ideas, aiming to bring about a transvaluation of values, they have gained sustenance from intimate commerce with fellow sectarians.

To be sure, cliques and coteries, political parties and various other types of groups have at times performed functions similar to those of political sects, yet the sect has had a special attraction for political intellectuals in search of utopia. Its single-minded devotion to an exclusive set of ideas, its tendency to embrace not only segments of the personality of each member but also the whole man, its morality of extremes, and its natural tendency to regard the "insider" as morally superior to "outsiders" who have not yet received "the message," all these characteristics have made the sect especially appealing to men in search of salvation.

A sect, as its Latin etymology suggests, consists of men who have cut themselves off from the main body of society. They have formed a restricted group that rejects the norms of the inclusive society and proclaims its adherence to a special set of values and rules of conduct. The religious sect, as distinct from the church, which contains within its fold both sinners and saints, consists of the visible community of pure saints. The political sect, as distinct from the modern political party, which aims at encompassing a high proportion of the mass of electors, consists of specifically qualified members only. The party is inclusive, the sect exclusive. Churches and parties aim at attracting all men of good will; sects aim at recruiting elites of religiously or politically qualified "performers."

The members of a political sect relish the comforting assurance that they are "in the know," that they have attained an esoteric knowledge denied to nonmembers. They are thus enabled to turn the tables on a society that has rejected them. While, in their previous isolation, they may have felt frustrated, insignificant, and powerless, they come to feel that in their reborn state they partake of the collective strength of the community of believers. Fortified by exclusive knowledge of certain hidden mysteries still unknown to the vulgus, they see themselves as a true elite.

Many political sects, far from wishing to withhold from outsiders the knowledge of their vision, have actively proselytized. Yet, by a paradox of which the sectarians themselves were never aware, the structure of the sect, even though it may have been deliberately designed to spread their message, has in fact impeded the wide diffusion of their ideas or at least prevented the attraction of a wider membership. Their almost total absorption with one another has forced them into ever larger departures from the norms of behavior governing the outside world. Conflict with the hostile outer world has reinforced absorption into the inner world of the sect—and has made it progressively more difficult to find a common universe of discourse with potential converts.

The original radical impulse of the political sectarian of the left was born out of revolt against injustice, cruelty, and disorder; it was nourished by moral indignation and utopian idealism and motivated by the desire to change the world. But, as the sect developed, it tended progressively to absorb its members' activities and succumbed to an "autonomy of motive": At first a platform in the struggle for a better world, it became a kind of retreat, a home away from home in which members could cultivate concern for their own salvation and gradually lose interest in the world at large. At this point, in its natural history, the sect was likely to experience a short period of tremendous collective excitement, of heightened experience, of ecstatic communion. But this period typically was brief. Soon the sect would be split and torn by internal dissension.

In groups in which the total personalities of members are involved, any internal conflict readily becomes imbued with a whole array of affective involvements. Such groups cannot afford the tolerance of large organizations based only on the segmental participation of the membership, for any internal conflict necessarily cuts so deep that it endangers the very basis of the sectarian consensus. Dissent cannot be tolerated, and the dissenter must be forced to withdraw. The sect continually expels heretics in an effort to maintain or increase cohesion among the remaining "worthy" participants.[2] But when too many members have been lost, the remaining sectarians may awake to the fact that the protective covering that the sect provided for them has disappeared. They are again alone in the world. In most sects and for most members, there finally comes that gray morning when, as one of the Saint-Simonians, Jules Le Chevalier, poignantly expressed it, "I doubt everything. I am becoming a *philosophe* again . . . I am once more alone in the world."[3]

Post-Napoleonic France, the France of Stendhal and Balzac, seemed to many young intellectuals a moral vacuum. Young men born too late to participate in the exciting days of the Revolution and Napoléon felt, amid the acquisitive fervor of *bourgeois* society, suddenly free of traditional restraints, as if all guiding moral values had been shattered, all ideals smashed, all purposes rendered senseless. The Revolution had destroyed those bonds of sentiment and devotion that had survived the corruption and corrosion of the *ancien régime*. The counterrevolution had disintegrated the fraternity born of revolutionary ardor. The world seemed devoid of generous emotion, of fraternal bonds, of ideas and ideals worthy of devotion. Alfred de Musset expressed it well: "Alas! Alas! Religion is vanishing . . . We no longer have either hope or expectation, not even two little pieces of black wood in a cross before which to wring our hands . . . Everything that was is no more. All that will be is not yet."[4] Disorder seemed loose upon the world. In a society dominated by *nouveau riche* financiers and corrupt or vacillating politicians, in which the Guizots egged on the new *bourgeoisie* to "enrich itself" and the Nucingens and César Birotteaus took them at their word, there seemed no place for virtue, fraternity, love, or justice.

Poets and artists might attempt to escape the *mal du siècle* by taking refuge in a world of art for art's sake; they might escape into the romantic cultivation of artistic sensibility and might sublimate their inner despair in the fashioning of romantic heroes and the pursuit of exquisite emotion. But such avenues were barred to other types of intellectuals. Mathematicians, lawyers, medical men, economists, and scientists were denied access to the realm of art. What were they to do? For some, the Saint-Simonians seemed to provide an answer.

On May 22, 1825, a few faithful friends gathered at the deathbed of Henri de Saint-Simon. This erratic genius, one of the great eccentrics of history, prophet of a new industrial age at a time (1814) when France boasted only fifteen steam engines, annunciator of the proximate day when government would be replaced by administration, when social science wedded to industrial energies would usher in the reign of social harmony to replace the disorder of the present, had, during most of his life, few disciples. But toward the very end of his career and after his most illustrious disciples, Augustin Thierry and Auguste Comte, had left him, he succeeded in attracting a new group of devotees. His last work, *Nouveau Christianisme*, preached a humanitarian religion devoted to material betterment and increased power over nature. Saint-Simon's new gospel enjoined men to behave toward one another as brothers and to reorganize their society in order to take care of *la classe la plus nombreuse et la plus pauvre*, that is, of the swarming multitudes of the disinherited and humiliated who were being neglected in the great scramble for wealth that characterized the age. This goal captured the imagination of a new crop of disciples.

These disciples were young men. The most active among them and the nearest to the founder in his last years, Olive Rodrigues, was thirty-one years old when Saint-Simon died. Bazard and Enfantin, who were soon to displace him as leaders of the Saint-Simonians, were born in 1791 and 1796 respectively. Hardly one of them was more than thirty-five years old at the time of Saint-Simon's death. A very high proportion (their total number was never more than 100) was trained in the natural sciences or had some ties to the world of business. Rodrigues had been a mathematics instructor at the Ecole Polytechnique and had become a bank director. Enfantin, the son of a banker, had studied at the Ecole Polytechnique and had led a somewhat adventuresome life in the world of commerce and banking. Buchez was a medical man; D'Eichthal and the Pereire brothers were bankers. There were others of course, journalists, artists, and literary men. Some were dedicated to politics—Bazard, for example, who came to the movement from a turbulent period of revolutionary activity in the Carbonaro movement. Nevertheless, most of these young men were trained in the sciences both natural and economic. And this common background, in addition to revulsion against the disorder of the day, explains their common infatuation with planning and order. To scientifically trained men, to men taught in the Ecole Polytechnique and similar institutions that the world of natural phenomena was governed by orderly laws, it must have been particularly galling that disorder still prevailed in the social world, that society continued to be governed by the erratic movements of the market, that it lacked purpose and plan. What they found in the truncated and fragmentary lessons of Saint-Simon was an appeal to science and a prophecy of a new age in which the affairs of men would be regulated according to the same scientific laws that governed the world of nature.

The need for some kind of new order to overcome the prevailing anomie was felt by many young intellectuals of divergent political orientation. Many of them were led to some form of counterrevolutionary vision, to belief in a possible return to the well regulated and secure world of the *ancien régime*. But young scientists or men imbued with the scientific spirit could hardly be expected to relish a vision of return to a prescientific age. To them, as to Saint-Simon, the golden age was in the future, not in the past. They might admire the orderly hierarchy of the Roman Catholic Church, but they could not imagine a return to Church domination. They envisaged a new and stable order to replace the anarchy around them, but this order would have to embody science and progress, the deities they had worshiped at the Ecole Polytechnique and other scientific schools. To them, science was holy, as was industry, but the most consecrated task was to bring to France a new integration, a drawing together of all its citizens. In particular, the many millions of Frenchmen who had previously been neglected by all the statesmen and most of the thinkers, the swarming multitudes of powerless and pitiable men on whom the ascending *bourgeoisie* had battened, was to be reintegrated into the community.

The Saint-Simonians were not equalitarian in their outlook. They were much too sure of their superiority to the common run of men, of their inherent intellectual pre-eminence, to partake in the sentimental adoration of "the people" that characterized a number of contemporary radical tendencies. They were willing to do a great deal for the people, but they were convinced that none of these advances could be brought about *by* the people. There ought to be full equality of opportunity in the good society. But, because equality of endowment was nothing but a sentimental pipe dream, those who had what it takes should take what opportunities there were.

Yet, lest we conceive of these young Saint-Simonians as technocrats bent solely on coldly rational reorganization of society, it must be added that they decried not only the anarchy of their age but also its lack of community and brotherhood. The sickness of the age, they believed, could be traced to the atrophy of love, a dryness of heart. When community withers away, they preached, the impulse of egotism dominates, and the ties of sympathy among men relax. In their passionate desire to renovate society, they were always moved to escape the desert of love that was, to them, contemporary France. If science and industry were not joined to the cultivation of generous emotions, to the task of bringing together the men and women of France in a joyous and loving community, they would be of no use. Reason, science, and industrial capacity would remain barren if not tied to feelings of love and fraternity.

This book is not the place to discuss in fuller detail the sometimes quite subtle elements of the Saint-Simonian doctrine; only a few major points have been sketched here. What is of central concern is the fact that, in Frank Manuel's words, "The members of the movement practiced those virtues which would become normal among mankind in the future. The movement, the religion, was the new world in miniature."[5] Having projected a City of God into the future of mankind, they proceeded to live the ideal in the here and now, to reproduce the macroscopic vision of regenerated humanity in the microcosm of the Saint-Simonian sect.

What started as a propagandistic enterprise in the journals, *Le Producteur* and *Le Globe*, and in a series of conferences and lectures in which the new doctrine was expounded, clarified, and elaborated soon led to the foundation of a Saint-Simonian "church." From 1826 to 1829, Saint-Simonianism made a considerable impact on the advanced younger intellectuals of the day. It attracted a number of devoted disciples, especially from the ranks of young scientists at the Ecole Polytechnique, but it was still only a loose grouping of theoreticians preoccupied with tracing the outlines of the new doctrine and evolving the major dogmatic formulas for the new practice of the future. But, in this effort, these intellectuals had grown very close to one another. Linked by emotional bonds, they now began to feel the necessity of building an edifice that would represent to the world the visible community of new saints. And, as the doctrine insisted on the principle of hierarchy, the organization would have to be strongly hierarchical. The oldest members formed a "college" of sixteen Fathers; at the next lower level, there were twenty-two members of the "Second Degree"; and below them were thirty-nine members of the "Third Degree." On top of the structure, Enfantin and Bazard, after election by the Fathers, reigned as Supreme Fathers. The whole constituted what was called the "Saint-Simonian Family." This sacred college of apostles, a brotherhood of dedicated saints, was from now on to carry the gospel to the gentiles.

One is tempted to smile at the weird and sometimes almost incredible proceedings of the "church" and to dismiss them as the products of disordered minds. The accounts of many Saint-Simonian gatherings read like records of the outpourings of madmen. These activities were no longer, one feels, the mere eccentricities of youthful enthusiasts. The apostles claimed that they were a clergy similar to the regular clergy and therefore subject to the same immunities. They adopted strange costumes—among others a garment that could only be buttoned in the back, which symbolized fraternity, for to get dressed one needed a brother. They sported long beards and addressed Enfantin with all the reverence due a new pope. They paraded through the streets of Paris, a little band of prophets, chanting the new gospel in ritual unison. They sent missions to the gentiles of provincial France and of foreign countries. They finally decided upon a collective retreat into the celibate monastic life on a suburban estate in Ménilmontant. They organized a vain quest for a female messiah to share a double throne with the male Father. The record of their schisms and internal feuding, of their violent rivalries and personal antagonisms is one of intense emotion brought to a kind of paroxysm in the feverish environment of the "church." The intimacy and involvement with each other, which they preached and practiced, generated collective delusions and inhibited the operation of the "reality principle." Each new schism—the departure of Bazard, of Rodrigues, of many others—increased the common exaltation of the remnant still huddled around Father Enfantin.

George Santayana once defined a fanatic as "a man who redoubles his efforts when he has forgotten his ends." This definition applies exactly to the last stages of the Saint-Simonian Church. The Saint-Simonians began by laying great stress on the authority of science, but they proved ever more incapable of correcting their vision in the light of evidence or experience. Faith replaced science and ended in exotic rituals, strange new symbols, and veritable orgies of dreamlike trances. But this phase proved to be short-lived. Late in 1832, the disciples, one after the other, left the Ménilmontant "monastery." On December 15, 1832, Enfantin and Michel Chevalier entered Saint-Pelagie prison to serve one-year sentences for having violated a law forbidding meetings of more than twenty persons. Father Enfantin abdicated. "It is now necessary," he wrote, "that the Children find in themselves and without the Father the inspiration of what they must do."[6] Soon, almost all the disciples awakened to the realization that, in the words of one, the Father was "neither Moses nor Christ, neither Charlemagne nor Napoleon —that he was only Enfantin, only Enfantin."[7]

Much of what happened in the last stages of their infatuation appears almost purely pathological. Yet, if illness there was, it was a temporary, a situational illness. Most of the men who participated in the wildest manias had been, only a few years earlier, among the flower of scientific and intellectual France. Soon they would again be among the most successful engineers, journalists, bankers, and even politicians of Napoleon's Empire. The young men who became Saint-Simonians were by no means intellectual misfits or social outcasts. Most had left professional activities that seemed to assure promising careers to join the "Family"—and most achieved high status after they left it. Let us follow a few of these careers.

Henri Fournel was graduated from the Ecole Polytechnique in 1820 as a mining engineer, became director of a metal factory, and, as early as 1825, designed a railroad network for the Champagne.

In 1828, he became director of the Creusot, a huge metallurgical enterprise then employing 2500 workers. He left this brilliant career to join the Saint-Simonian "Family" in 1830. Later he was again to become a high official in the mining industry. Michel Chevalier, recruited at the same time as Fournel, was an engineer in charge of the mines of the Department of the North before joining the "Family." By 1860, he was a senator and a close economic advisor of the Emperor. Enfantin himself became in later years an administrator of the Paris-Lyon-Marseille railroad, and the Pereire brothers built a powerful banking empire rivaled only by the Rothschilds.

Even before they joined, the Saint-Simonians had been alienated from the values of dominant society. They sacrificed their careers because of their yearning for fraternal bonds that could not be realized in a society increasingly reliant on the cash nexus. Self-interest clearly played no part in their motivations. On the contrary, in the few years in which the Saint-Simonians held their allegiance, they were moved by a sense of self-sacrifice, of self-transcendence. They found in the dedicated brotherhood rewards incomparably more valuable to them than the paltry compensations profane society had to offer. Once they had joined the "Family," mutual stimulation led to a hypertrophy of generous emotions previously repressed. It led to an exaltation of precisely those elements of its members' personalities that had been neglected and curbed, whether because of rigorous scientific training or of the general repression of instinctual gratification and emotional warmth in the society at large. This collective exaltation of the emotions undoubtedly led in some cases, though not in all, to temporary unhinging of the mind.

It also led the Saint-Simonians to the elaboration of a system of ideas that would leave its mark on subsequent intellectual history. Marxism, welfare-state planning, and Stalinism were all to borrow significant ideas from the Saint-Simonian inheritance. The romantics, from Heinrich Heine to Vigny and Sainte-Beuve, weaved strains of Saint-Simonian doctrine—especially its glorification of sexual love, the "rehabilitation of the flesh," into the texture of modern literature. The idea that art has a social mission and that the artist has priestly functions, which is at the center of Victor Hugo's philosophy, among others, owes a great deal to the Saint-Simonians. After they broke with their brothers and succumbed again to the lure of the quotidian world, these once exalted secretaries became the animators of significant industrial and financial enterprises that made the France of Napoleon III into an economic world power. They built banks and railroads, manufacturing enterprises and modern centers of distribution. They had already planned the Suez Canal and had helped to construct dams on the Nile while still seeking for the female messiah. Finally, shorn of their illusions —or delusions—they kept on building dams and laying plans for the industrialization of "underdeveloped areas." They elaborated an ethic of organized large-scale enterprise that would provide, in a Catholic country like France, some of the incentives for worldly activities that the Protestant Ethic had provided in Protestant countries.

It might of course be said that individual Saint-Simonians would have made quite similar contributions had they pursued their initial careers without the strange interludes with the "Family." One can never fully disprove such contentions. But the record of their discussions and correspondence suggests strongly that the ideology of scientific planning in the interest of *la classe la plus nombreuse et la plus pauvre* that they developed was the fruit of their close involvement with one another. It evolved in the mutual stimulation of the members of the "Family." Their very isolation from outside contact, their very social distance from the uninitiated led to more than feverish pathologies; it also led to an intensity of concern with ideas that is only rarely achieved by ordinary men distracted from intellectual tasks by rival claims and social responsibilities. Their final move to the physical isolation of a celibate monastery only highlighted tendencies already present earlier in their history. They desired to dedicate themselves with single-minded passion to the one great task at hand: the elaboration of a new, all-encompassing vision of a planned and fraternal world.

To be sure, some contributed more to the collective enterprise than did others—Bazard was responsible for many, perhaps most, of the seminal ideas, whereas Enfantin contributed more than his share of the bizarre elements—yet it is beyond dispute that the doctrine as a whole could flower only in that hothouse of collective emotions, mutual involvement, and give-and-take of ideas that was the Saint-Simonian movement. Strange and exotic plants grew in the artificial atmosphere of the "Family," no doubt. But who is to say today whether or not the varieties that proved to have more enduring life spans would ever have been produced except in symbiosis with the more aberrant species?

Finally, one might ask, Was it not precisely the bizarre aspects of the movement that helped the wider diffusion of Saint-Simonian ideas. At times the sectaries proved to be experts in showmanship. But even when they were not consciously engaged in *épater les bourgeois*, even when they were genuinely driven by inner visions or collective rituals, they unwittingly attracted the attention of an audience that might otherwise have remained indifferent. On a tide of irrationality, there floated rational proposals, and many of those who originally came only to watch the show absorbed the more enduring parts of the message. A subsequent generation found no difficulty in peeling off the hull of absurdities and extracting the core of seminal ideas. The "Family," with all its fantastic accompaniments, served as midwife at the birth of Saint-Simonian ideas, which were to spread over much of the Western world.

NOTES

1. The classic study of the Saint-Simonians remains Sébastien Charléty, *Histoire du Saint-Simonisme* (Paris: P. Hartmann, 1931). I have profited a great deal from Frank E. Manuel's fine chapter on the Saint-Simonians in his recent *Prophets of Paris* (Cambridge, Mass.: Harvard University Press, 1962). His earlier definitive work on Henri de Saint-Simon, *The New World of Saint-Simon* (Cambridge, Mass.: Harvard University Press, 1956), has also been most helpful. George G. Iggers, *The Cult of Authority* (The Hague: Martinus Nijhoff, 1958), is a stimulating though somewhat biased discussion of the Saint-Simonians. *The Doctrine of Saint-Simon: An Exposition, First Year, 1828–1829*, the most important of all Saint-Simonian writings, has finally been rendered into English by Iggers and published by Beacon Press (Boston: 1958).
2. For a fuller discussion of the sociology of the sect and for relevant bibliographical material, see Lewis A. Coser, *The Functions of Social Conflict* (New York: The Free Press, 1956), especially pp. 98–103; and Coser, "Sects and Sectarians," *Dissent*, I (Autumn, 1954), 360–9.
3. Quoted in Manuel, *op. cit.*, p. 149.
4. Alfred de Musset, *Confessions of a Child of the Century* (London: J. M. Dent & Sons, Ltd., Publishers, 1912).
5. Manuel, *op. cit.*, p. 175.
6. Quoted in Charléty, *op. cit.*, p. 201.
7. Quoted in Manuel, *op. cit.*, p. 193; and in Charléty, *op. cit.*, p. 324.

Chapter 10

LITERARY BOHEMIA: THE EARLY YEARS OF GREENWICH VILLAGE

WHEN MEN STRUGGLE AGAINST A SOCIAL ENVIRONMENT that they judge to be crippling and confining and in which they do not receive the sustaining response they crave, they are likely to experience social claustrophobia. They feel that, if they are not to exhaust themselves in vain endeavors to assert their individualities in a hostile environment, they must go elsewhere, to a social scene where they can receive response and recognition from like-minded rebels against the conventions of the "home town." The young men and women who began flocking to Greenwich Village about 1910 were in revolt against small-town philistinism and in search of a community of the unconventional. "One cannot understand Greenwich Village without understanding Kansas City."[1]

"The generation to which Waldo Frank and I belong," wrote Floyd Dell, one of the major literary figures of the early Greenwich Village, "is a peculiar and unhappy generation and I don't wonder that the older generation looks at it askance. It is a generation of individuals who through the long years of their youth felt themselves in solitary conflict with a hostile environment. There was a boy in Chicago, and a boy in Oshkosh, and a boy in Steubenville, Indiana, and so on—one here and there, and all very lonely and unhappy. . . . They were idealists and lovers of beauty and aspirants toward freedom; and it seemed to them that the whole world was in a gigantic conspiracy to thwart ideals and trample beauty under foot and make life merely a kind of life imprisonment. . . . This generation had to make, painfully enough, two important discoveries. It has had, in the first place, to discover its own corporate existence, to merge its individual existences together, and get the confidence and courage that can come only from the sense of mass thought and mass action. But the trouble is that each one of us, in our loneliness, has become a little odd, a little peculiar, and more than a little suspicious . . . Individualism is the very fabric of our lives, we who have brooded too long apart to become without pain a part of the social group to which we belong."[2]

The young denizens of the Village mostly came not from New York City but from the provinces. Max Eastman, the editor of *The Masses*, came from upstate New York; Floyd Dell from Davenport, Iowa; Hutchins Hapgood, a leading Village journalist, from Alton, Illinois; Sherwood Anderson, whose *Winesburg, Ohio* was to provide an almost clinical description of the stultifying effects of the small town on unconventional deviants, from Clyde, Ohio; Margaret Anderson, founder of the influential *Little Review*, from Columbus, Indiana. The list could be extended at will. These provincial rebels were joined in New York by a group of college rebels: Walter Lippmann, Van Wyck Brooks, and John Reed from Harvard and Sinclair Lewis and Waldo Frank from Yale, to name only a few. In the Village, the young men and women from these two sources encountered two separate but not unrelated worlds. "One was," says the sensitive historian of this period, Henry F. May, "the young literary and artistic world which had sprung into existence in the shadow of the old centers of polite culture, a world suddenly complete, with its own theatres, galleries, publishers, customers, and leaders. The other was the world of the American radical movement. At the intersection of these two, the Young Intellectuals created the most typical and important expressions of the prewar rebellion."[3]

Why did they come to Greenwich Village? First, because living there was inexpensive. The rush of traffic could not make its way through the many twisted streets that crossed and recrossed the area, and so, as New York expanded northward, what had once been a fashionable residential district decayed into a picturesque slum. One of Floyd Dell's poems captures the Village atmosphere:

> There was a Greenwich Village then—
> A refuge for tormented men
> Whose heads were full of dreams, whose hands
> Were weak to do the world's commands;
> Builders of palaces on sands—
> These, needful of a place to sleep
> Came here because the rents were cheap.[4]

For $30 a month one could rent a whole floor in an old house with enormous high-ceilinged rooms and huge fireplaces. And these rooms could be decorated in any way one wanted. "There were," wrote Malcolm Cowley, "two schools among us: those who painted the floors black (they were the last of the esthetes) and those who did not paint the floors."[5] The sober superintendents of these apartment houses took unconventionality for granted, and landlords did not mind when couples put their different names next to the common apartment bells. The first evening Floyd Dell spent in the Village, he was taken to call upon a beautiful girl dancer who kept a pet alligator in her bathtub. : . .

But the Village was not only a place where one could live outside the reigning conventions. It was a community, and residence there implied commitment to a life style. It was indeed "the homeland of the uprooted where everyone you met came from another town and tried to forget it; where nobody seemed to have parents, or a past more distant than last night's swell party . . ."[6] But it was more than that.

The Village was not merely a temporary home for impecunious and unconventional folk; it tried to embody a set of ideas. Grub Street, a crowded quarter that houses an intellectual proletariat trying to make a precarious living out of the trade of letters, has a very long history. Bohemia, on the other hand, dates only from the nineteenth-century revolt against *bourgeois* civilization. Grub Street implies a way of life unwillingly followed from necessity; Bohemia involves life styles adopted by choice. Bohemia, in other words, attempts to create countersymbols and a special and distinct culture of rebellion.[7] The Village provided a refuge from middle-class philistinism and permitted the widest experimentation in dress, sexual mores, and life styles generally. It created its own peculiar system of values.

The idea of experimentation, whether in literature, sex, politics, or the arts, provided the common denominator for otherwise di-

vergent groups and personalities in the Village. The new and the
untried attracted the typical Villager, often simply because it was
new and untried. This iconoclasm is why many would in short
succession be anarchists and socialists in politics and realists, imagists,
and vorticists in literature. It seemed not incongruous to move
within a few months from the cult of the body beautiful to the
cult of the proletariat, from "art for art's sake" to the syndicalism
of the I.W.W. Nonpolitical Bohemianism and political radicalism,
the revolt against puritanism and the revolt against capitalism were
to diverge after the war, but they mingled in the prewar Village.
Free love, free verse, anarchism, and syndicalism were all part of
one current. Margaret Anderson put the matter very nicely when
she wrote, "When 'they' ask you what anarchism is, and you scuffle
around for the most convincing definition, why don't you merely
ask instead: 'What is art?' Because anarchism and art are in the
world for exactly the same reason." Hutchins Hapgood discovered
that anarchism was "the fine art of the proletariat."[8] And when
Emma Goldman lectured, it was quite often not on political topics
but rather on Strindberg and Nietzsche, on the modern drama, or
on "The Limitation of Offspring" and "Is Man a Varietist or a
Monogamist?"

The Village creed may be summarized, as Malcolm Cowley
suggests, in a few articles of belief: 1) The idea of self-expression:
Each man's and woman's purpose in life is fully to express himself,
to realize his full individuality. 2) The idea of living for the moment, the rejection of the puritan ethos of deferred gratification:
One should burn one's candle at both ends. 3) The idea of female
equality: Women should be the economic and moral equals of men
and should have the same opportunities for making a living, smoking, drinking, and taking or dismissing lovers. 4) The idea of psychological adjustment: We are maladjusted because we are repressed;
the removal of repression liberates the true man. 5) The idea of
salvation by the child: If children are encouraged by new educational methods to realize their full personalities, they will bring
forth a new and freer world. 6) The idea of liberty: All laws and
conventions that hamper free expression should be abolished, for
puritanism is the great enemy. 7) The idea of cosmopolitanism:
the rejection of American cultural provincialism.

Nonconformity bred its own type of conformity. Certain of
the libertarian creeds of the Village were held with quite doctrinaire rigidity. When Floyd Dell wrote a theoretical defense of

marriage, he was viciously attacked. Bohemia's protest against the violation of its codes could be as violent as Main Street's reaction against the violation of the code of the middle class. And, as Joseph Freeman shrewdly remarked, "Like all codes, this one produced its own hypocrisies. In the bourgeois world, a girl concealed her vices; in Bohemia she concealed her virtue. The bourgeois lady, secretly deflowered, marched to the altar pretending to be a virgin; the girl poet or painter, still a virgin, pretended to be a Messalina. Bohemia demanded, whether we liked it or not, that we be Great Lovers."[9] When that staunch Marxist editor and poet Max Eastman got married, he felt "that I had betrayed my ideals."[10]

The Village not only had its own ideas; it had its own institutions. The famous "evenings" at the Fifth Avenue apartment of Mabel Dodge, a wealthy and eccentric patroness of the arts and of left politics, provided one of the settings for the intermingling of intellectual currents. In her beautiful white room with its Venetian décor, anarchists like Emma Goldman and Alexander Berkman and leaders of the I.W.W. like Bill Haywood would meet with middle-class reformers like Frederick Howe and Amos Pinchot, young radical intellectuals like John Reed, Walter Lippmann, and Max Eastman, *avant garde* artists from the Stieglitz group, and scores of younger writers and poets. There women in evening dresses talked with unemployed men and I.W.W. organizers about the coming revolution. And on different evenings, the assembled anarchists, cubists, feminists, poets, painters, and reformers might discuss penal reform or birth control, the Paterson strike or the Armory show. There middle-class rebels could mingle with authentic believers in the propaganda of the deed. "You might find one evening," reads a contemporary account, "a learned and eminent professor from Columbia University holding forth enthusiastically on Freud's theory of psychoanalysis to a room full of absorbed highbrows. Or it might be that Mr. Haywood of the I.W.W. would be expounding to the uninitiated what the I.W.W. really stood for. Or Lincoln Steffens, or Walter Lippmann, would be talking about 'Good Government'; a correspondent just back from Mexico would be telling about the war, or a scientist from England would make eugenics a topic; or it might be feminism, or primitive life, or perhaps anarchism would bring a queer but harmless looking crowd."[11]

Mabel Dodge's salon, important though it was in defining a peculiar Bohemian attitude out of many intermingling crosscurrents, could not have sufficed as an institutional setting for the young rebels. They needed one another, and so, despite their intense individualism, they created a whole network of community institutions in which they attempted to embody the values that sustained them in their common alienation from middle-class America.

The new Liberal Club became a common meeting place. In the fall of 1913, a young, intensely serious high-school teacher, Henrietta Rodman, broke up the old Liberal Club, a respectable uptown club devoted to the gradual improvement of mankind. Half the membership resigned, and she took the other half down to Mac-Dougal Street in the heart of the Village. Up till then, the Village had been split into tiny cliques and grouplets often mutually indifferent or secretly suspicious of one another. The Liberal Club built bridges among them. There social-settlement workers, reformers, and socialists mingled freely with artists and writers. "Why," asked Henrietta Rodman, "shouldn't intelligent people today have the same chance to know each other that the church and the tavern gave their grandparents?"[12] And indeed, this club, with its debates, its plays (impromptu lines and no props), its dances, its opportunities for discussion among strangers became a functional equivalent for the church or the lodge of the respectable.

In the basement of the Liberal Club flourished a restaurant run by two anarchists from Evanston, Illinois, Polly Holliday and Hippolyte Havel. There the young rebels would gather before an evening's debate or a dance or play upstairs. There for a while was the real center of the Village, although similar small eating places, featuring cheap food and plenty of opportunity for talk, soon sprang up elsewhere.

The Provincetown Players' theater became another meeting ground for the various factions in the Village. In the early years, Floyd Dell produced plays right at the Liberal Club. He served as playwright, stage designer, scene painter, stage manager, and actor all at the same time. But in 1916, the Provincetown Players moved to the Village. This amateur theater had been started in 1910 by a group of artists and writers spending their summer at Provincetown, Massachusetts. In 1916, a young man named Eugene O'Neill approached the group with a trunkful of unpublished and unproduced plays and became its most prominent member. In the same year, the group made the daring decision to move to New York for the winter. Its leading spirit, George Cook, a somewhat older rebel intellectual from Iowa, managed to find a building on Mac-Dougal Street and to convert an abandoned stable into a theater.

There many of the Village's writers and artists like Floyd Dell and Max Eastman, Maxwell Bodenheim and Harry Kemp acted modern plays written by themselves or by such relative Village newcomers as O'Neill. The audience and the actors belonged to the same *milieu*, were in fact almost interchangeable, so that this theater in its turn became a vital center strengthening the Villagers' common bonds of fraternity.

And then, of course, there were the Village magazines, from *The Masses* (which we shall discuss later) up on Greenwich Avenue to *The Little Review* on West Sixteenth Street, which first introduced James Joyce's *Ulysses* to America—and the multitude of ephemeral little Village magazines like *Rogue*, *Pagan*, and *Quill*. Village magazines engaged in a lively war with the more staid uptown publications and found allies and reluctant supporters among the writers for such liberal magazines as *The New Republic*. In their rebellious pages, Marx, Freud, and Bergson were celebrated as the liberators, and the new poetry of Pound and Eliot, of William Carlos Williams and Amy Lowell was printed. And most of the major prose writers of the succeeding period first appeared in little magazines in and around the Village. These magazines were irreverent, irresponsible, typically short-lived, and usually full of printing errors. But even now, their yellowed pages hint at how much fun it must have been to put them out. And in these magazines, as in the theater, there was no clear separation between producers and consumers, writers and audience. The young newcomer from Iowa would not for long gape in wonderment at the old-timers who wrote for these magazines; soon he too would have his poetry or book reviews printed.

Many denizens of the Village dreamed of the classless society of the future. In the meantime—and this fact is most significant—they already lived in an approximation of such a society. The Village had indeed leveled the barriers that habitually shield members of different classes from intimate contact with one another. "The poor," wrote Joseph Freeman, "came to the Village to escape the burdens of poverty, the rich, the burdens of boredom."[13] A common life style, based in part on common economic conditions, leveled the differences between the young middle-class radicals from the Midwest and the sons and daughters of the urban lower classes and of recent immigrants. Whatever differences in background the Villagers had, their common bond was distaste for the environments from which they came. And this agreement on the situation obliterated to a very large extent any class distinctions among them. It is therefore hardly surprising that they naïvely believed that what they had accomplished for themselves by acts of will could be extended with relative ease to the society at large.

The salon, the club, the theater, the editorial office, and, of course, the café, all provided meeting grounds for the Villagers and helped to mold what had initially been only a collection of intensely individualistic rebels into a community with its own institutions and symbols. The war and the postwar influx of a different type of Bohemian seeking pleasure and shunning "causes" were to change all that. But for a few years the Village embodied the full flowering of an intellectual, artistic, political, and emotional counterculture that gave sustenance and support to the assault against the dominant values of nineteenth-century America and opened the way for the major currents of modern culture.

Almost all the themes that animated the young rebels of the Village were later absorbed and assimilated by the dominant culture. And in the process, they were often cheapened and vulgarized, for too often they entered the mainstream only after much of their radical vigor was softened and domesticated. It remains true, however, that without the Village rebellion, neither American literature nor American painting, neither American politics nor American social reform would have become what it in fact became. The Village community did not last long, but, as long as it did last, it provided indispensable institutional settings for the radicals' and artistic innovators' successful assault on the proprieties of Iowa and Indiana, of Harvard and Yale. The Village revolt helped to put an end to the age of American innocence.

NOTES

1. Peter L. Berger, *Invitation to Sociology* (Anchor ed.; Garden City, N.Y: Doubleday & Company, Inc., 1964), p. 58.

2. Quoted in Joseph Freeman, *An American Testament* (New York: Farrar, Straus & Cudahy, Inc., 1936), p. 266.

3. Henry F. May, *The End of American Innocence* (New York: Alfred A. Knopf, Inc., 1959), p. 301. I have relied heavily on this fine volume throughout this chapter. Also *cf.* Daniel Aaron, *Writers on the Left* (New York: Harcourt, Brace & World, Inc., 1961). Among the older treatments, I found most useful Lilian Symes and Travers Clement, *Rebel America* (New York: Harper & Row, Publishers, 1934). For an

excellent community study of the Village, *cf.* Caroline F. Ware, *Greenwich Village 1920–1930* (Boston: Houghton Mifflin Company, 1935). *Cf.* also Allen Churchill's journalistic but lively *The Improper Bohemians* (New York: E. P. Dutton & Co., Inc., 1959).

4. Floyd Dell, *Love in Greenwich Village* (Garden City, N.Y.: Doubleday & Company, Inc., 1926). This book and Dell's later autobiography, *Homecoming* (New York: Farrar, Straus & Cudahy, Inc., 1933), are indispensable source books.

5. Malcolm Cowley, *Exile's Return* (New York: W. W. Norton & Company, Inc., 1934), p. 57.

6. *Ibid.*, p. 56.

7. For the above distinction, as well as for the later enumeration of the Village credo, I am indebted to Malcolm Cowley's *Exile's Return.*

8. *Cf.* May, *op. cit.*, p. 306.

9. Freeman, *op. cit.*, p. 273.

10. Max Eastman, *Enjoyment of Living* (New York: Harper & Row, Publishers, 1958), p. 358. This book is another most revealing autobiography by a major Village figure.

11. Quoted in Mabel Dodge Luhan, *Movers and Shakers* (New York: Harcourt, Brace & World, Inc., 1936), p. 82. This third volume of Mabel Dodge's verbose and detailed autobiography is a valuable source.

12. Quoted in Dell, *Love in Greenwich Village*, p. 20.

13. Freeman, *op. cit.*, p. 267.

Chapter 11

THE LITTLE MAGAZINE: *THE MASSES* AND *THE LITTLE REVIEW*

WHEREAS THE GREAT ENGLISH REVIEWS OF THE nineteenth century endeavored to speak for wide strata of educated middle-class opinion, the "little magazines" of the twentieth century set themselves a very different task. They did not endeavor to reach a large audience. On the contrary, they relished the fact that they were read by only very small minorities. The little magazine came upon the scene after considerable differentiation had taken place among the audience for literary, artistic, and, to a degree, political writing. In the twentieth century, most larger American publishing enterprises, as well as the major reviews, attempted to reach the widest possible audience and in that effort diluted their offerings to serve the lowest common denominator. Others like *The Atlantic* or *Scribner's* continued to cater to the genteel tastes of the traditional elites. The little magazines, which began to appear around 1912, set themselves a very different task.

The staffs of these magazines considered themselves enlisted in the vanguard of the war against established literary, artistic, or political proprieties. They therefore had to limit their appeals to a relatively restricted audience of unconventional readers. They aimed at printing the works of those writers who were found unacceptable by the commercial publishers. The more than 600 little magazines published in English between 1912 and 1945 came into being, to quote their historian Frederick C. Hoffman, "for the purpose of attacking conventional modes of expression and of bringing into the open new and unorthodox literary theories and practices. . . . Little magazines have been founded for two reasons: rebellion against traditional modes of expression and the wish to experiment with novel (and sometimes unintelligible) forms; and a desire to overcome the commercial and material difficulties which are caused by the introduction of any writing whose commercial merits have not been proved."[1] They were, in other words, a response and a challenge to the commercialization of literature that has marked the history of the arts in the West ever since the beginning of the *bourgeois* age.

While a great many of these magazines limited themselves to literature and the arts, others opened their pages freely to political argument. And, given the fact that the revolt against the genteel tradition in literature was carried on by writers deeply contemptuous of middle-class philistinism, it is not surprising that the politics of most of the little magazines tended to be radical. Most of the editors and writers of these magazines, although apparently not all of them, no matter what their specific political views, would have agreed with Flaubert's famous outburst: "I call bourgeois all that is mean."

The two magazines that will be discussed here in some detail, *The Masses* and *The Little Review*, cannot be said to be "typical" —nothing can ever be considered typical of the intensely individualistic world of these magazines—but they may be considered fairly representative of the early reviews. They set the tone for many that followed in their wake. Furthermore, although most of the little magazines had very short life spans, they all may be said to have had common functions. To discuss two of them thus enables us to capture at least some of their common qualities. Morton Dauwen Zabel has written, "It becomes apparent that the multiplication of these periodicals atones for their individual impermanence; that despite their varying shades of policy and opinion, their functions are ultimately identical and their activities continuous."[2]

To understand the impacts and functions of the little magazines, it is necessary to pay some attention to the structural conditions in which they arose, the cultural atmosphere that surrounded them, the different audiences to which they addressed themselves, and the social and economic arrangements that underpinned their existence. *The Little Review* and *The Masses*, though belonging to the same genus, represented in fact rather different species in terms of most of the variables just mentioned. The first was an intensely personal magazine mainly reflecting the idiosyncratic views of its editor; the other was a group enterprise. The first reached out for the extremely restricted audience of an artistic and intellectual elite; the other wished to be read by all those who revolted against the ugliness, philistinism, and middle-class domination of contemporary America.

THE MASSES

The Masses was the organ not of a national culture, not of a religious or ethnic community, not—despite its extreme left politics —of a class. It was the voice of provincial middle-class rebels who, in their revolt against the genteel tradition and the philistinism of the small town, had come to look at America through lenses ground in their novel metropolitan experiences. It reflected the encounters of men brought up in the values of gentility and respectability with the harshness, the shrillness, the terror, and the appeal of metropolitan New York.

The Masses first appeared in New York in January, 1911, under the guidance of Piet Vlag, a Dutchman who ran a co-operative restaurant in the basement of the Rand School of Social Science, and Thomas Seltzer, a young publisher. It was financed by a socialist vice-president of the New York Life Insurance Company. Unorthodox methods of finance were to mark its entire career. It was co-operatively owned by a group of writers and artists—among them the artists John Sloan and Art Young, the poet Louis Untermeyer, and the labor journalist Mary Heaton Vorse—and published on a nonprofit basis. It stood for a fairly mild brand of reform socialism, realism in the arts—it serialized Zola's *Germinal* and printed Tolstoy and Suderman—and a general anticapitalist attitude. Although it claimed to have reached a circulation of 10,000, it soon ran into the usual difficulties that afflict most such magazines: a shortage of money. And in August, 1912, it folded. But in December of the same year it was brought back to life when the co-operative owners elected as editor Max Eastman, a young lecturer in aesthetics at Columbia University. Then the real history of *The Masses* began.[3]

Under Piet Vlag, *The Masses* had talked socialism and had advertised Karl Marx cigars, but it had in fact been a fairly mild affair. Under Eastman, *The Masses* moved to the extreme left of the socialist spectrum. And Eastman moved it, quite aware of the symbolic significance, from Nassau Street to Greenwich Village. The magazine printed aggressive contributions by I.W.W. sympathizers and philosophical anarchists and emphasized its desire to "conciliate nobody." But above all, the magazine moved from somewhat moralistic earnestness to gay and often slightly irresponsible criticism. It had irrepressible energy and infectious liveliness. It was profusely illustrated and managed to draw on the best of the Ash Can School artists for its cartoons. The elaborate two- or three-line dialogues under the pictures ("My dear, I'll be economically independent if I have to borrow every cent!" or "Did you know that I am an Anarchist and a Free-Lover?" "Oh, indeed!—I thought you were a Boy Scout.") became its special trademark. Max Eastman's famous masthead defines the magazine:

A REVOLUTIONARY AND NOT A REFORM MAGAZINE: A MAGAZINE WITH A SENSE OF HUMOR AND NO RESPECT FOR THE RESPECTABLE: FRANK, ARROGANT, IMPERTINENT, SEARCHING FOR THE TRUE CAUSES: A MAGAZINE DIRECTED AGAINST RIGIDITY AND DOGMA WHEREVER IT IS FOUND: PRINTING WHAT IS TOO NAKED OR TRUE FOR A MONEY-MAKING PRESS: A MAGAZINE WHOSE FINAL POLICY IS TO DO AS IT PLEASES AND CONCILIATE NOBODY, NOT EVEN ITS READERS.

The Masses under Eastman, soon to be joined by John Reed as managing editor and Floyd Dell as associate editor, reported on the class war in Paterson, on the Mexican Revolution, on unemployment and sweatshops, on exploitation, and on the trials and tribulations of the I.W.W. But it also interested itself in nonpolitical causes, from feminism to psychoanalysis and free speech. In fact—and here was perhaps the major reason for its appeal—it managed to gather the main strands of *avant garde* ideas as they emerged among the young rebels who had come to live in Chicago's Bohemia, in Provincetown, and especially in Greenwich Village. Menckenians, socialists, anarchists, apolitical Bohemians, all appeared in the magazine, and, although they differed considerably in their positive goals, they all knew what they were against—middle-class culture. Although its editors had no particular liking for the more thoroughgoing experimentation in writing or the cubist art that had just begun to gain notice in America, the magazine nevertheless managed to print some of the earliest work of Sherwood Anderson, Vachel Lindsay, Djuna Barnes, Amy Lowell, Babette Deutsch, Randolph Bourne, Carl Sandburg, and William Carlos Williams. And its cartoonists included Art Young and John Sloan, Stuart Davis and Jo Davidson, Robert Minor and Boardman Robinson, in fact most of the "realist" artists of the time.

The almost instantaneous success of the magazine was probably due to the fact that it became a meeting ground for the revolutionary labor movement and the radical intelligentsia in the arts. Earlier socialist publications had had too much moral uplift to appeal to artists and writers. *The Masses*, by fusing revolution and socialism with wit and humor, by engaging in many a crusade with gay laughter, by earnestly pleading for revolution while yet enjoying life and refusing to take itself too seriously, succeeded in brewing a heady mixture of art and life, of experimentation and rebellion, which caught the spirit of the alienated young reformers, radicals, and artists who were its readers. Like them, it had, as Granville Hicks wrote, "The seriousness of strong convictions and the gayety of great hopes."[4]

The Masses was run in ways that would have appalled more conservative publications; it was run "like a circus wagon."[5] Its editorial board usually met once a month in some author's apartment or artist's studio. Manuscripts were read and pictures exhibited and then voted upon. In addition to the editors, many friends of the magazine—a good part of New York's radical intelligentsia—came to these meetings from time to time. And they were encouraged to vote too. Art Young tells how, at one of the meetings, after a vote on a poem, a man from the corner of the studio, the anarchist poet and restaurant manager Hippolyte Havel, shouted contemptuously: "Bourgeois! Voting! Voting on poetry! Poetry is something for the soul. You can't vote on poetry!"[6] These meetings were always jovial and gay. "Everybody was playing," Geneviève Taggard recalled, "and the editors of *The Masses* were playing hardest of all."[7] But this gay mood did not mean that there were no quarrels. The art editors quarreled with the literary editors, and at one time some members of the staff came close to throwing Eastman out. But the editors seemed able to take all this conflict in their stride.

Nobody was ever paid for anything published in the magazine. Eastman and Dell did receive meager salaries for their editorial

work because it was considered uncreative dirty work that ought
to be compensated. Nevertheless, the magazine at no time made
money and always had to be subsidized. Money came from rather
unexpected sources. The $3000 that started it came from Mrs. O. H.
P. Belmont, divorced wife of W. K. Vanderbilt and an ardent
feminist, and from the most respectable southern novelist, John
Fox, Jr.[8] Later, in what he called his "career in high finance,"
Eastman managed to get money from such unlikely sources as the
sister of newspaper king E. W. Scripps, reformer Amos Pinchot,
and respectable philanthropists like Samuel Untermeyer and Adolph
Lewisohn.

The Masses had unconventional editors, was financed by unconventional methods, and waged an unceasing war against the
conventions of American philistinism. No wonder then that its
audience was to be found mainly among the unconventional folk
of Greenwich Village and their uptown spiritual allies who wished
to identify themselves with the experimental life style and the urge
toward greater freedom that defined the Village community. It
appealed, above all, to the young not yet caught in the routines of
steady jobs and the servitudes usually imposed by family life and
responsibilities.

The youth of the audience was matched by that of the editors.
Max Eastman was just thirty when he took over the magazine. John
Reed and Floyd Dell were twenty-six when they joined The
Masses. And very few of the other staff members and writers were
past thirty. While editors, writers, and audience belonged to the
same generation, sharing a common feeling that they represented a
"new wave," they also had many background features in common.
They came mainly from provincial middle-class Anglo-Saxon backgrounds. Max Eastman was the son of two Congregational ministers
in upstate New York. Reed came from a wealthy upper middle-
class family in Portland, Oregon. Floyd Dell's father was a "respectable" businessman in Illinois, who had been hit by the panic
in 1873 and had become a foreman in a woolen mill but who still
clung to "respectable" status.

By and large, these young men were from the provinces, not
from New York. They were of middle-class origin, not from the
working class. No wonder, then, that they at first reacted to New
York as if it were a strange country and reveled in exploring its
disreputable "underbelly." Much of The Masses' best reportage
about New York sweatshops and the slums, about the misery of

immigrant living and the harshness of the class war in the textile mills owes its freshness to the sense of discovery among these young men from the provinces. They could still react vividly to an urban landscape that was commonplace to the born New Yorker. Where the New Yorker might perceive only grayness and dullness, the young middle-class rebels from the small towns saw color and exotic appeal.

Karl Mannheim has made the point that what distinguishes a "generation unit" from a merely chronological generation is "the great similarity in the data making up the consciousness of its members."[9] Similarity of perceptions leads to similarities of responses, and such "formative and interpretative principles . . . form a link between sparsely separated individuals who may never come into personal contact at all."[10] "The generation-unit tends to impose a much more concrete and binding tie on its members [than does an actual generation] because of the parallelism of responses it involves."[11] These young rebels belonged to such a "generation unit," which united them despite their concrete differences. The fact that the bulk of their readers belonged to the same generation unit made for the close bonds between magazine and audience.

The Masses defined and clarified the experience of a "generation unit" and became the mouthpiece of the Greenwich Village Bohemian community. In the process, it added one highly differentiated chord to the complex response evoked by the social and cultural realities of early twentieth-century America.

Subsequent history proved that the mixture of rebel art and rebel politics was not a stable one. These two elements would again diverge in the Twenties. But while *The Masses* lasted (it was barred from the mails because of alleged violations of the Espionage Act, and its second-class mailing privileges were withdrawn in October, 1917, because of its criticism of the war), it established a significant connection between radical aesthetics and political rebellion, a connection that helped to fashion many aspects of modern American writing well beyond the brief years of its publication.

THE LITTLE REVIEW

While *The Masses* was indifferent to experimental writers and poets, *The Little Review* was one of the very first publications to provide them with an audience—even though it was an audience of

only about 2000 readers. *The Little Review* was belligerently experimental, sponsoring the new and the esoteric, often for no better
reason than that it was new and esoteric. The famous exchange
between Upton Sinclair and Margaret Anderson, editor of *The
Little Review*, is indicative. Wrote Sinclair: "Please cease sending
me the *Little Review*. I no longer understand anything in it, so it
no longer interests me." Margaret Anderson replied: "Please cease
sending me your socialist paper. I understand everything in it, therefore it no longer interests me."[12] For a while, the masthead heralded
*The Little Review, a Magazine of the Arts. Making No Compro-
mise with the Public Taste*, and this slogan did indeed quite adequately describe the contents.

The Masses, although dominated by Eastman, was always a co-
operative enterprise; *The Little Review* was Margaret Anderson's
very personal magazine, reflecting on every page her moods, her
enthusiasms, her rhapsodic admiration of a variety of "causes."
Reflecting upon Margaret Anderson's career as an editor, one is
forcibly moved to consider the crucial role of deviant individuals
in intellectual and cultural life. She certainly refused to live up to
any of the current expectations concerning the role of editor. But
it was precisely this deviant behavior that allowed her to make a
lasting impact. Her nonconformity and her cultivation of originality made her a "marginal woman," but this very marginality was the
basis of her creative performance. Had she been less idiosyncratic,
she would have been less potent an influence on her own generation
and the one that followed.

Margaret Anderson was only twenty-one when she started her
magazine. A refugee from Columbus, Indiana, she had come to
Chicago's Bohemia in 1913 and had started to earn a livelihood of
sorts writing book reviews for *The Dial*. On the spur of the moment, she decided that a new magazine was needed and that she
was going to create it. Her enthusiasm was infectious; a young
journalist on the staff of an agricultural journal offered to put aside
enough of his monthly salary to pay the printer and the office rent.
A trip to New York to solicit advertising from publishers netted
$450. The magazine was on its way. No contributor would be paid,
of course, but the magazine would print all those authors who could
not get a hearing elsewhere. "Practically everything *The Little Review* published during its first year," Margaret Anderson wrote
later, "was material that would have been accepted by no other
magazine in the world at the moment."[13] The first issue on March,

1914, and those that followed were long on enthusiasm and rather short on critical detachment. The editor's articles used terms like "beauty" and "passion" in every second phrase. Her editorials in favor of "the splendor of life" quoted indiscriminately from Maeterlinck and Bergson, from Samuel Butler and George Moore, even from Emerson. Other contributors wrote about Nietzsche ("The Prophet of a New Culture"), "The Meaning of Bergsonism," and the "cubist literature" of Gertrude Stein. Much of this work was adolescent, gushy, sometimes even bordering on the childish. Yet from the very beginning, Margaret Anderson managed to attract major writers who, partly thanks to her, were soon to win a wider audience. Vachel Lindsay had one of his earliest poems printed in the first issue. Sherwood Anderson discussed "The New Note" in literature. In the second number, William Butler Yeats praised the new American poetry of Lindsay and Pound. After the first few issues were out, it was already apparent that, in spite of or perhaps because of, the editor's chaotic passions and enthusiasms—"My attitude during this epoch was," she wrote, "life is just one ecstasy after another."—here was a most important new voice in American literature.

When the third number was going to press, the editor "heard Emma Goldman lecture and had just time to turn anarchist before the presses closed."[14] From then on, the magazine would sponsor all the "causes" of the rebellion: feminism, sexual freedom, the new paganism. One month there would be paeans to Emma Goldman and the next to the Nietzschean superman. And there were even more literary causes. The magazine sponsored imagism and futurism, later vorticism, cubism, and German expressionism, and still later dadaism. Margaret Anderson thought nothing of heralding the most extreme forms of aestheticism (*"The Little Review* is a magazine that believes in life for Art's sake," wrote the editor), while sponsoring at the same time the most variegated social causes. But the magazine was always vibrant and alive, responding "eagerly to every new tremor in the international avant-garde."[15] It printed Sherwood Anderson when his "fleshy" stories scared away most other editors. It printed Ezra Pound's poetry and many of his critical papers. Ford Madox Ford's *Men and Women* appeared first in *The Little Review,* William Butler Yeats contributed stories and plays. One issue printed no fewer than twenty-four photographs of Brancusi's sculpture. Much of the early work of T. S. Eliot, William Carlos Williams, Aldous Huxley, Jean Cocteau, Louis Aragon, and Djuna

Barnes appeared first in its pages. It was the first to publish *Ulysses* and to fight for Hart Crane. And when, one month, nothing worth while seemed to have come to the editor's attention, she brought out an issue filled largely with blank pages. . . .

The magazine's finances were, predictably enough, even more erratic than its content. It cost over $10,000 a year to put out *The Little Review*. So Margaret Anderson and her assistant-companion Jane Heap would sometimes eat nothing but biscuits for days, make their own clothes, do their own housework, and even cut their own hair. For a while, editorial offices and "home" consisted of a tent on the shores of Lake Michigan. At one time, the only clothes Margaret Anderson possessed were a hat, a blouse, and a tailored suit. The subscriptions from the approximately 2000 subscribers did not pay for even half the magazine's cost—so the editors experimented with a book-mail service and later with a bookstore to make up the deficit. And, of course, Margaret Anderson was always trying to get money from wealthier friends. Once she took the subway to the heart of Wall Street, chose the largest building in sight, and began to canvass the whole building for subscriptions.

"We published a hundred dollars' worth of *Ulysses*," she wrote, "and settled again into poverty." And yet the magazine, apparently relying on a modern miracle of loaves and fishes, kept alive.

In 1917, *The Little Review* was moved to New York and was published on the borders of Greenwich Village. In 1920, it was indicted and fined as a purveyor of "lascivious" writings—by one James Joyce. It became a quarterly in the fall of 1921 and moved to Paris in 1922, ceased publication from the winter of 1926 to May, 1929, and finally, in 1929, printed its last issue (Vol. XII, 5-6) with a farewell piece by Jane Heap appropriately entitled "Lost: A Renaissance." "We have given space in *The Little Review*," she wrote, "to 23 new systems of art (all now dead), representing 19 countries. In all of this we have not brought forward anything approaching a masterpiece except *Ulysses* of Mr. Joyce. . . . Self-expression is not enough; experiment is not enough . . . Masterpieces are not made from chaos . . . you can't get race horses from mules." This outburst was a very discouraging *finis* to what had begun as so enthusiastic a voyage, but it was by no means a correct assessment of the importance of *The Little Review*.

A few years before the demise of the magazine, Margaret Anderson wrote, "My idea of a magazine which makes any claim to artistic value is that . . . it should suggest, not conclude; that it should stimulate to thinking rather than dictate thought."[16] This assessment of *The Little Review*'s functions is much better than the one Jane Heap provided in her *post mortem*. *The Little Review* constantly fed new ideas into the stream of American culture. It provided a gateway for ideas and techniques that were to have revolutionary impact on American writing, even though it also printed much that was simply silly and had, at best, ephemeral shock value. Without *The Little Review*, postwar fiction and poetry would ultimately have taken its experimental course in any case, but *The Little Review* became a "midwife of history," accelerating a course that would otherwise have been delayed or beset with greater difficulties. The time was ripe for it, of course, and *The Little Review* actively helped to determine the literary renewal of the postwar years. It was a kind of informal college in which young writers who were to leave their marks on later literary history acquired the tools of their trade and sharpened their sensibilities as well as their techniques.

The Little Review never reached an audience as wide as that of *The Masses*, and *The Masses*' audience, as we have seen, was not very wide. *The Little Review* had none of the political and social effects that we might associate with *The Masses*. It was essentially a literary man's literary magazine. It consciously chose to address only the small elite of cultivated taste that concerned itself with artistic experimentation. But within these chosen limitations of appeal and audience, it managed to be amazingly effective as a taste-maker and pace-setter for the culture of postwar America.

NOTES

1. Frederick J. Hoffman, *et al.*, *The Little Magazine* (Princeton: Princeton University Press, 1946), pp. 2, 4. I have used this excellent book throughout this discussion.
2. Quoted in *ibid.*, p. 5.
3. For the early history of *The Masses*, see Walter B. Rideout, *The Radical Novel* (Cambridge, Mass.: Harvard University Press, 1956), Chapter IV. I have also used Daniel Aaron, *Writers on the Left* (New York: Harcourt, Brace & World, Inc., 1961); and Henry F. May, *The End of American Innocence* (New York: Alfred A. Knopf, Inc., 1959). Important materials can be found in Floyd Dell's autobiography, *Homecoming* (New York: Farrar, Straus & Cudahy, Inc., 1933), and in Granville Hicks's *John Reed* (New York: The Macmillan Company, 1937). The most valuable information is to be found in Max Eastman's *Enjoy-*

ment of Living (New York: Harper & Row, Publishers, 1958). Also *cf.*
Allen Churchill, *The Improper Bohemians* (New York: E. P. Dutton &
Co., Inc., 1959).

4. Granville Hicks, *op. cit.*, p. 93.

5. Alfred Kazin, *On Native Grounds* (Anchor ed.; Garden City, N.Y.:
Doubleday & Company, Inc., 1956), p. 136.

6. Eastman, *op. cit.*, p. 439.

7. Quoted in Kazin, *op. cit.*, p. 137.

8. Eastman, *op. cit.*, pp. 403–4.

9. Karl Mannheim, "The Problem of Generations," *Essays on the
Sociology of Knowledge* (New York: Oxford University Press, Inc.,
1952), p. 304.

10. *Ibid.*, p. 306.

11. *Ibid.*, p. 307.

12. Margaret Anderson, *My Thirty Years' War, An Autobiography*
(New York: Alfred A. Knopf, Inc., 1930), p. 128. This delightful auto-
biography has been my major source in the discussion of *The Little
Review*. Additional data were provided by the chapter, "The Little
Review," in Hoffman, *et al.*, *op. cit.*, as well as by others of the works
cited earlier.

13. Anderson, *op. cit.*, p. 44.

14. *Ibid.*, p. 54.

15. Kazin, *op. cit.*, p. 139.

16. Quoted in Hoffman, *et al.*, *op. cit.*, p. 60.

Part Two

Intellectuals and the
House of Power

Chapter 12

INTRODUCTION

KNOWLEDGE MAY BRING POWER, BUT, EVEN SO, MEN of knowledge have only rarely been men of power. A few individual intellectuals have wielded power without losing their intellectual qualities: Masaryk, Wilson, Léon Blum, Nehru, Disraeli, and Gladstone come readily to mind. Occasionally even groups of intellectuals have moved into the house of power: the Girondins and the Jacobins, the Bolsheviks, and, nearer to home, the founding fathers. But, except in the last case, such forays by intellectuals into the political domain have usually ended rather disastrously.

Although intellectuals have often been fascinated with power, although they have felt that power without knowledge is apt to lead to calamity, they have in the main shied away from the temptation to conquer power for themselves. They have more frequently attempted to exercise influence on the men of power, to make them instruments in their designs. They have often been advisers to the powerful, hoping to make them espouse their causes. We are reminded of Plato in Syracuse, Hobbes and Charles II before the Restoration, Turgot under Louis XVI, Lord Keynes and the Treasury, the Webbs and successive British Liberal governments, and the "Brain Trust" under F. D. Roosevelt. But even in these cases the relationship between power and intellect usually proved to be unstable. The general tension between the intellectuals' preoccupation with general and abstract values and the routine institutions of society asserted itself. Intellectuals tended to turn in disdain from the practical concerns of decision-makers immersed in day-to-day compromise and adjustments, and men of power were wary of what they called the impracticality and the lack of realism of intellectuals. Power holders and intellectuals have traditionally looked upon each other with a measure of mistrust and mutual incomprehension. To be sure, there have been short periods of honeymoon, but no stable union has ever been achieved.

A number of modalities characterize the relations between men of power and men of ideas. Intellectuals may hold power, as did the Jacobins and the early Bolsheviks. They may attempt to direct and advise the men of power, as did the Fabians or the members of Roosevelt's "Brain Trust." They may serve to legitimize the men of power and provide them with ideological justifications. The *idéologues* under Napoléon and the Polish "revisionists" under Gomulka are prime examples. They may be critics of power, and, like Old Testament prophets, they may castigate political men for the errors of their ways, attempting to shame men committed to an ethos of compromise by holding up absolute standards of moral righteousness. The Dreyfusards and the Abolitionists played such roles. Finally, they may despair of exercising influence at home and may turn to political systems abroad that seem more nearly to embody the image of their desire.

Other types of relation between the men of power and the men of intellect are naturally conceivable and have been embodied in historical experience. There are, for example, intellectuals who, like the upholders of "art for art's sake" have no relationship whatever with things political, for whom the world of politics is like a nightmare. And there are intellectuals who, without aspiring to power or influence, fashion countersymbols that undermine the legitimations of the men of power. Radical sectarians as well as conservative mugwumps may fall in this category.

We shall now examine this gamut of typical relationships between intellectual and men of power in greater detail.

INTELLECTUALS IN POWER

There have been intellectuals ever since Plato who have believed that, "until philosophers bear rule, State and individuals will have no rest from evil." As in the seventeenth century the rebellious Calabrian monk Campanella had dreamed of a City of the Sun dominated by a Great Metaphysicus, Saint-Simon at the beginning of the nineteenth century evolved a vision of the benevolent dictatorship of a college of Great Physicus-Engineers: Scientists whose inventions had just begun to make the wheels of industry turn should, he held, become the regulators of society. A few decades later Auguste Comte pursued the megalomaniacal vision of High Priests of Humanity directing mankind according to a positive theory of authority; politics, thought Comte, would become a sort of applied social physics, and reliance on the spiritual guidance of the elite of social scientists would become a matter of course. In the United States, Lester Ward dreamed his complicated dreams of a sociocratic world in which the primacy of knowledge over power would finally be achieved. And in our days, Karl Mannheim has movingly argued the need for an elite of intellectuals to put their hands on the tiller of the state.

These men and many others dreamed Plato's dream—although none had a chance of enacting it into reality.

In periods marked by relatively stable social structures and routinized politics, the affairs of state prove recalcitrant to intellectuals' attempts to gain political ascendance. But revolutionary periods may afford them the chance to gain state power. In ordinary periods, individual intellectuals may upon occasion be co-opted into seats of power, but only in revolutionary times will groups of intellectuals be in a position to conquer the state. It is then that revolutionary intellectuals wrest power and rule society, even if only for a short but pregnant moment in history. We can witness this process in many of the new nations of the contemporary world. The founding fathers were similarly a group of revolutionary intellectuals who bore rule. But the Jacobins and the Bolsheviks remain the prime historical examples.

The Jacobin men of virtue, sons of the Enlightenment, found it possible to impress their political will upon the polity of revolutionary France, making and remaking the fabric and structure of French society and politics. They attempted to rebuild this society in terms of a rational model derived from the seminal ideas of the *philosophes*. But their reign was brief, and even before their fall they had already compromised and tainted their vision. A century later, Lenin's Bolshevist "leaders and teachers of the masses," a vanguard of intellectuals armed with "scientific knowledge," succeeded in their turn to grasp state power. But soon the domination of the high priests of the historical *logos* was replaced by a brutal dictatorship of bureaucratic practitioners.

During brief periods of revolutionary exhilaration and upsurge, when everything seems possible and men ache with the desire to make the world over, intellectuals have succeeded in taking power. But they have failed to hold it when subsequent routinized exigencies brought to the fore political practitioners unhampered by intellect but endowed with the requisite practical skills.

BORING FROM WITHIN

When the times seem inconspicuous for revolutionary upheavals and intellectuals yet feel that it is imperative to bring about major changes in the operation of society, they may turn from attempts to gain power for themselves to the task of converting and advising the men of power. They then endeavor to become spiritual guides, directors of conscience, or chiefs of staff to the power holders. Despairing that their blueprints can be realized directly, they conceive of the notion that they may slowly mold reality to their liking by becoming gray eminences, powers behind the throne.

This urge to influence powerful men characterized many utopian intellectuals just as it spread among intellectuals given to a more "moderate" vision of the good society. Charles Fourier, that man with the terrible imagination who was convinced that he alone had "overcome twenty centuries of political imbecility" and that to him "present and future generations will owe the initiative for their immense happiness,"[1] made it known most humbly that he would be home daily at a certain hour in order that his expected political patron, who was to mold his flights of imagination in the thick paste of everyday reality, not be inconvenienced. Saint-Simon and Robert Owen bombarded the crowned heads of Europe with memoranda and unsolicited advice. Auguste Comte sent a copy of his *Positive Philosophy* to Emperor Nicholas I of Russia with an accompanying letter in which he took for granted that the Emperor would avail himself of the proffered advice in order to institute the reforms necessary to elevate Russia to a positive society.

Utopian blueprints naturally remained without immediate impact among the robust men of power to whom they were addressed. Yet intellectuals less absolutist in their doctrine, more flexible in their orientations, more willing to consider the exigencies of practical politics while yet bent on bringing about major reforms, even, as it were, through the back door, proved at times more successful. By slow infiltration into the seats of government, by permeating the higher civil service and the major ministries, by cautious advice and careful documentation, the Fabians succeeded in changing the climate of British politics around the turn of the century and in infusing the British polity with belief in a large part of their blueprint for a welfare state.

The early "Brain Trusters," though never wholly capturing the intensely pragmatic mind of F. D. Roosevelt, were partly responsible for the many daring departures from tradition that marked the early years of the New Deal. Turgot was able, for a short period, to help infiltrate the machinery of the French monarchy with a considerable number of his fellow intellectuals and to bring a semblance of rational order into the creaking machinery of the French *ancien régime*. Historical examples of the influence of individual intellectuals on political decision-makers abound, from Hobbes to Lord Keynes.

But even though their roles as advisers to the men of power may often have brought some success to intellectuals bent on influencing the march of political events, their relationships with the men of power usually proved highly unstable. Sooner or later most of them found that they were forced to make the choice of either saying "yes" to power and hence becoming courtiers, experts, or technicians or reverting to the status of unattached, autonomous, and critical intellectuals. The fate of Thomas More is a paradigm in this respect.

The Webbs were successful in their chosen roles partly because they steadfastly refused to become officially attached to the machinery of government. They might serve on an official inquiry or prepare memoranda for the use of a ministry, but they would not themselves become civil servants or assume direct governmental responsibilities. They therefore enjoyed an independent basis of operation. The matter is very different, however, for those intellectuals who, in their desire to influence the decision-makers, consent to join the machinery of administration. Then the pressures to conform to the demands of day-to-day political requirements almost always lead to high tension, which can be resolved either by the self-transformation of detached intellectuals into attached staff men—or by a more or less dramatic parting of the ways. When intellectual autonomy is relinquished and the constraints on inquiry imposed by policy-makers are accepted, when no independent basis of power is available, the intellectual becomes an expert. When the intellectual is not allowed to select his own problems and is forced by the exigencies of the situation to work on the problems posed to him by the policy-maker, his role comes to resemble that of a public servant who possesses peculiar skills but who must execute whatever the policy-maker may dictate.

Particular individuals or even groups of individuals—one thinks of the English Utilitarians in the India Office, of Macaulay or Charles Trevelyan—may at times succeed in impressing their ideas on initially reluctant and recalcitrant policy-makers. Yet, in the great majority of cases, it remains true, in Robert K. Merton's words, that the union of policy-makers and intellectuals tends to be nasty, brutish, and short.[2]

LEGITIMIZING POWER

A third typical relationship between power and intellect is one in which intellectuals fashion a system of symbols, tissues of legitimating ideas, to clothe the exercise of power. Such systems of legitimation may be broadly classified into two subcategories: Intellectuals may fashion new legitimations in historical situations in which the old ones no longer seem sufficient to shore up the edifice of power, or they may create entirely novel systems of legitimation in order to justify new systems of power. Conservative thought is essentially of the first kind; I shall illustrate the second by reference to the roles of the *idéologues* under Napoleon and of the Marxist revisionists in contemporary Poland.

Modern conservatism, as Karl Mannheim has shown, is to be distinguished from traditionalism.[3] The latter tends to be unreflective and unself-conscious, a simple turning to the ideas and styles of thought of the past as sufficient guides for conduct in the present. Traditional societies are governed by the eternal yesterdays of custom and precedence. The matter is very different in the case of modern conservatism, which arose as a mode of defense when the old values and traditions were threatened and called into question by the Enlightenment and the French Revolution. "Conservatism," writes Karl Mannheim, "is conscious and reflective from the first, since it arises as a counter-movement in conscious opposition to the highly organized, coherent and systematic 'progressive' movement."[4] Conservative thought then, whether expressed by Burke in England or Chateaubriand in France, by Adam Mueller, Justus Moeser, and Treitschke in Germany or by William Graham Sumner and Friedrich Hayek in this country, is always a defense of the existing state of affairs in general and of the prevailing relations of power in particular against critical streams of thought that call them into question. By preaching with Hegel that "what exists is rational" or with William Graham Sumner that "it is the greatest folly of which a man can be capable, to sit down with a slate and pencil to plan out a new social world,"[5] conservative thinkers have always, whether consciously or not, furnished justifications for the powers that be.

Conservative thinkers have been studied so often and in such great detail, there seems no need to add here to the vast and exhaustive literature on the subject. The second type of legitimizing intellectual, however, the kind of man who erects systems of justification for new systems of power, has been much less studied and is accordingly given more sustained attention here. I have in mind such efforts at legitimation as those of certain Bolshevist Russian intellectuals who, after the seizure of power by a new revolutionary government, fashioned the intellectual tools needed for its defense against those who disputed its legitimacy. One may think here of men like Leon Trotsky, who, long after having lost his position of power and even after having become exceedingly critical of the new men of power in the Soviet Union, still provided certain major intellectual arguments to defend its character as a "workers' state." One thinks of many of his former coworkers —Radek, Bucharin, Zinoviev—all of whom provided ideological legitimations for Stalin's regime. These men had their earlier counterparts, of course, in the French Revolution and among the Puritan ideologists of the English Revolution. Milton may serve as their prototype.

Regimes needing ideological legitimation are not necessarily revolutionary, of course. Counterrevolutions, personal dictatorships, and new liberal regimes alike require legitimation. I have chosen to examine in some detail two relatively little known groups of intellectual legitimizers, the *idéologues* under Napoleon and the "revisionist" Marxists in the Poland of Gomulka. In both cases, the new regimes required ideologies to legitimize their seizures of power. In both cases also the intellectuals who rose to the task initially misunderstood the new regimes, believing them to be steps on the road toward greater freedom, liberalism, and justice—only to discover that, after they had done their work, they were to be discarded together with major aspects of the liberal ideologies that they had at first provided. Again the unstable relationship between policymakers and intellectuals becomes apparent. Even those, it turns out, who welcome new systems of domination and provide them with symbolic justification are apt, if not sufficiently pliable to become uncritical propagandists, to end up with the bitter taste of disillusionment in their mouths.

At the accession of Napoleon, the *idéologues* fancied they had found the "man on horseback" who would usher in the reign of reason, but there soon came a time when the "hero of liberal ideas" turned against the "vermin" of *idéologues* and made it clear that there was no middle way between submission and exclusion from official cultural life. Many submitted, but many others chose such exclusion in order to keep alive the liberal vision in an autocratic age. Many young Polish Communist intellectuals believed for a brief moment and made others believe that Gomulka would bring libertarian socialism, but most of them soon realized that the regime, though "liberalized" in certain respects, was far from libertarian. Most of them withdrew from public political activity; others became propagandists for the regime and in this way surrendered freedom of action and critical distance.

CRITICS OF POWER

Many intellectuals did not need disillusionment to convince them of the long-range incompatibility of power and intellect. They saw themselves *ab initio* as the bearers of the consciousness and conscience of the society, in permanent readiness, if need be, to descend into the political arena to battle against those who held power.

The Russian radical intellectuals of the nineteenth century considered themselves permanently mobilized against an autocratic regime that, in its every motion, denied the claims of the intellect and its aspirations toward freedom and justice. In liberal societies, similar types of intellectual do not as a rule consider themselves in comparable permanent mobilization. They tend to become concerned with public and political matters only in situations of particular stress and strain. They may, in fact, be barely distinguishable from apolitical intellectuals as long as the times are ordinary. It is only extraordinary events that mobilize them and cause them to forsake the quiet of the study for the political battlefield. Only, in other words, when the political events of the day have produced an issue that transcends humdrum politics and illuminates larger and transcendent concerns do such intellectuals become actively engaged. It is during such major junctures in a nation's politics that this type of intellectual appears on the scene as spokesman for sets of abstract ideas and ideals that are endangered by the men of power. The Dreyfusard intellectuals, who defended the ideal of justice against tradition-bound judges and the ideal of truth against those who would make it subservient to reasons of state, were such men. The Abolitionists, rising in holy wrath against the abomination of slavery, were of an essentially similar type. In our days, those who have become spokesmen for the peace movement, protesting the suicidal madness of the men of power in an age of overkill, may be said to be their successors. And certain contemporary Polish and Russian intellectuals who have lately raised their voices against the iniquities, barbarities, and sheer stupidity of their own rulers belong to the same breed.

SALVATION ABROAD

Finally, a very special type of intellectual will be considered here. I have in mind men of ideas who, while highly critical of and alienated from their own culture, while assuming a critical stance toward the men of power in their own society, tend to transfer their allegiance to the foreign scene, becoming, in effect, legitimizers of the power structures of nations not their own, while, at the same time, undermining the legitimations of their own society.

Efforts to contrast the decadence and disorders of one's own age with the splendor and health of other ages run throughout human history. Such are the myths of a bygone golden age, of a bygone age of chivalry, and the eighteenth-century adoration of Roman virtue or Spartan simplicity. Men of ideas have used the splendors of other ages as foils for their own decayed societies to shame their contemporaries into recognizing their fall from virtue. Another and perhaps less studied kind of comparison is made not over time but in space, between the disorders of one's own society and the superior virtues of another across the borders. We notice then the curious phenomenon of intellectuals estranged from their own culture turning to another for spiritual haven and point of repair. Such efforts usually involve undue idealization of the external society of reference; blemishes that are clearly perceived at home are often overlooked abroad. It is as if, by a curious alchemy, the very things that are seen as vices at home are transmuted into virtues when perceived in the context of an admired foreign society.

Cases in point can be found in the anglomania of many French eighteenth-century intellectuals, in the twentieth-century infatuation with supposedly "experienced" Europe among expatriate or would-be expatriate American literary men in revolt against the uncouth "innocence" of the United States. I choose to deal with two examples of more immediate political import: the admiration for Russia and China among a wide group of French intellectuals of the Enlightenment and the Russophilia of English and American intellectuals during the 1930s. These groups, despite widely different historical circumstances, show a rather astonishing sociological parallelism. In both cases, anarchy and disorder at home were contrasted with supposed harmony and order in the countersocieties. In both cases, the lowly and neglected role of intellectuals at home was contrasted with the supposedly elevated status that they enjoyed abroad. In both cases, intellectuals committed to rejecting the pieties of their own societies were able to construct powerful myths about others. In both cases, finally, intellectuals were led by estrangement from men of power at home to justify and legitimize the brutal exercise of power abroad.

NOTES

1. Quoted in Alexander Gray, *The Socialist Tradition* (London: Longmans, Green & Co., Ltd., 1946), p. 170.

2. Robert K. Merton, "Role of the Intellectual in Public Bureaucracy," *Social Theory and Social Structure* (Rev. ed.; New York: The Free Press, 1957), pp. 207–24. I have learned a great deal from this essay.

3. Karl Mannheim, "Conservative Thought," *Essays in Sociology and Social Psychology* (New York: Oxford University Press, Inc., 1953), pp. 74–164.

4. *Ibid.*, p. 99.

5. William Graham Sumner, "The Absurd Effort to Make the World Over," *Social Darwinism, Selected Essays of William Graham Sumner* (Englewood Cliffs, N.J.: Prentice-Hall, Inc., 1963), p. 180.

Chapter 13

INTELLECTUALS
IN POWER

THE JACOBIN INTELLECTUALS OR THE
POLITICS OF VIRTUE

THE MAIN ACTORS IN THE JACOBIN DRAMA, ALTHOUGH
not the majority of Jacobins, were disaffected intellectuals, marginal
to the society of the *ancien régime* for a variety of reasons, some
private, some public. They were dissatisfied in various degrees with
the old institutions and desired to alter them in a fundamental
manner. But none was consciously prepared to play the role he
actually played during the Revolution. Unlike the Bolsheviks, the
Jacobins were not "professional revolutionists" prior to 1789. Events
cast them into parts for which they had not prepared themselves.
They were forced to enact their historic roles without even the
benefits of dress rehearsal. Yet, when they finally achieved power,
they showed that, as ruling intellectuals, they were not content
with the humdrum activities of daily politics: They had a grand
design; they wanted to remake France according to the dictates of
reason and of natural virtue.

The roughly 500,000 enrolled Jacobins in France, on the other
hand, were not, for the most part, intellectuals. They represented a
fair cross section of the urban population, with wide ranges of
income and occupation.[1] Of course, there were few aristocrats

among them and few of the desperately poor; most were of the
middle class. In the early years of the Revolution, they were mainly
of upper middle-class origin; later, petty tradesmen, small shopkeepers, and other lower middle-class people joined them, along
with cobblers, masons, carpenters, and other artisans. (The new
industrial proletariat, numerically still very feeble, was hardly represented.) In the leadership groups and among the most active
members, men with some education prevailed. But even they seem
to have represented the whole range of occupations and professions
that literate men might occupy. Given the fact that between 1793
and 1795 about one male in twelve was a member of the Jacobins,
it would be quite wrong to picture them as a small sect, an inter-
nally homogeneous group of professional revolutionaries.

The number of intellectuals increased as one moved up the
pyramid of power. Radical physicians were quite numerous among
the leaders, as were ex-priests. There was also a sprinkling of lawyers and men of the theater, as well as of teachers and notaries.
It would be unwarranted to assume that they were all disaffected
under the *ancien régime*, but many had been part of that minority
of *frondeurs* that had helped to undermine its legitimations in the
years before the Revolution. Many, perhaps most, had been members of the various provincial literary societies, debating clubs, provincial academies, and Masonic lodges in which the ideas of the
Enlightenment had been discussed and which had served to dis-
seminate these ideas among wider strata. In all these groups, intellectuals had played leading roles, even though in most the majority
probably consisted of solid middle-class burghers.

As one moved, then, from the rank and file of the Jacobins to
the leadership of the various local societies, the proportion of intellectuals increased. And if one moved from provincial leadership
groups to the men who enacted the key political roles—deputies of
the Mountain in the Convention, major agitators and journalists,
even leaders of the Parisian popular masses and of the Paris Commune—intellectuals became predominant: lawyers like Danton, frustrated scientists like Marat, journalists like Desmoulins and Hébert,
ex-priests like Jacques Roux, or former playwrights like the Revolutionary general Ronsin. If we finally consider the very top group,
those twelve men who constituted the Committee of Public Safety
during the Terror, we encounter only intellectuals, most of whom
had grounds for considerable disgruntlement and dissatisfaction

with the regime in the years before the Revolution. This small group deserves closer analysis.[2]

Of these twelve men, seven were lawyers, and an eighth had taken a law degree, although he had never practiced. Two were army officers and engineers, one an actor and playwright, and one a Protestant minister. Only one, Collot d'Herbois, had ever experienced economic insecurity; the others had been fairly well off, some even possessing moderate wealth. All except Hérault de Séchelles, a nobleman, were members of the middle class. All except Collot d'Herbois had received a good deal of formal schooling. They had studied rhetoric and philosophy and had, in addition, been graduated from professional studies in law, engineering, and theology. All were steeped in the works of the *philosophes*. Almost all had lived fairly comfortable lives. Most were probably better off economically than their fathers. Yet they had all become dissatisfied in one way or another with the *ancien régime*. A somewhat closer look at their careers prior to the Revolution may provide an explanation.

Lazare Carnot, later to be called the "organizer of victory," was a professional army man, a first-rate mathematician, and author of several mathematical treatises. Few army officers of *bourgeois* origin had any chance to climb the ladder of advancement in the *ancien régime*. Only in the corps of engineers, where technical knowledge was indispensable, did they have any chance at all. But Carnot, a captain before the Revolution, had already reached the highest rank a commoner could attain. His further career was effectively blocked, although he was still only in his thirties.

Saint-Just, the Benjamin of the group, was, before the Revolution, an unruly youngster who revolted against the narrowness of small-town life in Picardy. He had run away to Paris at the age of nineteen, taking some of his mother's silver with him. Upon the complaint of his mother, he was arrested and kept in protective custody under a *lettre de cachet*. Returned home, he studied law but made no move to practice it, writing instead a poem in twenty cantos, *Organt*, a compound of pornography and violent attacks against kings, courtiers, and nobles. He went to Paris to get it published just before the Revolution began. He was a rebel before he became a revolutionary.

Jeanbon Saint-André was a Protestant minister, the son of an artisan. The Huguenots were officially outlaws under the *ancien régime*, although they were not much molested at the end. As a Protestant, he was effectively barred from participation in civic affairs and had to live, at least so far as the law was concerned, in the interstices of society.

Billaud-Varenne, a trained lawyer, had not succeeded in establishing a secure law practice. Instead he had written a comedy, which had failed, and several violent philosophical tracts against Church and government, all of which lacked originality and brought him no success. He lived precariously on the margin of society.

Barère, Couthon, and Robespierre were moderately successful provincial lawyers who belonged to the "advanced set" in the literary societies of their towns. Imbued with modern philosophy, committed to thoroughgoing reforms and curbs on Church and nobility, at odds with dominant values, they, though by no means consciously revolutionary, were immediately sensitive to the first revolutionary stirrings.

Hérault de Séchelles, the only nobleman in the group, was a rich man about town. Much admired by the women of Parisian society, a smiling libertine, a highly cultivated lover of books, the author of a cynical work called *Theory of Ambition*, he was an egotist of pure water, a man few would have expected to turn up, even for a short period, among the stern champions of republican virtue. During the *ancien régime*, Hérault, unlike all the others, did not reject the cultural goals of the society in the name of counter-values but retreated instead into anomic withdrawal.

Collot d'Herbois, a native of Paris, had for years prior to the Revolution toured the provinces as a professional actor. Under the *ancien régime*, such men were discriminated against in a variety of ways, both legal and social. Collot suffered from awareness that he had been welcomed to *bourgeois* or noble homes only as an entertainer to contribute amusement but never as an equal. He had written plays that had had only moderate success. He had been a theater manager twice, and both ventures had ended in failure through no fault of his own. He was filled with resentment not only against the nobility but also against the well-to-do middle classes from whom he had unsuccessfully craved recognition.

Too little is known about three of the twelve, the two Prieurs and Robert Lindet, to establish their prerevolutionary careers.

It should be clear that most of these men had experienced cir-

cumstances that alienated them from the basic values of their society. Not all of them had made large and dramatic departures
from institutional norms, yet they were all deviants, at least in
terms of ideas, from the currently dominant values. Some had been
thwarted in their ambitions; others felt that there was no relationship between their own worth and the consequences of their actions.
The social structure in which they were placed exerted definite
pressure upon them to engage in nonconformist rather than con-
formist conduct.³ As members of the middle class shut off from
some of the prerequisites of status in a society still granting premium honor to the nobility, even those among them whose careers
had been fairly regular were deeply involved with the reforming
ideas of the *philosophes*, which provided them with countersymbols
against the current values. Being intellectuals, they seized upon the
values inherent in the writings of the *philosophes* to construct reasoned images of alternatives to contemporary reality. They were in
regular contact with other men of advanced ideas in the literary
societies and academies of their provincial towns, so that they did
not feel that they were simply isolated malcontents. All, in one
way or another, laid claim to participation in the Enlightenment;
all were involved in a common effort to reappraise critically received ideas and assumptions in the light of reason and nature. They
were all to some extent alienated intellectuals—alienated intellectuals,
moreover, with at least the rudiments of an alternative system in
their minds.

This book is not the place to follow their subsequent revolutionary careers in detail. It suffices to say that they all played active
roles in the Revolution, always on its left wing (although, of
course, the Left at the time of the Constituent Assembly resembled
but little the Mountain of the Convention). Some of the twelve
had been in the forefront of Jacobin politics since the early days
of the Jacobin Society; others had been limited at first to more obscure tasks. Robespierre was a key figure among the Jacobins almost
from the very beginning, whereas the young Saint-Just entered the
national scene only upon his election to the Convention in September, 1792. But from the middle of 1793 (most were elected in July
but some not until August and September) till 9 *thermidor* (July)
of the following year, these men, with the exception of Hérault,
who was guillotined as a traitor in April, 1794, were re-elected
each month to the all-powerful Committee of Public Safety, which

ruled France absolutely as no monarch had ever been able to rule
it. For one year, France bore the rule of Jacobin intellectuals. For
one year these men of the word were men of power.

Being intellectuals rather than realistic politicians—and intellectuals reared in the spirit of the Enlightenment—they used this power
in an attempt to make France over in the image of pure reason. I
cannot enter here into the specialized quarrels of historians about
the degree to which Jacobin doctrine and the Terror can be accounted for in terms of the compulsions of foreign war and internal
subversion. Nor do I intend to discuss here whether or not they
aimed to build a truly equalitarian republic or whether or not the
laws of *ventôse* providing for distribution among the poor of the
property of suspects were intended only as emergency legislation.
It suffices for our purpose to document the fact that these men
attempted to transform radically the very fabric of French society
and to transform it in the image of reason and virtue, as interpreted
by the philosophers, especially Rousseau.

The Jacobins in power were determined to make a clean break
with the immediate past, to kill that past, to write on a clean sheet
of history.[4] This determination is perhaps best symbolized by their
changing of the calendar. They sought to do away with the symbolic associations between the old calendar and the obscurantist
past, so they made twelve new months and named them, not after
old gods or dead tyrants, but after the works of beneficent nature
—*germinal*, the month of buds, or *fructidor*, the month of ripening, for example. The very continuity between past and present
was thus to be broken; the citizens of the new republic were ever
to be reminded that they were living in that exhilarating moment
when a totally new society was being born, cleansed of the vices of
the old.

New republican rituals and ceremonies were to replace collective memories encrusted with the vices of an oppressive past. It
was ordained that "festivals shall be instituted to remind men of
the Deity, and of the dignity of their state . . . these festivals shall
be named after the glorious events of our Revolution . . ." On specific days, there were to be festivals honoring, among many others,
the Supreme Being, nature, the human race, the French people,
liberty and equality, hatred of tyrants and traitors, friendship, temperance, mother-love, filial piety, and so forth.

The Jacobins changed forms of dress as well as forms of address.
One greeted one's fellow as *citoyen*, rather than as *monsieur*. The

virtuous *citoyen* was to wear the simple long trousers of the *sans-culottes*, rather than the knee breeches of the aristocracy, and a Phrygian bonnet or liberty cap in the place of the elaborate head-pieces of bygone eras.

The rage for renaming did not stop at the calendar: Streets were also renamed, and men who had the misfortune to carry such names as Leroy changed them to Laloy. Christian names like Louis were changed to Brutus or Gracchus. Infants were named Constitution, Marat, Montagne, and Spartacus. Even the kings and queens of playing cards were replaced by republican symbols. Such changes, and there were others, were meant to destroy historical continuity. In an urge to clear the road to the millennium of reason and virtue, the Jacobins smashed the traditional symbols. Trained and skilled in the manipulation of symbols, these intellectuals were well aware of the power of symbols over the minds of men.

Secularized millenarianism also helps to account for the Terror. Terror had become, especially in the last months before their fall, the Jacobins' *ultima ratio regum*. It would be superficial to explain this fact by the exigencies of the emergency alone; terrorism became in fact an integral part of Jacobin ideology. "At the harvest-time one must pluck the weeds out of God's vineyard," Thomas Muenzer, the chiliastic leader of the German peasant uprising, had written almost 300 years before their day. The Jacobins echoed him in their secularized terminology. The structural similarities among millenarian movements assert themselves beyond the particularities of historical circumstance.[5] The Jacobins sincerely believed that their dictatorship was nothing but a prelude to a harmonious society in which all coercion would become unnecessary. But precisely the striving for so exalted a goal legitimized for them the recourse to terroristic means. "The Revolution will come to an end," said Robespierre in his speech on the principles of political morality, "in a very simple way . . . when all people will have become equally devoted to their country and its laws. But we are still far from having reached that point . . . The Republican government is not yet well established, and there are factions." Only when unanimity had been attained among the people would the Republic of Virtue prevail, but, for the time being, conspirators, factionalists, and enemies of reason were hiding everywhere, and so the guillotine had to continue its work. "There is only one remedy," declared Robespierre, "for all our ills: it consists in obedience to the law of nature, which intends every man to be just, and to live a virtuous life, the foundation of all society." But as long as the demands of nature were violated, as long as there were corruption and rascals and lukewarm concern with public virtue, the purge must continue. And after each orgy of violence, the blessed goal seemed to recede further into the future. "The craving for violence," writes Robespierre's biographer J. M. Thompson, "returns at shorter intervals; the reign of virtue seems, not less desirable, but harder to achieve."[6]

A few among the Jacobins came, toward the end, to understand the folly of establishing morality by fiat. "Let us beware of connecting politics with moral regeneration—a thing at present impracticable. Moralism is fatal to freedom," wrote Camille Desmoulins, erstwhile friend of Robespierre, shortly before he too was to die under the guillotine. He had indeed uncovered the mainsprings of Robespierre's orientation, an orientation shared in varying degrees by the other members of the Committee until the last few months of its reign. Eager to regenerate the French citizenry in the image of virtuous Romans and Spartans, they sought to institute fraternity and friendship by legislative decree, to legislate morality into existence. In the pursuit of so exalted an aim, men invested with high purpose and morally invulnerable need feel no pity. Their opponents were not only in error; they were in sin. They could therefore be exterminated in good conscience. Those swine, vermin, reptiles who aimed to subvert the good work were enemies of mankind on whom no human pity need be wasted.

The Jacobins had begun as sincere democrats, and one might suppose that they considered themselves democrats to the very end. But while they held total power, a short interval that they seemed to project ever further into the future, they felt the need to impose freedom and virtue on recalcitrant men. They became not wicked tyrants oppressing for personal ends but conscientious inquisitors torturing men to save their souls.[7] Robespierre was not a bloodthirsty man; he was, as contemporaries have testified, a man of great sweetness of character. But once his scheme came to be applied by Jacobins with a monopoly on the exercise of power, the politics of this virtuous lawyer became monstrous. The Jacobins exemplify the certain consequences of allowing intellectuals, possessed by the hubris of reason, to remake society—and the character of man—by decree. Once they had achieved total power, once they had moved from the role of critic to that of dictator, the humanitarian, democratic, progressive men of the early Revolutionary Left became men who killed in a purely disinterested manner.

The Jacobin intellectuals, fanatic apostles of reason, attempted to impose a preconceived pattern on recalcitrant social reality. It matters little that they believed the pattern confirmed to the "true nature" of society, which had been perverted by unreasonable customs and unenlightened policies. The fact remains that they believed themselves the only men who understood the ways of nature. "The revolutionary doctrinaire," writes J. L. Talmon, "is convinced that his pencil sketch is the only real thing . . . He experiences reality, not as an inchoate static mass, but as a *dénouement*, a dynamic movement towards a rational solution. The amorphous flesh mass is unreal, and can be brought into shape in accordance with the pencil pattern. It is not something that is, but something that fails to be, that is not yet what it should be . . . When the revolutionary doctrinaire is thwarted by the inchoate, 'unreal' mass of flesh and the 'irrational' egotistic behavior of men, his impatience turns into exasperation."[8]

Does Talmon describe a mere psychological characteristic of the revolutionary doctrinaire, or does he refer to the attributes of a social role?

The doctrinaire in power plays the role of the bureaucrat. Bureaucracy, Karl Marx wrote, is distinguished by the fact that "it wishes to do *everything*, i.e., that it makes *will* the *causa prima* . . . The bureaucrat views the world as a mere object of his manipulation."[9] Karl Mannheim has also remarked that "the mechanistic, rationalist, and centralizing impulse in the French Revolution . . . finds its exponent in the bureaucracy . . ."[10] The bureaucrat "does not understand that every rationalized order is only one of many in which socially conflicting irrational forces are reconciled."[11] Indeed, the Jacobin regime became increasingly a regime of bureaucrats.

Jacobinism had been primarily based on the *sociétés populaires*, the revolutionary clubs. As the old state machinery gradually broke down, the network of citizens' associations covering all of France served as the basis of Revolutionary government. But as one faction after another was liquidated, as terror heaped upon terror finally smothered all free expression within the clubs, as the press was muzzled and only a few official journals remained, active rank-and-file participation ceased. There remained only professional politicians and functionaries of the Revolution. Crane Brinton describes the situation: "We have seen how exacting were the self-imposed duties of these Jacobins of 1794—the committees, the missions to the infidel peasantry, the commissions, the clerkships, the investigations into markets, army supplies, hospitals. It is too much to expect citizens of a modern state already in the beginning of the industrial revolution to take self-government in the Athenian sense. Even before thermidor, then, the Jacobin government was increasingly a government of *fonctionnaires* . . . Nothing can be more illuminating in this respect than a study of the after careers of the more active local Jacobin leaders. Man after man assumes an appointive position under the Directory, and ends up as a Napoleonic official . . . Napoleon was as indebted to the Jacobin government for his civil administration as he was to the revolutionary armies for his military leaders. . . . Even had they not been suppressed, the *sociétés populaires* must have become what they were fast becoming in 1794, mere syndicates of civil servants."[12]

Brinton's view is not based solely on the hindsight of the historian; some of the participants were aware of these trends. Saint-Just, the most vigorous exponent of terror, the spokesman of the most determined centralizing wing of the Jacobins, jotted down during the last months of the regime a series of notes, later published as "Fragments sur les institutions républicaines,"[13] in which one finds entries like this one: "The Revolution has grown cold; all its principles are weakened; there remain only the red caps worn by intriguers. The exercise of terror has made crime blasé, as strong liquor makes the palate blasé." Saint-Just complained that the laws were revolutionary but that the organs of the law were not. What he clearly had in mind was the growth of bureaucracy. Earlier he had said that "the ministry is a mountain of paper. I don't know how the governments of Egypt and Rome managed without paper . . . Deputies, generals, functionaries are surrounded by bureaus just like the men of the old regime were surrounded by palaces; nothing happens, but the apparatus costs enormously. . . . The bureaus have replaced monarchism." Saint-Just did not exaggerate. There were only twelve men on the Committee of Public Safety, but it employed 114 functionaries, office heads, secretaries, translators. And every day a new increase in the scope of the Committee's activities, whether in price control or security, increased the need for functionaries.

Not only did the Jacobins require more and more bureaucrats

to execute their orders in an ever widening sphere. In their mania for order, plan, and rationality and in their contempt for the ordinary, still insufficiently enlightened citizen, the top Jacobins themselves increasingly exhibited the bureaucratic mentality. To them also the world became "a mere object of manipulation." This point is also best illustrated in Saint-Just's *Fragments*. At the same time that he jotted down his despair about the lack of popular participation in the Revolution, at the same time that he vehemently attacked the bureaucrats, Saint-Just laid down bureaucratic rules to guide the citizens' public behavior and their private behavior as well: ". . . he who strikes a child will be banished." ". . . every man aged 21 is required to declare in the temple the name of his friends. . . . If a man leaves his friend he must declare his motives before the people." "A married couple who have no children in the first seven years of their union and have adopted none will be separated by law and must leave each other . . ." "Nobody shall eat meat on the third, sixth and ninth day of the decade." These rules were written by the same man who wrote in the same *Fragments*, "The freedom of the people resides in their private lives, don't disturb it."

Saint-Just exemplified more than any other Jacobin the dilemma of the revolutionary gripped by the bureaucratic mania to remake the world in the image of his will, while hating bureaucracy that restricts his own attempts. "He who fights against monsters," wrote Nietzsche, "should look out that he does not turn into a monster in the process." That is what happened to the Jacobins. They set up a bureaucracy to implement their plans, yet the very bureaucratic apparatus they had called into being resisted their further innovations. To the extent that bureaucracy is committed to ritualistic practice in terms of methodical adherence to rigid rules, it proves recalcitrant to men who seek to fashion the world beyond bureaucratically set limits. It is thus no paradox to assert that the Jacobins fostered bureaucratization and fought its consequences. Already in his *Rapport* of October 10, 1793, Saint-Just had written, "A people has only one dangerous enemy: its government."[14] In his *Rapport* of February 26, 1794, he reiterated, "The more the functionaries take over the place of the people, the less democracy we are going to have. In the Popular Societies the people watch the functionaries instead of judging them."[15] Again, somewhat later, in his *Rapport sur les factions de l'étranger*, he stated, "Democracy is dead in France if the functionaries have more power than the people; it is no longer the people who judge the government: rather the functionaries who have now coalesced impose silence upon the people." These thoughts culminated in violent outpourings in the *Fragments* against the functionaries: "Whoever is a functionary no longer belongs to the people. . . . When one speaks to a functionary one should not call him citizen; this title is too great for him."[16]

Saint-Just deplored the lack of participation in the *sociétés populaires*, the drying-up of the wellsprings of popular enthusiasm, yet he had no other remedy than to call for a dictator: "In every revolution a dictator is needed to save the state by force, or censors are needed to save it by virtue. . . . The most severe censorship must be exercised over the functionaries of the government—we must instill fear in those who govern . . ." When the bureaucratic mind encounters an obstacle, it calls for yet another committee to supervise the rest; Saint-Just called for dictators or censors, and at the same time he wrote, "We have too many laws and too few civil institutions."

In the spring of 1794, the Committee of Public Safety had become almost totally isolated from the citizenry, a tutelary power legislating bureaucratically amid the disaffection of large segments of erstwhile supporters and the swelling hatred of a growing number of enemies. When finally the majority of the Convention and of their own colleagues turned against Robespierre, Couthon, and Saint-Just, the Paris Commune attempted to rouse the people to a new insurrection in order to save their former heroes. But the *sections* did not respond, and the people remained apathetic. When one of Robespierre's supporters, Hanriot, rode on horseback through the streets of Paris shouting, "The people is lost because its protector Robespierre is oppressed," he met some twenty workers busy repairing the pavement of the rue Saint-Honoré. He called them to arms; the workers looked up with astonishment, listened to the flood of words, then shouted a noncommittal "vive la République" and went back to work.[17]

The Republic of Virtue had come to an end, and the people, lectured at, exhorted, coerced, and terrorized for so long, looked on with indifference. The Jacobins had defeated the foreign enemies of France, they had for a time inspired its citizens to acts of heroic valor, and they had forged a nation. But they failed to remake France on the basis of reason. "I am not made to govern," Robespierre said in his last speech, "but only to combat crime." But he and his associates had in fact governed. They had had total power. The world had been an object of their manipulation.

After the despots of virtue had fallen, what had been most substantial in their work remained standing. Their government was dead, but their administration survived. They had attempted to storm heaven and to make men virtuous but had succeeded only in laying the groundwork for a regime that would administer them rationally, bureaucratically, methodically. They cleared the way for the military dictatorship of the man whom Mme. de Staël called mockingly, "a Robespierre on horseback." In later years, sovereigns and political constitutions would change, but the administrative bureaucracy of France remained.[18] The Jacobin intellectuals had started out with a burning belief in substantial rationality as the guide to political action; they ended as the main promoters of the "functional rationality" of the bureaucrat.

THE BOLSHEVIKS: INTELLECTUALS AS PROFESSIONAL REVOLUTIONARIES

The small disciplined band of Russian revolutionaries who called themselves Bolsheviks were the Jacobins of the twentieth century. Their leaders and the majority of the professional revolutionists who constituted their organization prior to the revolutionary days of 1917 belonged to the Russian intelligentsia. Although committed to the building of a Socialist Republic of Workers and Peasants, although considering themselves orthodox Marxists, they were not themselves, with a few exceptions, sons of the class to whose dominance they were committed and on whose behalf they professed to act. Lenin made this point clear in the early days of Bolshevism (1902) when he called for a party created by and mainly composed, at least at the outset, of intellectuals: ". . . In Russia," he said, "the theoretical principles of Social Democracy originated *altogether independently* [my emphasis—L.C.] of the spontaneous growth of the workers' movement. They were a natural and inevitable result of the development of the ideas of the revolutionary socialist intelligentsia."[19] Only revolutionary intellectuals—professional revolutionists—Lenin believed, could transform the spontaneous trade-union consciousness of Russian workers into a political struggle for socialist goals.

Lenin used the rhetoric of Marxism, but his emphasis on the

creative role of the intelligentsia was rooted in the history of the
nineteenth-century Russian revolutionary movement. Peter Tkachev,
a non-Marxist revolutionary of an earlier generation, whom Lenin
admired, expressed a similar idea when he wrote, "We should not
deceive ourselves that the people by its own might can make a
social revolution. The people is of course necessary for a social
revolution. But only when the revolutionary minority assumes the
leadership in this revolution."[20] The intelligentsia assumed a saliency
in the Russian revolutionary movement, pre-Marxist as well as
Marxist, that has had no counterpart in the West—although we
may find similar trends in today's "underdeveloped countries." In
order to account for this fact, we must ask, Who were the Russian
intelligentsia? Where did they originate?

The Russian nineteenth-century intelligentsia were heterogeneous in social origins but united by education and an abiding concern
with social problems. They had been excluded from a society still
largely governed by the principles of a medieval estate order. They
were recruited both from "below" and from "above" in the social
pyramid. Those from "below" were sons of priests, merchants,
minor officials, impoverished squires, and even freed or runaway
serfs, that is, *raznochintsy* (literally, "men of many ranks" or "un-
rankables"). Belonging to no estate and to no class, with no specific
place in the traditional structure, they were in official society without being of it. The intelligentsia also included sons of the upper
class who had rejected their own class and were attempting to ex-
piate the sins of their fathers, who had battened on the misery of
the Russian people. The intelligentsia was bound together by common alienation from the core assumptions of official society and
also—and this feature distinguishes it from the French intellectuals
of the eighteenth century—from all classes of society. They were
balanced precariously between the nobility and officialdom, on the
one hand, and the mass of people, silent, untutored, stubbornly
clinging to the traditional way of life, on the other. They were
déclassé and rootless outcasts, leading lives of voluntary or involuntary separation. They were, as Bertram D. Wolfe has written,
"lawyers without a practice, graduate clerics without benefices and
often without religion, chemists without laboratories, technicians,
engineers, statisticians for whom industry had as yet no need,
journalists without a public, educators without schools, politicians
without parties, sociologists and statesmen rejected by the state and
ignored by the people."[21] Highly cultivated, possessed of exquisite

moral and social sensibilities, they lived in a society in which the uncouth brutality of the vast peasant mass was matched by the equally uncouth brutality or elephantine apathy of a decaying gentry that hardly succeeded in hiding its lack of moral fiber and social conscience behind a veneer of culture. These intellectuals could not, as in France, address themselves to a cultivated middle-class public. They were continually thrown back upon themselves, talking only to one another.

At first, they made efforts to arouse interest in reform among state officials, only to find themselves rebuffed by uncomprehending bureaucrats. They then came to feel, in the words of the liberal censor Nikitenko, that "we were expected to hold our tongues, that our talents and brains were condemned to petrify or putrify at the bottom of the heart . . . that every fresh thought proved a crime against the social order; when in short, we were told that educated men in our society were outlaws . . . then suddenly the whole young generation felt out of gear." Later, when they turned to the people and attempted to rouse the peasantry from its historic apathy and sloth, they met an equally hostile reception. Isolated, insulated, made to feel superfluous and besieged, they were torn between despair and messianic dreams of salvation. "By what magic have we become aliens among our own," wrote the playwright Griboyedev. ". . . a people of the same blood, our people is estranged from us; and for ever."[22]

In the first part of the nineteenth century, the socially conscious among the intelligentsia had mainly been idealistic and utopian dreamers, intoxicated by ideas, eagerly becoming in turn Fourierists, Saint-Simonians, Hegelians, and admirers of Schelling, as the winds of intellectual fashion dictated. They lived for ideas, only for ideas, perpetually involved in discussion, their lives spent in never-ceasing controversy. In the latter half of the century, they became more militant in their rejection of tsardom. They came to idealize in turn the peasants, science, machines—any instrument that seemed capable of rousing Russia from its stasis. Persecuted and hunted by the police, rebuffed in all their efforts to spread liberal enlightenment, the most active finally turned in desperation to the weapons of terrorism. Powerless, they attempted to compensate for their weakness by extolling the virtues of men of deeds who would fling themselves against a hostile world with passionate dedication and self-abnegation.[23] The terrorist revolutionaries were truly "possessed." Nechaev, Bakunin's one-time associate, summed up their creed: "The revolutionary is a dedicated man. He has no personal interests, no personal business, no sentiments, no attachments, no property, not even a name. Everything in him is absorbed by one single thought, one single passion: the revolution . . . The revolutionary considers himself a capital to be spent for the triumph of the revolution."[24]

Toward the end of the century, the fathers of Russian Marxism attempted to create a revolutionary movement in opposition to populism and revolutionary terrorism. Once industrialization had finally made its first tentative steps and promised to break the crust of Russian stagnation, they oriented themselves to the industrial workers. But, even though they disowned the nineteenth-century revolutionary movement and derided its representatives as unscientific, romantic, and idealistic, they could not in fact reject a heritage so peculiarly their own. Plechanov, Lenin, Trotsky, and the majority of Bolshevik leaders were the legitimate heirs of the Herzens, the Chernyshevskys, the Nechaevs. Even though they differed from them in program and orientation, they were also of the intelligentsia. They shared the perennial problems of the intelligentsia as well as the glory of its tradition of critical rejection.

Their fathers had, for the most part, been neither peasants nor workers but rather professionals. Lenin's father was a school inspector, Bukharin's a teacher, Kamenev's an engineer, Krestinsky's a teacher—although Stalin's father was a shoe worker of peasant background. Trotsky's father was a rich tenant farmer. Most of them had attended the university, and many had been expelled for revolutionary activities. Most of the leaders had done some "postgraduate studies" in the "university for revolutionaries" that Siberian exile provided for the Tsar's enemies.

The Bolshevists' orientation, even more than their origins, furnishes clues to their intimate familiarity with the problems of the intelligentsia. The very violence of their efforts to sever their ties with certain traditions of the intelligentsia testifies to the hold these traditions had on them.[25] Their emphasis on the supreme importance of *activity* can be interpreted as a reaction against the apathy and intense self-absorption of the nonpolitical intelligentsia. To Lenin, the heroes of Turgenev and Chekhov, so intensely introspective that they have no capacity to act, seemed the very embodiment of those pernicious tendencies that had to be rooted out if Russia was to be pushed forward. Turgenev's Rudin, of whom the author wrote that "nature has . . . denied . . . him the power of action, the ability to carry out his intentions";[26] the hero of *The Diary of a Superfluous Man*, who "analyzed [himself] to the last shred . . .";[27] Goncharov's Oblomov, that antihero, who consumes the first two hundred pages of the novel in an effort to get out of bed and the rest with vague dreams of what he will do, dreams he will obviously never realize—these characters were to the Bolshevists symbols of Russian passivity and sloth, which had to be fought.

While we may see the roots of Bolshevik thought in reaction to and rejection of the temptation to passivity among the intelligentsia, it later acquired a momentum of its own, as it became in effect the ideology of a political movement. In its later stages, this thought was, to use Freud's term, overdetermined. While still a function of the Bolshevist intellectuals' need to free themselves from the passivity of the nonpolitical intelligentsia, it also became the ideology of a militant minority intent upon acquiring power. Something had to be done, and it had to be done *now*. All energies had to be strained to the utmost in constant activity. Thought was of no worth if it did not serve as a prelude to action. The Bolshevist intellectual had no right to feelings or sentiments that would distract him from the urgent task at hand. Lenin's often quoted remarks about the danger of being distracted by listening to moving music are only one example. All activity, moreover, had to be *disciplined* and organized; spontaneity disperses energies and was therefore little better than inactivity. "Our task is to combat spontaneity," wrote Lenin. ". . . a desperate struggle against spontaneity has to be carried on."[28]

All intellectual effort was ultimately directed to serve the political goal. Out of this concentration emerged what may properly be called the "Bolshevik ethos." Although Lenin had called for a party of intellectuals, he regarded the intellect as subject to the need for action. The Bolshevist could not afford to follow at the tail of popular movements, for that would be "subservience to spontaneity" (Lenin). The party, "the great whole which we are creating for the first time"[29] as the embodiment of disciplined activistic drives, became the foremost instrument for achieving revolutionary goals. The true activist must devote his all to the party. The party would insure the single-minded pursuit of the revolutionary goal and would guarantee that the militant who was fully devoted to it would not succumb to the temptations of becoming the superfluous man. If commitment to the party was complete, then the life of the militant had a purpose, a purpose, furthermore, in tune with the trends of history. The party, to the Leninist, was the embodiment of the forces of progress. It could do no wrong, for by definition it was the very incarnation of historical reason in a world of irrationality.

The Bolshevists saw the surrounding world as an amorphous mass of enemies and the party as shock troops of historical necessity. Hence the prevalence of military rhetoric in the writings of the Bolshevist leaders, the stress on the necessity of hardness, of "iron discipline," of total commitment.

The political organization conceived by Lenin had many similarities to a religious sect. The sect is, in Max Weber's terminology, "an association of religiously qualified . . . [it has] the ideal of the 'ecclesia pura,' the visible community of saints."[30] The sect is an *ex*clusive body of special religious performers, a religious elite. Similarly, the Bolshevist party had, according to Lenin, to limit its membership to those "who shall devote to the party not only their spare evenings, but the whole of their lives."[31] It was "a militant organization of agents."[32] "Without the 'dozen' of tried and talented leaders . . . professionally trained," wrote Lenin, "schooled by long experience and working in perfect harmony, no class in modern history is capable of conducting a determined struggle."[33]

For fifteen years, the energy of Lenin and his collaborators was concentrated on the building of this party of professional revolutionaries. There were ups and downs, tactical advances and retreats, interminable doctrinal discussions, Byzantine quarrels over the meanings of particular passages in Marx (for such meanings had to be interpreted anew in terms of the political needs of the moment). But all this activity amounted to little in the perspective of the overriding aim: to forge the party. Once in possession of this perfected organizational tool, and given the right moment, the Bolshevists hoped finally to be able to escape the deadening weight of history, of the inactivity and isolation of the intelligentsia. "Hating the past and knowing how to discard its deadening decay, which strangles every living thing,"[34] the party would open the road to an active transformation of slothful Russia into a socialist democracy.

In 1917, the moment when the political sect could be tested in action finally came. On the eve of the February Revolution, Lenin said to a group of Zürich students, "we of the older generation may not live to see the decisive battles of this coming revolution."

But soon after February, he resolved that the time had arrived to use the party in an effort to gain state power. Most of the old Bolshevists who greeted Lenin at the Finland Station in St. Petersburg after his return from exile were stunned by the boldness of his program. Most had been working for the unification of Bolsheviks and Mensheviks, visualizing themselves as a leftist opposition to the liberal regime that the February Revolution had brought into being. Lenin therefore startled them with his: "We don't need any parliamentary republic. We don't need a bourgeois democracy. We don't need any government except the Soviet of Workers', Soldiers' and Peasants' Deputies." Lenin was, from the very beginning, intent upon preparing a new revolution controlled and directed by his party. He succeeded in welding the Bolsheviks, who quickly grew from a small conspiratorial organization into a party of several hundred thousand members, into an instrument capable of seizing power. Could the Bolsheviks alone attain state power? And even if they did, could they retain it? asked the skeptics. Lenin answered, "Russia was ruled by 130,000 landowners . . . and yet we are told that Russia will not be able to be governed by the 240,000 members of the Bolshevik Party—governing in the interest of the poor against the rich."[35] Passages like this one have often been quoted as proof that Lenin was from the outset intent upon erecting in Russia a new dictatorial absolutism, a dictatorship over, rather than of, the proletariat. Matters were more complicated, however.

As an intellectual, Lenin needed reflection before embarking upon action; in order to clarify his own ideas on the character of the regime he was about to bring into being, he wrote *State and Revolution* in August and September, 1917. In this book, more clearly than elsewhere before or after, he gave free expression to his profoundly democratic sentiments. In communist society, he averred, there would be no domination of man over man, and the state would thus become unnecessary and obsolete. The "*mass of the population will be raised to independent participation not only in voting and elections, but in day-to-day administration. Under socialism, all will administer in turn and will quickly become accustomed to nobody administering.*" In the transitional period, state power of the type held by the Paris Commune of 1871 would still be necessary, but "the proletarian state will begin to die away immediately after its victory, since in a society without class contradictions, the state is unnecessary and impossible."[36] But these reflections did not in fact inform Lenin's subsequent actions. The party in motion exemplified what Lenin had stressed earlier: the primacy of action over thought.

When the Bolshevists attained state power, they postponed the application of ideas like those Lenin had expressed in *State and Revolution* to an ever receding morrow. They could not yet trust the errant impulses of peasant masses held in subjection for centuries. It was an emergency situation. The Revolution had not yet spread to the more advanced countries of the West, and it was still necessary to rely on the party to guide the masses as teachers and leaders. The party, not the masses, would have to be the "motor of history" in the period to come. Spontaneity, unguided, would mean the death of the Revolution. To be sure, the party must always feel the pulse of the masses, and its tactical course must be dictated by the circumstances of the moment, but it alone must finally take decisive action, for it alone was the embodiment of historical consciousness.

In November, 1917, 240,000 members of the Bolshevik Party—their numbers were soon to grow—assumed control of Russia. Within a few days, the Council of People's Commissars issued decrees changing the institutions of the old order from top to bottom. "Henceforth all authority belongs to the Soviets." "Landed proprietorship is abolished forthwith without compensation." "All the classes of society existing up till now in Russia, and all divisions of citizens, all class distinctions and privileges, class organizations and institutions . . . are abolished." "All ranks are abolished." "The Council of People's Commissars resolves to abolish all existing general legal institutions, such as district courts, courts of appeal . . . and to replace all these institutions with courts established on the basis of democratic elections."[37] In one gigantic sweep, the Bolsheviks cleared away the heritage of Russia's past. In the first few weeks and months of their reign, they were ready to remake Russia in the image of their desires.

We cannot follow the story of their efforts. We need only recall that, by 1922, after the incredible years of famine and civil war, after years of inhuman hardship and chaos, of bitter struggle with White Guards and opposition within, after factional struggles that often threatened the unity of the party, the Bolshevists succeeded in consolidating their regime.

With the end of civil war and the beginning of economic recovery, a relaxation of the tight terroristic rein might have been conceivable, just as it might have been conceivable after the Jacobins' decisive military victories. But relaxation did not occur in either case. The machinery of power had acquired an impetus of its own, a functional autonomy no longer dependent upon external circumstance. It is to these dynamics that we now turn.

The Revolution had been carried forward and consolidated by a very small number of activists within the party and on its fringes, but masses of other people had participated actively in the heroic exertions of the first few years. As the revolution went on, however, the leading Bolshevists sensed that popular participation was falling off. "So far we have not managed," said Lenin already in 1919, "to get the toiling masses to participate in the work of government. . . . The result . . . is that the Soviets which by virtue of their program are organs of government *by the toilers*, are in fact organs of government *for the toilers* . . . the stratum of workers who are governing is an inordinately, incredibly, thin one."[38] He was to return repeatedly to the discrepancy between the small number of activists and the vast mass of passive workers and peasants. And with a strange ambivalence that is most characteristic of his political program, he sometimes noted this fact with pride and sometimes with dismay. "This grain of salt," he said in 1922, with evident complacency, "has taken the task of transforming everything, and it will perform it."[39] But in the same year, there also appeared a note of anxious concern, even of panic, in Lenin's speeches: "The state has not acted according to our will . . . We are losing control of the machine. It would seem that the man sitting at the wheel is directing it. But in reality the machine is not moving in the direction we want it to, but where something or other is directing it . . . This mass of bureaucrats—who is leading whom? The 4,700 responsible Communists [in Moscow], the mass of bureaucrats, or the other way around? To put it honestly they are not leaders but led."[40] The Leninists took the driver's seat believing that possession of the steering wheel ensured control—only to discover that the machinery of government was in fact responsive to the remote control of unobtrusive, almost invisible, functionaries.

Like Saint-Just in his day, Lenin, for similar reasons, began to fulminate against bureaucratization. At first he limited himself to attacks upon the bureaucracy in state administration, but in 1923, he wrote, ". . . We have a bureaucracy not only in the Soviet institutions, but in the institutions of the party."[41] Degeneracy had spread to the very instrument in which the purpose and direction of the Revolution was vested. Bukharin had already said in a bitter joke that the history of mankind was divided into three great periods: the "matriarchat," the "patriarchat," and the secretariat. With the mass of the population worn out, tired, weary of its exertions, and with the unorthodox in the Soviets and even within the party itself silenced by terror or administrative fiat, the bureaucrats came into their own. Lenin sensed all this change and suffered forebodings that the Revolution might be buried in bureaucratic administration. Yet he still believed that the isolation of Russia and its backwardness, along with the regime's need for the services of functionaries of the old order for want of trained new men, accounted for these developments. He never understood that bureaucratization followed directly from his own principles. Like the Jacobins, the Bolshevik intellectuals who led the party had, in the process of action, fallen victim to domination by the tools they had employed. He who desires to make the world over through the decisive action of a chosen elite, even though his intentions may be idealistic and democratic, is finally caught in the inherent logic of his actions: Without participation of the governed in the political process, the tools of political action appropriate power. Then, as Robert Michels had written a few years before the Revolution, "mechanism becomes an end in itself."[42]

Lenin died early in 1924. "The government was dead, the administration survived." The anti-intellectual element among the Bolsheviks won the upper hand. Stalin, Secretary General of the Party, waited in the wings. No intellectual but a patient, methodical organizer, he shuffled his file cards filled with the personal histories of all Party members, appointed his men to key posts, ensured that the Party's activity would thenceforth be controlled from his Moscow office. Trotsky waged an intellectually brilliant battle against the growing bureaucratization and gathered around him the elite of the younger intellectuals as well as many of the older Bolshevists. But many may have asked themselves why they should now trust Trotsky who had previously been among the most extreme advocates of action by administrative fiat. Trotsky was defeated and driven into exile. Many of the old Bolsheviks resigned themselves to serve the regime in various capacities—a few years later most of them were purged after mock trials or by gunshots in the cellars of the G.P.U. "The old Bolshevik Party," wrote

Trotsky in his last book, "and its old heroic cadres went the way of all flesh; shaken by fever and spasms and excruciatingly painful attacks, it finally died."[43]

Of the members of the highest council in the party, the Politburo, between 1917 and 1923, three died natural deaths, one committed suicide, five were executed by Stalin, and one, Trotsky, was murdered upon Stalin's orders. Their successors were no longer cosmopolitan theoreticians and revolutionary intellectuals but organizers and administrators without higher education and of lowly social origins.[44] Critical intellect was no longer at a premium; it had in fact become a liability. Authority was in the hands of tough men of power.

The Bolsheviks were consistent exemplars of scientific millenarianism. Among them, belief in completely rational state power wielded by militant intellectuals attained its highest and fullest development. With them, belief in the scientific application and manipulation of objective laws of history reached its high point—only to degenerate abruptly into a new system based on bureaucratic formulas for the guidance of political action, replacing reason and inquiry with shibboleths. Their program had been based on the idea that, armed with correct insights, the "leaders and teachers of the masses" would be able to lead Russia into the promised land. They held that their dictatorship would open up backward Russia so that reason could proceed unhampered and triumphant to bring that land into the forefront of social progress.

But this last and most grandiose attempt to realize a utopia of revolutionary intellectuals was destined, paradoxically, almost to erase utopias from the map of ideas. Only the apparatus of power has survived its creators. The domination of the high priests of "rational historical knowledge" has been replaced by the dictatorship of the men of naked power—no utopians they. The spirit of bureaucracy has now come fully into its own.[45]

NOTES

1. For my description of the backgrounds and orientation of the Jacobins, I have relied heavily on Crane Brinton's seminal *The Jacobins* (New York: The Macmillan Company, 1930). I also have consulted Gérard Walter's *Histoire des jacobins* (Paris: Somogy, 1946). Walter limits himself to discussion of the Parisian Society.

2. This discussion of the characteristics of members of the Committee of Public Safety owes much to R. R. Palmer's *Twelve Who Ruled* (Princeton: Princeton University Press, 1941).

3. *Cf.* Robert K. Merton's illuminating discussion in "Social Structure and Anomie," *Social Theory and Social Structure* (Rev. ed.; New York: The Free Press, 1957), pp. 131–60.

4. *Cf.* Brinton's *The Anatomy of a Revolution* (Vintage ed.; New York: Random House, Inc., 1957), especially pp. 186ff.; Brinton, *The Jacobins;* and Brinton, *A Decade of Revolution* (New York: Harper & Row, Publishers, 1934), especially pp. 142ff.

5. *Cf.* Norman Cohn, *The Pursuit of the Millennium* (Fairlawn, N.J.: Essential Books, Inc., 1957).

6. J. M. Thompson, *Robespierre*, II (New York: Appleton-Century-Crofts, 1936), 169. I have used this splendid book throughout this chapter and owe it many insights.

7. I have borrowed this sentence from Thompson's characterization of Robespierre, *ibid.*, p. 276.

8. J. L. Talmon, *The Rise of Totalitarian Democracy* (Boston: Beacon Press, 1952), p. 136. This book is one of the most important modern works on Jacobinism and related creeds.

9. Karl Marx, "Kritik der Hegelschen Staatsphilosophie," S. Landshut, ed., *Die Fruehschriften* (Stuttgart: Koerner, 1953), pp. 61–2.

10. Karl Mannheim, *Essays on Sociology and Social Psychology* (New York: Oxford University Press, Inc., 1953).

11. Mannheim, *Ideology and Utopia* (New York: Harcourt, Brace & World, Inc., 1936), p. 105.

12. Brinton, *The Jacobins*, pp. 230–1.

13. Louis Antoine de Saint-Just, "Fragments sur les institutions républicaines." These fragments were first published in 1800. I translate from *Oeuvres Complètes* (Paris: Charpentier et Fasquelle, 1908). *Cf.* Eugene Newton Curtis, *Saint-Just, Colleague of Robespierre* (New York: Columbia University Press, 1935), especially Chapter XX.

14. Saint-Just, *Oeuvres Complètes*, II, 76.

15. *Ibid.*, p. 239.

16. *Ibid.*, p. 265.

17. Paul Sainte-Claire Deville, quoted in Daniel Guerin, *La lutte des classes sous la première république*, II (Paris: Gallimard, 1946), 295.

18. *Cf.* Alexis de Tocqueville, *L'ancien régime* (Oxford: Basil Blackwell & Mott, Ltd., 1949), p. 212.

19. V. I. Lenin, "What Is To Be Done," *Collected Works*, IV, Book 2 (New York: International Publishers Co., Inc., 1929).

20. Quoted in David Shub, *Lenin* (Garden City, N.Y.: Doubleday & Company, Inc., 1948), p. 54.

21. Bertram D. Wolfe, *Three Who Made a Revolution* (Boston: Beacon Press, 1955), p. 33. I have borrowed freely from Mr. Wolfe's excellent treatment of the intelligentsia. *Cf.* Leopold H. Haimson, *The*

Russian Marxists (Cambridge, Mass.: Harvard University Press, 1955); and Nicolas Berdyaev, *The Origin of Russian Communism* (Ann Arbor: The University of Michigan Press, 1960).

22. Quoted in Irving Howe, *Politics and the Novel* (New York: Horizon Press, Inc., 1957), p. 116.

23. *Cf.* Albert Camus, *The Rebel* (Vintage ed.; New York: Random House, Inc., 1956).

24. Mikhail Bakunin, *Sozial-politischer Briefwechsel mit A.I. Herzen und Ogarjow*, pp. 374–5, quoted in Nathan Leites, *A Study of Bolshevism* (New York: The Free Press, 1954), p. 132. Mr. Leites's study is a fine source for key quotations from the Bolshevists and also from other Russian thinkers. I found many of his leads most valuable, although I cannot subscribe to his central thesis.

25. *Cf. ibid.*, especially Part I.

26. I. Turgenev, *Rudin*, Constance Garnett, transl. (London: W. Heinemann, 1894).

27. Turgenev, *The Diary of a Superfluous Man* (New York: Charles Scribner's Sons, 1904), p. 15.

28. Lenin, *op. cit.*, pp. 123–4.

29. Lenin, "One Step Forward, Two Steps Back," *Selected Works*, II (New York: International Publishers Co., Inc., n. d.), 464.

30. Max Weber, *Wirtschaft und Gesellschaft* (Tübingen: J. C. B. Mohr, 1922), pp. 198–9.

31. Lenin, *Collected Works*, IV, Part 1, 57.

32. Lenin, "What Is To Be Done," p. 246. For further discussion of the sect-like characteristics of the Bolshevik organization, *cf.* Lewis A. Coser, *The Functions of Social Conflict* (New York: The Free Press, 1956), pp. 97–9.

33. Lenin, "What Is To Be Done," p. 196.

34. Lenin, *Selected Works*, IV, 307.

35. Lenin, *Will the Bolsheviks Retain State Power?* (New York: International Publishers Co., Inc., 1932), p. 25.

36. Lenin, *State and Revolution* (New York: International Publishers Co., Inc., 1930).

37. Quoted from translations in James Meisel and Edward Kozera, eds., *Materials for the Study of the Soviet System* (Ann Arbor: George Wahr, 1953), pp. 15–30.

38. Lenin, *Selected Works*, VIII, 353–4.

39. *Ibid.*, IX, 380.

40. Quoted in Leon Trotsky, *The New Course*, in Max Shachtman, *The Struggle for the New Course* (New York: International Publishers Co., Inc., 1943), p. 176.

41. *Ibid.*, p. 177.

42. Robert Michels, *Political Parties* (New York: The Free Press, 1949), p. 187.

43. Trotsky, *Stalin* (New York: Harper & Row, Publishers, 1946), p. 403.

44. *Cf.* George Schueller, *The Politburo* (Stanford: Stanford University Press, 1951).

45. The last two paragraphs are a modified version of a few passages of "Utopia Revisited," by Coser and Henry Jacoby, in *Common Cause*, IV (February, 1951), 7, 370–8.

Chapter 14

BORING FROM WITHIN

THE FABIANS: INTELLIGENCE OFFICERS
WITHOUT AN ARMY

"The Fabians," writes the British historian G. M.
Trevelyan, "were intelligence officers without an army . . . but
they influenced the strategy and even the direction of the great
hosts moving under other banners."[1] Through patient and plodding
penetration of the seats of power, the Fabians, like Bentham and
Mill in an earlier time, helped to shape and change the body politic
of England. They wanted to transform British society, not through
violent revolution, but through practical and unobtrusive advice to
the men of power. They did not aspire to gain power for themselves, and they were singularly devoid of belief in the charisma of
the powerful; such men were to be used, not worshiped; to be
pulled and maneuvered rather than admired and served.

"The Fabians," wrote Edward Pease, the earliest historian of
the Fabian Society and one of its founding members, "were mostly
civil servants or clerks in private employ. The methods of agitation
congenial to them were compatible with their occupation."[2] Although convinced socialists, they rejected the traditional socialist
methods of mass organization and revolutionary propaganda. They
had concluded quite early in their lives that, if they were to make

an impact on the political and intellectual scene, it would have to be through methods congenial to their peculiar gifts and their particular stations and training. They meant to mobilize the energy of trained and organized reason to subvert and neutralize the untrained rhetoric of the men of power. The troubled conscience of late Victorian middle-class society gave them their chance.

The early Fabians—Sidney Webb, Bernard Shaw, Graham Wallas, and Sidney Olivier—were, of course, uncommonly gifted men. But Fabian ideas and Fabian methods and doctrine cannot be said to have been the product of any individual thinker. They emerged as the genuine results of close partnership among these men. "It was this exceptional group of leaders," wrote Pease, "all intimate friends, all loyal to each other, and to the cause they were associated to advocate . . . that in a few years turned an obscure drawing-room society into a factor in national politics."[3] The Fabians pooled their brains in a concerted effort to permeate the fabric of British political and social life. As individuals, they might well have remained without influence; as a group, they proved capable of controverting once and for all the legend of the inherent incapacity of men of knowledge to act upon the body politic. Fabianism was a collective phenomenon.

The Fabians' close partnership can be related in turn to similarity among their key members in social background and station, as well as in ideas. The Fabians were, in their large majority, middle-class thinkers whose social consciences had been aroused in the social and intellectual crisis of the 1880s. In the period that saw the birth and growth of the Fabian Society, the long domination of middle-class liberalism had come to an end. Many diverse thinkers were groping for a doctrine to replace the *laissez-faire* that had characterized the preceding age.[4] Social reform was in the air, and the Victorian mind was slowly awakening from its dogmatic slumbers. Young middle-class rebels looked at the ugliness of slums, the poverty that seemed never to decrease despite the vaunted glories of progress, the general squalor that appeared to be the result of domination by the "shopkeeper mentality" over the preceding half century. Many young rebels turned toward social-reform movements of various kinds, from settlement houses to the Salvation Army or other church work. Others were attracted by the Marxist socialism of H. M. Hyndman or the utopian romantic socialism of William Morris. But Sidney Webb, Sidney Olivier, and Frank Podmore—

who gave the Fabians their name—were men trained in the rigorous routines of the civil service, as were many other less known Fabians. Not for them the romantic visions of the disciples of Morris or the Marxian ideology of class struggle put forth by Hyndman's followers in the Social Democratic Federation. They searched for a solution less utopian, less visionary, more practical and hard-headed. Their socialism was to be anchored in concern for rigorous administrative method and empiricism. They drew on the heritage of Bentham and Mill rather than on that of Hegel and Marx.

Fabian doctrine, as it slowly developed, emphasized the "inevitability of gradualness" and the prosaic task of providing those who make decisions in the body politic with facts and reasoned arguments in order to sway them in the direction of socialist reform. When H. G. Wells challenged Fabian doctrine and admonished his fellow Fabians, "Make socialists and you will achieve socialism," the majority of Fabians agreed with Pease's rejoinder: "The work of the Fabian Society has been not to make socialists, but to make socialism." G. B. Shaw, the Fabians' major spokesman, revealed the crux of their political attitude when he wrote, "We set ourselves two definite tasks: first, to provide a parliamentary program for a Prime Minister converted to Socialism as Peel was converted to Free Trade; and second, to make it as easy and a matter of course for the ordinary respectable Englishman to be a Socialist as to be a Liberal or Conservative."[5] The Fabians, at least before the World War, did not wish to create a mass movement—the Society never numbered more than a few thousand members. They wished instead to create a socialist brain trust. "[The Society] does not ask the English people to join the Fabian Society. It urges its members to join other Societies—Socialist or non-Socialist—in which Fabian work can be done."[6]

The Fabians' favorite word was "permeation." "Permeation," wrote Shaw, "as applied to Parliament means wire-pulling the Government in order to get Socialistic measures passed, and stimulating the opposition to denounce the Government for neglecting the grievances of the people."[7] But Fabian permeation was by no means limited to parliament. Wrote Beatrice Webb, in her diary, about the trade unionist James Mawdsley, "Whether or not we use Mawdsley, we may rest assured that he will use us: which after all is all we desire."[8] The Fabians translated socialist economics and collectivism into the language of unionists, town councilors, and vestrymen. They were ready to provide facts, statistics, and out-lines of reform projects to anybody who was interested. Amending poor laws and factory acts, municipalizing gas and water supplies, revamping the educational system, social-security legislation—such were their immediate concerns.

Men of power are too often hampered in their work by insuffi-cient factual information, which bureaucratic experts attempt to monopolize. In Max Weber's words, "The 'political master' finds himself in the position of the 'dilettante' who stands opposite the 'expert,' facing the trained official . . . every bureaucracy seeks to increase the superiority of the professionally informed by keeping their knowledge and intentions secret."[9] The Fabians' peculiar role was to function as unofficial expert "clerks" to any decision-maker hampered by lack of expert advice. Beatrice Webb may have been a bit too sanguine when she noted in her diary that ". . . no young man or woman who is anxious to study or to work in public affairs can fail to come under our influence."[10] But even if this phrase does not quite describe a reality, it describes an ambition. When the radicals on the London County Council needed a platform, the Fabians provided the London Program for them; they were simi-larly instrumental in promoting the Local Government Act of 1888. The Education Acts of 1902 and 1903, which fundamentally altered the British educational system, were partly based on a Fabian tract written by Sidney Webb. Examples could be multiplied. Once a reform act was passed, it had to be made to work, and the Fabians therefore published series of tracts explaining its operation to the local people who were to apply it: *The Parish Councils Act: What It Is and How To Work It* (Fabian Tract # 53—more than 30,000 copies sold in five months); *Question for Parish Council Candi-dates* (Tract 56), *Parish Council Cottages and How To Get Them* (Tract 63), *Parish Councils and Village Life* (Tract 106), and so on. Tirelessly the Fabians published pamphlet after pamphlet and addressed meeting after meeting explaining the intricacies of gov-ernmental procedure or reform legislation. During 1891–1892, 3339 lectures were given by 117 Fabian Society members. In 1891, ten new tracts, four pamphlets, and six leaflets, as well as reissues of all the old ones, were published, 333,500 copies printed, and 98,349 distributed; 378,281 tracts were distributed in 1891–1892.[11] In addition, many Fabians wrote for the various liberal dailies and weeklies, published books and reports, gave advice, drafted programs and proposals, and sat on innumerable committees.*

Yet, in a certain sense, this incessant public agitation was perhaps not even the most important of the Fabians' activities. Much of their enduring influence came through private contact in clubs and country houses, in smoking rooms and at carefully selected social gatherings. "Winston Churchill dined with us last night," wrote Beatrice Webb in a typical diary entry. ". . . we talked exclusively shop. He has swallowed whole Sidney's scheme for boy labour and unemployment, had even dished it up in an article in *The Nation . . .*"[13] Again and again we find entries along the same line in these revealing diaries. "Lord George gives me unhesitating support; my difficulty is with Sir Samuel Provis. But I had the most friendly chat with him this afternoon, and *he comes to dine to meet a carefully selected dinner party.*"[14] Or, "As luck would have it, Dr. Downes had to give evidence and was puzzled to know what to talk about. He had dined here, and I brought forward all my instances . . . In the witness box, he made this . . . part of his thesis."[15] Lord Asquith, Arthur Balfour, Winston Churchill, Lloyd George, Lord Haldane, Herbert Samuel, almost all the leading Liberal politicians, and a goodly number of Conservatives as well, at one time or another came under the Webb influence. They were invited to the Webbs' parties, where the food left much to be desired but where they were subtly fed the "right ideas." "The truth is," wrote Beatrice Webb, "that we want the things done and we

---

* From 1892 to 1898, Sidney Webb was the Chairman of the Technical Education Board of the London County Council and was a member of the caucus that determined the policy of the Progressives in the L.C.C. In addition, he served on the following committees:[12]

Appeal Committee   1892–1893
Corporate Property Committee   1895–1898
County Rate Committee   1896–1898
Establishment Committee   1892–1893
Finance Committee   1893–1895
General Purposes Committee   1892–1898
Local Government and Taxation Committee   1892–1898
   (Vice-Chairman   1892–1894)
Parliamentary Committee   1892–1898
Public Health and Housing Committee   1892–1893
Rivers Committee   1894–1895
Water Committee   1892–1895
London Government Special Committee   1894–1895
Thames Conservacy Special Committee   1893–1894

don't much care what persons or which party gets the credit."[16] "Moreover," she wrote somewhat later, "we resolutely refuse to believe that any good person *properly* informed could be otherwise than a Progressive."[17] Still later, she declared, "We should continue our policy of inoculation—of giving to each class, to each person, coming under our influence, the exact dose of collectivism that they were prepared to assimilate."[18]

After the founding of the Labour Party, the Fabians in general and the Webbs in particular worked less closely with the Liberal and Conservative politicians, but even then their essential method and creed did not change in any fundamental way. "We staked our hopes on the organized working class," wrote Beatrice Webb, "served and guided, it is true, by an *elite* of unassuming experts who would make no claim to superior social status, but would content themselves with exercising the power inherent in superior knowledge and longer administrative experience."[19]

H. G. Wells, in *The New Machiavellians*, drew a fiercely satiric pen portrait of the Webbs. Two typical passages bear quoting here because they convey much of the character of Fabian method.

At the Bailey's one always seemed to be getting one's hand on the very strings that guided the world. You heard legislation projected to affect this "type" or that; statistics marched by you with sin and shame and injustice and misery reduced to quite manageable percentages, you found men who were to frame or amend bills in grave and intimate exchange with Bailey's omniscience, you heard Altiora canvassing approaching resignations and possible appointments that might make or mar a revolution in administrative methods, and doing it with a vigorous directness that manifestly swayed the decision; you felt you were in a sort of signal box with levers all about you, and the world outside there . . . running on its lines in ready obedience to these unhesitating lights, true and steady to trim termini.[20]

I can still recall little Bailey, glib and winking, explaining that democracy was really just a dodge for getting assent to the ordinances of the expert official by means of the polling booth.[21]

The total personalities of Fabians like Sidney Webb were harnessed to the tasks of reform through persuasion and permeation. He went only once in his life to hear a Wagnerian opera. When asked whether or not he had enjoyed it, he replied, "Oh, yes, we had a most enjoyable evening. We happened to be sitting just behind Herbert Samuel. I was able to have a most useful conversation with him in the interval on the incidence of sickness in pregnancy."[22]

Reasons why. What, beyond the great ability of their main leaders, accounts for the amazing success of the Fabians? Perhaps nothing so much as the fact that, though they were rebels against middle-class society, they were nevertheless, as G. B. Shaw has said, "middle-class all through."[23] While other socialists advocated a thorough subversion of the class order, the Fabians used methods of propaganda designed to disarm middle-class suspicions. When they based their appeal on such ideals as efficiency and rationality, they relied on guiding norms the middle class had long accepted, so that they seemed to imply that differences between them and those in power revolved around questions of proximate means rather than of ultimate goals. Their resolute constitutionalism, their emphasis on the inevitability of gradualness made it possible for them to advocate a socialist transformation while accepting the rules of the political game. They opposed the prevailing social order without cutting themselves off from it. "Should you become a convert to Socialism," G. B. Shaw advised his "intelligent woman," "you will not be committed to any change in your private life, nor indeed will you find yourself able to make any change that would be of the smallest use in that direction."[24] The Fabians made use of the bad conscience of middle-class England, but they also soothed it.

One marvels at the incredible amount the Fabian pioneers were able to accomplish. Granted that men like Webb and Shaw possessed amazing resources of energy, one feels that, in the contemporary world, much of this energy would probably have been absorbed in professional and occupational life. But things were different in the leisurely atmosphere of nineteenth-century England. The amount of leisure time available to professionals and intellectuals was much greater than it is in the twentieth century. When we read that James Mill or John Stuart Mill worked for many years in the India Office or that Sidney Webb and his colleague and friend Sidney Olivier worked at the Colonial Office, we must understand that these offices were not making such strict demands on their personnel as do modern bureaucracies. The Colonial Office did not open for public business before 11 A.M., although the clerks generally stayed till around 7 P.M.[25] And even while officially working at the Colonial Office, it was quite possible to conduct much of the business of the Fabian Society on the side. For some time, the scanty Fabian records were stored on a table in Downing Street.

Furthermore, many Fabians had money with which to buy time. After their marriage, Sidney and Beatrice Webb—Sidney had resigned from the Civil Service shortly before their engagement—had between them an income, mainly Beatrice's, of about £1000 a year, with income tax at sixpence on the pound.[26] On this sum they could live comfortably and with a sufficient margin to keep a secretary and domestic help. Not all Fabians lived in such comfort, but even in the early days of the society its key members were never so absorbed by the daily struggle to make a living as to have to restrict their activities for the Fabian Society. The Fabians could live "for," and not "off," politics, for they were economically independent of the income politics can bring.[27]

Another highly important factor was the amazing *esprit de corps* among the key Fabians. Although the Society was naturally not free from rivalries and enmities, Webb, Shaw, Wallas, and Olivier were bound to one another by close ties of personal friendship, so that, "For many years there were probably few evenings and few holidays which two or more of them did not spend together."[28] The key figures in the movement were united not only by common ideas but by complex ties of sentiment and affection. The Fabian society, especially in its early years, was a kind of fraternity.

Although the Fabian rank and file did not have the exceptional abilities of the main leaders, they nevertheless formed an unusually talented group. But, whatever the natural intellectual endowments of its members, the very structure of the Society fostered the growth and display of trained intelligence. The frequent meetings revealed a high and exacting standard of debate. The numbers attending were most of the time not very great—forty or fifty usually—but they were not passive audiences, for nearly all attending were practiced debaters and speakers.[29] Much like American Trotskyism in a later day, Fabianism proved to be a demanding school of rhetoric; it sharpened dialectical skills and taught its members the art of persuasion. Many of the Fabians, in addition, were trained, as Bernard Shaw had been, in the bracing school of open-air propaganda.[30] And writing a Fabian tract or pamphlet meant that one had to submit to the exacting criticism and scrutiny of scores of fellow Fabians.

The Society instilled in its members a sense of dedication, a pride in the high seriousness of their calling and tasks. Though very loose in structure and therefore quite different from religious sects, it nevertheless fulfilled certain functions of "socialization" for its members that were none too different from those fulfilled by religious orders. The Society served as a most potent means of social control over the activities of its members; it was a reference group whose exacting standards became firmly internalized. Its strict criteria of admission, its very limitation in size instilled in the members a sense of belonging to an intellectual and moral elite. This shared feeling explains why the structure and functions of the Society served to maximize the productivity, the effectiveness, and the missionary ardor of its members.

Another reason for the Fabians' amazing success must be sought in the intellectual climate of late Victorian and Edwardian England. It was an age in which the "social question" loomed large, in which the ruling circles had awakened to an awareness of the need for serious reform. At the same time, the prestige of science was still unimpaired. A group of men, undoubtedly experts in the science of society, not visionary dreamers but hard-headed empiricists, found ready access to the seats of power, especially when, as in the case of the Webbs, they exhibited all the virtues of middle-class respectability. The rough workmen of the Independent Labour Party, the street corner orators of the Social Democratic Federation would never be admitted even to the antechambers of the establishment, but the civil servants, the professors, the journalists and writers of the Fabian Society did not find it hard to force their way in—especially if they came with bulky portfolios full of significant statistics.

Assessment. The Fabians did for British Socialism at the end of the nineteenth century what the Utilitarians had done for British Liberalism at its beginning. Through permeation of the Civil Service and of Royal Commissions, through advice to the politically influential, through lectures and pamphlets, through research and writing, they transformed the intellectual climate of British political life. They founded *The New Statesman* and the London School of Economics; they were the intellectual godfathers of the modern Labour Party.

As early as 1900, Beatrice Webb shrewdly assessed the Fabians' strength and their limitations when she wrote, "We realize every day more strongly, that we can never get hold of 'the man in the street': we are 'too damned intellectual.' All we can hope to do is to find out for ourselves the actual facts and embody them in a more or less scientific form, and to trust other people to get this knowledge translated into popular proposals."[31] Such widespread use of their knowledge contributed materially to that transformation of law, government, and public opinion that changed the England of Gladstone into the England of Attlee and of Wilson. In the light of this historical example, it is hard to maintain that intellectuals are inherently incapable of influencing the course of political events. Boring from within the house of power, the Fabians permeated it and managed to twist its inhabitants to many of their own ends. They did not institute collectivist socialism in England, but they laid the foundations on which the welfare state was later built.

THE BRAIN TRUST COURTS POWER

"A plague of young lawyers settled on Washington," wrote George Peck, the veteran farm leader, sourly recalling the early days of the New Deal, and "they all claimed to be friends of somebody or other, mostly of Felix Frankfurter and Jerome Frank. They floated airily into offices, took desks, asked for papers and found no end of things to be busy about."[32] Nor were these young lawyers the only group of intellectuals who swarmed to Washington in the first months and years of the New Deal administration. Young economists from Columbia and Harvard, agricultural experts from Cornell, monetary experts, social workers, sociologists, and political scientists came by the hundreds. Before they arrived, three brilliant younger intellectuals from Columbia—Raymond Moley, Rexford Tugwell, and Adolf Berle—had already constituted the Brain Trust that had developed many of the ideas Roosevelt had used so effectively during his campaign.

The Columbia trio recruited many of their friends; Felix Frankfurter recommended brilliant young lawyers with whom he had worked; Justice Brandeis suggested former law clerks and associates. Within a few months, the whole staid atmosphere of Washington officialdom was utterly transformed by scores upon scores of brash young men who had descended upon the scene. These young men fresh from the campus and the classroom were joined by others—militant midwestern progressives, agrarian reformers, former Bull Moose champions, municipal reformers, veterans of all the liberal causes since the days of Theodore Roosevelt. But the younger men gave the Washington scene its characteristic new atmosphere.

These young journalists, administrators, lawyers, economists, and social scientists, though possessed of diverse backgrounds, experiences, and training were bound together not only by a certain similarity in ideas and middle-class backgrounds but by membership in a common generation unit.[33] Born mainly between 1895 and 1905, they shared a common experience of recent historical events. Although they might never have come into personal contact with one another prior to 1933, the very fact that they had perceived the events of recent history and had been marked by them in similar ways created bonds among them and distinguished them from an older generation. This similar location in generational terms, despite diversity in other aspects, created a similarity of outlook. Although some had already made impacts in their respective fields, few were yet frozen into permanent careers. Many had drifted from one field to another in the Twenties, restless and vaguely discontented; others came straight from the campus open to new winds of doctrine, alienated from the business civilization that seemed to have failed the country so signally in Mr. Hoover's days. For most, the Depression had been a major trauma, which had marked them more deeply than it had marked the older generation. Older men faced the Depression more adequately protected by mental routines and professional reputations.

A very significant number of the younger men—and this point is of some sociological importance—came from those minority groups whose members had not so far secured significant places in the machinery of government. For the first time, the many informal and not so informal barriers that had prevented young Jewish intellectuals from making their contribution to government seemed about to tumble. Jews and Catholics, who in an earlier day had been effectively confined to careers in commerce, law, or local politics, now felt that they would be welcome in Washington for the first time. Particularistic criteria of recruitment were giving way to universalistic standards of achievement.

These young intellectuals had worked in diverse political organizations: There were among them former Socialists and former Republicans, Progressives as well as Democrats. Many, on the other hand, had never yet taken part in political activities. Most came because the scarring experiences of the Depression and the Hoover years of inaction had inspired in them a concern with social reform. By no means revolutionaries but alienated from the assumptions and objectives of unrestricted private enterprise, estranged from the prevailing institutional pieties through the political and social dislocations of the previous few years, they believed that business could no longer be trusted to set its own house in order. They had quite divergent ideas on what should be done. Some continued to think in the Brandeis tradition of trust-busting and "the curse of bigness"; others, with visions of the World War I War Industries Board dancing in their heads, dreamed of vastly more ambitious schemes to replace the old competitive system by some kind of self-government in industry under Washington's supervision. But whatever their differences, they all felt the urgency of the situation; something had to be done, and it had to be done *now*.

To be sure, the newcomers did not take over the administration. The Bureau of the Budget, the Treasury, the Federal Reserve Board, and the Department of Commerce were still manned by conservative old hands, but the new men were in urgent demand in the new agencies. Harry Hopkins, a crusading social worker from Iowa, was appointed Federal Relief Administrator. The Tennessee Valley Authority was run by Arthur Morgan, Antioch College president; Harcourt A. Morgan, President of the University of Tennessee; and a young lawyer protégé of Felix Frankfurter, David Lilienthal, who had worked with Governor Phil LaFollette of Wisconsin. In the National Recovery Administration, General Hugh Johnson was flanked by a young labor lawyer from Chicago, Donald Richberg. The young men assumed many staff positions in the older agencies as well. In the Department of Agriculture, Henry Wallace's new general counsel, a brilliant liberal lawyer named Jerome Frank, brought in Thurman Arnold and Abe Fortas from Yale Law School and Alger Hiss, Lee Pressman, John Abt, and Nathan Witt from Harvard Law School. The N.R.A. Consumer Advisory Board included such left-wing economists and sociologists as Paul H. Douglas, Dexter M. Keezer, and Robert S. Lynd. Leon Henderson, a young economist from the Russell Sage Foundation, headed the N.R.A. Research and Planning Division and became N.R.A.'s chief economist. In P.W.A. and W.P.A., in C.W.A., in C.C.C., in S.R.C.—in the whole bewildering array of new alphabetical agencies created from scratch in record time, the new men achieved rapid influence and eminence.

In the old established departments, it took many years to climb the bureaucratic ladder; no such handicaps prevailed in the new agencies and in the research staffs of the older ones. In the exhilarating atmosphere of New Deal Washington, it looked as if careers were at last fully open to talent, as if the barriers erected by precedence, tradition, and customs to ensure that only properly seasoned bureaucrats would get their hands on the tiller, had suddenly broken down. It looked as if suddenly *everything* had become possible. Even professional training no longer restricted the scope of a bright young man. Legal scholars and agricultural specialists suddenly had roles in determining monetary policy; social workers had opportunities to influence high-level policy decisions; young Harvard lawyers found themselves working on milk-market agreements, surplus relief, or mine wages.

The new young men brought to Washington alertness, excitement, and willingness to experiment and to improvise. They were at home in the world of ideas, capable of applying them in the solution of any problem at hand. They were generalists, not specialists. They talked and debated continuously. They fought, argued, and passed rapidly from feelings of grandeur and omnipotence to moods of frustration and despair. They were alive.

The vast majority of new men worked in the executive rather than the legislative branch of government. Only a very few initially had major executive responsibilities. They were researchers and advisors, they drafted laws and regulations, they originated the schemes that older and more seasoned administrators were to apply. They saw themselves mainly as "idea men" who could transform the apparatus of power by boring from within. In the exhilarating atmosphere of the early New Deal, it seemed quite possible to change the shape of America through well chosen moves on the Washington scene. For the first time, at least since World War I, no contradiction seemed to exist between working for reform and working for the government. The government itself seemed to be embarked on the gigantic enterprise of reforming the very structure of American society.

Two mutually reinforcing tendencies were at work in the early New Deal period. First, unattached, reform-minded intellectuals, far from being repelled by government service, tended to seek it, for the government had come to seem the major reform agency. And at the same time, autonomous reform movements were slowly absorbed by the political forces backing the New Deal, making it all the more plausible to believe that only commitment to a career in the governmental apparatus would make it possible to affect the course of political events in a progressive direction.

Differences from the Fabians. Although the political and social situations in the England of the 1880s and the United States of the

1930s were obviously quite different, we find a number of striking similarities between the Fabians and the early New Dealers. Both groups were recruited from young generations, both were mainly middle-class in origin, and both, whether by design or circumstance, had adopted a strategy of boring from within the house of power. Both were able, to significant extents, to change the social and political climates of their times. Yet their differences are even more striking than their similarities.

The New Dealers never created a coherent program or a common platform similar to that of the Fabians. As individuals, they achieved considerable influence in particular agencies; they shaped programs and influenced legislation and executive action, but they never had the coherence of outlook or the steadiness of aim that characterized the Fabians. The New Dealers were, from the beginning, individual intellectuals bound by no commitment to group discipline or group loyalty similar to that of the Fabians. They lacked a community that might have served as a means of social control, as a disciplining agent, as a common point of reference. They were, in essence, lone wolves bound to some colleagues by similar ideas in a particular venture but separated from others—who may have had essentially the same ideological orientations—by the requirements of departmental struggles and internal power alignments. When T.V.A. men were locked in battle with the Department of the Interior; when Lilienthal men fought Arthur Morgan men in T.V.A.; when Johnson men fought Richberg men in N.R.A., what divided them in most cases was not so much major intellectual orientations as the requirements of factional battle or departmental politics. The intensely ambitious young New Dealer was not restrained by allegiance to a systematic set of ideas and a coherent group of like-minded men, coparticipants in a crusade. The Fabians banded together in devotion to a common cause; the New Dealers were individual warriors fighting single combats as the exigencies of the moment required.

The Fabians, furthermore, limited themselves mainly to giving unobtrusive advice to the men of power. Although some of them, at times in their careers, achieved personal political power, they did so, as it were, only by historical accident. Fabian tactics and methods committed them to remaining in the background, free from the dramatic entanglements of open political battle, free also from the burdens and corruptions of power. Much of their effectiveness arose from the fact that they were not seen as serious contenders for power by their audience or by those over whom they exercised influence. The New Dealers were a different breed; many of them relished nothing so much as the sweet taste of personal power. They threw themselves into the battles of official Washington with zest and relish. Far from being only advisers to the men of power, they attempted, often quite successfully, to accumulate power for themselves. Not for them the role of unobtrusive "clerks."

But once they had entered the political battle they were faced with the stumbling block that has forever plagued intellectuals who aspire to exercise power on their own: the antagonism of power and intellect. When intellect is harnessed to the pursuit of power, it loses its essential character and necessarily becomes ancillary; to harness it to the chariot of power is to emasulate it. To the extent that New Deal intellectuals acquired power, they changed their roles: They became men of power, more cultivated perhaps than their predecessors, but not essentially different.

Yet not all, not even most, New Dealers ever achieved significant measures of political power. Why then did most of them soon lose many of the characteristics that had distinguished the enthusiastic young men who had arrived in Washington in the spring of 1933?

Those young men, impelled by idealistic motives and reformer's zeal, and the experts and technicians who had previously manned the various offices seemed very different breeds in 1933. But, as work in the new agencies became routinized and began to resemble the procedures of the older offices, it became apparent that the very requirements of bureaucratic functioning had begun to exert pressures upon the new intellectuals.[34] They had to accommodate themselves to the policies of those who make strategic decisions in any bureaucratic context. As top leadership in the new agencies became regularized and routinized, those who had put themselves at its service had to follow suit. In time, the role of the once unattached intellectual became indistinguishable from that of the old-time technician and expert.

Many of those who had come to Washington left again, often as disillusioned men. Those who remained accepted, by and large, their roles as technicians and no longer felt the need to question the ends of the policies they served. From goal-oriented intellectuals they were, by imperceptible steps, domesticated and came to accept the roles of means-oriented mental technicians. The reform orientation of the early New Deal legitimized work in public bureaucracies for intellectuals, much as the Protestant Ethic legitimized capitalist acquisitiveness for entrepreneurs. In both cases, what had earlier been considered a vice had become canonized as a virtue, and, in both cases, once the new pattern had been securely institutionalized, the practitioners no longer needed the support of a "calling."

"From time to time," wrote Robert Michels almost fifty years ago, "the state, embarrassed by the increasing demand for positions in its service, is forced to open the sluices of its bureaucratic canals in order to admit thousands of new postulants and thus to transform these from dangerous adversaries into zealous defenders and partisans. There are two classes of intellectuals. Those who have succeeded in securing a post at the manger of the state, whilst the others consist of those who . . . have assaulted the fortress without being able to force their way in."[35] The New Dealers who remained in the administration had forced their way in for the most idealistic of motives; they were nevertheless transformed from "dangerous adversaries" into "zealous defenders" by the pressures of bureaucratic machinery.

The bureaucratic intellectual allows the policy-maker to define the goals of his activities, thus implicitly lending his skill and knowledge to the preservation of institutional arrangements. He thus abdicates the critical role of the intellectual, for he is in effect barred from defining his own problems and choosing such problems in the light of his own values. Those New Deal intellectuals who had originally come to Washington because of their divorce from traditional values and who stayed on in the bureaucracy gradually came to accept the framework of the policy-makers. Many others left Washington in various degrees of frustration and disillusionment.

The exhilarating mood of the early New Deal could not be sustained for long. By the end of the decade, most of the hopeful young intellectuals of the early Thirties who had remained in Washington had been transformed into cynical operators or tame experts. Many of the central figures of the early New Deal, perhaps most, had long since left the Washington scene. The young New Deal intellectuals had made a significant impact on American political and social life, and the effects of their actions would be felt for a long time to come—but they had proved once again that the role of the man of power and the role of the intellectual cannot be successfully combined. Once again, it was shown that, in order to play one's role among the powerful successfully, as a participant or as a compliant expert, a *sacrificium intellectus* is required.

NOTES

1. G. M. Trevelyan, *British History in the Nineteenth Century* (London and New York: Longmans, Green & Co., Inc., 1922), p. 403.
2. Edward R. Pease, *The History of the Fabian Society* (2nd ed.; London: George Allen & Unwin, Ltd., 1925), p. 63.
3. *Ibid.*, p. 65.
4. *Cf.* Helen Merrell Lynd, *England in the Eighteen-Eighties* (New York: Oxford University Press, Inc., 1945).
5. George Bernard Shaw, "Fabian Essays Twenty Years Later," *Collected Works*, XXX (New York: Wm. H. Wise & Co., Inc., 1932), 304.
6. Quoted in Lynd, *op. cit.*, p. 401.
7. Margaret Cole, ed., *The Webbs and Their Work* (London: F. Muller, 1949), p. 11.
8. Beatrice Webb, *Our Partnership*, Barbara Drake and Margaret I. Cole, eds. (London: Longmans, Green & Co., Ltd., 1948), p. 48.
9. H. H. Gerth and C. W. Mills, trans. and eds., *From Max Weber, Essays in Sociology* (New York: Oxford University Press, Inc., 1947), pp. 232–3.
10. Webb, *op. cit.*, p. 82.
11. Anne Fremantle, *This Little Band of Prophets* (Mentor ed.; New York: New American Library of World Literature, Inc., 1960), p. 96.
12. Webb, *op. cit.*, p. 82.
13. *Ibid.*, p. 404.
14. Cole, *Beatrice Webb* (New York: Longmans, Green & Co., Inc., 1946), p. 98.
15. Webb, *op. cit.*, p. 349.
16. *Ibid.*, p. 67–8.
17. *Ibid.*, p. 70.
18. *Ibid.*, p. 122.
19. *Ibid.*, p. 87.
20. H. G. Wells, *The New Machiavellians* (New York: Duffield & Co., 1910), p. 202.
21. *Ibid.*, p. 327.
22. Cole, *The Webbs and Their Work*, p. 297.
23. Shaw, *op. cit.*, p. 130.
24. Shaw, *The Intelligent Woman's Guide to Socialism and Capitalism* (New York: Brentano's Publishers, 1928), p. 99.
25. Fremantle, *op. cit.*, p. 44.
26. Cole, *Beatrice Webb*, p. 59.
27. Gerth and Mills, *op. cit.*, pp. 84–5.
28. Pease, *op. cit.*, p. 64.

29. Cole, *The Webbs and Their Work*, p. 60.

30. *Ibid.*, p. 60.

31. Webb, *op. cit.*, p. 202.

32. Quoted in Arthur M. Schlesinger, Jr., *The Coming of the New Deal* (Boston: Houghton Mifflin Company, 1959), p. 16. I have drawn heavily on this evocation of the early days of the New Deal. I have also used James MacGregor Burns's *Roosevelt: The Lion and the Fox* (New York: Harcourt, Brace & World, Inc., 1956); Basil Rauch's *History of the New Deal 1933–1938* (New York: Creative Age Press, 1944); Schlesinger, *The Crisis of the Old Order* (Boston: Houghton Mifflin Company, 1957); and Schlesinger, *The Politics of Upheaval* (Boston: Houghton Mifflin Company, 1960). Richard Hofstadter's essay on Franklin D. Roosevelt in *The American Political Tradition* (Vintage ed.; New York: Random House, Inc., 1954) was also very helpful.

These autobiographies proved useful for an understanding of the mentality of the New Dealers: Raymond Moley, *After Seven Years* (New York: Harper & Row, Publishers, 1939); Donald R. Richberg, *My Hero* (New York: G. P. Putnam's Sons, 1954); and Charles Michelson, *The Ghost Talks* (New York: G. P. Putnam's Sons, 1944). *The New Dealers*, by the Unofficial Observer (John F. Carter) (New York: Simon and Schuster, Inc., 1934), is not always fully accurate but gives vivid sketches of the early New Dealers as they appeared to a contemporary. Ernest K. Lindley's *The Roosevelt Revolution* (New York: The Viking Press, Inc., 1933) is a lively contemporary account of the first phase of the New Deal.

33. *Cf.* Karl Mannheim's essay, "The Problem of Generations," *Essays on the Sociology of Knowledge* (New York: Oxford University Press, Inc., 1952).

34. I am deeply indebted to Robert K. Merton's "Role of the Intellectual in Public Bureaucracy," *Social Theory and Social Structure* (Rev. ed.; New York: The Free Press, 1957), for some of the major points in the following paragraphs.

35. Robert Michels, *Political Parties* (New York: The Free Press of Glencoe, 1949), p. 186.

Chapter 15

LEGITIMIZING POWER

NAPOLEON AND THE *IDEOLOGUES*

"IT IS TO IDEOLOGY," BARKED NAPOLEON IN 1812, "this gloomy metaphysics which subtly looks for first causes upon which to base the legislation of people instead of making the laws attune to knowledge of the human heart and the lessons of history, that all the misfortune of our beautiful France must be attributed."[1] It was not the first time that he had vented his spleen on the men whom he called derisively the *idéologues*. He had earlier spoken of "a dozen or fifteen metaphysicians who ought to be thrown into a pond. They are swarming like vermin around me."[2] He had referred to the *idéologues* as "a band of imbeciles who sigh from the bottom of their souls for liberty of the press and of speech, and believe in the omnipotence of public opinion."[3]

But the same men against whom the Emperor spoke with so much venom had been only a few years before his close friends and allies. He had sought their company and been honored by their attention.[4] By tracing the sources of this reversal, we may throw some light on certain aspects of the more general problem of the relations between intellectuals and men of power.

What was "ideology"? The term had been coined in 1802 by Antoine Destutt de Tracy, the major philosopher of the school, to denote a philosophical discipline that took as its goal to observe and describe the operation of the human mind in the strictly empirical manner appropriate to description of an object of nature, a mineral or a plant. Continuing the tradition of Condillac, Destutt and his cothinkers insisted that ideas must always be traced back to sensations. Analysis of the processes of the human mind in the formation of ideas would lead to a scientific discipline that would allow recognition of truth and detection of error in the world of ideas with as much accuracy as the physical sciences had attained in the study of natural phenomena. Ideology as a strictly empirical science of the formation of ideas sought to develop a universal methodology for testing their validity.

But ideological doctrine was not limited to purely theoretical consideration. The *idéologues*, true to the eighteenth-century tradition of the Enlightenment, taught that the systematic reduction of all ideas to their constituent sensations had immense practical importance for the reconstruction of political and social life. Only if the lawgiver were armed with a system that furnished him with indubitable knowledge about men and ideas could he erect a just and reasonable social order. But there could be no reasonable legislation without enlightened citizens. The education of the citizen must be a matter of central concern. Ideology thus became a philosophical discipline and a pedagogical one as well. It could serve its purpose only if the whole educational system, until then dominated by religious training and instruction in the classics, were reconstituted according to rational and scientific principles. The radical reduction of ideas was not a goal in itself; it was only a means for the thoroughly rational education of the citizen. Hence the *idéologues'* deep commitment to the reconstruction of the French educational system.

Education, however, was so intimately connected with politics that the ideologists were inevitably drawn in the political battle. As man could fully develop his faculties only in freedom, pedagogical freedom, they believed, was deeply tied to freedom in the political and the economic sphere. Not all Ideologists descended directly into the political arena, but their very pedagogical ideas, their very emphasis on the need for enlightenment forced them in effect to take a political stance.

Given these premises, it is not surprising to find the *idéologues*, from the onset of the Revolution, playing prominent roles in the various legislative committees—especially in those devoted to educational and constitutional affairs. Many were members of the Constituent and later of the Legislative Assemblies, and many of them sat in the Convention. Moderate liberal *bourgeois*, deeply devoted to the rational ideals of the Enlightenment, they were sympathetic first to Mirabeau and later to the Girondins. Most of them therefore incurred the wrath of the Mountain during the Terror: Volney, Daunou, Ginguené, and a number of others were imprisoned; Condorcet took poison; and Cabanis escaped only by virtue of his employment in a hospital commission. Not until *thermidor* did the *idéologues* again come into their own.

The *idéologues* differed from one another in many details, yet there was a remarkable cohesion among at least the central figures of the group. Such cohesion must be traced to three factors: a common tradition, close and intimate contact with one another, and the availability of a magazine to express the central lines of their doctrine and to adapt it to shifting events on the political scene.

It is important to note that these heirs of the eighteenth-century Enlightenment developed their peculiar doctrine while still in intimate contact with some of the major figures of the older generation. The famous salon of Madame Helvétius, where the ideological movement was born, was of special importance. In 1772, after the death of her husband, the great sensationalist philosopher, Madame Helvétius moved from Paris to the suburb of Auteuil, there to reopen the salon that, during the lifetime of her husband, had been a major nursery for the ideas of the Encyclopedists and in which Condillac, Diderot, and D'Alembert had often gathered to discuss with passion the philosophy of the Enlightenment. Old friends among the survivors again gathered at Auteuil, but a new group of younger intellectuals also began to make its appearance. Morellet, Volney, Turgot, Condorcet, the elderly Benjamin Franklin, along with Pierre Cabanis, the young physiologist and moral philosopher, Destutt de Tracy, the former cavalry officer turned philosopher, and a whole group of young men in the process of developing that particular philosophical doctrine that in later years was to be named the "ideological movement." This direct and immediate contact with their elders ensured that the younger *idéologues* would remain strongly imbued with consciousness of the continuity of the Enlightenment tradition, even when they were intent on giving new twists to traditional assumptions. They did not see themselves as radical innovators but as inheritors of a tradition to be put to their own use.

Auteuil allowed the young intellectuals to form close and enduring contacts with one another while remaining conscious of the pre-eminence of their elders. This drawing together in Mme. Helvétius's salon counterbalanced the disruptive tendencies of Parisian intellectual life and helped to give the doctrine the character of a collective enterprise.

For many of the ideologists, Auteuil came to mean more than a salon. Cabanis lived there for many years, as did Destutt de Tracy. Condorcet stayed there before he was forced to go into hiding. A considerable number of other *idéologues* lived for shorter or longer periods in Auteuil to be close to their friends. Marital alliances also strengthened the internal cohesion of the group: Cabanis married the sister of Condorcet's wife.

The considerable degree of cohesion derived from the Auteuil setting was further increased after the fall of the Jacobins. The Ideologists were again free to re-enact common public roles. The Constitution of the Year III was written by Daunou and was conceived as a kind of charter of the ideas of the Ideologists. The transformation of the French school system, which the Convention undertook after *thermidor*, was to a very large extent the work of the Ideologists. The Ecole Normale, the Ecole Centrale, and the Ecole Polytechnique were founded by men deeply imbued with Ideologist doctrine. Under Lakanal's leadership the Convention left as its academic testament a complete system of public instruction based on the blueprints of the *idéologues*. The Ecole Normale in particular was conceived as the keystone of the whole educational system. In this school, the analysis of ideas, taught as the central discipline, was expected to bring about the regeneration of morals and society of which the Ideologists had long dreamed.

The founding of a new learned society, the famous Institut National, was also the achievement of Ideologists, more particularly of Daunou. The Institut was divided into three classes: physical and mathematical science, moral and political science, and literature and the fine arts. Its Second Class, to which most of the Ideologists belonged, soon became the forum where the important works of the school were debated, and its *Mémoires* published the more important contributions. There analysis of sensations and ideas was the center of interest, although social science, legislation, history, and economy were also given full attention.

In the Ecole Normale, Cabanis taught hygiene, Volney history, and Garat philosophy. At the Council for Public Instruction, the key position was occupied by another Ideologist, Ginguené. The *idéologues* seemed to have triumphed. They had a considerable voice in the place of power; they lived under a constitution written by one of them; they dominated legislative committees; the new school system was under their influence; the new learned society was to a large extent dominated by them.

In addition to Auteuil and the Institut, the Ideologists had still another meeting ground: the offices of the *Décade philosophique, littéraire et politique*, their chief literary organ. This magazine, published from 1794 to 1807, served the development and refinement of Ideological thought and became the tribune from which they could make their critical comments on the political and intellectual scene.

As Ideologists were the leaders of the intellectual and political life of the France of the Directory, it is hardly surprising that the young Napoleon courted them assiduously. He had occasionally visited Cabanis at Mme. Helvétius's house in 1793. In the spring of 1795, the Ideologist Volney introduced the General, then in temporary disgrace, to republican deputies, who later were instrumental in putting him in charge of the Convention's troops against the Royalist uprising of 1795 and who thus launched him on his career.

When Bonaparte became commander of the Armies of Italy, he stepped up his courtship of the *idéologues*. He sent a letter to the Institut paying special tribute to Monge, one of its members, for his services in the Italian campaign; he paid similar tribute to enlightened Italian writers and thinkers. In turn, the *idéologues* joined in the widespread enthusiasm for the young general when he returned to Paris from his victorious campaign. Napoleon began to frequent Ideologist circles and to court the intellectuals who influenced public opinion. To be elected to the Institut seemed to him a most desirable goal. Such was the atmosphere of the time that successful generals needed the legitimation of the intellectual community. Napoleon's election campaign proved as successful as his recent Italian campaign: He was elected a member of the Institut's section on mechanics in December, 1797. Bonaparte was exceedingly proud of his membership and attended the meetings of the Institut up to the time he left for his Egyptian campaign. During this campaign, Napoleon behaved like an *idéologue* on horseback. It is hardly surprising that he appeared to the intellectuals as an incarnation of all the virtues they sought in enlightened men of power. Napoleon was wont to sign his proclamations to the army in the name of

"Bonaparte, général en chef, membre de l'Institut," thus symboliz-ing, or so his *idéologue* admirers believed, the union of power and intellect of which they had dreamed. And the Egyptian expedition far transcended the purely military sphere. Napoleon attempted to create in Egypt institutions like those the *idéologues* had been instrumental in creating in France. Scientists and other intellectuals were his companions and camp followers. He created an Ecole Centrale in Malta and primary schools in Malta and Gazo; he or-ganized an Institut du Caïre, patterned on the French model and designed to bring progress and enlightenment to Egypt. Finally Napoleon created a literary and philosophical journal, *Décade egyp-tienne*, a replica in title and general orientation of the Ideologists' Parisian magazine. The Ideologists saw in him their future philoso-pher-king.

When Napoleon returned to Paris, he had conquered the major figures in the world of letters. Scientists, poets, and philosophers were convinced that the young general would help to found the enlightened commonwealth of their dreams. Through Napoleon, the republic of letters was to dominate the body politic. It is hardly surprising that the *idéologues*, moderate republicans for the most part, acclaimed the 18th *brumaire* with enthusiasm. After Napoleon's *coup* (November 9, 1799), even more than after the fall of the Jacobins, they believed that their hour had finally come. The aris-tocracy of learning and intellect was now to be the governing elite, or so it seemed.

The *idéologues* had written the liberal yet undemocratic Con-stitution of the Year III. They now helped to write the illiberal and undemocratic Constitution of the Year VIII, and they acclaimed it with enthusiasm. The legislature under the new constitution in-cluded almost all major members of the Ideological school. They were to be found everywhere—in the Senate, in the Council of State, in the Tribunate.

Although a few of the Ideologists harbored suspicions of the general's true intentions, the great majority did not. But it soon became apparent that Napoleon, despite his earlier professions of amity, profoundly disliked these "men with a system" who exhibited insufficient flexibility in adapting themselves to the demands of the new regime. He preferred men "concerned with positive and exact facts" to Ideological analysts and enlightened dreamers. The whole elaborate system of political bodies set up by the Ideologist fathers of the constitution was soon converted to an instrument of dictatorship. Senate, Tribunate, and legislative body soon came to play only passive and ornamental roles. Pragmatic power considerations took precedence over ideological preferences. The First Consul soon realized that it would be to his advantage to make his peace with Rome. Religion was a useful buttress of power; critical thought was not. Napoleon needed legitimation for his regime, and religion seemed able to provide it. Philosophy could at best serve as a minor *ancilla politicae.*

The Concordat marked Napoleon's final rejection of the dreams of the Ideologists. He turned from the Enlightenment, using religious sentiment to bolster temporal power. The *Décade* voiced indignant criticism, and many *idéologues* protested in public or in private but to no avail. State power was firmly in Napoleon's hands. The consolidated regime no longer needed the support of liberal intellectuals. When the Senate rejected a few of Napoleon's proposals, he purged it of twenty of its more recalcitrant members, among them almost all the leading *idéologues.* Those *idéologues* or other intellectuals who clung to the anticlericalism, the liberalism of an earlier day, were dispersed and divided among themselves; they were no longer an effective force.

In 1797, Napoleon, the conqueror of Italy, had written to the Institut, "The only true conquests, the only ones which inspire no regret in me, are the conquests that are made over ignorance." When the Consulate was created, Napoleon had proclaimed: "We wish to have a true Republic founded in liberty," but the honeymoon between the Ideologists and the dictator had come to an end. On January 23, 1803, Napoleon dissolved the second section of the Institut, the section devoted to moral and political sciences, to which most of the major Ideologists belonged. New sections were given the innocuous tasks of writing a dictionary of the French language and of translating Greek, Latin, and Oriental authors.

The educational system, that masterpiece of Ideological longrange planning, was also abolished. Profoundly convinced of the need to instill authoritarian norms in the young, so that his order could perpetuate itself, Napoleon abolished the Ecoles Centrales, those nurseries of doubt, enlightenment, and the inquiring and skeptical spirit. His educational reforms between 1802 and 1806 were designed to train imperial subjects, not liberal citizens. The Ideologists were beaten on all fronts. It mattered little that some accommodated themselves and others withdrew from the public arena to devote themselves to private studies; whatever courses they chose, the movement was beaten. The time for the analysis of ideas was gone; they had now merely to be accepted.

Daunou, the proud republican enemy of Napoléon's imperial ambitions, who had held out longer than many others, was finally reduced to writing, "My intention is to publish nothing which might displease the government; I am hence disposed to make any changes that might be required in that respect."

Increasingly hampered by censorship, the *Décade* ceased to appear in 1807. Power had won over intellect.

It would be superficial to attribute the defeat of the *idéologues* solely to Napoléon's successful consolidation of his authoritarian regime. The whole climate of ideas in the beginning of the new century was no longer propitious to the *idéologues*. The young men who had begun to flock to the schools were tired of philosophical discussion and ideological contention. Careers seemed open to talent willing to engage in technical, military, administrative, or scientific pursuits. Students tended to neglect courses that dealt with cultural themes but flocked to the new polytechnical school. "The moral sciences are neglected," said the *Décade*, "the study of the arts and letters is neglected, only mathematics are studied."[5]

The civic enthusiasm of the revolutionary years had subsided. Students trained themselves to assume positions in business, the army, or governmental service. Vocational goals seemed far more important than general cultivation. As self-advancement absorbed the energies of a young postrevolutionary generation, the receptivity for liberal ideas declined. The enlightened ideology was faced, not only with the police measures of the men of power, but also with the apathy of a society of self-seeking, career-oriented subjects. The young sought training rather than cultivation, secure niches in the prevailing order rather than comprehensive ideas. As their audience slowly disappeared, the *idéologues* were unable to resist the demands of the men of power. The alternatives were accommodation or withdrawal from the public scene. The age of ideology was over.

Yet the Napoleonic ice age proved much less enduring than its creator had assumed. In 1814, Destutt de Tracy had the satisfaction of voting in the Senate for the deposition of the Emperor. Most of the surviving Ideologists remained as unreconciled to the Restoration as they had been to the Empire. And in 1830, "one saw circulating on the [revolutionary] barricades a very old man with white hair, almost blind, the eyes protected by a huge green eyeshade, sharing their dangers with the insurgents."[6] His name was Destutt de Tracy.

GOMULKA AND THE REVISIONISTS

"If a Party member disagrees with Party policy; if he does not submit to the Party majority on questions of principle," barked Wladyslaw Gomulka six months after the October, 1956, Polish revolution, "if his world view prevents him from accepting the Party's ideological principle, either he leaves the ranks, gives up his Party card, or the Party must expel him."[7] He then went on to attack "revisionism," which "crippled Marxist principles by introducing false theses that do not reflect social reality in Marxist teaching . . . Revisionism represents the ideology of capitulation because of the difficulties of building socialism." The main ideological spokesman of the Polish Communist Party, Adam Schaff, followed Gomulka in the same style. The Party, he said, could not allow "a camouflaged struggle against the policy of socialism to be carried on under the cloak of an alleged struggle for the freedom of spiritual creativity . . . True freedom for science depends on a clear and effective cultural policy of the Party . . . The absence of such a policy is not democracy and only leads to anarchy."

The men against whom Gomulka spoke with such venom had been his close friends and allies only a few months earlier. He had sought their support and had been strengthened by their adherence to his cause. The dialectic of the intellectuals' support of and alienation from power, which had stretched over several years in the case of Napoleon and the *idéologues*, was compressed into a much shorter span of time in the relations between Gomulka and the revisionists. But in the Polish case, as in the French, tracing the sources of the reversal may help to throw some light on the more general problem of the relations between intellectuals and men of power.

What was "revisionism"? The term came to designate the ideas of a wide and often quite heterogeneous group of Polish intellectuals within the Communist Party and around its fringes, who, in 1955, had begun to waken from their dogmatic slumbers and had become the ideological spokesmen for the October Revolution of 1956. The revisionist current had started as a protest against the Party's strangulation of cultural affairs, the regime of censorship, the enforced orthodoxy of a narrowly interpreted Marxism-Leninism, and the general absence of political and intellectual freedom. The first writer to present a revisionist thesis was the well known sociologist Jozef Chalasinski. Writing in 1955 in the journal *Nauka Polska*, Chalasinski, who had previously found ways to accommodate himself to the Stalinist regime, advanced the thesis that it was not incumbent upon supporters of historical materialism to accept uncritically every assertion of the founders of Marxism. He suggested that values cannot be deduced from Marxism, just as they cannot be deduced from physical science, and went on to denounce the stultifying effect of Marxist orthodoxies in the humanities and the sciences, the impersonal ritualistic style, the enforced unanimity, the absence of any real intellectual achievement in Communist Poland. This first attack gave the signal for similar assaults on the monopoly of the Party in the intellectual and literary fields. In the summer of 1955, the by now famous poem by Adam Wazyk, "A Poem for Adults," appeared. Wazyk had joined the Party before the war and had served with the Russian forces on the eastern front. His poem summed up the disillusion of the postwar decade: "They drink sea-water, and cry 'lemonade'! They return quietly home to vomit, to vomit."

It is important to note that the bitterly critical comments that appeared in the Polish press in 1955 and 1956 were written by men who still placed their hope in the Communist Party. "We appeal through our Party" is the closing line of Wazyk's poem. Another of his poems, published in April, 1956, closes with the lines, "The Party will liberate the sense of revolution until it is again as Lenin saw it."

After the Twentieth Congress of the C.P.S.U. and the shattering revelations of Khrushchev, attacks against dogmatism swelled. The revisionists engaged in a general assault against the tyranny of politics over science, art, and literature. Leszek Kolakowski, once the most brilliant of the young philosophical defenders of orthodoxy and soon to become the major philosopher of revisionism, wrote in the Party's theoretical journal in September, 1956, "Every petrifaction of doctrine necessarily leads to its transformation into mythology, surrounded by a ritual cult, turned into an object of devotion, and safeguarded from criticism. In this situation embarrassing platitudes are proclaimed as theoretical achievements. It is profoundly humiliating to have to be told that one should not falsify historical documents, that scientific opinion must be based on evidence, that criticism of scientific opponents should be to the point, etc."

The main attacks of the revisionists were directed against the ideological distortions of truth in the official *Dialectical Materialism* (*Diamat*), Russian style; but given the intellectual climate, the revisionist attack could not remain limited to purely theoretical concerns. The revisionist movement could no longer be contained within the scope of the official framework; it led to a general assault on orthodoxy in the sphere of political practice. The revisionists had been reared in an intellectual tradition in which the unity of theory and practice was considered axiomatic. The make-believe of the economic plans, the miserable conditions of the workers, the absence of any democracy, all were now attacked. When Wladyslaw Bienkowski lashed out at the Stalinist agricultural policy under the sarcastic title, "Moon Economy and Earthy Matters" (*Przeglad Kulturalny*, September 28, 1956), stating that "statistics are like courtesans who know how to give every man what he seeks," he followed an already established tradition.

In March, 1956, the Nineteenth Cultural Session of Polish Writers and Artists opened with a violent attack by the leading critic Jan Kott on party-line socialist realism, entitled "Mythology and Truth." The debates that followed showed that the bulk of Polish writers had joined the revisionist camp, that it was no longer possible to contain criticism in the comparatively safe channels of purely theoretical debate.

Had the revisionists been isolated critics, their impact would have been less shattering. But soon all the leading cultural periodicals like *Nowa Kultura*, *Przeglad Kulturalny*, and *Pro Postu*, became strongholds of the heresy. The young heretics had at their disposal several magazines that could express the central lines of revisionist doctrine and in which revisionism could be adapted to the shifting events of the day. And the writers' clubs and Warsaw cafés came to fulfill the same functions for revisionist intellectuals that the Parisian salons had served for the men of letters of the Enlightenment and *idéologie*.

Had revisionism been limited in its impact to older intellectuals in or around the Party, it probably would not have been so effective. But it became clear that the bulk of the students, especially at Warsaw University, stood behind the revisionists, and the student paper *Pro Postu* quickly became the main revisionist organ, reaching the unprecedented circulation of 150,000 copies.

In June, 1956, riots broke out in one of the main factories of Poznan. This outbreak revealed that the workers were as discontented with the regime as were the intellectuals. When one of the fathers of revisionism, Professor Chalasinski, was called as a witness for the defense, the emerging alliance between the discontented workers and the aroused intellectuals became clear. The link was fully forged in the days of October, 1956, which brought Gomulka to power. In those October days, the elite among Warsaw students and factory workers lined up behind Gomulka in his struggle against the Stalinist remnants of the Central Committee and against the Russians, headed by Khrushchev, who had flown to Warsaw in a last-minute effort to prevent both Gomulka's accession to power and the inauguration of an independent Polish policy.

Gomulka had been in disgrace and in prison since 1948. He had written in 1947, "We have chosen our Polish road of development which we have named popular democracy. In following this road, and under these conditions, the dictatorship of a single party is not essential, it is even superfluous. Poland can follow her own way, and she is doing precisely that." This "national communist deviation," which seemed to anticipate revisionism, earned him the hatred of the Stalinist die-hards who ruled Poland until October. Then the scorned prophet of a special Polish road to socialism was called into power at a moment of supreme crisis. The writers and scientists, the students as well as the workers who had chafed under the Stalinist regime saw in Gomulka the man who might return Poland to the path of a more humane socialism, a more democratic regime.

For the bulk of the Polish population, Gomulka represented resistance to Russian demands and the end of the hated regime of thought control, secret police, censorship, and ideological conformity. When Gomulka, soon after taking office, declared that "the only unalterable principle of socialism is the end of the exploitation of man by man," when he proceeded to engage in an unmerciful exposé of the errors and crimes of the previous ten years of the Stalinist regime's history, when he seemed to move toward democratization of political institutions and the extension of workers' control over industrial life, he became the hero of the intellectuals. Now at last, they thought, the union of theory and practice, of power and intellect of which the founders of Marxism had dreamed can be enacted. The reign of terror of the bureaucratic pseudo-Jacobins had, it seemed, come to an end, and the time for a humane socialist reconstruction under the revisionist aegis seemed to be at hand.

Until the elections of January, 1957, the revisionist intellectuals were the surest allies of Gomulka. He called many of them into the councils of government and relied on them to uncover the crimes and errors of the past. They served as his mouthpieces. Their passionate appeals contributed much to his election victory. But soon after the elections, Gomulka, his power consolidated and the diehard Stalinists eliminated, began to turn against the revisionist intellectuals. He apparently thought that, if he were to maintain the party apparatus at all, he would have to appease the old party functionaries, the *apparatchiki*. The revisionists and their principled attack against the whole *apparat* became an obstacle. Furthermore, Moscow, sensing the danger of contagion, launched a violent campaign against the revisionists, and Gomulka apparently believed that, if he must make gestures of appeasement toward Moscow, attacks on the intellectuals would be the least costly. Although Gomulka was feeling his way toward a somewhat more liberal Communist position, he was by no means prepared to condone the younger revisionists who were by then engaged in a general onslaught on any kind of dogmatism, whether of the Stalinist or any other variety.

In the days of October, when the whole regime threatened to crumble, the ideological support for reform that the revisionists had so passionately voiced had been invaluable to Gomulka. By attacking the old regime and reviving hopes for a fundamental revision of its policies, the young intellectuals had effectively labored for the legitimation of the new regime. But a consolidated government was no longer in need of the kind of legitimation critical intellectuals were able to supply; continued support from the Church was of considerably greater importance in this respect. Only a little over a year after the October days, the official party paper, *Trybuna Ludu*, stated categorically, "In October 1956, our Party did *not* proclaim a new revolution."

The consolidated regime needed to appeal to continuity of, rather than a break with, Party tradition. The functionaries who had been serving their Stalinist masters and who had been frightened and uprooted by the October events could thus be made to serve the new masters with devotion. That is why the *Trybuna Ludu* attacked the revisionist *Pro Postu* writings as "a complete negation of the thirteen year achievements of the Polish Peoples Republic and an apologia for the capitalist West."

The first sign of a new offensive against the revisionists was the creation of a new weekly, *Polityka*, designed to combat the other cultural periodicals, which were all more or less infested with revisionism. Soon the regime went further. Beginning in March, 1957, press censorship suppressed more than 50% of the contents of each number of *Pro Postu*. Finally, not quite a year after the October revolution, *Pro Postu* was closed down, and many members of its editorial board were expelled from the Party. Warsaw students rioted in the streets, but to no avail. The workers had become apathetic. Many students were beaten, and some were sentenced to years of imprisonment. During the months that followed, censorship again became rigorous. *Europa*, a new Western-oriented literary journal, to which authorization had at first been given, was prohibited. B. Werblan, a key Party official, announced that "in the future, neither time nor money would be wasted on the publication of demoralizing works which do not contribute to the socialist reconstruction of the state." In protest against these measures, some of the most famous among Polish writers, Adam Wazyk and Jan Kott among them, resigned from the Party.

A number of revisionist intellectuals still maintained positions of influence within the Party and the governmental machine between 1957 and 1959, hoping to influence them in a more liberal direction. But by 1959, a new tightening of Gomulka's grip resulted in the ouster of the last major revisionists. Professor Julian Hochfeld, a former socialist and a major figure in the liberalization of 1956, was dismissed as a director of the Institute of Foreign Affairs in Warsaw, and Wladyslaw Bienkowski, one of the major spokesmen of revisionism and a personal friend of Gomulka, was dismissed as Minister of Education.[8]

Gomulka had successfully consolidated his authoritarian regime. The revisionists were beaten on all fronts. It mattered little whether some accommodated themselves to the regime, serving it in various technical capacities, or withdrew from the public arena and devoted themselves to university teaching and private studies. Whatever personal courses they chose, the revisionist movement had come to an end. The time for a critical evaluation of Marxist ideology and Communist practice was gone. Gomulka's Poland was still much freer than Stalinist Poland, but Gomulka himself, once his regime had been consolidated and legitimated, turned against the intellectuals with the full force of his power. The free play of ideas that these men demanded would have undermined Gomulka's pragmatic course of accommodation to the powerful eastern neighbor, which seemed to him the only possible one.

Summing up the drama of revisionism, Leopold Labedz has written, "It may seem paradoxical that those who were most active in the revolt were the most vulnerable after it has partly succeeded, while those who were the least active and stood aside benefited most. The revisionists, the writers, the students, became a relatively easy target for attacks from the reconsolidated Party machine; their strength largely evaporated because of the general apathy of the population which, fearing Soviet intervention, reverted to an apolitical mood. By contrast, the peasantry, the Catholic Church, and petty bourgeois 'private initiative' all received important concessions which have so far been preserved. Their social weight or organizational strength makes them more formidable opponents and Gomulka was careful not to antagonize them, even though the long term costs of antagonizing the youth and intelligentsia may still have to be assessed."

Labedz puts his finger on one of the main reasons for the defeat of the revisionists. The political enthusiasm of the students and the younger intelligentsia had subsided, and political apathy had taken its place. Those who had been enthusiastic about Gomulka's emphasis on socialism as the end of the exploitation of man by man told a bitter joke about the fumbling *Diamat* teacher who, when asked to define capitalism, replies "correctly" that capitalism means the exploitation of man by man and, when asked to define socialism, says "the other way around."

Polish students are now intent on vocational training rather than on ideological discussion. Careers are open for technical and administrative talent, and as self-advancement absorbs the energies of the younger generation, receptivity to revisionist ideas has declined. In May, 1958, the Department of Sociology at the University of Warsaw made a survey of the political and social attitudes of Warsaw students. When asked about their activities in the October days, 45.5% indicated that they had been "very active" or "rather active" participants. But when asked whether they now considered themselves Marxists, only 1.8% answered "decidedly yes," and another 11.4% answered "rather yes." Sixty-eight per cent of the student sample declared themselves "rather not" or "definitely not" Marxist. While a vast majority of students stated that they believed it very important to abolish the exploitation of some men by others, a majority also felt that wide ranges of salaries and wages do not constitute an indirect form of exploitation. Eighty per cent of the students in the sample considered that professions and jobs requiring higher education ought to be paid much more than jobs not requiring higher education . . .[9] The students, in shedding whatever Marxist ideology they once had, have adapted to the realities of bureaucratic society and seek to prepare themselves for privileged status. In today's Poland, the bulk of the young seek training rather than cultivation, secure niches in the prevailing order rather than comprehensive ideas.

As their audience slowly disappeared, the revisionists were unable to resist the demands of the men of power. The alternatives were accommodation or withdrawal from the public scene. The age of revisionism was over.

NOTES

1. Quoted in Hippolyte Taine, *Les origines de la France contemporaine*, II (Paris: Hachette & Cie., 1898), 219–20.

2. Quoted in Charles Hunter Van Duzer, *The Contribution of the Idéologues to French Revolutionary Thought* (Baltimore: The Johns Hopkins Press, 1935), p. 151.

3. Quoted in *The Cambridge Modern History*, IX (Cambridge: Cambridge University Press, 1906), p. 132.

4. I am heavily indebted for the account that follows to Dr. Van Duzer's seminal work, *op. cit.* Hans Barth, *Wahrheit und Ideologie* (Zürich: Manesse Verlag, 1945), was also most helpful. Other important works for the understanding of the *idéologues'* thought and the *milieu* in which they functioned are François Picavet, *Les Idéologues* (Paris: F. Alcan, 1891); and Antonie Guillois, *Le Salon de Madame Helvétius* (Paris: Calmann Lévy, 1894). For a full bibliography, see Van Duzer, *op. cit.*

5. Quoted in Guillois, *op. cit.*, p. 206.

6. Maxime Leroy, *Histoire des idées sociales en France*, II (Paris: Gallimard, 1950), 167.

7. Among periodicals, *Soviet Survey*, published in London, was especially helpful for documentation of events in Poland since 1955. The American *Problems of Communism* has also carried a number of helpful articles. Interesting documentation can be found in *East Europe*, which is published in New York.

These books include translations from the works of revisionist writers: Pawel Mayewski, ed., *The Broken Mirror* (New York: Random

House, Inc., 1958); and Edmund Stillman, ed., *Bitter Harvest* (New York: Frederick A. Praeger, Inc., 1959). The special issue of *Les Temps Modernes* for February-March, 1957, has additional translations into French.

I have relied very heavily on K. A. Jelinski, "Revisionism, Pragmatism, Gomulkaism," *Problems of Communism*, VII (May-June, 1958), 3; Leopold Labedz, "The 'Polish Road to Socialism,'" *Soviet Survey*, II (January, 1957); and Labedz, "Poland: The Evasion of Freedom," *Dissent* (Spring, 1958). The quotations from Polish sources, unless otherwise indicated, are from these three articles.

8. *The New York Times*, October 30, 1959.

9. Excerpts from the study of Warsaw students by Stefan Nowak and Anna Pawelczynska were printed in *Esprit* (Paris), XXVI (November, 1958), 11. Other excerpts appeared in English translation in the monthly *Polish Perspectives*, 3–4, 7–8 (Warsaw, 1958). Cf. Nowak, "Egalitarian Attitudes of Warsaw Students," *American Sociological Review*, 25 (April, 1960), No. 2, 219–31.

Chapter 16

CRITICS OF POWER

THE ABOLITIONISTS

THE INTELLECTUAL AS ACTIVE CRITIC OF GOVERNMENT
and society, as agitator for a set of ideas, is not intent on power
but aims first at focusing the public mind upon a central issue and
then at bringing to bear the force of public opinion upon the makers
of policy. As an agitator, the intellectual plays a role fundamentally
different from the other roles we have considered. Wendell Phillips,
the most articulate and lucid of the Abolitionist leaders, formulated
this difference with great perspicacity, contrasting the reformer with
the politician: "The reformer is careless of numbers, disregards popularity, and deals only with ideas, conscience and common sense . . .
He neither expects nor is overanxious for success. The politician
dwells in an everlasting NOW . . . His object is not absolute right,
but . . . as much right as the people will sanction. His office is not
to instruct public opinion, but to represent it. Thus, in England,
Cobden, the reformer, created sentiment, and Peel, the politician,
stereotyped it into statutes."[1] Phillips had the intellectual agitator
in mind when he wrote elsewhere, "The difficulty of the present
day and with us is, we are bullied by institutions . . . Stand on
the pedestal of your own individual independence, summon these
institutions about you, and judge them."[2] And, "The agitator must

stand outside of organizations, with no bread to earn, no candidate
to elect, no party to save, no object but truth,—to tear a question
open and riddle it with light."[3] The agitator, in Max Weber's terms,
acts in tune with an ethic of ultimate ends, whereas the politician
must espouse an ethic of responsibility.[4] The politician has to weigh
consequences and adjust interests; the agitator stands for a set of
ultimate and absolute values that cannot be compromised. Theodore
Parker, a leading Abolitionist, summarized the ethic of ultimate
ends when he wrote, "In morals as in mathematics a straight line is
the shortest distance between two points."[5] Men who espouse such
an ethic can never expect to reach office or even to become counselors to those in the seat of power, but they can mobilize opinion
and prick the moral conscience of a nation—precisely, what the
Abolitionists accomplished.

The Abolitionist movement, as it first became articulate around
1830, differed significantly from earlier efforts aimed at gradual
emancipation and the colonization of freed Negroes in Africa. It
was a crusade rather than a tame proposal for gradual reform. The
Abolitionists demanded an unconditional and immediate end of
slavery, no matter what the cost. To be sure, their movement
formed part of the wider humanitarian reform movement for
temperance, prison reform, women's rights, and Sabbath observance, which arose around 1830. But it differed from all the others
in that its main proponents hammered away at one central fact:
Slavery was a sin, an absolute evil with which no compromise was
justifiable. This identification of the institution of slavery with sin
and evil gave the Abolitionists' efforts high moral purpose, a sense
of absolute rightness. Their insistence that slavery contradicted the
basic assumptions of Christian doctrine and of the philosophy of
natural right enabled them to attack those in power from the vantage point of ideas and doctrines that the power-holders themselves
pretended to profess. The Abolitionists utilized the discrepancy
between culturally accepted beliefs and actual patterns of behavior.
While other reformers argued that their causes would help to remove corrupting elements from this or that concrete aspect of
American society, the Abolitionists preached that, as long as slavery
persisted, all America was corrupt to the core, for it acted in basic
contravention of its own professed values.

The great majority of the leading Abolitionists in the 1830s came
from the northeastern states, primarily New England. They were
relatively young men. David Donald's study of the Abolitionist

leadership[6] shows that their median age in 1831, when the first issue
of Garrison's *Liberator* was published, was twenty-nine. They came
mostly from educated middle-class homes, many from old and distinguished New England families, and most had attended college,
university, or theological seminary. Few came from big cities; the
majority was from rural or small-town areas. Reaching maturity in
the 1830s, these young men faced a world for which they had not
been prepared in the genteel environments in which they had
grown up. They disdained the bustling new world of business,
with its unashamed money-grubbing, and yearned for the simpler
world of their fathers. Their zeal for reform was, in part at least,
a response to the dislocations of northern society under the impact
of industrialism, which they were witnessing. Many of these young
Abolitionists may have been motivated, though on a subconscious
level, by fears of losing status in a world of business that threatened
to submerge the genteel intellectual elite.

But such an explanation cannot do full justice to any group of
men; we must study the historical actor's own definition of the
situation, his own subjective orientation to the world around him,
if we wish to understand his actions. And it remains true that the
Abolitionists acted from deeply rooted ethical convictions, that
their politics was a politics of conscience, harnessing the total personality in the service of an impersonal goal. The unpopular cause
they espoused was unlikely to bring them status or reward. They
did not aspire to gain political power or to reach office, even though
they may have derived a measure of satisfaction from their ability
to influence an audience or to sway a crowd.

The case of Wendell Phillips, the scion of an old and wealthy
Boston family, furnishes an excellent example. His father had been
Mayor of Boston. Wendell had received the best and most refined
education that patrician Boston could provide. When he decided
in 1837, at the age of twenty-six, to abandon a promising law
practice, to break with the Boston aristocracy, and to devote himself to the cause of Abolitionism, he effectively blocked his access
to any of the careers normally open to a proper Bostonian. His
family seriously considered committing him to an asylum. Most
of his patrician friends shunned this man, who had abandoned his
class and had sought friends among the lunatic fringe of agitators.
Yet Phillips never wavered. From then on, he spoke at literally
thousands of meetings, went on hundreds of "abolitionizing" trips
through New England and the rest of the North, faced innumer-

able mobs, and led, throughout his long career, the nerve-racking life of a professional agitator.

Or there were the many young evangelists first stirred by Charles Finney's Great Revival, then converted by Theodore Dwight Weld to the antislavery cause. These young divinity students, who spread first from Lane Seminary and later from Oberlin throughout the Middle West, converted thousands to the cause of Abolitionism as a revival in religious benevblence. Many of them could have looked forward confidently to successful careers as respected clergymen in Presbyterian or Congregational churches. As preachers of Abolitionism, they were often not even allowed to approach the pulpits of respectable churches.

Or there was the case of William Lloyd Garrison, who came from a less favored background than most of the others. Garrison was a former printer's apprentice and a largely self-taught journalist. When he was very young, his father, a Newburyport seaman, had abandoned his mother, and young Garrison had grown up in miserable circumstances. A man with his rhetorical gifts might well have looked forward to a promising career in politics. Instead he turned to Abolitionism.[7]

In 1830 Abolitionism appeared a forlorn cause indeed. Although earlier, around the turn of the century, it had seemed that slavery was soon to disappear in the United States, subsequent improvement in cotton culture and increased manufacturing had made it again a flourishing institution. The southern slave-owners had joined forces with the northern captains of industry, and "the Lords of the Lash and the Lords of the Loom," to use Wendell Phillips's striking phrase, held practically undisputed mastery. Yet when Garrison put out the first issue of *The Liberator*, the first Abolitionist journal, on January 1, 1831, he deliberately chose a most uncompromising and militant line. The first editorial explained that the paper favored immediate emancipation and opposed the "popular but pernicious doctrine of gradual abolition." It ended with the famous affirmation, "I will be as harsh as truth, and as uncompromising as justice. On this subject I do not wish to think, or speak, or write with moderation . . . I am in earnest—I will not equivocate —I will not excuse—I will not retreat a single inch—AND I *WILL* BE HEARD." The unknown young man, only twenty-five years old, who penned this article seemed a madman, a self-destructive fanatic, even to otherwise sympathetic reformers.

The Liberator hardly created a stir in Boston or elsewhere. Men of sober common sense among the reformers were repelled by the violence of its language and the intransigence of its policies. A few of Garrison's more affluent friends sent money for the rent of his primitive editorial office and for a second-hand printing press. But subscriptions came in very slowly, and the paper was perpetually in debt. After two years, in 1833, it had only about 1400 readers, fewer than 400 of them white and the rest Negro freedmen. The whole venture seemed a dismal failure.

Garrison, with his bitter passion and fanatic belief in the righteousness of his cause, met violent opposition not only from street mobs and local bullies but also from the "respectable" elements among the New England intellectual elite. Almost all Boston churches were closed to the Abolitionists; most Christian gentlemen of the cloth considered Garrison's followers queer zealots speaking an objectionably violent language. Their moral passion was disturbing. They seemed unsound men with unsound minds.

It is true that the Abolitionists attracted, as any radical movement is apt to do, a good number of unbalanced and unhinged minds. It is hardly surprising that a movement that attacks some of the central assumptions of an age attracts men who are plagued by inner conflicts, guilt, diffuse hostility, and marked ambivalence toward authority. Many of them may, to use Harold Lasswell's formulation, have displaced private motives onto public objects, rationalizing this displacement in terms of the public interest.[8] But we must remind ourselves, lest we be carried into an unwarranted equation of radical politics with emotional sickness, that radicals have never had a monopoly on madness, that the defenders of the *status quo* have also had their share of disturbed individuals. And when a moral order has been called into question, when it no longer functions with spontaneous smoothness, we can only expect that ensuing conflicts will bring to the fore many of the irrational forces that, in calmer times, operate below the surface. Violent and even irrational conflict in times of moral crisis may be the means by which a new moral consensus is reached.

The intensely devoted band of followers who gathered around Garrison belonged mainly to the solid middle class. There were among them prosperous lawyers, successful businessmen, and well known educators. Persecution might often have deflected them from the pursuit of their ordinary careers and, temporarily at least, stamped them as marginal men, but in terms of background they were by no means underprivileged. On the other hand, the movement also attracted street-corner agitators, revivalist preachers, and professional advocates of women's rights, labor unions, and the like, who had led marginal lives from the very beginnings of their careers.

The Abolitionists thrived in an atmosphere of controversy. To make themselves heard, they had to attract attention. Young theology students who would force their way into congregations and demand to be heard from the pews used such shock tactics quite advisedly. In fact, the persecution the Abolitionists suffered and the martyrdom of some of their spokesmen helped greatly to further their cause. When one of their band disturbed a religious service and was thrown out of church, when one was attacked by street crowds, when Elijah Lovejoy was murdered by an anti-Abolitionist mob, greater attention was paid to the movement. William Channing, a leading Abolitionist, saw this point clearly. He wrote in 1836, "One kidnapped, murdered abolitionist, would do more for the violent destruction of slavery than a thousand abolitionist societies."[9]

In the beginning, the majority of northerners saw in the Abolitionists only troublemakers who disturbed the pleasant routines of ordinary living. At first, the ordinary northerner was inclined to see in the anti-Abolitionist mobs defenders of law and order against those noisy busybodies who disturbed them. But, as the crusade progressed, the temper in the North slowly began to change, and the audience for the Abolitionists began to expand.

The increasing receptivity of a growing audience cannot be explained by the zeal of the Abolitionists alone. No doubt, their courageous stand moved many to grudging admiration; their lecturers spoke at meeting after meeting in all the Free States; magazines, tracts, articles, and pamphlets spread Abolitionist doctrine. Yet all this activity would have been of little avail had there been no expansion of a receptive audience from other sources. The fact is that, between 1830 and 1860, American society was in the grip of a strong reform impulse. The old institutional balance was upset, and the structure of society had become fluid and loose-jointed. The decline of federalism, the triumph of Jacksonian democracy, the extension of economic opportunity, the consequent decline of the old merchant families, the loss of authority of traditional Calvinistic doctrine—these and many other causes forced upon the nation and especially upon its educated and articulate segments the need to re-examine old beliefs in the light of new experience. The customary adjustments could no longer be taken for granted in an age that saw the emergence of universal suffrage, mass parties, and political machines. As the old forms of traditional integration broke down, thoughtful men were open to the winds of new doctrine, ready to consider new solutions to novel problems. We must also consider the crucial role religion played in the America of the 1830s. De Tocqueville remarked with his customary shrewdness that, "in the United States religion exercises but little influence upon the laws, and upon the details of public opinion; but it directs the manners of the community . . ." As the new Jacksonian faith in the common man threatened traditional Calvinist ascendancy, as traditional predestinarian ideas of sin, righteousness, and salvation were put in question by religious revivals stressing individual responsibility and the co-operative activity of men in the work of salvation, the Protestant churches became battlegrounds of ideas. When the Abolitionists raised the antislavery issue and couched it in the language of Christian principle, they found an audience already prepared to examine the problems of the day in the light of religious precepts. The Abolitionists thus faced, without at first realizing it, what turned out to be prepared and potentially receptive listeners.

The propagandistic efforts of the Abolitionists were prodigious. In January, 1832, Garrison and his associates organized The New England Anti-Slavery Society devoted to immediate and unconditional emancipation. The Society, originally composed of fifteen young men, mainly journalists, lawyers, teachers, philanthropists, and reformers, nearly all of them of old Yankee stock, was to grow within only eight years into a national movement with a quarter of a million members and nearly 2000 branches in all the Free States. There were only sixty Abolitionist societies in the nation in 1835; by 1838, there were 1300 with more than 100,000 members. During 1837–1838, 412,000 antislavery petitions reached the House, and two-thirds of that number reached the Senate. In 1838–1839, two million signatures for Abolition were gathered. In 1835 alone, the American Anti-Slavery Society printed and circulated more than a million pieces of Abolitionist literature. The Abolitionists had thirty or forty newspapers.[10] There was a plethora of antislavery meetings, antislavery celebrations, antislavery bazaars, antislavery *soirées*, and antislavery festivals.

The Abolitionists used all means of propaganda available to them, often with amazing skill, but above all the intensity of their moral conviction, their simple-minded devotion to their appointed task, their stern Old Testament Hebraism made their impacts. Those who felt safely installed in the world and felt no need to question its arrangements might not be disturbed by the Abolitionist message, but men whose moral sensibilities were more fully developed could not remain insensitive.

Their very unwillingness to compromise assured the early Abolitionists their success in gaining a hearing. Then, as now, there were many who would assert that politics was the art of the possible and that it was therefore necessary to go forward cautiously, step by step. Garrison had only contempt for such counsel. "These are young men of 'caution,' " he wrote, "and 'prudence' and 'judiciousness.' Sir, I have learned to hate these words. Whenever we attempt to imitate our great Exemplar, and press the truth of God, in all its plainness, upon the conscience, why, we are very imprudent; because forsooth, a great excitement will ensue. Sir, slavery will not be overthrown without excitement, a most tremendous excitement."[11] Garrison knew that compromise is essential in daily political affairs, but he also knew that his movement would fail if it entangled itself in daily politics.

Historians lately have argued that the influence of Garrison on the Abolitionist movement has been overstated,[12] that his individualism, his sectarianism, the wide variety of his peripheral enthusiasms —for such causes as women's rights and nonresistance—and his unbending antipolitical attitudes limited his influence, especially after 1840, when most Abolitionists began to take more active interest in political movements. It is quite true that the western Abolitionists never followed Garrison's lead, but nevertheless Garrison and Phillips and their followers dramatized the cause of Abolitionism, furnished it with the key symbols, defined it as a moral crusade, built the fires of enthusiasm that, many years later, would eventuate in victory. The early Abolitionists were by no means clear on how the slaves were to be freed or how, once free, they were to be made self-reliant citizens. They hardly thought in institutional terms. They were often utterly lacking in a sense of reality and proportion. No doubt, many of them were fanatics, seething with a repressed violence not devoid of certain paranoid features. Had they attained power, they might have exercised it with the same ruthlessness that has marked the regimes of other "true believers." The fact is, however, that they did not aspire to power. They lacked in fact all the qualities of the successful politician.[13] Rather than politicians, they were agitators and prophets, and as such they

were superbly successful. The moral atmosphere of America ten
or fifteen years after *The Liberator*'s birth was drastically changed,
and in this change their labors had counted for much.

After 1840, the center of antislavery agitation shifted to Washington. Congressional lobbies emerged. Abolitionist congressmen led
by John Quincy Adams formed an antislavery bloc in the House.
After the middle 1830s, volunteers from all over the North brought
petitions to Washington demanding an end to slavery. Thenceforth Abolitionism became a political issue. But would it ever have
entered the realm of politics had it not first been raised by agitators who lacked all the virtues of politicians but possessed to a
supreme degree the gifts to raise a moral question to the status of a
public issue?

THE DREYFUSARDS

The intellectuals who took up the defense of Alfred Dreyfus
and proclaimed his innocence were, for the most part, not activated
by narrowly political motives. Much like the Abolitionists, they
descended into the political arena to defend a set of principles rather
than to gain personal advantage or political power. Theirs was a
politics of conscience. They opposed the men of power in the name
of universal ideas and ideals. The Dreyfus Affair became a watershed in modern intellectual history because in its course a fundamental distinction between two attitudes toward political power,
the social order, and the national state was articulated. The very
term "intellectual" owes its present-day connotations, both favorable and pejorative, to the Dreyfus Affair.

The anti-Dreyfusards, true to a conservative tradition with deep
roots in French political history, affirmed that the claims of the
state and its major institutions, above all of the army and judiciary,
were superior to claims made in the name of such abstract ideals
as justice and individual right. To them, social order was higher
and morally superior to the injunctions of abstract morality or disinterested thought. The Dreyfusard intellectuals, on the other hand,
defended universal, abstract values against the claims of the state
and the social order. They defended what they considered the cause
of justice, even against the judiciary. They upheld the rights of
man, even when such defense might be considered harmful to the
state. When the men of power traduced the cause of justice, then

it behooved the men of intellect, as the guardians of universal values, to call them to order—which they did in the Dreyfus case.

At the end of 1894, Alfred Dreyfus, a Jewish officer of the French General Staff, was convicted of espionage for Germany and condemned to lifelong incarceration on Devil's Island. The trial was secret, but it was known that the major incriminating document, the so-called *bordereau*, was a letter supposedly written by Dreyfus to the German military attaché. In the summer of 1896, Colonel Picguart, who had in the meantime become head of the Information Division of the General Staff, informed his superiors that he believed the *bordereau* to have been written by a Major Esterhazy and that Dreyfus was innocent. The military leaders believed, however, that an admission of error would hurt the cause of the army. In December, 1896, Picguart was sent on a dangerous mission to Tunisia.

In November of that year, Bernard Lazare, a young Jewish writer, published the first Dreyfusard pamphlet, *The Truth about the Dreyfus Affair, a Judiciary Error*, but it had little impact. In June, 1897, Picguart convinced Scheurer-Kestner, Vice-President of the Senate, of Dreyfus's innocence. Slowly the defenders of Dreyfus increased in number. In November, Clemenceau started the fight for revision of the trial in the paper *L'Aurore*. At the same time, the press campaign against the Dreyfusards rapidly gained in volume in such papers as Drumont's *Libre Parole* and Rochefort's *Intransigeant*.

On January 13, 1898, Zola printed his "J'accuse" in *L'Aurore*. On the same day, Picguart was arrested; soon after, he was dismissed from service. The army and the government remained adamant. Zola, tried for calumny of the army, which he had accused of shielding the real author of the *bordereau*, was convicted. Early in 1898, a manifesto in favor of a new trial was signed by a galaxy of well known intellectuals, among whom were Anatole France, Marcel Proust, André Gide, Claude Monet, Lucien Herr, Charles Péguy, Jules Renard, Gabriel Monod, Ferdinand Brunot, Emile Duclaux (Pasteur's successor and Director of the Institut), and a great many others. The Zola trial helped further to mobilize the Dreyfusard intellectuals and to cement the ranks of the antirevisionists. In August, 1898, Esterhazy was dismissed from service for embezzlement and fled to Belgium. A few days later, Colonel Henry, a key member of the counterespionage department, con-

fessed to having forged several pieces of the secret Dreyfus dossier
and committed suicide.

The court of appeals ordered a new investigation and, in June,
1899, annulled the original sentence. In a retrial at Rennes, Dreyfus
was condemned to ten years' imprisonment because of "alleviating
circumstances." Shortly thereafter he was pardoned by the President of the Republic. The major battle was over. Finally, in 1906
another court of appeals squashed the Rennes verdict and fully
rehabilitated Dreyfus.[14]

The Affair assumed so central a place in French political history
partly because it revealed and accentuated deep fissures in the
French body politic. After more than twenty years, the Third
Republic was still not considered legitimate by a considerable part
of the population. The monarchist cause was no longer so powerful
as it had been in the early days of the Republic, yet large numbers of influential Catholics, despite the Pope's recent policy of
accommodation with the Republic, had not yet made their peace
with a Republic that, in its educational system and in other areas,
rejected Catholic claims to control. The supporters of Boulanger's
plebiscitary dictatorship were still not fully reconciled to the Republic, despite their hero's spectacular failure in 1889 to carry out
his promised *coup d'état*. In the early 1890s, France was still in the
midst of an economic depression, and the socialist and union movements began to re-emerge with some force after the bloodletting of
the Commune. There had been a number of spectacular failures
and scandals in the financial world, climaxed by the Panama scandal,
in which a number of members of parliament were deeply impli-
cated. The Third Republic, under attack from left and right, seemed
unsure in its course, vacillating in its policies, unstable in its governing personnel, and unclear in its ideological orientation. The
army, the diplomacy, and the magistrature harbored many who, in
their hearts, despised the Republic they served.

When legitimation wavers, intellectuals are called upon to clarify
the resulting moral disorder. Albert Thibaudet has aptly called the
Dreyfus Affair a "tumult of intellectuals."[15] It was a battle in
which rival factions of intellectuals were standard bearers and
symbols-makers. The Affair agitated the whole of French society,
splitting the French polity into two warring "spiritual families"
who fought in so violent a manner that the effects of their battle
can still be felt in contemporary French politics. Such deep scars

were possible only because intellectuals transformed what was originally a concrete debate over a possible miscarriage of justice into a controversy over basic principles. Who were the Dreyfusards, and what moved them to descend into the arena?

Those who took their stands in the defense of Captain Dreyfus were by no means a homogeneous group—in later years, they were to follow divergent paths and to engage in widely differing courses of action. But, during the years of the agitation around the Affair, they battled unitedly not only for Dreyfus but for justice. Their final victory had long-lasting effects on the balance of power in France and prepared the ground for the dominance of the anticlerical left over the Church and the General Staff, which marked the early years of the twentieth century. Yet those who fought for Dreyfus were, for the most part, not motivated by narrowly defined political considerations.

"The generations which have followed us," wrote Léon Blum many years later, "can no longer understand that during two interminable years, between the beginning of the campaign for the revision and the pardon, life was so to speak suspended, everything converged toward one unique question, in intimate sentiments and interhuman relations everything was interrupted, perturbed, reclassified. One was a Dreyfusard or one was not."[16] I can think of few instances in modern history in which ideological passions were aroused to such a fever pitch. Friendships were destroyed, families divided, old associations broken. And while these conflicts wrecked old allegiances, they led to new alliances among men who had had little in common before the Affair brought them together. When Marcel Proust, long after Dreyfus's pardon, gave a dinner party to which he invited both Dreyfusards and anti-Dreyfusards, Léon Daudet wrote, "I doubt if anyone except Proust could have accomplished that feat." It was years before the antirevisionist Auguste Rodin agreed to visit again his old friend Anatole France, who had been an ardent Dreyfusard. Jules Renard, an active Dreyfusard writer, rejected ten years after the pardon the friendly overtures of a major literary critic, Jules Lemaître, because Lemaître had been an antirevisionist.[17] Julien Benda, the author of *Treason of the Clerks* and a most antipolitical intellectual, confessed in his autobiography that, "The Dreyfus affair taught me that I was capable of true ideological fanaticism. I knew moments when I would have with pleasure killed general Mercier [Minister of War during Dreyfus's first trial]. . . . I love those who, unable to hurt a fly, are capable of becoming ferocious in the name of an idea."[18]

Though, by and large, Catholic intellectuals turned up in the anti-Dreyfusard camp, while anticlericals and those indifferent in matters of religion were attracted to the Dreyfusards, it was by no means always predictable what stand an individual would take. Anatole France, who had been a political cynic, a critic of parliamentarianism, and an advocate of plebiscitary Boulangism, became one of the most impassioned defenders of Dreyfus; even anti-Semites like the novelist Octave Mirbeau and Bonapartists like the journalist Paul de Cassagnac joined the Dreyfusards. Léon Blum recalled many years later that he expected Barrès—who was to become a spokesman for the antirevisionists—to sign a petition for Dreyfus. He was also most surprised to find that such men as Jules Lemaître and the journalist Rochefort had become banner-bearers of the anti-Dreyfusard cause.[19] André Gide, until then quite unconcerned with public affairs, was among the first to come out for Dreyfus, but his intimate friend, the novelist Pierre Louys, joined the opposing camp.

It would be unprofitable to attempt to locate the split between Dreyfusards and anti-Dreyfusards along class lines. The aristocracy and upper *bourgeoisie* were mainly antirevisionist, but the working class was at best neutral, and even many Socialist leaders, like Millerand and Viviani, were by no means favorable to the cause of Dreyfus. Jean Jaurès did not speak for a united Socialist Party when he took up the cudgel for Dreyfus. The two violently opposed ideological factions split the middle classes. Nevertheless, the defenders of Dreyfus and his enemies were not distributed at random throughout the social structure.

The Dreyfusards were especially strong among both professors and students in the university system. But not all Faculties were equally represented. In Paris, for example, there were relatively few Dreyfusards in the Faculties of Law and Medicine. These Faculties were usually frequented by the sons of the well-to-do, for plebeian children could not afford such expensive studies. The Dreyfusards were strongest at the Ecole Normale Supérieure, which was frequented by students, mainly from lower middle-class backgrounds, who had gained entry through competitive examinations and had won fellowships. Almost the whole faculty of the Ecole Normale Supérieure, that Port Royal of the anticlerical intellectual

elite, was ardently Dreyfusard. A high proportion of both teachers
and students at the Sorbonne and at provincial faculties of letters
and sciences was also ranged behind the Dreyfusard banner. Teachers in Parisian public and provincial secondary and primary schools
were mainly Dreyfusard, if only because they felt moved to range
themselves against the Catholic antirevisionists in the private schools.

"The Dreyfus Affair," wrote Thibaudet, "made the professors
rivals and competitors of the lawyers."[20] The teachers, that is, were
from then on to play a public role in the defense of secular values
and ideals against lawyers wedded to conservatism and the defense
of the *status quo*. By and large, the generalization holds that the
main strength of the Dreyfusards was in the world of schools and
universities—though not in the professional schools of law and medicine—among convinced republicans especially in the provinces,
among intellectuals of lower middle-class and plebeian backgrounds,
and among those whose training had made them sensitive to general
ideas rather than to the requirements of practicality. The 300,000
readers of Clemenceau's editorials in *L'Aurore* and the 200,000 who
read "J'accuse" on the day it appeared came mainly from these
groups. The vocal antirevisionists, on the other hand, were largely
from the Parisian upper and upper middle classes, churchmen, lawyers, army officers, and activist students mainly of law and medicine. The bulk of the Royalists and those who had been Boulangists
a few years earlier were on the antirevisionist side, as were the
anti-Semitic superpatriots who dreamed of "revenge" and war
against Germany. The literary world was split, some of the leading
critics being in the antirevisionist camp but a high proportion of
both young and established writers siding with the Dreyfusards.
The French Academy, a mainstay of traditionalism and *bourgeois*
respectability, was heavily antirevisionist.

Turning to the climate of ideas, the defenders of Dreyfus, with
some exceptions were recruited from those intellectuals who traced
their spiritual inheritance to the eighteenth century and to the
Revolution, whereas the proponents of the antirevisionist cause
upheld the ideas of the *ancien régime* and anti-Revolutionary
thought, having been reared in the traditions of Gallican or Ultra-
montane Catholicism. Much of their thought, with its emphasis on
the necessity for maintaining social order above all, can be traced
to De Maistre and De Bonald and sometimes, as in the case of
Charles Maurras, to Auguste Comte or Taine. The Dreyfusards'

most immediate spiritual ancestor, on the other hand, was the Voltaire of the Callas Affair, of *écrasez l'infâme.*

It would be very hard to say how many of those who opposed a revision of the trial of Dreyfus believed in his guilt till the end of the affair. One ought never to underestimate man's capacity for self-deception even in the face of overwhelming evidence. But no doubt many agreed with the leading antirevisionist novelist Paul Bourget when he said, in 1899, ". . . the cause of justice. Well, I don't care a fig for justice. Remember Goethe's admirable saying at the siege of Mainz: 'I prefer an injustice to a disorder'?"[21] When the Dreyfusard writer Jules Renard asked the antirevisionist Paul Claudel, who had talked about the harm the Affair had done to France abroad, "Mais la tolérance?" there came the unbelievably crude reply, "Il y a des maisons pour ça."[22] It is in these terms, the claims of justice against the claims of order, that the Affair must be defined. When Barrès called the Dreyfusards *déracinés* (uprooted), he meant that they were enemies of the established order, of collective discipline and national purpose. When Lucien Herr, a major Dreyfusard spokesman, replied that they were *désinteressés* (selfless), he meant to imply that they were cosmopolitan defenders of moral and cultural standards, disinterested guardians of ideals and ideas acting as true "clerks" out of conscience and a sense of moral duty. While the antirevisionist right took its stand with Goethe's defense of order, the Dreyfusard left believed that *fiat justitia, pereat mundus.*

The case of Emile Zola, the most widely read and most deeply detested novelist of his day, is illustrative. When he heard that Esterhazy had been acquitted by a court-martial of all charges against him, he composed during two nights and a day his letter to the President of the Republic, "J'accuse," in which he attacked the War Office and a number of top members of the General Staff for deliberately obstructing justice and covering up the facts of the case to save the reputation of the army. "As for the people I accuse," he wrote, "I do not know them; I have never seen them. I bear them neither ill-will nor hatred. For me they are no more than entities, spirits of social evil . . ." To Zola, as well as to the great majority of his comrades in arms, what was at stake was less the crimes or errors of particular men than the very idea of justice, though only through exposure of such particular crimes or errors could the general cause of justice be served. This ideal lent peculiar force to his appeal. Zola touched a most sensitive nerve in his audience when he suggested that a polity could not endure and must inevitably decay if it did not inspire respect in its citizens. When force and fraud had become the instruments of government, he argued, the political order had lost its moral justification; it had become the duty of the citizen to oppose it. The political order, Zola and the other Dreyfusards suggested, could not claim the obedience of the citizen if it acted in contravention to the requirements of justice, for then it lost its sacred character, and the citizen had the right to oppose it by all means at his command.

After the Dreyfus Affair, the noun *intellectual*, which had until then been used quite infrequently, came into general usage. It referred, as Victor Brombert has shown, to the Dreyfusards.[23] There were, of course, many intellectuals—in the sense in which I employ the term—in the antirevisionist camp, but they called themselves "men of letters," "literary critics," "writers," and the like and gave a pejorative connotation to the term "intellectual"; the Dreyfusards proudly adopted it. The reason for this attitude becomes clear when we consider Maurice Paléologue's vivid account of a dinner at which Ferdinand Brunetière, a famous literary critic and leading anti-Dreyfusard, commented upon Zola's "J'accuse," which had just been published. "And what is Zola up to? His letter, *J'accuse*, is a monument of stupidity, presumptuousness and absurdity. This novelist meddling in a problem of military justice seems to me no less impertinent and preposterous than the intervention of a captain of gendarmerie in a question of syntax or prosody . . . And this petition which is being circulated among the 'intellectuals.' The sole fact that the word 'intellectual' has recently been coined for the purpose of setting apart in a kind of exalted social category people who spend their lives in laboratories and libraries points to one of the most absurd eccentricities of our time, namely, the claims that writers, scientists, professors, philologists should be elevated to the rank of supermen. I certainly do not despise intellectual abilities, but their value is only relative. I place will power, force of character, sureness of judgment, practical experience, higher in the social scale."[24]

Brunetière clearly defined the issue as it was joined. The anti-Dreyfusards reasoned in terms of a vision of an ordered society in which the various professions and occupations should restrict themselves to performing their tasks. They believed that everyone should cultivate his own garden and be respectful of those who were entrusted with high national purpose. When intellectuals set concern for abstract justice above respect for the decisions of the national judiciary, they were subversive of the social order and set themselves above the national community, presuming to judge it in terms of supernational standards. No specific professional category had a right to such presumption. If men were to attempt to transcend their occupational and professional roles, the social order, which rested on a clear-cut division of labor, would be weakened. When Zola answered the judge at his trial, "I don't know the law and don't want to know it," he offered the antirevisionists a prime example of the presumption of intellectuals who dared to intervene in public affairs without the requisite occupational qualifications.

The Dreyfusard intellectuals, on the other hand, believed that it was by virtue of their immersion in the world of ideas that they had the right, nay the moral duty, to uphold universal ideas and ideals against even the claims of the state. In defending Dreyfus, they believed that they were at the same time defending their own claim to represent the realm of ideas beyond narrow specialization. Their defense of Dreyfus was meant to justify their very mode of existence. As true inheritors of the tradition of the Enlightenment, they believed their mission was to criticize the ruling powers when they interfered with reason or justice. They saw themselves as deeply committed to the defense of disinterested inquiry and skeptical scrutiny of traditional and "sacred" verities. Commitment to reason, even if it should prove corrosive of stability and social order, had priority over national concerns. Faith in the efficacy of universal ideas and dedication to their defense were the hallmarks of the Dreyfusard orientation to the public world.

Many social struggles would have taken place even without intellectuals' verbalizations and symbolizing. That is emphatically not true of the Dreyfus Affair. Perhaps Dreyfus might finally have been released without the agitation of the intellectuals; such questions are difficult to answer. But there would have been no Dreyfus Affair; there would have been only the private sorrows and tribulations of an individual suffering from a miscarriage of justice. The Affair was the peculiar creation of intellectuals. In a number of instances, spokesmen for the Dreyfus family wished to refrain from too much public agitation and sought to limit the issue to the guilt or innocence of the Captain; but in every case they were opposed by the Dreyfusard intellectuals, for whom the case surpassed the man and had assumed an autonomy of its own. This attitude ex-

plains the disappointment of many when Dreyfus finally accepted
the pardon of the President of the Republic instead of fighting for
full vindication. It may seem that the intellectuals were sometimes
rather callous about Dreyfus's personal fate—he was, by the way, a
rather average man who never fully understood the symbolic role
he was asked to assume—but that is understandable when we realize
that, to the intellectuals, the Dreyfus Affair far transcended Dreyfus
the man.

The Affair led to a tremendous exaltation of moral energies. It
was one of these extraordinary times when men are carried beyond
the ordinary routines of their lives to devote themselves to a cause
that is in no way connected with their immediate personal interests.
The young students who fought in the battles of the Sorbonne to
defend their professors against mobs of antirevisionists, the young
professors grouped around Charles Péguy, for whom the cause of
Dreyfus was for a few years the very core of their lives, were
marked forever by the impact of these days. Péguy has written
movingly about the Dreyfus "mystique" of those years and has
sharply contrasted it with the "politique" of those Dreyfusards
who, after the end of the Affair, rode to political power on the
Dreyfus case. The very depth of Péguy's later disappointment testifies to the strength of his initial commitment. Men who had been
abused in public, attacked by mobs, cashiered from their positions
in the diplomatic corps, or suspended from their university positions by a vindictive government, men who had had to part company with friends and loved ones because of the Affair carried the
scars to the ends of their lives.

The very intensity of the conflict led to a revitalization of public life. For a while, the intellectuals were truly drawn into the
public arena, becoming guides and mentors for masses of men to
whom, perhaps suddenly, the cause of justice had become a vital
and immediate concern. A recent historian, Michael Curtis, writes
quite correctly that "The Affair was to give a new lease on life
to the Republic, to provide it with an enthusiastic vigor equivalent
in many ways to the Wesleyan revivals in the Anglo-Saxon
countries."[25]

The parallel between the roles of the Dreyfusards and the Abolitionists is striking, even though these two groups have very little
else in common. Both groups raised moral issues to the level of
public problems. They upset habitual adjustments by injecting profound moral questions into routine discussions of public affairs.

They forced men to rethink the very bases of their political allegiances, to re-evaluate the political order before the tribunals of their consciences. By challenging precedent and tradition they shocked men out of their customary passivity and helped to shape their political and moral consciousness. When they finally succeeded in bringing to bear the force of public opinion upon the men of power, they forced them to desist from courses that sacrificed justice to expediency. The Affair proved that intellectuals, backed by the force of public opinion, could prevail over the men of power. Justice triumphed despite the obstructions of the judiciary.

NOTES

1. Quoted in Richard Hofstadter's perceptive essay, "Wendell Phillips: The Patrician as Agitator," which is Chapter VI in his *The American Political Tradition* (Vintage ed.; New York: Random House, Inc., 1954), p. 138. I have learned much from this essay.

2. Quoted in *ibid.*, p. 139.

3. Quoted in Ralph Korngold's *Two Friends of Man* (Boston: Little, Brown & Co., 1950), p. 181. The "two friends" are Garrison and Phillips.

4. *Cf.* Max Weber, "Politics as a Vocation," H. H. Gerth and C. W. Mills, trans. and eds., *From Max Weber, Essays in Sociology* (New York: Oxford University Press, Inc., 1948).

5. Quoted in Oscar Sherwin's *Prophet of Liberty* (New York: Bookman Associates, 1958), p. 98. This book is a detailed scholarly study of Phillips and his times.

6. David Donald, "Toward a Reconsideration of Abolitionists," in his *Lincoln Reconsidered* (New York: Alfred A. Knopf, Inc., 1956).

7. On Garrison, I have consulted, in addition to the works already cited, Russel B. Nye's *William Lloyd Garrison and the Humanitarian Reformers* (Boston: Little, Brown & Co., 1955).

8. Harold D. Lasswell, *Psychopathology and Politics* (New ed.; New York: The Viking Press, Inc., 1960), especially pp. 74ff.

9. Quoted in Hazel C. Wolf, *On Freedom's Altar* (Madison: University of Wisconsin Press, 1952), p. 32.

10. Sherwin, *op. cit.*, pp. 100ff. This book contains a wealth of data on the propaganda efforts of the Abolitionists.

11. Quoted in V. L. Parrington's portrait of Garrison in *Main Currents in American Thought*, II (Harvest ed.; New York: Harcourt, Brace & World, Inc., 1954), 348.

12. *Cf.* Gilbert H. Barnes, *The Antislavery Impulse* (New York: Appleton-Century-Crofts, 1933).

13. I have profited much from Stanley M. Elkins's discussion of the Abolitionist intellectuals in his *Slavery* (Chicago: University of Chicago

Press, 1959). I cannot, however, follow Mr. Elkins when he criticizes the Abolitionist intellectuals for their lack of involvement in institutionalized politics, for their individualism, and for the abstractness of their program. No doubt, in England's rich institutional life, Abolitionism became a more reasoned, concrete, reformist movement and was less given to extremes of moralistic crusading. But, as Mr. Elkins himself demonstrates, such a life simply did not exist in the United States of the 1830s, so that a fairly uncomplicated appeal to individual conscience remained the only way to bring the issue to the attention of the nation.

14. I have consulted several general histories of the Dreyfus case. The most objective recent study is Guy Chapman's *The Dreyfus Case* (London: Rupert Hart-Davis, Limited, Publishers, 1955).

15. Albert Thibaudet, *La république des professeurs* (Paris: Grasset, 1927).

16. Léon Blum, *Souvenirs sur l'Affaire* (Paris: Gallimard, 1935), p. 13.

17. These incidents are described in Michael Curtis, *Three Against the Republic* (Princeton: Princeton University Press, 1960), p. 34. I have learned much from this study of the thought of Sorel, Maurras, and Barrès.

18. Julien Benda, *La jeunesse d'un clerc* (Paris: Gallimard, 1936), pp. 201–2.

19. Cf. Blum, *op. cit.*, pp. 73ff.

20. Thibaudet, *op. cit.*, p. 23. Thibaudet's book is most important for an understanding of the atmosphere at the Ecole Normale Supérieure. Cf. also the biased yet quite revealing study by Hubert Bourgin, *De Jaurès à Léon Blum* (Paris: Fayard, 1938).

21. This conversation is reported in Maurice Paléologue, *An Intimate Journal of the Dreyfus Case* (New York: Criterion Books, Inc., 1957), p. 217.

22. Quoted in Curtis, *op. cit.*, p. 35.

23. Victor Brombert, "Toward a Portrait of the French Intellectual," *Partisan Review*, XXVII (Summer, 1960), No. 3, 480–502. I have borrowed heavily from this extremely valuable article.

24. Quoted in Paléologue, *op. cit.*, p. 113.

25. Curtis, *op. cit.*, p. 42.

Chapter 17

SALVATION ABROAD

RAGE FOR ORDER: THE *PHILOSOPHES'* LOVE AFFAIR WITH CHINA AND RUSSIA

THE FRENCH *philosophes*, SO THE SCHOOLBOOKS usually say, were mighty champions of liberty; they preached the defense of freedom against the arbitrary powers of the state. Did not Diderot write, "Each century is characterized by a specific spirit. The spirit of ours seems to be that of liberty"?[1] It comes therefore as a shock to realize that many of the *philosophes*, as well as such other champions of liberalism and individualism as the physiocrats, the ancestors of classical economics, admired the societies of China and Russia above all others in their day. This paradox is worthy of some attention.

When intellectuals are out of tune with political trends at home, they are apt to look for more congenial harmonies abroad. "Not finding anything about them which seemed to conform to their ideals," wrote Tocqueville of the physiocrats, "they went to search for it in the heart of Asia. It is no exaggeration to say that everyone of them in some part of his writings passes an emphatic eulogy on China. . . . That imbecile and barbarous government . . . appeared to them the most perfect model for all of the nations of the world to copy."[2] And l'Abbé Baudeau, one of the principal members of the physiocrats' circle, wrote, "More than three hundred twenty million people live there [in China] as wisely, happily and freely as men can ever be. They live under a most absolute but most just government, under the richest, the most powerful, the most humane and the most welfare-conscious monarch."[3] The *intendant* Poivre, whose writings were considered authoritative by the physiocrats, went so far as to assert in his *Travels of a Philosopher* that, "China offers an enchanting picture of what the world might become, if the laws of that empire were to become the laws of all nations."[4] To the father of physiocratic doctrine, Quesnay, China was a model state "founded on science and natural law."

This strange Sinophilia was not limited to the physiocrats; it was in fact shared by a great many among the eighteenth-century *philosophes*. Voltaire in particular never tired of singing the praises of China, "the widest and best policed nation of the world."[5] "One need not be obsessed with the merits of the Chinese," he wrote, "to recognize at least that the organization of their empire is in truth the best that the world has ever seen, and moreover the only one founded on paternal authority."[6] There is almost equally enthusiastic language about the Chinese in the writings of Diderot and Helvétius. Leibniz had already expressed similar enthusiasm in an earlier day.[7]

French knowledge of Chinese affairs was, of course, fragmentary. Most of it came from Jesuit missionaries, and their accounts were, to say the least, not always free from a bias imposed by the need to defend themselves against their theological adversaries in the famous quarrel over the Chinese ceremonies. The Jesuits had been led to make a number of major concessions to traditional Confucian culture in their effort to bring the Chinese to the Faith, and they had therefore a vested interest in presenting an idealized picture of the country of Confucius. Such idealization by the philosophers was not, however, due to ignorance alone. Russia was much better known, yet we find idealizations of Russian conditions in the writings of Voltaire, Diderot, Helvétius, Grimm, and many others that fully match their unrealistic ideas of China.

A certain degree of self-interest helps to account for this Russophilia. Catherine II assiduously courted the Parisian enlighteners. In 1763, she bought Diderot's library for 15,000 francs but left it in his possession—giving him a pension of 1000 francs a year for assuming the task of librarian. Two years later, she gave him 50,000 francs for fifty years in advance.[8] D'Alembert was offered the tutorship to the heir of the Russian throne; others were given similar tangible proofs of the Empress's support. Yet it would certainly be most unfair to aver that self-interest was the main spur to admiration of Catherine and her administration. Not all admirers of Catherine derived such material benefits from their commerce with the Empress, and, further, Voltaire and many of his friends admired the long-dead Peter the Great as much as his successor.

Voltaire never tired in his praise of Catherine. He was a kind of unofficial public-relations expert for her until her death. "What times are these," he wrote to D'Alembert. "France persecutes the philosophers and the scyths favor them." "I admire Catherine, I love her to folly," he wrote a few years later, "the scyths become our masters in everything."[9] He compared Catherine to Lycurgus and Solon and was never at a loss to explain away her failings. He acknowledged that she had had a hand in the assassination of her husband but referred to this event as "family quarrels" and "bagatelles."[10] His admiration for Peter the Great was equally unbounded. The Empress Elizabeth had commissioned his biography of Peter and had liberally rewarded him after that piece of hack work had turned out to her satisfaction. But even before he had any relations with the Russian court, he had written that Peter "resolved to be a man, to command men, and to create a nation," that Peter had single-handedly changed the greatest empire in the world, had "civilized his people."[11] Marmontel, whose *Bélisaire* Catherine herself had translated into Russian, and Grimm, her most assiduous correspondent, never tired in their championship of the virtues of the Empress's regime. Although some of the *philosophes* were not beyond opportunism and even venality, other factors must also have been at work.

The social position of the man of letters in the eighteenth century helps to account for his fascination with "enlightened rulers." In his isolation at home, persecuted, censored, forbidden to publish his books in France, he was naturally prone to look abroad for encouragement and support. Interest on the part of powerful foreigners flattered him and bolstered a self-esteem that was often badly shaken by discouragement at home. Such treatment, according to Peter Gay, "created some false impressions among the philosophers . . . they were all too easily tempted to imagine themselves, at least on occasion, in the role of Plato and Aristotle, and to imagine their royal friends as a Numa or Lycurgus."[12] But why did the *philosophes* turn specifically to Russia, and how does

one account for their Sinophilia, for clearly no tangible or even
intangible benefits could have been expected to descend upon de-
serving philosophers from the Son of Heaven, even when similar
benefits were possible from the Semiramis of the North?

Suffering from a multiplicity of laws and authorities, fragmentation of political will, lack of concerted planning in governmental
affairs, and all the privileges accruing to favored estates and orders,
the philosophers yearned for a body politic that would be efficiently
run by a central administration. Such an administration would
know how to deal with the obstructions of rank and birth and how
to order the affairs of the state in the mirror image of universal
reason. Reason could not be expected to prevail in a society split
into autonomous, warring powers, in which *parlements* checked the
court and the clergy, subservient to Rome, utilized the secular arm
in its struggle against the Enlightenment.

Frederick the Great, in one of his letters to Voltaire, provides
us with a first clue for understanding Voltaire's infatuation with
China. Frederick wrote that he visualized Voltaire ever repeating
to his friends, "Seeing that only one law prevails throughout the
whole vast empire of China, must you not desire, oh my country-
men, to imitate them in your little kingdom."[13] China seemed to
the *philosophes* a society in which things got done. They got done,
moreover, with the help and under the guidance of wise scholars,
of fellow *philosophes*. What impressed Voltaire even more than the
beneficent rule of a benevolent Emperor was the fact that the Emperor was surrounded by men of letters, an official class of literati
chosen on a rational basis, free from the corruptions of organized
religion and the particularistic criteria of rank and birth. And
imagine, said Voltaire, that the Emperor could do nothing without
consulting "these men educated in the law," who would check all
tendencies toward arbitrary action.[14]

The same reasoning seems to account, in somewhat modified
form, for the philosophers' Russophilia. Everything, they argued,
is possible if, in a country that had been until recently wholly
barbaric, one man aided by right reason could transform a whole
people. Russia had made enormous progress within the short span
of a few decades; to use modern terminology, it seemed to have
jumped many stages of development. It moved ahead so fast that,
in many respects, it was already a model for countries of much
older civilization. And what, if not enlightened despotism, had
allowed the Russians to make such giant steps forward? Despotism,

of course, if properly enlightened, turned out upon inspection to be by no means so horrible as Montesquieu had pictured it; it was, in fact, one of the most impressive means of progress. Even though such despotism might not be wholly suitable at home, it certainly was the most potent means to allow "underdeveloped countries" to reach quickly and even to surpass the lands of older civilization. If Russia had succeeded in thirty or forty years, through enlightened legislation, in overcoming a lag of three centuries, then indeed one could continue to believe in the perfectibility of man and be optimistic about progress. Russia's advance revived the spirits of those discouraged by the anarchy and apparent hopelessness of the political scene at home.

In enlightened Russia, in contrast to Western Europe, the sovereign was not hindered by all sorts of obsolete and obsolescent resistance to his beneficent actions. There one could paint with broad strokes upon the canvas of the future. In Russia—and in the other enlightened despotisms of the North—the ancient alliance of the throne and the altar seemed about to be replaced by the alliance of throne and philosophy. "The greatest happiness of a nation," wrote D'Alembert, "is realized when those who govern agree with those who instruct it."[15] To enlighten an absolute monarch appeared a most advantageous short cut on the road to the universal reign of reason. To instruct the people would take centuries, to enlighten an elite was a most arduous task, and the shortest route was, in Voltaire's words, "to make a revolution . . . in the spirit of those who are made to govern."[16] Leibniz had already said it: "To win the spirit of a single man such as the Czar or the monarch of China . . . is to do more than to win a hundred battles, because millions of others depend on the will of such men."[17]

China and Russia, to the *philosophes*, were unlike in many respects, but they had one thing in common and a most important thing at that: In both those great empires, the men of letters served in places of eminence, at the very center of things. In China, the literati, wise and incorruptible counselors to the Emperor, exercised both administrative and judicial power. There the powerful knew how to give due honor to the men of letters. In consequence, the country was well ordered and well policed, the customs agreeable and refined, the mores simple, and the people content. And, according to Voltaire, if a certain lack of progress might be discerned, it was due to the fact that they had attained so high a point of perfection that they saw no need to push any further. . . .[18] In Russia, on the other hand, the necessary progress was assured because despots, enriched by the advice of the enlightened from abroad, could freely knead with their own hands the paste of the future.

Almost all the *philosophes* were royalists at home, usually supporting the King's party against *parlements* and estates. But at home, their scope of action seemed fatally limited because the King was prevented from right action not only by personal insufficiency but also by built-in checks to his power. "The sole remedy against all the ills involved by the immensity of our States, the multiplicity of our laws, the slowness and uncertainty of our justice, the impunity of resourceful and clandestine crime and the favor of unjust power," wrote Grimm, the confidant of Catherine, "the sole remedy, if it exists, must be sought in the heart and character of him to whom the right to rule has come with his birth."[19] Louis XV, of whom so many had expected so much, had turned out to be vacillating and corrupt. His successor was an honest simpleton. But how could even wiser kings prevail against the domination of the "eternal yesterday" in the old countries of the West? What then was more rational than to turn in admiration and respect to those countries in which enlightened rulers, unhampered by tradition and precedence, were willing to accept the advice of philosophers? "It is most advantageous for the prince and the state," wrote Voltaire, "when there are many philosophers. The philosophers having no particular interest to defend, can only speak up in favor of reason and the public interest."[20]

Tocqueville summed it all up in his continuation of the passage quoted at the beginning of this chapter. He wrote, "They were moved with rapture at the vision of a country in which the sovereign [is] absolute but free from prejudice . . . and in which all offices are obtained by written examinations; which has for religion only a philosophy, and for an administration only men of letters."[21] In their rage for order, they were wont to forget their passion for liberty. "You might have thought," writes Paul Hazard, the great intellectual historian, "that you were looking at a minuet: the Princes bow to the philosophers, the philosophers return the bow. . . . As if the mighty ones had forgotten how they had persecuted, and were still persecuting, writers who were trying to undermine their authority; and as if the writers had forgotten about the furious rhetoric they had hurled, and were still hurling, against the tyrants."[22]

The philosophers' hopes, of course, came to nought. They

"thought they were using the kings; and it was the kings who were using them."[23] Catherine ruled Russia with rude and despotic practicality; enlightenment was a sport of kings but hardly a matter for realistic guidance. In the meantime, it was good indeed to have respected philosophers who could find enlightened arguments for calling crimes "family quarrels" and for justifying wars of aggression or the pitiless suppression of peasant *jacqueries*. Intellectuals who had sought to guide power managed in the end only to legitimize it.

A modern political scientist, Suzanne Labin, has written, "The contributions of Voltaire's vigorous mind were not approved by an ancient society stuffed with traditions, but his light was accepted in the faintly illuminated North, where a despot, free from the shackles of an ancient civilization, could smile prettily at his theories. *The elite of the word tries to establish its ascendancy where there is no elite of any other kind.*"[24] The "elite of the word" cannot be said, as Miss Labin seems to have assumed, to have a single, unified orientation toward the men of power. Rousseau and Montesquieu, for different reasons, never shared their contemporaries' enthusiasm for Russia and China. The orientation that has been sketched here, however, though not the only possible one, is significant, especially as we encounter a very similar one among European and American intellectuals almost 200 years after the encyclopedists and the physiocrats.

RIDING THE WAVE OF THE FUTURE IN THE THIRTIES

In the 1930s, a great number of British and American intellectuals, previously aloof from or hostile to Communism, suddenly "discovered" the Soviet Union. Beatrice Webb, who had previously considered the Russian revolution "the greatest misfortune in the history of the labor movement,"[25] fell in love with the Soviet Union. She and her husband saw there the emergence of a new civilization that embodied, through its planning, its application of science to the reconstruction of society, its moral dynamism, and its puritanical morality, the emergence of a true welfare state. Harold Laski, previously the most consistent advocate of political pluralism and a champion of reason in politics, of gradualism and legal adjustment, suddenly lost confidence in democratic institutions and began to vaunt the virtues of Russian-style Marxism. John Strachey, a former Labor M.P., wrote *The Coming Struggle for Power*, a most able popularization of Communism, which contributed much to making it respectable in the West. Scores of young men fresh from Oxford and Cambridge, poets, novelists, and scientists, became for shorter or longer periods enthusiastic devotees of the cult of Russia. W. H. Auden, Stephen Spender, Day Lewis, Christopher Isherwood, and a whole galaxy of young British intellectuals extolled Communism. Hugh MacDiarmid wrote a "First Hymn to Lenin," and Michael Roberts called upon fellow intellectuals to prepare the way for an English Lenin.[26] Even a liberal like E. M. Forster could consider at that time that Communism was the only political creed that offered hope for the future, although he added that he himself would not be a Communist.[27] Eminent scientists gathered around J. D. Bernal, who proclaimed the dictum that "science is communism." J. B. S. Haldane, J. G. Crowther, and other renowned scientists joined Bernal to create the Social Relations of Science Movement, which, partly through its influence on the editorial policies of the eminent scientific journal *Nature*, succeeded in nearly dominating the world of British natural science and in steering it into a pro-Soviet orbit.[28]

In the United States, a parallel development took place. Theodore Dreiser, who earlier had written a rather hostile account of his trip to the Soviet Union, now became one of Russia's spokesmen. Sherwood Anderson put to himself the question, What is the difference between a Socialist and a Communist? and answered, "I guess the Communists mean it." John Dos Passos, Sherwood Anderson, Erskine Caldwell, Edmund Wilson, Malcolm Cowley, Granville Hicks, and many others endorsed Communist William Z. Foster's campaign for the presidency in 1932.[29] Lincoln Steffens, the grand old fighter against corruption, finally arrived at the conclusion that in Russia he had seen the Future and that it *worked*. "Nobody in the world," he said, "proposes anything basic and real except the Communists."[30] Ruth McKenney, a young Communist writer, bubbled over with enthusiasm: "Communists today are in the great stream of humanity, brothers to the forgotten man who invented speech, comrades to the Greek architects who discovered form . . . They have discovered the direction in which production is changing, from the anarchy of capitalism to the logic of socialism. Communists can make history, and so transcend their lives by knowing the only immortality open to human beings—putting a mark on to-morrow."[31]

In Britain and the United States alike, books and articles extolling the new civilization of the Soviet Union kept pouring from the presses; the audience for such writings seemed to expand each year. Maurice Hindus, Louis Fischer, Ella Winter, Anna Louise Strong, Jerome Davis, and many others wrote as if they were press agents for the Russian future. The liberal weeklies, *The Nation, The New Republic*, and *The New Statesman*, hardly let a week pass without some enthusiastic or at least apologetic report about Russia. Friends of the Soviet Union, Russian-American institutes, British-Soviet friendship societies, somnolent until then, suddenly blossomed and attracted large numbers of passionately interested intellectuals. Russian movies played for weeks in the *avant-garde* houses. Literary magazines, theater groups, and dance groups all extolling Russian art, Russian culture, and Russian advances in all spheres of human endeavor mushroomed. Thousands of intellectuals, and not they alone, were turning with glee from old moorings, transferring their enthusiastic loyalties to the Soviet Union. The British poet Day Lewis summed it all up:

> Revolution, revolution
> Is the one correct solution—
> We've found it and we know it's bound to win.
> Whatever's biting you, here's a something will
>   put life in you.[32]

What was "biting" these men? What accounts for this truly remarkable outbreak? What, in particular, accounts for the fact that no similar enthusiasm for the Soviet Union had been discernable among wider circles of intellectuals in the Twenties?

The Depression was the traumatic event that marked the intellectuals of the Thirties. Not all of them reacted in the same manner, of course, but the shock was general. The Wall Street crash of 1929 meant the end of an era, the breakdown of an order. They saw the breadlines lengthening and watched, like Auden, "smokeless chimneys, damaged bridges, rotting wharves and choked canals, . . . power-stations locked, deserted, since they drew the boiler fires."[33] Like Spender, they saw the unemployed lounging "at corners of the street . . . they sleep long nights and rise at ten to watch the hours that drain away . . . I'm hounded by these images, I'm haunted by their emptiness."[34] They listened to the inanities of Herbert Hoover and his silver line just beyond the horizon; they felt contempt for Ramsay MacDonald's National government, which was so obviously unable to cope with the national disaster. They were filled with bitter loathing of such figures as former "Labour," now "National," Chancellor Philip Snowden, who proclaimed, at a time when in Britain's distressed areas 60% of the work force was unemployed: "Britain could not afford to have an unbalanced budget. An unbalanced budget is regarded as a sign of impending national bankruptcy."[35] They jeered when they heard Hoover's Secretary of Commerce Lamont state at the beginning of 1930, "There is nothing in the situation to be disturbed about . . . There are grounds for assuming that this is about a normal year."[36]

It was perhaps not the economic Depression itself that caused the intellectuals' disaffection but the accompanying social disorder. The times were hopelessly out of joint, and nobody seemed able to put them together again. It seemed to many intellectuals that the Western world was drifting without plan, guidance, or goal. The Depression revealed the apparent shipwreck of Western assumptions and values. The whole house of liberal civilization, which had been patiently erected by generations of eminent Victorians and their successors, seemed suddenly to collapse. What use was the whole framework of safeguards for the individual, of concern with the reign of law and freedom and democratic process, what use were all these traditional pieties, this conventional wisdom, when people were hungry and lived without hope or purpose, when men out of work sold apples in the streets and shuffled in bread lines? What use all the niceties of civil liberties and political freedom when young talented writers could not publish, when it seemed impossible to find a job even with the highest professional degree, when nobody seemed to be able to answer the insistent question, What of tomorrow?

Many young American intellectuals, especially among social scientists and lawyers, were soon to drift to Washington in the wake of the New Deal. They were to find there a climate that would allow them to act out their recently acquired antagonism to the values of a decaying business civilization in an effort to help plan a new, more humane, and more co-operative society. But to many others, to artists and literary men in particular, there was no such way out. And in Depression England, there was only the Old Deal of MacDonald and Baldwin.

There seemed to be only drift at home. But over the horizon, in a country that few had seriously noticed before and to which most had looked with a mixture of amusement and contempt—in the Soviet Union—there seemed to be mastery. The streams of visitors who toured the Soviet Union in that period—H. G. Wells and G. B. Shaw, Beatrice and Sidney Webb, Lady Astor, John Strachey and Aneurin Bevan, Walter Reuther and Paul Robeson, Mary Heaton Vorse and Ella Winter, Dr. Henry E. Sigerist, Corliss Lamont, and George Counts—varied in their reactions, but they were almost unanimously impressed by the evidence of Soviet power and purposefulness.[37] There was a society without bankers, trusts, and stock markets that got things done. Russia had an administration that was manifestly planning for a better future; national energy seemed truly harnessed to the service of the common weal. Visitors to Russia perceived none of the disillusionment, the cynicism, the impotence that reigned in the West. In the words of the Webbs, "What is really significant [in the Soviet Union] is the economic discovery that the substitution, for profitmaking manufacturing, of planned production for community consumption frees the nation not only from the alternation of booms and slumps, but also . . . from the hitherto incessant social malady of involuntary mass unemployment. . . . Soviet Communism has the guarantee, not only of a continuous advance of technical science, but also of the psychological discovery by the workers that the planning system eliminates the enemy party from distribution."[38] No wonder that the second edition (1937) of the Webbs' *Soviet Communism: A New Civilization?* dropped the question mark from the original title.

Like the Encyclopedists of an earlier day, the new fellow travelers of the Russian enterprise were not always completely disinterested. Authors could get their socially conscious works published in Russian translations, using the proceeds for extended Russian holidays; foreign correspondents who sent home the "right" copy found easy access to the powerful; writers and artists who had despaired of an audience at home were showered with flattering attention. At home, "proper" attitudes on Russia led to preferment and advance in many cultural enterprises fully or partly controlled by the Communist Party. Types of pressure that would have been rejected with contempt had they come from *bourgeois* institutions were accepted with good conscience if they came from those who represented the Russian camp.

Yet one should not overestimate the element of self-interest. Much more important than private advantage was the fact that most of the intellectual admirers of the Soviet Union seemed able to reach an audience not previously accessible. They felt that they could at last communicate their ideas to vast masses of men from whom they had previously been separated by class restrictions. The insistent question, For whom does one write? seemed at last to have received an adequate answer: for all progressive mankind.

In addition, Russia seemed to present to many professionals and intellectuals the image of a society in which their own roles would be fully recognized, in which they would be accorded the prestige they so sorely lacked at home. Prof. J. B. S. Haldane, then a leading British Communist, put the matter rather bluntly in *Why Professional Workers Should be Communists:* "You may ask: 'If the Communists succeed in their aims, what would be my position?' The answer is that if you are good at your job you would have more power and more responsibility than you have now. The leading commissars in the Soviet Union, who direct great socialized industries, compared to which I.C.I. [Imperial Chemical Industries] or any of the British railways are small fry, are business executives, mostly trained as engineers. The leading scientists, writers, artists, are very important people."[39]

Scientists seem at times especially likely to be out of sympathy with the apparent irrationalities and the slowness of adjustment in democratic polities. In the United States, many became fellow travelers for a time. In Britain, even more were easily lured into that version of Marxism *cum* technocracy that Prof. J. D. Bernal, a pioneer in the X-ray analysis of matter, and his friends expounded so forcibly. Dreaming of a well ordered polity in which the key decisions would be made on a scientific basis rather than in accord with the vagaries of the electoral process, they believed that the Soviet Union was the embodiment of those societies run by scientists and managers of whom Saint-Simon and Auguste Comte had dreamed in their day. Comte had believed that in the "stage of positive science" politics would become a sort of applied physics. Freedom of conscience would no longer play a progressive part because it would be absurd to oppose a scientifically managed state, just as it would be absurd to oppose a scientifically established law of nature. The British followers of Bernal, in their rationalism run amok, followed in Comte's footsteps. Democratic politics, wrote the Cambridge embryologist C. H. Waddington, was a "pulsing pusillanimous rigmarole." Communism offered science the ideal of an equalitarian world in which the scientist would no longer be restricted in his efforts. "Scientists," he wrote, "have long been used to inhabiting a world in which the final word is left to the test of experience, but such a test is inevitably incompatible with a world ordered in accordance with official status and personal prestige."[40] Professor Hyman Levy, a member of the Communist Party, went one step further, stating bluntly that social experimentation required a change in the *status quo* and that scientists should therefore attach themselves to the Communist movement. Only in that way would it be possible to achieve government by science, with society as the laboratory and mankind as the human material for experimentation.[41] These British scientists felt that men of science would become the "new masters" in a new "rational" order. There was much self-deception involved in Bernal's and his friends' imaginings that Stalin's Central Committee was a reasonable approximation of Bacon's Salomon's House, but the fact is that they believed it firmly —at least for a time.

These new masters, moreover, were not only ready to build new institutions; they were engineers of the soul prepared to fashion new men out of semibarbarous peasants. "Within the short space of sixteen years," wrote Maurice Hindus, "[the Revolution] has so 'reboiled,' or 'reforged,' the human being in Russia that he is a new personage on this earth, with a body of new aims, attitudes and responses."[42] "Is it possible for human nature to change with sufficient rapidity and depth to attain those revolutionary goals which constitute the essence of the communist program?" asked the social philosopher Edward C. Lindeman and answered with a resounding "yes."[43]

It was disorder at home, as we have already pointed out, that motivated admiration for orderly, planned Russian society. A decade earlier, most of the new admirers had been indifferent or hostile to that society, appalled at the disorder, the instability, the unpredictability of the heroic years of the Revolution. But things were different by the 1930s. "In the first place," wrote Lindeman, "there is stability in contemporary Russia and there is solidarity."[44] The Russia of the Thirties had settled down under the bureaucratic routines of Stalin's apparatus. Things were orderly there, as orderly, as rationalized, and as routinized as even the Webbs could have hoped for. Admiration for Russia could thus satisfy at the same time two apparently contradictory sentiments: rage for order and support for revolution. Stalin's bureaucrats, like the New Samurai that H. G. Wells had depicted many years earlier in his *New World for Old* (1908), seemed to their admirers an elite of technological planners, a corps of specially selected scientists, with a guiding ideology wholly devoted to making the world over. But they were not wild revolutionaries. Unhampered by encrusted prejudices, traditions, and checks and balances, which made such revolutionary endeavors impossible in the West, they were free to act. They would by force and cunning, coercion and manipulation achieve control over the wavering, the misguided, the perplexed, and the timid— and they would plan for everyone. These surgeons of politics, men beyond good and evil, would operate upon the body of Russia as it lay etherized upon the table of history. The Russian planners of the future were powerful men. That secret fascination with power that intellectuals so often harbor—and most of the time must repress at home—could blossom fully in relation to Russia. There were men of power who seemed to have pushed aside in one gigantic sweep all the cobwebs of the past.

In the West, huge industrial capacity rotted unutilized. In Russia, industry was burgeoning. Even those among the fellow-traveling intellectuals who were sometimes assailed by doubts warded them off by eulogizing industrial progress. Dnieperstroi seemed an irresistible argument. The long tradition of optimistic theories of progress in the West was finally put to use to justify Stalinism. For, if all change tended to be impelled by the logic of history in a progressive direction, those who seemed to stand for the most change would also seem the greatest progressives. They were simply fellow progressives in a hurry.[45]

The fellow travelers were, of course, aware of the absence of political freedom in Russia. But because they associated freedom in the political arena with the breakdown they had witnessed in Europe, they tended to explain away the need for "formal freedom" as unimportant compared to the "higher democracy," which they fancied they discerned in Russia. "If by the word liberalism we mean tolerance of opposition," wrote Maurice Hindus, "then there is not a vestige of it in Russia. But if we mean by it advanced ideas and practices in social accommodation, then the Russian dictatorship has outliberalized the most liberal statesmen in the world."[46]

John Strachey summed up the feelings of many: "To travel from the capitalist world into Soviet territory is to pass from death to birth."[47] Stalinism promised to satisfy the two basic needs of modern man: the economic and the spiritual. It laid claim to a world of planning and plenty, and it offered the vision of a life of community in which intellectuals would be duly honored. It organized and legitimated a break from the *status quo*. But all these elements were appealing only as long as intellectuals felt weak and impotent, unable to order their own destinies and to affect those of their fellows. The Russian myth held full sway at the peak of the sickness of Western society, but it began to recede as life in the West began again to acquire a semblance of normality. The Moscow trials and the Stalin-Hitler pact did the rest. Finally, the bulk of British and American intellectuals woke up from the Russian dream and recognized that the god had failed. But even as I write, a new crop of intellectuals, much less numerous, much less important so far than their predecessors in the Thirties, are turning, as Voltaire once did, to China. Writes the sociologist Arthur K. Davis with evident satisfaction, "Present indications suggest that the leadership of world civilization, held by Western nations during the last two or three centuries, is returning to the East—where indeed it has generally resided during most history."[48] The myth of the virtuous Mao may in time succeed the myth of the virtuous emperor.

NOTES

1. Quoted in André Lortholary, *Le mirage russe en France au xviiiè siècle* (Paris: Boivin, 1951), p. 135. I have used this book extensively throughout this chapter.

2. Alexis de Tocqueville, *L'ancien régime*, M. W. Paterson, trans. (Oxford: Basil Blackwell & Mott, Ltd., 1949), p. 172.

3. Quoted in George Weulersee, *Le mouvement physiocratique en France*, II (Paris: Alcan, 1910), 172.

4. Quoted in Adolf Reichwein, *China and Europe* (London: Routledge & Kegan Paul, Ltd., 1925), p. 92.

5. François Voltaire, *Lettres philosophiques*, Lanson, ed. (Paris: E. Cornély, 1909), lettre xi.

6. Quoted in Reichwein, *op. cit.*, p. 89.

7. *Cf.* Reichwein, *op. cit.*; Virgile Pinot, *La Chine et la formation de l'esprit philosophique en France* (Paris: Paul Geuthner, 1932); and R. Etiemble, "L'Orient philosophique au xviiiè siècle" (*Les cours de la Sorbonne*, mimeographed [Paris: Centre de Documentation Universitaire, 1958]), Part II.

8. *Cf.* Dimitri S. von Mohrenschildt, *Russia in the Intellectual Life of Eighteenth Century France* (New York: Columbia University Press, 1936), p. 74.

9. Quoted in *ibid.*, p. 142.

10. Quoted in Lortholary, *op. cit.*, p. 159.

11. Quoted in Peter Gay, *Voltaire's Politics* (Princeton: Princeton University Press, 1959), p. 182. I have found Mr. Gay's book most helpful, even though I cannot agree with some of his interpretations of Voltaire's politics.

12. *Ibid.*, p. 167.

13. Quoted in Reichwein, *op. cit.*, p. 94.

14. Voltaire, "Essai sur les moeurs," *Oeuvres*, XIII (Paris: Garnier, 1883–85), p. 162.

15. Quoted in Lortholary, *op. cit.*, p. 147.

16. Quoted in *ibid.*, p. 145.

17. Quoted in *ibid.*, p. 342.

18. *Cf.* Arnold Rowbotham, "Voltaire, Sinophile," *PMLA*, XLVII (1932), 1050–65, especially 1060.

19. Quoted in Marius Roustan, *The Pioneers of the French Revolution* (Boston: Little, Brown & Co., 1926), p. 64.

20. Quoted in Lortholary, *op. cit.*, p. 148.

21. Tocqueville, *op. cit.*, pp. 172–3.

22. Paul Hazard, *European Thought in the Eighteenth Century* (New Haven: Yale University Press, 1954), p. 328.

23. *Ibid.*, p. 334.

24. Suzanne Labin, "Advanced Intellectuals and Backward Countries," *Dissent*, VI (Summer, 1959), No. 3, 240.

25. Quoted in Margaret Cole, *Beatrice Webb* (New York: Longmans, Green & Co., Inc., 1945), p. 166.

26. *Cf.* Neal Wood, *Communism and British Intellectuals* (New York: Columbia University Press, 1959), especially p. 41. I have used this excellent volume throughout my discussion of British intellectuals and am much indebted to it.

27. Stephen Spender relates this declaration in his contribution to Richard Crossman, ed., *The God That Failed* (New York: Bantam Books, Inc., 1952), p. 246.

28. *Cf.* Wood, "Utopians of Science," *op. cit.*

29. *Cf.* Irving Howe and Lewis Coser, *The American Communist Party* (Boston: Beacon Press, 1957), especially Chapter VII.

30. Quoted in Granville Hicks, "Communism and the American Intellectuals," Irving DeWitt Talmadge, ed., *Whose Revolution* (New York: Howell, Soskin, 1941), p. 82.

31. Quoted in Malcolm Cowley, "Faith and the Future," *ibid.*, p. 145.

32. C. Day Lewis, "A Time to Dance," *A Time to Dance and Other Poems* (London: Hogarth Press, 1935), p. 62.

33. From W. H. Auden, *Poems* (London: Faber & Faber, Ltd., 1933), p. 73.

34. From Spender, *Collected Poems* (London: Faber & Faber, Ltd., 1933), p. 29.

35. Quoted in Adolf Sturmthal, *The Tragedy of European Labor* (New York: Columbia University Press, 1943), p. 126.

36. Quoted in Frederick Lewis Allen, *Only Yesterday* (New York: Bantam Books, Inc., 1946), p. 378.

37. Louis Fischer has given a good description of these pilgrims in *Men and Politics* (New York: Duell, Sloan & Pearce, Inc., 1941), pp. 189–201.

38. Sidney and Beatrice Webb, *Soviet Communism: A New Civilization* (3rd ed.; New York: Longmans, Green & Co., Inc., 1944), p. 972.

39. Cited in Wood, *Communism and British Intellectuals*, pp. 150–1.

40. *Ibid.*, p. 132.

41. *Ibid.*, p. 127.

42. Maurice Hindus, *The Great Offensive* (New York: Harrison Smith, 1933), p. vii.

43. Quoted in Eugene Lyons, *The Red Decade* (New York and Indianapolis: The Bobbs-Merrill Company, Inc., 1941), p. 106.

44. *Ibid.*

45. A few sentences in the preceding and following paragraphs have been adapted from Howe and Coser, *op. cit.*, Chapter XI.

46. Hindus, *op. cit.*, p. viii.

47. John Strachey, *The Coming Struggle for Power* (Modern Library ed.; New York: Random House, Inc., 1935), p. 360.

48. Arthur K. Davis, "Sociology without Clothes," *Monthly Review* (November, 1959), p. 262.

Part Three

The Intellectual in
Contemporary
America

Chapter 18

INTRODUCTION

D**ISPASSIONATE ANALYSIS OF THE ROLE AND POSITION** of intellectuals in contemporary America is hampered by major obstacles. The problem is especially difficult for those, like this writer, who have commitments predisposing them to take sides in the heated controversies over this topic among intellectuals and the public at large. Yet a writer dealing with the role of intellectuals would clearly shirk one of his major tasks were he to eschew discussing contemporary problems under the pretext that "not all the facts are in" or that personal involvement precludes the possibility of balanced assessment. No doubt only future historians, writing with the benefit of hindsight, will be able to evaluate fully trends in our culture that can be only dimly perceived by those actively involved in it. Yet the sociologist would be untrue to his calling were he not to attempt to delineate, to the limits of his ability and with the highest possible degree of objectivity, the main role and position of the intellectual in his own time and society. It is indeed easier to study social roles and status positions ranked lower than one's own, which is one reason why sociologists have typically been drawn to the study of prostitutes and hoboes, mental patients and juvenile delinquents. To turn the spotlight upon roles and people whose ranks are more nearly equal to one's own is a much more complicated and demanding task, making more stringent de-

247

mands on one's ability to remain detached and objective. To study congeries of roles that one plays oneself is, finally, the most exacting and difficult. Nevertheless, it cannot be avoided if the sociologist is to live up to the ancient injunction to "know thyself."

Much controversy regarding the current position of American intellectuals has been unnecessarily confused for lack of agreement about the denotations of the very term "intellectual." When, for example, Seymour M. Lipset argues that, in effect, intellectuals "never had it so good" as in contemporary America,[1] while C. Wright Mills asserts that "American intellectuals are suffering the tremors of men who face overwhelming defeat,"[2] their differing diagnoses are partially explainable by the fact that they have simply not been attending the same patient. Lipset refers to the very large stratum of "those who create, distribute, and apply culture," while Mills clearly had in mind a more restricted category of "creative" men of knowledge. Similarly, when Richard Hofstadter[3] gives a guardedly optimistic answer to H. Stuart Hughes's anguished question, "Is the intellectual obsolete?"[4] one senses again that the two men are not fully agreed on the object of their concerns. Hughes is preoccupied with "the freely speculating mind" in America, while Hofstadter is disposed to include among his "intellectuals" many experts who, according to Hughes, are "mental technicians."

While disagreement about the very connotations and denotations of the term "intellectual" has often led to widely differing assessments, it is not, of course, the only cause of difficulty. It would be naïve to believe, as do certain semanticists, that, once terms have been properly defined and clarified and channels of communication cleared of unnecessary and distracting "noise," all differences among observers can be eliminated. The values and the material and ideal interests of the analyst color his perceptions, and intellectual perspectives have a way of directing as well as of deflecting observers in their assessments of relevant data. Men like C. Wright Mills,[5] guided by apocalyptic visions of the imminent collapse of American culture, are likely to focus on certain dismal aspects of American intellectual life to the exclusion of more hopeful indicators, while writers like Edward Shils,[6] committed to a determinedly sanguine vision of the prospects of American culture, are likely to neglect the more disturbing factors. I myself cannot claim to have attained an Olympian vantage point from which to survey the mundane scene *sine ira et studio*. Yet, in the pages that follow, I shall attempt to delineate the contemporary situation of the American intellectual with as much critical detachment and objectivity as I am able. I am aware that not to take positions on certain issues is in itself a way of taking positions. Although I do not strive for a kind of disembodied neutral view, I do attempt not to slight those "inconvenient" facts that may fail to fit my own scheme of values.

INTELLECTUAL TYPES AND INSTITUTIONAL SETTINGS

It stands to reason that, in a society as highly differentiated and complex as contemporary America, intellectuals are located in a great variety of institutional settings as well as in the interstices between a number of institutional orders. To cover all these locations is plainly impossible here. I have chosen instead to deal only with a certain limited number of such locations and settings, which I believe are the most important and representative, but I am also fully prepared to grant that others might reveal different facets of the role and function of contemporary American intellectuals.

In earlier periods, unattached intellectuals, with whom I shall deal in Chapter 20, made up the bulk of all intellectuals. In an age dominated by large-scale organizations, their specific weight has declined markedly. Yet even today their importance looms large in assessments of the future of the intellectual vocation. Academic intellectuals, with whom I shall deal in Chapter 21, are numerically and strategically the most important group among contemporary intellectuals, so that a fairly extended discussion of the academy as a setting seems in order. Scientific intellectuals, although many of them operate within the academic community, are often located outside it, and a separate chapter is therefore devoted to a discussion of this category. Two subsequent chapters discuss the status and role of intellectuals in the bureaucratic settings of the mass-culture industries and of public administration. These settings, especially the second, have recently attracted considerable numbers of intellectuals, and it seems mandatory to inquire into how far they are conducive to the enhancement or, alternatively, the inhibition of the intellectual's tasks and vocation.

Finally, a chapter is devoted to examination of an institution that impinges with peculiar force on contemporary intellectual activities: the foundations.

Before the specific discussion of institutional settings is undertaken it is useful to confront the major assessments of the general cultural scene now current in America. The next chapter undertakes this task.

NOTES

1. See Seymour M. Lipset, "American Intellectuals: Their Politics and Status," *Political Man* (New York: Doubleday & Company, Inc., 1960).

2. C. Wright Mills, *Power, Politics and People* (New York: Ballantine Books, Inc., 1962), p. 292.

3. Richard Hofstadter, *Anti-Intellectualism in American Life* (New York: Alfred A. Knopf, Inc., 1963).

4. H. Stuart Hughes, "Is the Intellectual Obsolete?" *Commentary* (October, 1956).

5. Mills, *op. cit.*

6. See Edward Shils, "Mass Society and Its Culture," *Daedalus*, 89 (Spring, 1960), 2.

Chapter 19

THE SCENE AND PROSPECT
BEFORE US: TWO
CONTRASTING PERSPECTIVES

SOCIOLOGICAL OBSERVERS, AMONG OTHERS, HAVE COME forward in recent years with sharply conflicting views of the American cultural scene. They have painted pictures of the present condition and future prospects of cultural life in America so widely divergent in assessment and prognosis that they seem hardly to share any common criteria. Intellectual confrontation, however, becomes possible only when there is at least a shared framework of assumptions. If it is absent, the dialogue, as Albert Camus used to say, is impossible.

Whether or not there are really no common grounds between the antagonistic interpretations of American culture may be a matter for debate, but it is undeniable that the divergencies are major. Under these conditions, taking sides on the level of generality at which the debate is usually carried on can serve no purpose. Instead, I shall briefly summarize these clashing views and then analyze in some detail the current role and position of American intellectuals in a series of concrete institutional settings. Such particularized study may allow us ultimately to confront again the more generalized pronouncements. It is not to be expected that, even after more detailed study, these contradictory assessments can be reconciled. It is much more likely indeed that they reflect contradictory tendencies embedded in the very reality they purport to describe.

At any rate, evaluation of the evidence may at least help to dispel some current ambiguities of appraisal. As to the real ambiguities that will still remain, they will have to be suffered. After all, tolerance of ambiguity has always been a distinguishing mark of the educated man.

AMERICA AS A BUREAUCRATIZED MASS SOCIETY: THE OBSOLESCENCE OF THE INTELLECTUAL

Modern industrial societies, and American society in particular, are characterized by a comprehensive bureaucratization of social and cultural life. Not only their technological apparatus but their cultural apparatus as well is highly complex and integrated and confronts the individual as an alien and oppressive power. A corollary of increasing industrialization and rationalization is the fact that the ratio of organized activities to unorganized, spontaneous ones increases and that the individual is deprived of autonomy.

Cultural activities that are relatively uncontrolled in earlier stages tend to become highly organized, directed, and consciously fostered in fully developed industrial societies. Much cultural productivity that may once have been a matter of handicrafts, so to speak, becomes rationalized so that the production of ideas resembles in major respects the production of other commodities.

Some elements of this trend were clearly discerned by social analysts of the nineteenth century, although they had not yet confronted the fully developed bureaucratized industrial society of today. In particular, the Marxist notion of alienation permits us to discern the lineaments of the cultural situation we face in the modern world. Marx highlighted the effects of a social process in which the creations of man have become an alien power that dominates their creator. Before Marx, such German idealists as Schiller and Hegel had already focused attention on the dehumanizing consequences of the division of labor in modern society. "Eternally bound to a small fragment of the totality," Schiller wrote, "man himself develops only a fragmentary existence . . . he never develops the harmony of his being . . . and becomes a mere replica of his business or of his science."¹ Marx broadened the indictment and located the causes of modern alienation in the capitalist mode of production: "In what does this alienation of labor consist? First,

that the work is *external* to the worker, that it i[s not a part of his]
nature, that consequently he does not fulfill hi[mself in his work]
but denies himself, has a feeling of misery, not [of well-being, does]
not develop freely a physical and mental energy [but is physically]
exhausted and mentally debased. The worker the[refore feels himself]
at home only during his leisure, whereas at wor[k he feels homeless.]
. . . The alienated character of work for the worker appears in the
fact that it is not his work but work for someone else, that in work
he does not belong to himself but to another person."[2] Marx's
major criticism of capitalism was aimed not at injustice in the distribution of wealth, but rather, as Erich Fromm has noted, "it is
the perversion of labor into forced, alienated, meaningless labor,
hence the transformation of man into a 'crippled monstrosity.'"[3]
Marx's analysis centered on the condition of the manual worker in
capitalist society, but he saw the worker's alienation as the proto-
typical condition confronting all participants in industrial capitalism,
whether they be workers or intellectuals.

Max Weber's analysis of industrial society, although starting
from very different ideological and political premises, confirmed
Marx's central view by deliberately extending it from the world
of the worker to that of all men involved in bureaucratized society.
Weber showed that the wage worker's "separation" from the means
of production was only a special case of a more general trend; in
highly developed industrial societies, he claimed, scientists are
equally "separated" from the means of research and inquiry and
public officials from the means of administration.[4] To Weber, the
progressive rationalization of human activities, whether in the cultural, the administrative, or the technological sphere, involved a
regimentation of life and thought that, while making for previously
unreachable technological progress and the highly efficient pursuit
of productive goals, also threatened a "parcelling of souls" that
would dry up the springs of individual creativity.[5]

Georg Simmel, Weber's contemporary and friend, based his
critique of modern cultural trends on similar anxiety about the fate
of autonomy in an increasingly "objectified" cultural process. The
"objectivization of cultural contents," he wrote, "is brought about
by specialization and creates an ever increasing estrangement between the subject and his products."[6] "Cultural objects crystallize
increasingly into an interconnected world which has fewer and
fewer contacts with the subjective soul and its willing and feeling."[7]

Some twenty years later, Karl Mannheim echoed Weber's and

...mel's anguished concerns. "Increasing industrialization . . . implies functional rationality, i.e., the organization of the activities of
the members of society with reference to objective ends. It does
not to the same extent promote 'substantial rationality,' i.e., the
capacity to act intelligently in a given situation on the basis of one's
own insight into the interrelations of events . . . The average person
surrenders part of his own cultural identity with every new act of
integration into a functionally rationalized complex of activities."[8]

Still nearer to our own days, C. Wright Mills reaffirmed the
prognoses and the fears of his intellectual forebears: "The means
of effective communication are being expropriated from the intellectual worker. The material basis of his initiative and intellectual
freedom is no longer in his hands. Some intellectuals feel these processes in their work. They know more than they say and they are
powerless and afraid."[9] "Between the intellectual and his potential
public stand technical, economic, and social structures which are
owned and operated by others . . . The craftsmanship which is
central to all intellectual and artistic gratification is thwarted for an
increasing number of intellectual workers."[10]

Similar assessments, whether based on the notion of alienation
derived from Marx or on Weberian and post-Weberian analyses of
the trend toward bureaucratization, have become the common coin
of much intellectual discourse in our time. Furthermore, they have
been powerfully reinforced by thinking from the separate, though
related, literary and humanistic critiques of modern industrial society. This tradition, as Raymond Williams has shown in his *Culture
and Society*,[11] goes back to the romantics, to the critics of Utilitarianism, from Coleridge and Carlyle to Matthew Arnold, Ruskin,
and Morris. In more recent times, it has been a common element
in the otherwise divergent orientations of T. S. Eliot, D. H. Lawrence, R. H. Tawney, F. R. Leavis, and George Orwell. All of them
have attacked in one way or another the dehumanizing and stultifying effects of modern industrial society, the decline of standards of
excellence and meaning in the wasteland of modern culture. To all
of them, industrialization and the mass society that grew in its wake
have led to the destruction of common sensibilities once rooted in
a shared community of culture. *Gesellschaft*, to use the German
idiom of analysis, has destroyed *Gemeinschaft*, and the immense,
objectified cultural process now stands, like an overpowering monster, over individuals deprived of communal protection, isolated,

unable to find anchorage in tradition or community, overwhelmed
by processes that they can no longer influence or control.

Certain writers in this tradition—we think of T. S. Eliot, or Or-
tega y Gasset—espouse an elitist approach to the problem and claim
that mass society has come about through the decay of elites that,
in previous ages, held special responsibilities for maintaining cultural
standards. Others, like Erich Fromm or C. Wright Mills, are democrats or socialists who argue from the precisely opposite point of
view that mass societies dissolve those proximate units that cushion
and envelop the individual and therefore make meaningful participation in public affairs possible.[12] But no matter what the political
or ideological stances of these critics, no matter what traditions
they draw upon, they are united in deeply pessimistic diagnoses
of the possibilities for creative achievement in mass society. By de-
stroying articulated groupings, mass society, according to their
indictments, has made it impossible for elites to maintain standards;
it has eroded the public at large and communal audiences as well.
The weakening of traditional bonds, the growth of rationalization,
and the highly developed division of labor have created societies in
which individuals are only loosely bound to one another by increasingly attenuated and fragile ties. In mass society, the individual
becomes a faceless cipher, and those who hold the levers of control
increasingly resemble the totalitarian masters so frighteningly depicted in the anti-utopias of Zamiatin, Aldous Huxley, and Orwell.

If the trends described by these analysts should represent the
main drift of modern history, it would follow that the institutional
setting that permitted the development of the intellectual vocation
in the last 200 or 300 years is about to disappear or is, at least,
seriously weakened. The increasing bureaucratic integration of society and its progressive closure, as well as the parallel development
of mass culture, would then drive the intellectual from the position
he has occupied in the modern Western world. Even if totalitarian
developments could be avoided, the intellectuals would at best be
able to operate only within the interstices of society, leading more
or less tolerated marginal existences, while the center of the stage
would be occupied by mental technicians, specialized brain workers,
and experts of various kinds. Production engineers and engineers
of the soul would then be in high demand, but in such a "brave
new world" intellectuals would indeed be obsolete. Surviving speci-
mens, finding no resonance among an appreciative audience would

be, at best, quaint survivors of earlier stages of civilization. In Weber's "cage of the future," in the disenchanted ice age of managerially dominated mass societies, autonomy, creativity, and substantial rationality would be regarded as potential disturbers of peace of mind. Much like hunchbacks today, surviving intellectuals would meet a mixture of pity and awe on the part of the settled denizens of the world. Such a society would truly resemble the nightmare that Irving Howe recently evoked as *one* possibility for the development of the modern world: "We are moving toward a quiet desert of moderation where men will forget the passion of moral and spiritual restlessness that has characterized Western society . . . The human creature, no longer a Quixote or a Faust, will become a docile attendant to an automated civilization . . . The 'aura of the human' will be replaced by the nihilism of satiety. . . . High culture as we understand it will become increasingly problematic and perhaps reach some point of obsolescence."[13]

AMERICA AS A PLURALISTIC SOCIETY: SANGUINE PROSPECTS FOR SUPERIOR CULTURE

Significant numbers of sociologists have rejected the diagnosis of the critics of mass culture and bureaucratized society. Among them, Talcott Parsons, Edward Shils, Daniel Bell, and some of their students are perhaps the most prominent. To these men, the position of the Cassandras reeks of intolerable romanticism. Rather than confronting the challenge and promise of the present, such critics, it is claimed, retreat into a nostalgic vision of a supposedly less complicated past. They pass off as analysis of current trends what is in fact ideology. There are indeed many strains and tensions in the current social and cultural situation, but the diagnosis offered by the critics, far from correctly identifying these strains, is but an ideological defense mechanism for certain intellectuals torn from their accustomed moorings.[14]

Among the most important characteristics of industrial societies are increasing social complexity and resulting structural differentiation. This development "can result in (and, for American society *has* resulted in) greater mobilization of resources, increased capacity to pursue whatever goals are deemed desirable, and greater freedom

& you're lucky.

of choice for more individuals."[15] Those who claim that modern men suffer from the effects of alienation, those who dream of the restoration of community ties may think of themselves as "progressives," but they adhere in fact to a basically regressive view. They want to return to less differentiated social structures.

In less complex societies, men necessarily play less segregated roles. In primitive societies, for example, priestly duties, magical performances, artistic creation, technical expertise, and so forth, are still so undifferentiated that they may form part of the expected performance of the same role incumbent. In later stages of evolution, these roles are gradually differentiated and compose the separate duties of particular specialists, whose roles do not overlap. Priests are no longer expected also to be artistic performers, and artists no longer have priestly functions. Similarly, it becomes apparent that, in comparison with earlier stages of Western history, continued differentiations in task performance and role allocations have taken place. Whereas, in Newton's time, it was still possible for particular individuals to be proficient in all the sciences, his kind of generalized knowledge has become impossible in our own day. Science has now become so complex an enterprise that scientific roles have of necessity become highly specialized. A chemist may have only a rudimentary knowledge of nuclear physics, and a biologist may have only nodding acquaintance with the current state of the social sciences. Even within particular scientific disciplines, there is such accumulation of specialized knowledge that it can no longer be mastered by single individuals. Even more differentiated roles have thus grown up within scientific disciplines. Organic chemists may know little about the frontiers of knowledge in inorganic chemistry, and demographers may be almost totally ignorant of current work in social psychology.

The processes of differentiation of structure and specialization of function in modern industrial society have, naturally, brought in their wake considerable strains and tensions. In particular, when men accustomed to playing relatively undifferentiated roles have been threatened by the emergence of more specialized practitioners in fields they once dominated, they have reacted with resentment and generalized feelings of malice and frustration. In medicine, general practitioners resent the fact that more and more medical tasks are being performed by specialists. In similar ways, generalizing intellectuals react with anger to the fact that sectors of cultural activity that they dominated in the past are being increasingly pre-empted by specialized experts. This displacement explains at least in part their nostalgia for a simpler past.

The disgruntled critics of modern society focus their attention upon the loss of the individual's communal embeddedness and complain about conformity in mass society. This focus leads them to bypass the major gains for societies—and for individuals as well—that increasing differentiation has brought about; they do not acknowledge that there can now be greater freedom of choice for more individuals, that more individuals than ever before can pursue goals they consider desirable. Even if it is true that no individual can encompass any longer the great variety of intellectual tasks once performed by a Voltaire, for example, or a Newton or a Diderot, it is also true that in our age an incomparably greater proportion of the population has a choice of occupations that permit the development of mental capacities to the fullest. Far from leading to leveling, modern trends have in fact led to the proliferation of differentiated tasks. Furthermore, the very division of labor about which the critics complain has made possible a mobilization of resources and therefore an economic abundance that enable all men to attain comforts hitherto reserved for the elite few. Finally, by reducing work loads, technical civilization has increased in revolutionary ways the leisure time available to all. The bulk of mankind in highly developed societies is no longer forced to spend its life in backbreaking and uncongenial labor; the hours devoted to work have been drastically reduced, and the increasing range of career choices available enables men to work in areas truly in tune with their personal desires. All such change is laying the groundwork for a future flowering of cultural life, that is, for a wide expansion of the horizon of cultural creation.

Dire predictions about conformity and uniformity to the contrary, we have witnessed in recent years a qualitative upgrading, as well as a wider spread, of cultural offerings. "The rising levels of education," writes Daniel Bell, "have meant a rising appreciation of culture. In the United States, more dollars are spent on concerts of classical music than on baseball. Sales of books have doubled in a decade. There are over a thousand symphony orchestras, and several hundred museums, institutes, and colleges are purchasing art in the United States today . . . And in coming years, with steadily increasing productivity and leisure, the United States will become an even more active consumer of culture."[16] "With rising educational levels, more people are able to indulge a wide variety of interests. ('Twenty years ago you couldn't sell Beethoven out of New York,' reports a record salesman. 'Today we sell Palestrina, Monteverdi, Gabrielli, and Renaissance and Baroque music in large quantities.')"[17]

The assertion that ours is an "atomized" society rests on foundations as shaky as those of the conformity thesis. "It is asserted," writes Daniel Bell, "that the United States is an 'atomized' society composed of lonely, isolated individuals. One forgets the truism . . . that Americans are a nation of joiners. In no country in the world, probably, is there such a high degree of voluntary communal activity, expressed sometimes in absurd rituals, yet often providing real satisfactions for real needs."[18] Talcott Parsons and Winston White echo Bell: "Most fundamental of the fallacies underlying the biases of the mass culture theorists seems to us to be the assumption that this is an 'atomized' mass society where the relations of one individual to another have become increasingly amorphous. Quite the contrary . . . American society is one of the preeminent examples of a *pluralist* society in which—through the course of structural differentiation—an increasingly ramified network of criss-crossing solidarities has been developing."[19] Men are no longer enveloped by restricting communal institutions that claim all their loyalties in return for protection and security, but instead a huge number of fragmented and differentiated groupings now allow the individual to pursue his aims, make his choices, and allocate his loyalties and allegiances. There may be strains and conflicts in such pluralistic societies; individual life may be more complicated now than when men pursued their careers within the predictable routines prescribed by uniform communal associations. But the varieties of choices, of pathways, of challenges in associational and pluralistic society allow men to live more variegated and more stimulating lives. "This new order of society," writes Edward Shils,* "despite all its internal conflicts, discloses in the individual a greater sense of attachment to the society as a whole, and of affinity with his fellows. As a result,

* The following quotations from Edward Shils are reprinted from his "Mass Society and Its Culture," which appeared in *Daedalus*, Journal of the American Academy of Arts and Sciences, 89 (Spring, 1960), 2; and in *Culture for the Millions?* edited by Norman Jacobs, Copyright 1961, D. Van Nostrand Company, Inc., Princeton, N. J.

perhaps for the first time in history, large aggregations of human beings living over an extensive territory have been able to enter into relatively free and uncoerced associations."[20]

It is not true that mass society has dehumanized man and robbed him of autonomy. On the contrary, "it has aroused and enhanced individuality. Individuality is characterized by an openness to experience, an efflorescence of sensation and sensibility; a sensitivity to other minds and personalities. It gives rise to, and lives in, personal attachments; it grows from the expansion of the emphatic capacities of the human being. Mass society has liberated the cognitive, appreciative, and moral capacities of individuals."[21]

The decline in generalized roles and the increase of specialized activities associated with differentiation of societal functions do not necessarily destroy opportunities for a creative intelligentsia. Rather, the intelligentsia, which was once a small and fairly homogeneous stratum, is itself differentiated. We now have, according to Edward Shils,[22] a high intelligentsia, a mediocre intelligentsia, and a brutal intelligentsia. A wall now separates the producers of brutal culture from the producers of superior culture, and their audiences are, in the main, separated from each other. The professional producer of mediocre culture, on the other hand, although he has developed traditions, standards, and models of his own, remains exposed to the standards of superior culture and cannot entirely escape their pressure. The practitioner of mediocre culture suffers from a "troubling juxtaposition of two consciences," which provides "an increasing stimulus to an awareness of and a concern for high standards, even when they are not observed." The high intelligentsia, finally, far from atrophying in modern society, is now far broader than it ever was before. "There is today more internal specialization than in the past: it is impossible for any one man to be fully conversant with the inherited and currently produced stock of cultural objects. The productive intelligentsia is perhaps less intensely like-minded now than in the past, when it was smaller and the body of what it had to master was smaller. Nonetheless, despite changes in society, in the modes of financial support and in the organization of intellectual life, this creative stratum is constantly reproducing and increasing."

If the critics of mass society are right, we should expect a decline in science and scholarship, in artistic production and general cultural creativity. But there is no conclusive evidence that this decline has occurred. "In every field of science and scholarship into which so much of our contemporary genius flows . . . outstanding work is being done, not only in the older centers not yet afflicted by the culture of mass society, but in the United States as well, that most massive of all mass societies." In other fields as well, be it in the novel, in painting, or in political philosophy, the level of contemporary achievement is high, and there is no evidence of a general decline in the quality of the products of superior culture in our own time. In one sense, superior culture always has been in danger. "Since it never is and never has been the culture of an entire society, it must necessarily be in a state of tension vis-à-vis the rest of society. If the producers and consumers of superior culture see further and deeper than their contemporaries, if they have a more subtle and more lively sensitivity, if they do not accept the received traditions and the acknowledged deities of their fellow country-men, whatever they say or believe or discover is bound to create tensions." If intellectuals avail themselves of the new possibilities that mass society offers to them, while turning to their own creative uses the very tensions that will inevitably continue to beset them, "the prospects for superior culture seem to be reasonably good."

NOTES

1. Friedrich Schiller, "Ueber die Aesthetische Erziehung des Menschen," *Philosophische Schriften* (Leipzig: Inselverlag, n.d.), 6. Brief, pp. 385–6.

2. Quoted in Karl Marx, *Selected Writings in Sociology and Social Philosophy*, T. B. Bottomore and Maximilian Rubel, eds. (London: C. A. Watts & Co., Ltd., 1956), pp. 169–70.

3. Erich Fromm, *Marx's Concept of Man* (New York: Frederick Ungar Publishing Co., Inc., 1962), p. 42.

4. H. H. Gerth and C. W. Mills, trans. and eds., *From Max Weber* (New York: Oxford University Press, Inc., 1947), *passim*, especially p. 50.

5. See Max Weber, "Some Consequences of Bureaucratization," Lewis A. Coser and Bernard Rosenberg, eds., *Sociological Theory* (New York: The Macmillan Company, 1957), pp. 442–3.

6. Georg Simmel, *Philosophie des Geldes* (Leipzig: Duncker and Humblot, 1900), p. 491.

7. *Ibid.*, p. 492.

8. Karl Mannheim, *Man and Society in an Age of Reconstruction* (London: Routledge & Kegan Paul, Ltd., 1940), pp. 58–9.

9. C. Wright Mills, *Power, Politics and People* (New York: Ballantine Books, Inc., 1962), p. 297.

10. *Ibid.*, p. 296.

...ond Williams, *Culture and Society* (New York: Columbia ...ess, 1958).

...illiam Kornhauser, *The Politics of Mass Society* (New ...ee Press, 1959), especially pp. 21–38. *Cf.* also the special ...ca, Mass Society and Mass Media," of *The Journal of Social Issues*, XVI, No. 3, which contains a long paper by Raymond and Alice Bauer and critical comments by Talcott Parsons and Winston White and by Lewis A. Coser.

13. Irving Howe, "Mass Society and Post-Modern Fiction," *A World More Attractive* (New York: Horizon Press, Inc., 1963), p. 97.

14. Winston White, *Beyond Conformity* (New York: The Free Press, 1961), p. 168. White has been a disciple of Talcott Parsons, and they share common views. See also the essay by Parsons and White in *The Journal of Social Issues*, XVI, No. 3; and their contribution to Seymour M. Lipset and L. Lowenthal, *Culture and Social Character* (New York: The Free Press, 1961), pp. 89–135.

15. White, *Beyond Conformity*, p. 211.

16. Daniel Bell, *The End of Ideology* (New York: The Free Press, 1960), p. 32.

17. *Ibid.*, p. 33.

18. *Ibid.*, p. 31.

19. *The Journal of Social Issues*, XVI, No. 3.

20. Edward Shils, "Mass Society and Its Culture," *Daedalus*, 89 (Spring, 1960) 2.

21. *Ibid.*

22. *Ibid.* All the quotes that follow are from this essay.

Chapter 20

UNATTACHED INTELLECTUALS

ONE OF THE MOST IMPORTANT OBSERVATIONS THAT
can be made about unattached intellectuals in contemporary America is that there are so very few of them. Although over the last
two centuries unattached intellectuals have constituted the core of
the intelligentsia in the Western world, they have shrunk in this
country to a relatively small—though still qualitatively important—
group. There were about 28,000 people who defined themselves as
professional authors for the 1960 Census, but many, perhaps the
majority, held salaried positions in various organizations, so that only
a fraction may be considered truly independent. In addition, of
course, not all professional authors can be called "intellectuals." On
the other hand, there are, conceivably, independent intellectuals who
are not writers. Even if we add their number to that of the professional writer-intellectuals, we are not likely to arrive at more than
a few thousand in the whole United States. Numbers, however,
hardly tell the full story. The relative decline of unattached intellectuals over the last thirty or forty years must be explained by
both structural and ideological factors. It is part of the growing
institutionalization and, more particularly, academization of intellect
in America, and it is also a result of the decline of the *avant-garde*
and of radical ideology in American culture.

As long as the *avant-garde* was in sharp conflict with the surrounding genteel culture, it developed its own peculiar group norms and standards, and it supported a "tradition of the new" that distinguished its adherents from those outside. In its battle against a hostile majority culture, the *avant-garde* developed an intensely polemical relation to those who upheld majority values. Not only in their intellectual productions but also in their personal life styles, members of the *avant-garde* did shut themselves off as far as possible from contamination by genteel culture and accentuated their social distance from its bearers. The Village Bohemians before World War I, the expatriates or would-be expatriates of the Twenties, the "socially conscious" writers of the Thirties, though they adhered to different artistic orientations and had differing moral concerns, all shared a sense of belonging to a world different from, and in opposition to, the world in which the great majority of their countrymen lived everyday lives. They managed, in one way or another, a kind of inner emigration. They shunned affiliation with the "establishment" of America, nor would they have been acceptable to it. To be sure, many of the *avant-garde* might from time to time work in publishing houses or on magazines or might even teach in universities, yet they generally attempted to avoid such involvements and valued their independence from institutional pressures. Even though they might make compromises with the surrounding society, their self-image was that of unattached men of letters, independent soldiers in the battle for "modernism."

By the Fifties and Sixties the battle for modernism had been won. And, as with every successful innovating movement, this one has been incorporated and assimilated into the common culture. "The insurgent movement in this country which defended 'modernism'—that is, the esthetic experimentalism and social protest of the period between 1912 and 1950," writes Richard Chase, "has expired of its own success."[1] As a result, there has occurred what Isaac Rosenfeld once called "a shrinkage of extremes."[2] The modernist writer, who once stood at a considerable remove from society, has moved nearer to the center. The correlate of this decreased distance between the modern writer and the surrounding society is the institutionalization of modernism and the absorption of its main exponents by universities and other cultural establishments.

What has happened to modernism in the arts has also happened to radicalism in the ideological realm. It was once true that, as Joseph Schumpeter wrote, "capitalism inevitably . . . creates, educates, subsidizes a vested interest in social unrest."[3] This generalization is valid for the past history of capitalism, even for most capitalist countries of Europe today, but it holds up less well in contemporary America. We need not subscribe to the extreme claims for the "end of ideology" that have recently been made by such writers as Raymond Aron, Daniel Bell, Seymour Lipset, and Edward Shils in order to recognize that, in contemporary America, though not in the rest of the world, critical left-wing ideologies have lost much of their appeal among intellectuals. This book is not the place to investigate this phenomenon in any detail. It might suffice to note that the disillusionment of left-wing intellectuals with the Russian gods; the prosperity of American society; its apparent ability to hobble along on a pragmatic mixture of free enterprise, government intervention, and defense spending; the whole climate of the Cold War, with its polarization of the world into two camps—all have played their parts.[4] In any case, radicalism and socialism as ideologies have markedly declined in contemporary America, and most intellectuals who once subscribed to or sympathized with these movements have by now found havens in one or another position on that wide spectrum that in America is called "liberalism."

Although the loss of the radical impulse readily explains why many ex-radicals became eager to leave their isolation on the margin of American cultural life, it still does not explain why the main institutions of official culture were willing to welcome them and to make them comfortable. Here we must take into account the structural changes that have occurred on the American scene over the last few decades. In a fairly short span of time, the United States has moved from a self-absorbed and inward-looking posture to a dominant position on the world scene. Although foreign affairs could be conducted in a more or less parochial, unco-ordinated, and leisurely manner in earlier periods, the world position that the United States has now assumed requires co-ordination of effort, planning, and the deliberate implementation of predetermined policy. Similarly, on the domestic scene, the move from unfettered free enterprise to a mixed economy in which key decisions must be co-ordinated and implemented by the federal government has lent planning a new urgency. The mobilization of economic resources is no longer left to the free play of the market; the last few decades have seen the emergence of a variety of co-ordinating agencies, both public and private, which have attempted to plan the growth and expansion of the national economy. The husbanding of human resources, moreover, has been accompanied by deliberate social-welfare and social-security policies at the federal, as well as on lower governmental, level. In turn, all these requirements for planning, coupled with the more highly developed technological stage reached by modern industrial society, have led to the upgrading of many technical skills and to demand for persons with the sophistication necessary to operate the intricate and complicated machinery of bureaucratic administration, both private and public. The rewards for intellectual performance have therefore increased drastically, both directly because positions are constantly being created for "manipulators of symbols," and indirectly because the training of new generations of such "symbol manipulators" has provided the opportunity to increase teaching staffs at colleges and universities. Educational institutions have had to assume a crucial role in training the sophisticated manpower now required. Universities can therefore no longer limit themselves to the education of an elite of gentlemen and scholars. These factors help to explain why intellectuals are now eagerly sought by the powers that be.

Many old-style radicals who, in an earlier period, maintained wide social distance between themselves and the *bourgeoisie*, marking themselves off from the main currents of American thought and from the main institutions that embodied it, have now moved into the mainstream. They have done so, not only because they themselves have lost the radical impulse, but also because they have been welcomed by those who operate major institutions. In fact, the very tendency to large-scale generalization, the capacity, as it were, to stand back from immediate day-to-day experience and to take a wider view, which had been fostered in an environment of the radical sects and grouplets, makes intellectuals very valuable to a more sophisticated establishment in desperate need of men with the wider vision to meet the research, planning and co-ordinating requirements of modern America. The very broadness of concerns that went together with allegiance to innovating movements can be used, and the ex-radical's or radical's knowledgeability can be divorced from its iconoclastic origin and intent. To be sure, most of these men— except in the academy—have to become experts, for they are not being offered a chance to continue their free-wheeling intellectualism. But if they are willing to accept this change in roles, they are welcomed. No one has as yet written about the contribution of ex-radicals to American social and cultural life, but I suspect that it will on balance appear at least as important as the contribution of the external migration of European refugees. In any case, the decline of modernism and radicalism and the eagerness of decision-makers within the establishment to utilize the contributions of formerly unattached intellectuals have led to the absorption of large parts of an earlier *avant-garde* into the major institutions of American society. Countercultures have been integrated into the common culture.

While ex-members of the literary or radical vanguard have moved into a great variety of institutionalized positions, both public and private, the major intellectual movement has clearly been into the academy. Previously, to become a member of the academy one needed qualifications unrelated either to modernism or to radicalism. Today, a broad and innovating orientation in the arts or social sciences is believed to contribute to educating men with a "flexible outlook" and a variety of "human relations skills." A literary critic who used to look at literature from the vantage point of radicalism or modernism can now become a teacher of English—which is why literary critics, who until recently were predominantly nonacademic men, have now, with some exceptions, moved into academic positions. Men like Edmund Wilson, who has consistently refused such attachment, have come to look like monuments of a half-forgotten past.

A study of the proportion of academicians among the contributors to little magazines in the Twenties and Fifties shows, for example, that only 9% were teachers in the Twenties, while 40% were academicians in the Fifties.[5] It is no longer unusual to find literary critics on English faculties that were once the exclusive preserve of literary historians. There are few good colleges in America that do not boast of writers-in-residence or artists-in-residence. To the extent that modernism has conquered, those who represent its spirit have been welcomed into the groves of academe. It is symptomatic in this respect that *Partisan Review*, which for almost thirty years has been the gathering ground and central core of a certain strand of radical modernism among independent New York-centered intellectuals, is now being published by a university press, while its major editors at a fairly late stage in their careers have become professors at leading universities. Similarly, there are few major university departments in the social sciences or the humanities in which we do not find radicals or ex-radicals who at one time attempted to make livings as unattached intellectuals in the interstices of official society. Among the thirteen members of the editorial board of *Dissent*, a magazine that endeavors to uphold radical values, seven are university teachers.

Nor is the academy the only institution that has welcomed radical or ex-radical intellectuals. They are frequently found in the publishing industry—two editors of *Dissent* work there—in government, and in the world of the mass media. As Irving Howe has remarked, "What has actually been taking place is the absorption of large numbers of intellectuals, previously independent, into the world of government bureaucracy and public committees; into the constantly growing industries of pseudo-culture; into the adult education business . . ."[6]

The ranks of unattached intellectuals of an older generation have been depleted by the steady flow to the universities and other institutions. In addition, the supply of younger men, who flocked in the past to New York City to become independent intellectuals seems to have declined. To be sure, there are "hipsters" or "beat" writers who live on the edges of Greenwich Village or hitchhike across the continent to the subliterary havens of California, but few of them seem to have serious intellectual concerns or even pretensions. They wish to "express themselves," but they seem for the most part to lack the personal and artistic discipline necessary for serious intellectual work. As Malcolm Cowley has written, "the fact remains that this bohemian path to recognition no longer seems attractive or even possible to most young writers."[7] Those young and aspiring non-Bohemian intellectuals who continue to come to the metropolis, on the other hand, usually seek employment in publishing or the mass-culture industries. They do not typically envisage careers as independent and unattached intellectuals. The small number of young free-lance intellectuals among New York writers has often been remarked.

The death of "modernism" and the decline of ideology, as well as the pressures of an affluent society, seem responsible for this change in the orientation of young writers. As long as such writers could feel committed to a cause, be it the *avant-garde* in literature and the arts or social protest, they could accept a great deal of material deprivation in the interest of that cause. Such commitment and the involvement in the countercultures that it implied naturally led to further alienation from the common culture and to further social distance from those who adhered to it. The decline of ideology and the end of modernism naturally brought in their wake the decline of willingness and ability to share the material burdens of

Bohemian or semi-Bohemian existence. Furthermore, in an affluent society, even the standards of those who are willing to forgo some of the lures of middle-class culture tend to increase. Aspiring young writers, who might have put up with minimal creature comforts in a less well-to-do society, expect higher "minimal" standards of living today. The "poverty" they are willing to accept is different from the poverty that marked the lives of earlier generations of aspiring writers. As Isaac Rosenfeld once shrewdly observed, "with the rise in the cost of living, the cost of poverty itself has gone up. It costs, it seems to me, around $3,500 a year just to be poor . . . but if you want to be poor on that amount you have to make concessions to employment that were unheard of in the old days." "The garret still exists, but the rent has gone up in Bohemia."[8]

It is hard now to stay in the garret, "because there are so many temptations to come out of the garret, to come out of one's self-employment and self-consideration as a writer and accept the definition of the writer and the use for the writer which society is now willing to give him. The writer can now work at a great number of things. He can work in . . . the symbol manipulation industries. He can work in television, in radio, for the movies; he can work in advertising, in public relations, he can get himself some sort of a job as an editor almost anywhere—in a publishing house, for a slick magazine . . . The writer very seldom stands over against the world . . ."[9]

These are some of the reasons that account for the decline in the numbers of unattached intellectuals in both older and younger generations. Nevertheless, independent intellectuals still play key roles in American cultural life. What are the conditions under which they live today?

There are very few contemporary authors who live solely on the sales of their books. Authors' royalties are now paid at lower rates than they were in 1910. Before the First World War, 20% of the retail price was a common royalty for popular novels. Now 15% is the maximum, and many contracts call for 10% royalties on the first 2500 or even 5000 copies sold, 15% being reached only after 5000 or even 10,000 copies have been sold. This drop means that a novel priced at $3.50 will earn its author about $1750 on the first 5000 copies and a little less than $4000 on the first 10,000.[10] Very few books of any intellectual distinction sell more than 10,000 copies, and most sell a good deal fewer. The writer who is not a best seller can hardly expect to make a living from the hard-cover sales of his books. Nowadays, many books are, of course, brought out in soft-cover editions not long after the original editions have appeared. But contrary to popular belief, soft-cover royalties are not likely to be very high. To be sure, there have been some startling successes among "high-brow" books in soft-cover formats. *Dr. Zhivago* sold 1,500,000 copies in paper at 95 cents a copy; Ruth Benedict's *Patterns of Culture* sold 1,250,000 copies at 50 cents. But the great majority of paperbacks brought out each year sell no more than their original printings of 150,000 to 200,000 copies, netting the author (on a 50-cent book) $2250 at most. With the more expensive "quality reprints," which sell at a $1.45 and up, a sale of 10,000 is considered better than average. The author's royalties on such a book would be in the neighborhood of $500.[11] Altogether, then, the sales of his books cannot support an author, except in special cases.

Book publishing is not the only source of income for modern unattached intellectuals. In fact, it may only be a minor source for many. Book reviews bring in some income. But leading intellectual magazines like *Partisan Review* pay only nominal fees, and book-review payments from such media as *The New Republic*, *Commentary*, *The Reporter*, *The New York Review of Books*, and even the *New York Times Book Review* are most of the time not likely to amount to more than $100 each. Articles or essays for such magazines may, however, bring several hundred dollars. Short stories in the little magazines are likely to net only very small returns. It is only when a writer succeeds in placing an article or a story in one of the mass-circulation magazines like *Esquire* and *The New Yorker* that his returns are apt to be substantial. James Baldwin and Hannah Arendt are said to have received fees in five figures for their contributions to *The New Yorker*. For the run-of-the-mill author, however, income derived from short stories, essays, articles, and book reviews may be welcome additions to family income, but it is not likely to sustain them fully. Edmund Wilson, perhaps our most representative independent man of letters, reports that his total income between 1947 and 1951 averaged $2000 a year (although it has risen considerably since).[12]

For a writer living in New York and a few other metropolitan areas, there are a number of other sources of income. He may serve as a publisher's manuscript reader; he may be called in as a publisher's consultant for revision of a manuscript; he may be asked to write introductions to hard-cover, or more frequently soft-cover, editions of classic writers of the past; he may be paid a fee for serving on the selection board of a book club; he may be asked to lecture before women's clubs or university audiences; he may serve during a summer on the staff of a writers' conference; he may occasionally appear in a television discussion or a radio debate; he may give a series of lectures or even a regular course at one of the local universities; he may, finally, receive a foundation fellowship allowing him to take a year off from other work. There are today a great variety of sources of income for the independent writer. Those who have the capacity to profit from all or most of them can probably piece together fairly comfortable livings, yet very few reach incomes comparable to those now paid to senior men on university faculties. In addition, of course, they rarely attain economic security, being always dependent on the momentary chance and the special opportunity.

The relatively insecure economic position of the independent intellectual, together with his interstitial social position and the decline of modernism and radicalism, explain his style of life. New York writers hardly constitute a subcultural community as Parisian writers still do. They may see one another at publishers' cocktail parties, they may exchange gossip at prize juries and at art shows, or they may meet at various parties, but there is none of the cohesiveness in the literary world that the salon or the club provided in an earlier age. Most of the older writers live fairly isolated and insulated lives, and even the younger Bohemian writers maintain only sporadic contacts with one another in restaurants, bars, and *espresso* parlors in and around Greenwich Village.

At one time, most independent writers lived in or near Greenwich Village. Nowadays many have moved to the suburbs of Fairfield County and Bucks County, to Hudson or to Nyack, and those who have remained in New York City have been dispersed to upper Manhattan, the East Side, or the suburbs. Writers still seem to prefer the "district abandoned by the rich and taken over by the poor—like Greenwich Village—or else on the dividing line between rich and poor neighborhoods, as in the far-east Seventies of Manhattan, the Near North Side of Chicago, and in Boston on the wrong slope of Beacon Hill."[13] But the combined effects of high-rent apartments and urban renewal have driven many away from these areas. Residential interstices have declined along with institutional interstices, and this ecological dispersion has added further to the fragmentation of intellectual life among independent writers.

To be sure, cliques, coteries, and factions, which have never been absent from modern literary life, continue to exist today. Such cliques arise on the basis of mutual interests both real and ideal, and they provide a measure of mutual protection and reciprocal enhancement. They help to open channels for the emergence of new talent and to provide a medium in which new ideas can be tested before being exposed to a wider public. Although such cliques have not disappeared, they have declined in importance. What holds them together today seems less a commitment to particular sets of ideas than a common defense of "high-brow" culture against the invasion of "middle-brow" standards; their character is defensive rather than offensive, and their power to shape intellectual life has declined in consequence.

Finally, since so many intellectuals have moved to the academy or to other types of salaried employments, the remaining group of unattached intellectuals can no longer maintain its previous isolation but must mingle with a heterogeneous group of men from the academy, from the worlds of editing and publishing, of research, and the like, among whom they are a minority. The interstices have shrunk, and those still willing to operate within them have lost group cohesion and much of their former sense of mission.

Unattached intellectuals now display a kind of nervous irritability and edginess in their relations with academic men. This uneasiness may be connected with a half-acknowledged feeling of *ressentiment*. The domain of cultural criticism and social commentary has traditionally been the almost exclusive preserve of the independent literary critic and other unattached intellectuals. But lately economists, historians, sociologists, and other academic professionals have invaded this field. Threatened with the loss of what once were claims to exclusive possession, literary men have reacted with some violence against the intruders. It is interesting to note that much of their criticism of academics centers on language and style of presentation rather than on subject matter. Literary men often make a sport of mocking these invading savages, much as the British upper classes make merry over the non-U manners of the *nouveaux riches*. Unattached intellectuals seem to feel that they are the guardians of the word, craftsmen whose medium is the written language, and that they must preserve its purity against men who tend to debase it. Yet one cannot but feel that behind this concern with style of presentation there often lurks an uneasy feeling that the literary man is no longer able to compete with the academic expert in terms of content. The specialized knowledge now available to the academic man, the statistical methods, quantifiable variables, and complex research designs he has at his disposal make the literary intellectual fear that he himself is on his way to obsolescence and that "his technical incompetence paralyzes his capacity for insight."[14] Literary men tend in defense to react to this newfangled weaponry much as medieval knights reacted to the invention of cannon and muskets. A kind of secret fear of technological unemployment seems to lurk behind much of the aggressiveness that often marks the relationship between unattached intellectuals and academic men.[15]

Dispersion, the loss of clear-cut causes and ideologies, the fear of displacement, and undoubtedly many other factors, account for the high degree of unease that we are likely to encounter today among unaffiliated intellectuals. They still live on the periphery of the common culture and in critical distance from it, yet they find it hard to resist its inducement. Theirs has become a much more difficult position to maintain than it was in the past. They seem to fear popular success as much as failure, for popular success is equated in their minds with critical failure and the abandonment of standards. Whenever an author reaches a large public, there immediately arises the suspicion that he has done so only at the price of inadmissible concessions. It is indeed hard to resist the lure of a culture that has become as absorptive as our own.

Unattached intellectuals continue to think of themselves as the "salt of the earth." But they also fear that "if the salt have lost his savour, wherewith shall it be salted: It is henceforth good for nothing, but to be cast out, and to be trodden under foot of men."

Although unattached intellectuals have declined in their specific weight within the total culture, they may continue to provide some of the major critical ideas that later spread to a wider public and to public decision-makers, and they may continue to help set standards and influence ideological trends. They are in a privileged position to do so because they are less restrained by institutional pressures, more mobile because of their freedom from institutional roots, less subject to regular obligations and routines than are other categories of intellectuals. Their lack of firmly structured positions in society allows them a freedom to look at the world from a variety of perspectives and to be freer from the pressures to adhere to tradition. Yet they are hampered by a lack of expert knowledge in a society in which such knowledge is increasingly required in most spheres. That is why unattached intellectuals must now compete with academic men and salaried intellectuals in the very spheres in which they used to be fully in command. An Edmund Wilson, a Harold Rosenberg, a Paul Goodman may still be highly creative and innovative, but even innovation has been successfully institutionalized in America, and the majority of their peers can now be found in the universities.

NOTES

1. Richard Chase, "The Fate of the Avant-Garde," *Partisan Review*, XXIV (Summer, 1957), No. 3, 367.
2. Isaac Rosenfeld, "On the Role of the Writer and the Little Magazines," *Chicago Review*, II (Summer, 1957), 4.
3. Joseph Schumpeter, *Capitalism, Socialism and Democracy* (3rd [Torchbook] ed.; New York: Harper & Row, Publishers, 1962), p. 146.
4. *Cf.* the instructive symposium, "Our Country and Our Culture," in *Partisan Review*, XIX (May–June, 1952), No. 3 and subsequent issues.
5. Ferdinand Kolegar, "From Bohemia to Organization: A Sociological Study of the Trend Toward Institutionalization in American Literature as Reflected in the 'Little Magazines'" (Unpublished ms., mimeographed [Chicago: Roosevelt University, n.d.]).
6. Irving Howe, *A World More Attractive* (New York: Horizon Press, Inc., 1963), p. 258.
7. Malcolm Cowley, *The Literary Situation* (New York: The Viking Press, Inc., 1958), p. 167. I have used this excellent book throughout this section.
8. Rosenfeld, *op. cit.*, pp. 4–5.
9. *Ibid.*, p. 5.
10. Cowley, *op. cit.*, p. 173.
11. David Dempsey, "What's In It for Authors?" *The New York Times Book Review Paperback Book Section*, January 5, 1964.
12. Edmund Wilson, *The Cold War and the Income Tax: A Protest* (New York: Farrar, Straus & Cudahy, Inc., 1963).
13. Cowley, *op. cit.*, p. 216.
14. Merle Kling, "The Intellectual: Will He Wither Away?" *The New Republic*, April 8, 1957.
15. *Cf.* Bennett M. Berger, "Sociology and the Intellectuals: An Analysis of a Stereotype," *Antioch Review*, XVII (1957), pp. 275–90; and Lewis Coser, "The Uses of Sociology," *Partisan Review*, XXVII (Winter, 1960), No. 1, 166–73. I have used a few lines from the latter essay here.

Chapter 21

ACADEMIC INTELLECTUALS

THE MODERN UNIVERSITY IS A HUGE, SPRAWLING, AND multifaceted institution. It is devoted to teaching as well as to research, and it includes academic departments as well as professional schools. Some departments within it may live up to the traditional aim of the scholar, the disinterested pursuit of truth, while others may be only vocational schools in disguise.

Given these many aspects of the modern university, it stands to reason that its personnel is also varied. Most professors hold Ph.D. degrees, but there are obvious differences between a man who teaches Sanskrit and one engaged in research on soil conservation. Not all those holding Ph.D. degrees or all those teaching within a university can be considered intellectuals—not only because the activities and professional involvements of many readily suggest that they have narrow intellectual horizons, but also because they do not define themselves as intellectuals. One study of the self-images of academicians in a variety of fields excluding the natural sciences, engineering, and applied fields, concludes: "Indeed, one of the real surprises, during the course of these interviews, was the rarity of real acceptance of intellectual status. This non-acceptance is revealed in several ways. First, there is the frequency with which this freely offered remark appears: 'Intellectuals, I hate the word!' Second, there are the direct denials to the question, 'Do you consider

yourself an intellectual?' . . . A third denial of membership is shown
in the efforts that are made to avoid having one's affiliation publicly known."[1] Even people who may be publicly defined as intellectuals may not have corresponding self-definitions. An excellent
example is provided by the poet and novelist Randall Jarrell, who
says of one of his academic characters, "He had never been what
intellectuals consider an intellectual, but other people had thought
him one, and he had had to suffer the consequences of their
mistake."[2]

In order to account for the heterogeneity in the staff of the
modern university, we must first consider the heterogeneity in its
structure.

The historical development of the American academy can give
us some clues to its present condition. The contemporary university grew from at least two different historical roots, the early
college and the modern professional and graduate school. Until
roughly the middle of the last century, the American college was
mainly a school for training clergymen, lawyers, and gentlemen. It
was dominated by theologians, legal scholars, and classicists, united,
in most cases, in a common contempt for science and technology,
in fact, for anything that might be considered even remotely practical and useful. The men who set the tone in these colleges were
considered, and considered themselves, an intellectual elite. Their
training was often narrow, and it was circumscribed by often rigid
standards of gentility. This narrowness led to estrangement from
the social and economic realities of the country at large. But within
these confines, the colleges harbored professors who displayed concern with the major values of the society, endeavored to preserve
and extend its cultural heritage, and strove to define standards of
moral excellence appropriate for gentlemen.

After the Civil War, when industrialization began to make major
strides in America, a new type of university emerged. Instruction
and research in scientific and technological subjects were required
by growing industry, and they began to achieve ascendancy over
the traditional academic disciplines. "So," to quote Veblen, "the
university of that era unavoidably came to be organized as a more
or less comprehensive federation of professional schools or faculties
devoted to such branches of practical knowledge as the ruling utilitarian interests of the time demanded."[3] After Johns Hopkins University and the University of Chicago had taken the lead, the major
colleges were gradually turned into universities and graduate schools

in emulation of the great German universities. They conducted research and offered instruction in many subjects, ranging from the nonutilitarian and scholarly to the near vocational. In the process, the university lost its character as a relatively homogeneous community of like-minded scholars and became a federation of faculties and professional schools staffed by professors of heterogeneous training, background, and cultivation.

Its twin historical roots in a community of genteel scholars and loosely grouped purveyors of professional training help to explain the present diversity within the American academy. Yet historical antecedents cannot fully account for present operation. It is to the present functions of universities that we must now turn.

THE UNIVERSITY TODAY

The contemporary American university is a multifunctional organization. First, it provides undergraduate and graduate instruction for rising numbers of students. Between 1939 and 1961, the number of students enrolled in colleges and universities and earning credits toward degrees rose from about 1.3 million to more than 3.9 million. In 1939, college and university enrollments composed about 14% of the population between eighteen and twenty-one years old, while by 1961 that figure was about 38%. The majority of these students are enrolled in undergraduate colleges, but graduate students numbered about 280,000.[4] These enormous numbers of students are offered instruction of great variety in quality as well as in content. For most of them, college education is closely geared to occupational aspirations and achievements. Since the beginning of the century, new units designed to fit students for specific occupations have appeared and have become respectable: schools of journalism, business, librarianship, social work, education, dentistry, nursing, forestry, diplomacy, pharmacy, veterinary surgery, and public administration.[5] The college of liberal arts, on the other hand, attracts those undergraduates who seek education less directly geared to future occupational roles. These colleges allow their students a period before occupational placement, in which more generalized cultural concerns can be cultivated alongside preparation for later professional careers. Most of these colleges, however, tend to be partly high school, partly university, partly general, partly special in character.[6] Finally, advanced instruction is offered in such traditional professional schools as law and medicine, in the newer professional schools, and in the graduate departments offering M.A. and Ph.D. degrees. Given this variety, it stands to reason that standards and expectations differ widely among the branches of a single university and among similar departments or schools in different universities. Only the foolhardy would venture to assess the general level of instruction in America; in dealing with such widely different types, no useful comparisons can be made. It is, of course, possible to rank American universities in terms of some particular criterion, the number of Ph.D. degrees given, for example, and such rankings have in fact often been attempted.[7] What emerges in such comparisons is the enormous gap between the head and the tail of the academic procession, to use David Riesman's vivid image.[8] To sum up, the American university is at present geared to serve the education of very diverse students. It is therefore highly differentiated functionally, split into a number of segments usually only loosely connected, offering specialized types of instruction that may or may not be geared toward occupational or professional preparation and that differ considerably in quality.

Education, however, is only one of the functions a modern university performs. In addition, the university is the major locale for research. Such research, however, like teaching, differs widely in the various segments of the university. In some, research may be neatly articulated with the requirements of particular occupational or professional fields. In others, the emphasis may be on more general cultural or theoretical pursuits. In some, the pursuit of knowledge for its own sake predominates. To quote Veblen again, "from the first this quest of ideal learning has sought shelter in the universities as the only establishment in which it could find a domicile, even on sufferance, and so could achieve that footing of consecutive intellectual enterprise running through successive generations of scholars which is above all else indispensable to the advancement of knowledge."[9] In other areas, the research carried out has none of the qualities suggested by Veblen. There may be instead concern with the useful arts, from agriculture and forestry to "police science" or dental surgery. The general term "research" covers so many disparate activities that we must conclude, as we did about the educational aspect of the university, that it is vain to venture generalizations. University research today is carried on by many professionals and specialists who seem to have little in common beyond the fact that they all operate within the confines of particular universities.

When an organization is divided into a great number of differentiated parts, a need for co-ordination develops. This need explains the rise of academic bureaucracy. As long as universities were relatively small communities of scholars, they could run their affairs with a minimum of formal structure and needed few specialized administrators. They were institutions in which administrative functions, beyond those vested in the office of the president, were mainly performed by professors on a part-time and rotating basis—a pattern that partly survives in the various colleges of Oxbridge. Modern American universities, however, have reached a size, both in student enrollment and research operation, that precludes the possibility of self-administration by professors. Hence the rise of a huge academic bureaucracy made up of deans, registrars, bursars, research administrators, and the like. All these men are not directly involved in the main activities of the university, teaching and research, yet these activities could not be pursued if nobody were in charge of the administrative problems that large-scale organization naturally brings in its wake.

The power that administrators have attained in the modern university by the simple fact of their indispensability has naturally led to tensions between them and the faculty. Much of the history of modern academic institutions could be written in terms of such tensions. In particular, administrators are naturally intent on reducing the sprawling diversity of the university by imposing a minimum of patterned uniformity on the whole enterprise. They attempt to introduce tables of organization and well defined channels of authority and communication to combat what may seem to them at times the chaotic *laissez-faire* of the academician. The faculty, on the other hand, may feel that routinization and bureaucratization reduce its scholarly prerogatives and academic license. Thorstein Veblen's *The Higher Learning in America*, though written a half-century ago, remains the classic statement of the scholar's case against the "captains of erudition": "In order to their best efficiency, and indeed in the degree in which efficiency in this field of activity is to be attained at all, the executive officers of the university must stand in the relation of assistants serving the needs and catering to the idiosyncrasies of the body of scholars and scientists that make up the university; in the degree in which the converse relation is allowed to take effect, the unavoidable consequence is wasteful defeat. A free hand is the first and abiding requisite of scholarly and scientific work."[10]

THE UNIVERSITY AS A SETTING
FOR INTELLECTUALS

In the earlier type of college, intellectuals had pre-eminence and constituted the major body of teachers and scholars. But in the modern academy they do not. Today intellectuals may play a role within the university, they may benefit from affiliation with it, but they can no longer *be* the university.

Although the modern university has assumed a variety of tasks that call for unintellectual personnel, it remains, despite certain countertrends about which more will be said later, the most favorable institutional setting for American intellectuals today, for several reasons:

1. It provides a *milieu* in which men sharing a common concern with the untrammeled pursuit of knowledge can communicate with one another and thus sharpen their minds in continuous interchange.

2. It affords its professors regular remuneration, which, although far below that prevalent in a number of nonacademic professions, allows them a middle-class life style.

3. It provides security of tenure for senior academicians. This point and the last one together account for the fact that the academician is institutionally protected from the vagaries of the market place so that he can devote himself to his work without being distracted by economic pressures.

4. It has institutionalized the time allocation of academicians in such a way that they can devote a major part of their working time to independent thought and autonomous research.

5. Finally, and most important, it grants academic freedom to its members.

The freedom of speech, opinion, and publication claimed by the university professor is no different in principle from that claimed by other men in liberal society. The issue of academic freedom arises mainly from the fact that the academician is also a salaried employee who claims the license to disagree in his teaching and writing with the views of those who provide or administer the funds from which he is paid. Arthur O. Lovejoy put it neatly: "The principle of academic freedom asserts . . . that those who buy a certain service may not (in the most important particular) prescribe the nature of the service to be rendered."[11] Claims of this sort depart widely from the mores of a society based on the ethos of business. It is therefore hardly surprising that the American university, after it had successfully freed itself from clerical domination, found it difficult to impress on trustees, regents, and other representatives of fund-granting institutions, that he who paid the piper was not expected to call the tune. That the major American universities—though by no means all the minor or "middling" colleges and universities—have succeeded in imposing this principle is the foremost reason why they continue to be strongholds of intellectual activity. By and large, members of the academic professions have won freedom from outside control by successfully asserting the claim that their socially indispensable tasks cannot properly be carried out if their performance is dictated or controlled by those who pay for it.

Expectations concerning such matters as academic freedom, remuneration, tenure, teaching loads, and the like are not always met in all academic settings. But, more important, and quite independent from such departures from institutionalized expectations, there are a number of built-in countertrends within the very structure of the modern university that make it a somewhat less favorable environment for intellectual activity than its ideal image would lead one to expect. Such countertrends have not yet subverted other major forces operating within the academy, but they have often deflected them. It is to an examination of these countertrends that we must now turn.

CAREER PRESSURES AND THE DEPARTMENTALIZATION OF KNOWLEDGE

The career of the academician typically proceeds by a series of slow steps through the ranks up the academic ladder. This process may be an impediment to the achievement of intellectual excellence because the requirements for academic advancement and the optimal conditions for the advancement of knowledge do not necessarily coincide. It has been pointed out, for example, that Kant would probably not have achieved professorial rank in a modern university, for he published nothing of consequence until he was fifty-seven.

There is a built-in pressure on the young academician to publish. In other words, universities have institutionalized a graded system of advancement for professors in which each successive promotion is forthcoming only after a satisfactory publication record is achieved. The aspiring academician may be deflected from planning a large-scale intellectual undertaking that may take years to mature, in order to publish narrower contributions that can be of more direct use in the advancement of his career. As Logan Wilson says, "Disinterested activity and the slow ripening of long-term projects become well-nigh impossible as situational pressures call for quick results."[12]

Pressures from the requirements of academic promotion are not the only ones that may detract the scholar from pursuing broad-gauged intellectual undertakings. The modern academy is divided into a number of departments corresponding to scholarly disciplines and professional training centers. As the fields represented in these departments develop and as the departments grow, departmental boundaries tend to become rigid and to discourage intellectual curiosity beyond the administratively defined departmental settings. Lip service may be paid to "cross-fertilization," but in actual fact young scholars are generally advised to stay within the boundaries of the "field." In addition, as a particular academic field becomes professionalized, those active within it are expected to take their colleagues in the profession, as well as their professional clients, as their main reference groups. This expectation contributes further to the weakening of ties to the academy as a whole and to a tendency to eschew those intellectual undertakings that might cross departmental boundaries and not fit into the framework of the profession.

Expectations of colleagues and superiors within his department exert pressure upon the junior incumbent to play by the rules of the academic game. These rules require, among other things, intellectual discipline, the observance of fixed standards of scholarship, attention to the contributions of senior men, and, above all, respect for the boundaries of the various specialized fields. Those who attempt to create *ab ovo* are likely to be considered "unreliable" "outsiders" to be mistrusted.[13] Such an emphasis discourages potential generalizers, and young scholars may well feel that safety lies in involvement with narrow problems rather than with broad questions. What is at issue is not the necessary drift toward a measure of specialization that the rapid accumulation of knowledge in all fields has called forth but rather an additional source of professionalization that arises, not from the inherent development of knowledge, but from the specific organizational framework of the modern university.

TIME PRESSURES

Ideally the university affords its professors an environment in which only a fraction of their time is directly committed; a maximum of it remains institutionally unallocated and at their free disposal. Yet this ideal state, which was perhaps approximated in the leisurely styles of the eighteenth-century college, hardly prevails today. Not only have the demands of mass education, combined with the peculiarly American form of instruction through lecturing, led to an obligation to teach many more hours than is customary in European universities, for example, but the typical American professor is also involved with various types of committee work that require considerable chunks of his time.

Precisely because the modern university is no longer a community of scholars but a huge and heterogeneous assemblage of different schools, it requires large-scale efforts of administrative adjustment and regulation. If academicians are unwilling to let themselves be entirely regulated by professional administrators, they are forced to relinquish large parts of their own "free" time for administrative tasks. We face here an interesting paradox: The very effort among academic men to prevent the academy from becoming too highly bureaucratized leads them to engage in activities that necessarily distract them from those scholarly tasks that the academy is supposed to foster and protect.

Sheer scarcity of time may be a very serious impediment to intellectual activities in the modern university. In addition, alleged scarcity of time may be a kind of defense mechanism available to those academicians who wish to hide lack of scholarly productivity behind a respectable cloak. Anyone familiar with modern academic life knows of the well-nigh universal complaint among academicians about lack of time. But a great deal of familiarity with the case at hand is required in order to know whether or not those who complain actually are pressed for time or whether or not they involve themselves in time-consuming administrative tasks in order to distract attention from their sterility. The academy provides mechanisms that can be used for an institutionalized evasion of the academic norms of scholarly productivity. More generally, to the extent that the academy permits an allocation of the scarce time resources of its members in ways unconducive to intellectual activity, it hinders the intellectual vocation within its confines.

SKILL *VERSUS* CULTIVATION

In the nineteenth century, it was generally held that the university had functions other than those of inculcating specific skills. J. H. Newman may have provided a somewhat idealized picture in his *On the Scope and Nature of University Education:* "The culture of the intellect is a good in itself and its own end . . . As the body may be sacrificed to some manual or other toil . . . so may the intellect be devoted to some specific profession; and I do not call *this* the culture of the intellect . . ."[14] In actual fact, the nineteenth-century university did not fully live up to these high demands. But most cultivated opinion would at least have agreed with Newman's ideal. That is not true of contemporary America. In fact, an influential group of educators and academic decision-makers has now publicized the opinion that the university ought in fact to be nothing but a training ground for marketable skills and for the absorption of professional norms, beside being a locale for specialized research. Bernard Berelson, the author of a recent and influential study, *Graduate Education in the United States*, puts the matter with commendable frankness: "The graduate school should aim at training the skilled specialist—not . . . at producing the 'educated man,' the 'cultured man,' the 'wise man' (nor, for that matter, the 'mere technician,' either)."[15]

The reason for the shift in emphasis from cultivation to skill that Berelson represents, even while he aims to accentuate it, must be sought both inside the academy and outside. The increase in college and graduate-school enrollments has produced a student population qualitatively different from that of the nineteenth-century academy. An earlier student population may have gone to the university mainly in quest of genteel cultivation and the acquisition of gentlemanly graces, while a minority acquired broad skills in such professional fields as law, theology, and medicine. In contrast, the majority of present-day students goes to colleges and universities in order to acquire much wider ranges of diversified skills. No longer does only a small elite of wealth or of intelligence go to college and even graduate school; as indicated earlier, nearly 40% of the population between eighteen and twenty-one years old is now enrolled. Under this mass demand for higher degrees, both college and graduate school have increased enormously, and they have moved further in the direction of the kinds of specialization their students require. The demand for specialized training on the part of the majority of the student audience has accentuated more general trends toward the specialization of knowledge.

The shaping of the university by the demands of its student population is only a part of the story. External demands have also had a major part in the type of instruction offered. Berelson[16] specifies this point for the graduate school: The largest market for graduate students will no longer be college teaching, as it has been in the past. Only 20% of successful recent Ph.D. candidates have gone into undergraduate teaching in liberal arts colleges. The demands of industry and the government for Ph.D. holders have been increasing very rapidly. These "users" of academic products, however, want skilled specialists rather than cultivated generalists, and they therefore exercise pressures toward greater specialization paralleling those coming from vocationally oriented students.

The academy, though it is partially shielded from its surrounding social and economic environment, can hardly escape its influence. Although it may resist or lag behind the demands of society at large, it cannot fail to respond in some measure. And as it does so, it inevitably moves further in the shift from cultivation to the inculcation of usable skills. And the services it provides inevitably contribute to a certain reshaping in the roles of academicians; many of them are bound to become retailers of useful knowledge rather than producers of ideas.

THE CONSULTANT ROLE OF ACADEMIC MEN

The increasing recognition granted to academic men by decision-makers in business and government has had unanticipated consequences within the academy, consequences that may also decrease the chances for intellectuals within it. No longer do most professors lead lives sheltered behind academic walls. Many are now consultants to industry and the government, and their advice is eagerly sought by powerful decision-makers. Of course, in many branches of study—literature, history, the classics—professors have been unable to assume such extra-academic roles, but these roles have become almost routine in the natural and social sciences. As a consequence, many academicians have been able to widen their horizons and to shed a certain academic parochialism that clung to scholars of an earlier age. But those academicians who now move among decision-makers in the world of affairs have also acquired a new public, which affects their previous self-image.

The traditional audience of the scholar was found in the community of scholars. The sense of identity of the traditional man of knowledge was largely shaped through the rewards that recognition and esteem among his peers would bring him. But once a scholar acquires a new extra-academic audience, he is subject to new influences that reshape his self-image. When recognition is bestowed by extra-academic men whose problems the academician has helped solve, a tendency may arise for the academician to seek recognition less from his peers than from decision-makers who are able to reward him. As academicians are in increasing demand for the solution of problems in both private and business bureaucracies, they tend to be deflected from the pursuit of more general or theoretical problems for which there is no demand outside the academy. The fact that academicians are now being sought by industry and government to a greater extent than ever before accounts, at least in part, for their rising prestige in the community at large. When the academy can furnish so many men who can give advice on practical matters, the negative stereotype of the "impractical professor" tends to decline. Yet this greater acceptance of "practical professors" should not be mistaken for a general decline in anti-intellectualism in America. It is mainly those men of knowledge who have become more like the managers for whom they provide services that are now welcome and accepted in the community at large; those scholars who have eschewed extra-academic roles have not profited, nor can they be expected to profit, from such reappraisal of their worth among the decision-makers and the public.

In later chapters, we shall return to this problem in the context of the natural sciences and of the general public roles of intellectuals. Here we need note only the fact that the involvement of modern academicians with decision-makers in public and private organizations, while often broadening in its impact, has also led to increasing concern with applied problems and has therefore prevented certain academicians from turning to larger intellectual tasks.

RESEARCH ENTREPRENEURSHIP

In most academic fields outside the natural sciences, the dominant pattern of academic work in the past has been that of the researcher-writing-a-book-from-library-sources. But with the increasing complexity of research in the social sciences and even sometimes in the humanities, with the refinement of method and the attendant growth of necessary apparatus, researchers have found it more and more difficult to do their work without considerable outside aid. This necessity has led to the growth of research institutes within the academy and to the development of university research teams made up of professors, junior assistants, and auxiliary personnel.

The restriction of intellectual horizons and the fragmentation of research tasks that programed research entail will be discussed in detail in the next chapter. Here we need only note two additional impediments to intellectual growth that such programed research may bring in its wake. Insofar as senior members serving as research entrepreneurs are concerned, we may notice a significant diversion of their efforts from scholarly to administrative and fund-raising activities. Warren Bennis describes the problem: "[The new social scientist] cannot engage in successful research operations in the pristine isolation of his chambers . . . He has to interview subjects and 'establish rapport.' . . . Over thirty per cent of his day is spent in administrative tasks such as interviewing personnel; attending staff meetings and seminars; preparing speeches, consulting; meeting with important experts in his field . . . corresponding with colleagues, sponsors, and users of research. Much time is spent preparing research proposals for the Foundation. Here the research man has to balance budgets . . . choose personnel, and come up with a financial request."[17] A research entrepreneur so engaged will hardly be able to turn his full intellectual energies to the work at hand.

It might be objected that those who have chosen to play the new role of research entrepreneur are hardly predisposed to intellectual tasks in the first place. Yet anyone familiar with the current academic scene will not find it hard to name a number of instances in which men whose earlier contributions showed great intellectual promise failed to continue producing work of major importance once they became involved in directing research teams or institutes.

The possible negative effects of such research enterprises on the production of ideas of wider scope is perhaps more pronounced among junior academicians than among senior research leaders. The young scholar is unlikely to have much access to research funds of his own and is therefore generally forced to attach himself to a "collaborative" project headed by a senior member who has access to fund-granting institutions. As a result, he is likely, in the formative years of his career, to work on projects defined by others. That is, just at the stage of his career when a young scholar might be expected to "bubble over with ideas," he is constrained to fetter his creativity in order to fit into someone else's project. (By the time the young man has grown to head a project himself, the likelihood is great that he will be so absorbed in administrative tasks that he cannot fully devote himself to creative intellectual work.)

One of the traditional virtues of academic employment has been, as we have seen, the security it affords. But matters are different in research institutes. Here all but the top personnel, who hold full university appointments, suffer from chronic uncertainty, for each project is dependent on foundation or other support that may or may not be forthcoming next year. Bennis describes this uncertainty vividly: "The Development project was threatened by the yearly scrutiny of the Foundation, and consequently, an annual bout with uncertainty. For the past two years the Foundation has not announced the grant until the end of May . . . the Development personnel see the Foundation as a towering, overshadowing Moloch. Each year, during the past two years, with growing intensity from January to May, the payoff question raised by the Development personnel has been, 'will the funds come through?' "[18] One cannot help but feel that little work of intellectual stature on either senior or junior level is likely to be produced under the shadow of Moloch.

Not all research groups and institutions work in the extreme conditions of insecurity described by Bennis. But, in general, as the academician becomes a man with a staff and overhead, he faces pressures that, at least in many cases, stultify his own intellectual capacities, as well as those of his staff.[19] The dilemma seems inescapable: Much scholarly work nowadays requires sustained support from outside foundations and organization within bureaucratic settings, yet the very means of research may so affect the results and the practitioners that significant intellectual work is frustrated rather than sustained. A variant of Parkinson's Law seems to operate here: Research paraphernalia, routines, and overhead expand to use the funds available for the completion of the research. But too often, the more research there is, the less intellectual product.

BUREAUCRATIC IMPEDIMENTS

A few years ago, Jacques Barzun, the Provost of Columbia University, asked, "Why has the American college and university so little connection with intellect?"[20] His question was no doubt meant as rhetorical overstatement, but it is nevertheless relevant. I have already identified some potentials for anti-intellectualism in academic career requirements: time allocation, academic specialization, and the demand of the "users" of academic products for men with specialized skills rather than generalized cultivation. Still another source of pressure is located in academic bureaucratization itself. The vast internal bureaucratic apparatus of deans, directors, registrars, of administrators of the most variegated kind, today exercises a type of control over faculties that is quite different from that wielded by trustees and those "captains of erudition" with whom Veblen was familiar. They are not intent, in the vast majority of cases, upon restricting the expression of unpopular opinion within the university. But committed to a bureaucratic outlook on life, an outlook in which primary emphasis is given to smooth operation and in which the minimization of organizational friction is seen as a main task, academic administrators quite naturally distrust "trouble makers" who might upset the routines. It is not that they love academic freedom less than their colleagues on the faculty; it is that they love efficient operation more.

The internal operation of the academic bureaucracy is not the only issue to be considered here. Academic administrators are now part of a much wider web of power and influence that links them with their fellows in fund-granting institutions, whether public or private. In our days, no university has an independent budget sufficient to provide the necessary money. Institutional funds must be supplemented from the outside. And the administrators of foundation and government grants are likely to have criteria for the choice of recipients to match those of their colleagues within the academy.

They too are likely to distrust not unconventionality *per se*—in fact they have been known even to seek out an occasional "odd ball"— but those unconventional men who cannot be fitted into organizational plans of research teams or who do not stay within neatly circumscribed academic niches. We may therefore witness within the academy a selective process operating by means, as it were, of a series of close-meshed sieves through which the faculty is passed. Gradually the usable particles are separated from the coarser ones —and the latter are generally shunted to the sidelines.

Sixty years ago William James could proudly say at a Harvard Commencement Dinner, "Our undisciplinables are our proudest product."[21] It is no longer so—not because modern administrators possess vices from which earlier administrators were exempt but rather because the older pattern in a few elite universities could permit "undisciplinables" a freedom that has been much more difficult to grant in a highly bureaucraticized organization. In the modern, intricately organized university, men not fitted into tables of organization might create long-range administrative havoc far beyond their immediate and direct impact.

To be sure, modern universities have their share of "undisciplinable" intellectuals. Yet many observers have pointed out that, over the years, the denizens of faculty clubs, even in major universities, have tended to look more and more like the men one encounters in the executive cafeterias of major corporations. Kenneth Burke's memorable maxim—"People may be unfitted by being fit in an unfit fitness"[22]—seems to apply to the case at hand. The selection criteria typically applied by administrators and other bureaucratic officials contribute to the predominance of an academic type that, while admirably fitted into departmental tables of organization, may not be so fitted for creative scholarly tasks. The means of academic administration may be in danger of subverting the ends of the academy.

An unusually reflective participant-observer of the academic scene, Charles H. Cooley, once made an observation on the "genius on the faculty" that sums up much of what I have been trying to say, even though it was written in the Twenties when many of these developments were only beginning to appear. "It is strange that we have so few men of genius on our faculties; we are always trying to get them. Of course they must have undergone the regular academic training (say ten years in graduate study and subordinate positions) and be gentlemanly, dependable, pleasant to live with, and not apt to make trouble by urging eccentric ideas. Institutions and genius are in the nature of things antithetical, and if a man of genius is found in a university it is peculiarly creditable to both."[23] Not all intellectuals are geniuses, of course, yet what Cooley said applies to them too, to some extent. Although the university is theoretically the ideal environment for the intellectual, its institutionalized practices too often operate in such a way that the intellectual vocation within the academy is fraught with perils.

PROSPECTS

The picture of the academy that has gradually emerged from this review of trends and countertrends within it departs markedly from the picture that exclusive preoccupation with widely held ideals and generalized expectations about universities would suggest. "Academic organization is ideally expressed in the free association of equals, yet everywhere there is a hierarchical arrangement, in which independence is limited by the delegation of functions."[24] Ideally, the university is a community of equals, but in fact it may be only a loosely federated group of scholars, vocationally oriented teachers, and men concerned with practical arts. Ideally, it said to cultivate broadness, but practically it often cultivates narrow specialization. Ideally, it is devoted to disinterested scholarship, but practically it may often succumb to a variety of interests. Even its academic freedom, its greatest achievement, may degenerate through disuse into the mere freedom to be academic, to use Paul Goodman's phrase.[25] Despite all these flaws, the university remains today and is likely to remain in the future the major locale for intellect. There are two main reasons why: recognition of academic freedom by the society at large and the institutionalized removal of the academic man from the pressures of the market place.

The academician enjoys an unusual degree of freedom because, unlike most men, he receives a guaranteed salary that is not tied to the offering of particular products on the market. Or, to put the matter somewhat differently, the salary for his teaching furnishes the economic foundation for his free research and general scholarship.[26] Similarly, academic men are assured, in principle, freedom to pursue their scholarly tasks without regard for the opinions and desires of those who provide their funds. These twin rights, even though they may often be infringed in practice, make the academy a privileged locale for intellectuals. No doubt, in the future as in the past, many creative intellectuals will continue to make their contributions outside the academy. Comte, Marx, Darwin, Schopenhauer, Kierkegaard, Freud—those giants who shaped the modern mind—were not academic men, and upon occasion they would all pour scorn upon the academy and make fun of academic men. Yet their own achievements would hardly have been feasible had they not been able to stand on the shoulders of many others who did find in the academy the environment in which their talents could be sheltered and fostered. Genius may upon occasion transcend the limitations and do without the protection of institutional orders, but ordinary intellectuals, like ordinary men, need sustaining institutions. The academy is likely to continue as such an institution in the future. As long as free universities exist, the chances for intellect remain open.

NOTES

1. Melvin Seeman, "The Intellectual and the Language of Minorities," *American Journal of Sociology*, LXIV (July, 1958), No. 1, 25–35.

2. Quoted in *ibid.*, p. 27, from Jarrell's *Pictures from an Institution*, p. 110.

3. Thorstein Veblen, *The Higher Learning in America* (New ed.; New York: Sagamore Press, Inc., 1957), p. 26.

4. *Cf.* Martin Trow, "The Democratization of Higher Education in America," *Archives européennes de sociologie*, III (1962), No. 2, 213–62.

5. Robert M. Hutchins, *The Higher Learning in America* (New Haven: Yale University Press, 1936), pp. 33–4.

6. *Ibid.*, p. 2.

7. Bernard Berelson, *Graduate Education in the United States* (New York: McGraw-Hill Book Co., Inc., 1960), pp. 124ff.

8. David Riesman, *Constraint and Variety in American Education* (Anchor ed.; Doubleday & Company, Inc., 1958).

9. Veblen, *op. cit.*, p. 27.

10. *Ibid.*, p. 63.

11. Arthur O. Lovejoy, "Academic Freedom," *Encyclopedia of the Social Sciences*, I (New York: The Macmillan Company, 1942), 384–7.

12. Logan Wilson, *The Academic Man* (New York: Oxford University Press, Inc., 1942), p. 219. This volume, though somewhat dated, remains the major sociological study in this area.

13. *Cf.* my more detailed comments on this point in Lewis A. Coser, "Georg Simmel's Style of Work: A Contribution to the Sociology of

the Sociologist," *American Journal of Sociology*, LXIII (May, 1958), No. 6, pp. 635–40.

14. J. H. Newman, *On the Scope and Nature of University Education* (New York: E. P. Dutton & Co., Inc., 1915), p. 255.

15. Berelson, *op. cit.*, p. 222.

16. *Ibid.*

17. Warren G. Bennis, "The Social Scientist as Research Entrepreneur: A Case Study," *Social Problems*, III, No. 1, 44–9. See also Bennis, "Some Barriers to Team Work in Social Research," *Social Problems*, III, No. 4, 223–35.

18. *Ibid.*

19. *Cf.* C. Wright Mills, *White Collar* (New York: Oxford University Press, Inc., 1951), pp. 131–6.

20. Jacques Barzun, "Foreword," Theodore Caplow and Reece J. McGee, *The Academic Marketplace* (New York: Basic Books, Inc., 1958). This fine volume on the career patterns and working conditions of academic men has been valuable to me, although I have not dealt directly with these topics here.

21. William James, "The True Harvard," *Memories and Studies* (New York: Longmans, Green & Co., Ltd., 1911), p. 355.

22. Kenneth Burke, *Permanence and Change* (New York: The New Republic, 1936), p. 18.

23. Charles H. Cooley, *Life and the Student* (New York: Alfred A. Knopf, Inc., 1927), p. 184.

24. Wilson, *op. cit.*, p. 218.

25. Paul Goodman, "The Freedom To Be Academic," *Growing Up Absurd* (Vintage ed.; New York: Random House, Inc., 1962), pp. 256–79.

26. *Cf.* Theodor Geiger, *Aufgaben und Stellung der Intelligenz in der Gesellschaft* (Stuttgart: Enke Verlag, 1949), p. 109.

Chapter 22

SCIENTIFIC INTELLECTUALS

DURING THE SCIENTIFIC REVOLUTION OF THE SEVENteenth century and the period that preceded it, those who made major contributions to science were almost all creative intellectuals. In fact, as the very term "natural philosophy" indicates, scientific activities were not yet clearly differentiated from other intellectual pursuits. Since those days, of course, the character of science and of its practitioners has changed drastically. Science has become a specialized activity carried out by professionals. Norbert Wiener has depicted well the shift that has taken place: "Since Leibniz, there has perhaps been no man who has had a full command of the intellectual activity of his day. Since that time, science has been increasingly the task of specialists, in fields which show a tendency to grow progressively narrower." In the nineteenth century, he wrote, there were still men like Gauss, Faraday, or Darwin, who, while not encompassing all the sciences, were able to embrace large subdivisions of it. "Today," however, "there are few scholars who can call themselves mathematicians or physicists or biologists without restriction. A man may be a topologist or an acoustician or a coleopterist. He will be filled with the jargon of his field and will know all its literature, but, more frequently than not, he will regard the next subject as something belonging to his colleague three doors down the corridor."[1] Wiener, as was his habit, perhaps dramatized the issue unduly. He himself was the best example of the fact that scientific generalizers are by no means extinct. Yet he was undoubtedly correct in his assertion that the majority of scientists today, bent as they are on the pursuit of narrowly specialized problems in a professionalized occupational system, can hardly be called intellectuals.

THE PROFESSIONAL ROLE OF THE SCIENTIST

Science has become one of the major industries of America. It is, moreover, one of our fastest growing industries. Expenditures for research and development by government, industry, and university amounted to $900 million in 1941 and climbed to $10,230 million in 1958.[2] Most of this increase was, of course, spent for applied research, but even basic research is now supported by enormous funds. In 1953, total expenditures for basic research amounted to $432 million; four years later this amount had been almost doubled to $835 million.[3] Not only funds but also personnel devoted to scientific pursuits have increased at a rapid rate. The number of Ph.D. holders in scientific subjects, living in the United States, and under seventy years of age has increased from thirteen per million in 1900 to 182 per million in 1940 and to 257 per million in 1950.[4] There are now about 77,000 Ph.D. scientists in the United States, compared to 49,000 in 1953, that is, roughly 30,000 new Ph.D. degrees in scientific fields have been granted since 1953.[5] In 1954, a total of 223,200 scientists and engineers was employed by the government, industry, universities, and other nonprofit organizations; only four years later, that number had increased to 327,100, that is, by 47%.[6]

Most scientists now work in highly specialized fields in a vastly expanded world of research organizations and laboratories, which resembles but little the small workshops that lonely discoverers and inventors habitually used in the last century. Max Weber wrote about the process of routinization of charisma, the process through which the extraordinary appeal of religious innovators, for example, is gradually stabilized within the bureaucratic organization of a church. Something similar seems to be happening in the domain of science; we may speak of the routinization of invention and discovery. This routinization occurs not because invention and discovery flow automatically, so to speak, from large research organizations but because contributions can be made mainly by those who have access to the facilities provided by large-scale organizations. As J. K. Galbraith once wrote, "Most of the cheap and simple inventions have, to put it bluntly, been made."[7]

The inventor of the classical period of scientific invention could work almost singlehandedly; not so his modern counterpart. James Conant describes the change: "A barn or an attic and a small bank account, coupled with the rare combination of imagination, tough-mindedness, and perseverance, were sufficient. Not so today. By and large, the laboratory of applied research . . . has taken the place of the solitary inventor. This has been the result of a fusion of advance in science and progress in technology that has forced the inventor into partnership with other inventors with different skills and knowledge; the resulting requirements of equipment and supplies have necessitated new and enlarged method of financing inventions . . . The lone inventor and the scientific amateur are almost as extinct as the American buffalo."[8]

Three separate yet related developments seem to account for the changes Conant describes. First, the very rapid accumulation of knowledge in all spheres of science has made it very difficult for any individual to master more than one specialized area of research. Second, the expansion inherent in the development of science in a great number of fields requires a research apparatus so complicated, expensive, and difficult to handle that large-scale organization is needed to meet the exigencies of research. Third, even in those scientific fields in which such complicated and expensive apparatus may not be required, the bureaucratization of research has increased because of pressures from fund-granting institutions and research administrators, both public and private. Biologists may not need such huge outlays as those required by atomic physicists, yet they too can no longer operate without some supporting funds. Except among mathematicians, who "carry in their own minds all the essential instruments for their work," there is now a general need in science for "administrative outlays on a scale comparable to an industrial undertaking."[9]

The conditions under which scientific work must now be pursued have, of course, correspondingly deep repercussions on the role of the scientist and on his self-definition. The scientist of earlier days, although not exempt from social pressures, was largely guided by the play of his curiosity and imagination. The typical scientist today is a specialized research worker operating within a bureaucratic setting.

Certain exceptions to the specialization of scientific tasks must be noted. In the first place, a number of scientists have successfully moved from fields in which they were first trained to other areas of investigation. Such scientific hybrids have made many major contributions, and in recent years various foundations have therefore made efforts to support such "hybridization." Such transfers from one field to another, it is interesting to note, tend to be from areas with rigorous experimental techniques to fields in which such precision has not been the rule and in which more daring departures from routine still seem possible.[10] Second, a few generalists—one thinks of men like Leo Szilard—seem at home in many areas of science, although their own major productive contributions are usually in single areas. Altogether, even when these exceptions are noted, it remains true that the vast majority of scientists today works in fairly narrowly specialized areas of research.

Organized and programed research. More important even than specialization in science has been the growth of various types of organized research. Wherever research is organized, whether within institutes, research laboratories, or university teams, there exists a tendency to limit the scientist's freedom to choose his own problem. The more bureaucratic the organizational setting, the more stringent the limits imposed on his horizon of inquiry. In spite of the otherwise significant difference between, for example, university teams, who maintain the ideal of a "company of equals" and whose goals are defined in purely scientific terms, and industrial laboratories, in which scientific work is determined by business interests, the very dependence of scientific investigation on bureaucratic organization narrows the scope of individual practitioners. One example from an earlier stage of scientific research may help to clarify this point.

In his early scientific career, Louis Pasteur ranged widely over a number of areas that excited his curiosity. When his fame spread, a research institute was organized for him, and he became increasingly committed to the application of science to the improvement of human health. "Social pressures," writes James Conant, "of which he himself was only partly aware closed the gate to his returning to the investigation of those chemical phenomena connected with the optical activity of natural products."[11] If the social pressures thus generated within a research institute have influenced the direction of inquiry of the man for whom the institute was organized in the first place, it stands to reason that such pressures must, *a fortiori*, be powerful determinants for the great majority of scientists who work within organizational settings not specifically designed for them. What is involved is James Conant's distinction between uncommitted investigation and programed research.

A laboratory, a research institute, a hospital, or a university department "which has undertaken to explore a particular segment of a scientific field for whatever reason is committed to a program. The program may be defined broadly or narrowly, by explicit deed of gift, by contract, or implicitly by the goals proclaimed and the series of victories already won."[12] This type of programed research tends to predominate in all but a few branches of science. The reasons are several. The first, already mentioned, is the cost and scale of experimental work in many of the natural sciences. There are few men in physics, chemistry, and biochemistry who can make significant contributions singlehandedly. Large budgets for equipment and research teams made up of scientific collaborators, assistants, and ancillary personnel are therefore a *sine qua non* of almost all research in these areas today. The required expenditures of both money and manpower must of course be justified to the fund-granting organization, be it government, industry, or university. And, "once the expenditure of money becomes justified in terms of specified aims, the investigator is no longer uncommitted: programmatic research is at hand."[13]

The contrasting styles of programed and uncommitted research may be illustrated by the reflections of a great physicist, Percy W. Bridgman, whose major work was done before the advent of large-scale organized research in physics but who had occasion to watch its impact on a new generation of scientists. Bridgman's description of his own style of work is worth extended quotation: "In spite of the fact that I have in the main followed one guiding experimental idea, I have nevertheless at all times felt free to pursue other lines of interest, whether experiment, or theory, or fundamental criticism. Another outstanding characteristic of my work has been the smallness of its scale. Not only is the apparatus itself small . . . but I have never had more than two or three students at a time or a couple of assistants. The result has been that I have been able at all times to maintain the closest contact with the details of the work, and also have been able to conserve the requisite amount of leisure. Both of these features have been of the highest importance. In advancing into new territory . . . the necessity is continuous for the development of new methods and new ideas. For me, at least, new ideas germinate only in an atmosphere of leisure. I have to immerse myself in a problem and then let it gestate in my brain, without distraction of other interests, if I am to expect the solution to come sauntering into my mind when I wake up two or three mornings later . . . Adjoining my laboratory is my machine shop; in fact it is an integral part of the laboratory to which I can repair and stimulate inspiration by working out half-formed ideas with my own hands. Not only do I have enough leisure so that I can work in the shop with my own hands on occasion, but I am also able to carry through my own experiment, including making all the readings, myself . . . Another great advantage of working on a small scale is that one gives no hostage to one's own past. If I wake up in the morning with a new idea, the utilization of which involves scrapping elaborate preparations already made, I am free to scrap what I have done and start off on the new and better line. This would not be possible without crippling loss of morale if one were working on a large scale with a complex organization under one."[14]

After mentioning the enormous size and expense of the apparatus required, Bridgman comments on the work styles now required in most branches of physics. "Although we may recognize that such instruments are necessary, we may nevertheless deplore some of the consequences. Up to now ideas have been in such a rapid state of flux that the instrument itself has been continually evolving, with the result that most physicists in this field have been spending an increasingly large fraction of their time on the purely engineering job of the design and construction of new and better instruments, and correspondingly an increasingly small proportion of time on the calculation of results and rumination on their significance . . . The physicist who should be directing his team by his creative ideas is likely to be so swamped by the administrative details of the large enterprise under him that he is overwhelmed and his purely scientific activity destroyed."[15] Bridgman attributes the emergence of large-scale team research to World War II, when practically all the physicists in this country were diverted to war work. "The older men, who had previously worked on their own problems in their own laboratories, put up with this as a patriotic necessity, to be tolerated only while they must, and to be escaped from as soon as decent. But the younger men . . . had never experienced independent work and did not know what it was like . . . The result is that a generation of physicists is growing up who have never exercised any particular degree of individual initiative, who have had no opportunity to experience its satisfactions or its possibilities, and who regard cooperative work in large teams as the normal thing. It is a natural corollary for them to feel that the objectives of these large teams must be something of large social significance. The temper of the rising generation is recognizably different from that of the older."[16]

The emphasis on applied science. Pressures to deflect investigators from theoretical problems to those with practical applications are related to, but not identical with, those involved in programed research. Industrial laboratories, presumably mainly concerned with applied work, sometimes foster pure research. The Bell Telephone and General Electric laboratories come readily to mind. Conversely, much applied work is still done by lone inventors, as John Jewkes, *et al.* have recently shown in *The Sources of Invention.*[17] Nevertheless, most applied research today, be it within governmental or industrial contexts, is programed research. And organized applied research tends to involve even greater heteronomy for the scientist than does programed pure research. Whereas in the latter case, pressures may emanate from fund-granting institutions and from the exigencies of team research and programing, in the former case, additional and usually more direct and immediate pressures emanate from the obvious fact that the employing client must be satisfied and that such satisfaction is likely to derive from "practical results." A university department may "suggest" the problems for a university research team, but it is not likely to require concrete and practical results. The matter is very different for government administrators, who must justify their outlays before a Congress concerned with results of a practical nature, or for industrial administrators, who must justify their budgets in terms of their laboratories' contributions to the over-all productivity of their firms.

Why is it then that increasing numbers of young scientists are being attracted to applied rather than to pure research? Why is it, for example, that, in 1961, 250,000 of the 400,000 American scientists and engineers were working for government space and defense programs?[18] The reasons are probably complex, and only a few may be suggested here. Financial rewards in industry are, by and large, higher than in universities or institutes of pure research. Not only salaries, but general research budgets as well, are generally larger for men in applied research than are those for men concerned only with advancing science. Those scientists, for example, who are involved in current space programs enjoy practically unlimited funds for their work. A third factor, the audience of the applied, as distinct from the theoretical, scientist deserves separate consideration.

The audience of the scientist.   In a culture as pervasively pragmatic as our own, devotion to purely theoretical work requires an unusual effort to disregard the attitudes of the *milieu* of nonscientists, in which a scientist is necessarily involved through his relationships in the wider community. Given the strong anti-intellectual tendencies in the public at large, theoretical work requires of the scientist that he take other scientists as his almost exclusive reference group and that he thus isolate himself from people in the wider community. In contrast, work in an applied field promises more direct recognition by a public of nonscientific contemporaries. Involvement with practical problems that "pay off" in tangible results is thus more likely to bring a scientist status and prestige in the community, while theoretical work brings such rewards only in cases of exceptional achievement. Given the negative stereotypes surrounding the "impractical" scientist, it stands to reason that career choices tend, except for the especially dedicated, toward the applied rather than toward the "impractical" aspects of science.

Another source of the preference for applied work—also connected with prevailing anti-intellectual tendencies—lies in the school system. Children first learn about science primarily in relation to applied problems rather than to underlying theory. In fact, science and technology are too often hardly distinguishable in the curriculum. The hero of the young American interested in science is more often Thomas Edison than Willard Gibbs, Eli Whitney than Mendel, Von Braun than Einstein. In consequence, many young men are later attracted, whether from commendable concern with helping mankind or from more mundane motives, to careers in applied rather than in pure science.[19]

More important than these general considerations, however, is the increased demand for scientists in industry and government. Not only do these agencies provide important attractions for young scientists, but they also help to bring about changes in the scientist's role. What Robert K. Merton has said about the difference between unattached and bureaucratic intellectuals applies, with slight modifications, to the difference between theoretical and applied scientists. In both cases, the difference involves the distinctive audiences to which these scientists address themselves. "The distinction is pointed up," writes Merton, "by recognizing a difference in the 'client' of the two kinds of intellectuals: for the bureaucratic intellectual, it is those policy-makers in the organization for whom he is, directly or remotely, performing a staff function; for the unattached intellectual, the clientele is a public."[20] The unattached scientist, be he in programed or in unprogramed research, finds his rewards primarily within the community of other scientists, who grant him recognition and esteem for his achievements; only exceptionally high attainments may also be noted by the wider public, and a few scientists may then attain social prestige as symbolized, perhaps, by awards like the Nobel Prize. Matters are different, however, for the scientist working on practical problems in an industrial or governmental context. Although certain of these men may also be oriented toward the rewards that come from recognition by their peers or the public at large, they generally tend to be oriented toward the policy-makers in the employing organizations. Even if the scientists see themselves as scientific professionals rather than as mere technicians, the policy-makers remain the immediate reference group. Although such dual allegiance may be the source of a great deal of conflict,[21] the very terms of entry into industrial or governmental research are predicated on agreement that the scientist will orient his work toward the solution of problems posed for him by the policy-maker.

The importance of such a conflict of reference groups for scientists should not be underestimated, however, for it may readily become the source of a countertrend. If there is an increasing demand by industry and government for scarce top scientists, they will be in a position to impose some of their own terms. Some research organizations already allow company time to scientists for their own research;[22] this provision makes it possible for them to compete for the "best" men, that is, for those to whom the community of scientists provide the guiding standards.

Policy-makers in industrial and other applied laboratories have recently become more sensitive to the special requirements of scientists and have tended to restrict them less. The headlines of an article in *The Wall Street Journal* dealing with scientists in industry are quite revealing in this respect: "Handle With Care. Scientists in Industry Often Baffle the Boss, Force Policy Changes. Researchers Fret at Controls of Work, Fume at Locked Labs, Ignore Time Clocks. 'We tolerate the Screwballs.' "[23] Dr. C. E. K. Mees, vice-president in charge of research at the Eastman Kodak Company, is probably not representative of most policy-makers, but he may suggest a growing tendency: "The best person to decide what research work shall be done is the man who is doing the research. The next best is the head of the department. After that you leave the field of best persons and meet increasingly worse groups. The first of these is the research director, who is probably wrong more than half the time. Then comes a committee, which is wrong most of the time. Finally there is a committee of company vice-presidents which is wrong all the time."[24]

What, then, are the chances for scientific creativity of a high order in the world of the big laboratory? James Conant is undoubtedly correct that "History shows that the significant revolutions, the germinal ideas have come from the uncommitted investigator."[25] The question is, however, whether or not this statement must be true in the future. Conant believes that "the present trend holds grave dangers for the future of science in the United States," and many eminent scientists share his view.

The very fact that leading scientific spokesmen have expressed misgivings over current trends has, however, already begun to affect these trends. Such concern over the neglect of pure science probably accounts for the fact that basic research, although mainly programed, has in recent years received financial support not granted earlier. Although applied work attracts most recruits, there are more scientists working in pure science today than ever before. There has certainly been no decline in American contributions to science in recent years. Indeed, the number of Nobel Prizes awarded to American scientists points in an opposite direction. Since 1939, "scientists in the United States have won twenty-three full prizes, one half-prize and one third-of-a prize. Except for 1940 to 1942, when awarding was suspended . . . there has been only one year that brought no Nobel recognition to the United States."[26] Yet this evidence is far from conclusive. The mature scientists who have won recognition in recent years belong for the most part to a generation trained before the accelerated trend toward large-scale organized research was in full swing. It would be presumptuous for an outsider to make dogmatic statements in an area in which even experts disagree violently, but I think it is safe to say that, although the chances are very bright indeed that American science will advance on a very broad front in a great variety of areas, the chances for major theoretical breakthroughs are less bright. It might be well to close this section with a last quotation from Conant, on whom these pages have relied so heavily: "Undoubtedly over the years many uncommitted investigators who have made little or no contribution to science but only increased the amount of available information would have been more productive if their efforts had been part of a well-conceived program. But if science were too individualistic and anarchic fifty years ago, the danger now lies in the opposite direction."[27]

It seems that increasing specialization and professionalization, the trend toward large-scale programed research, and the disproportionate support granted to applied science all militate toward decreasing chances for the emergence within modern science of generalizers with broad-gauged knowledge and concerns. Does the increasing involvement of major sectors of the scientific community with questions of public policy constitute an effective counterweight to these tendencies?

THE NEW PUBLIC ROLE OF THE SCIENTIST

The atomic bombing of Hiroshima and Nagasaki served as a dramatic watershed in both the public appreciation of the role of science and the self-image and sense of social responsibility of the scientists themselves. Even as leading scientists were suddenly thrust into the limelight and emerged as public figures of almost heroic cast, many of them were inwardly troubled by anxiety and guilt at the consequences of their wartime activities. J. Robert Oppenheimer has expressed this feeling in a classic comment: "In some sense, which no vulgarity, no humour, no overstatement can quite extinguish, the physicists have known sin and this is a knowledge they cannot lose."[28]

Until the development of the atomic bomb, the scientific community adhered to a fairly unambiguous belief in progress. Science, thought practicing scientists with something near unanimity, automatically contributes to the benefit of mankind. There were differences among scientists as to the merits of pure research compared with those of applied work; some scientists were wont to put greater stress on the aesthetic rather than on the practical side of science or to emphasize the advancement of knowledge for its own sake rather than for the sake of its practical uses. But there was agreement that scientific knowledge could not but be beneficial to humanity. Earlier uses of science for the development of new and deadlier weapons had, upon occasion, brought forth critical comments by individual scientists; here and there, uncommonly reflective scientists had raised some doubts about the generalized philosophy of progress shared by most of the scientific community, but it was only in the aftermath of Hiroshima that large numbers of scientists were moved to reflect in sustained ways on the moral issues raised by their own activities. They had lost their naive belief in more or less automatic progress and were forced to examine anew their own roles and the functions of science in the community at large.

Although the new concern with public issues and social responsibility was not shared equally by all scientists, what is socially important is the fact that those who were drawn into the developing discussion were the leaders in the scientific community. Similarly, although not all branches of the sciences were equally involved, concern was most pronounced among those who had participated directly in the work that led to the production of the atom bomb and was, in general, stronger among theoretical physicists than among engineers, for example. That is, the strongest concern was voiced by those who had, as Richard L. Meier has suggested, the greatest scientific prestige and highest relative standing among the various branches of the sciences.[29] Indeed, Meier thinks that there is an informal hierarchy of intellect within the scientific community, with theoretical physicists, geneticists, and mathematical statisticians at the top and engineers and medical men at the bottom. He also suggests that the political attitudes of scientists generally vary according to the fields in which they are involved, the physicists tending on the whole toward liberalism, the chemists toward the middle of the road, and the engineers toward conservatism.[30] In any case, physicists, and more particularly those involved in atomic work, whether because of their positions at the top of the academic hierarchy, their liberalism, or their wartime involvements, were in the forefront of the re-examination of the public role of science and scientists.

In 1945, a group of atomic scientists under the leadership of James Franck took the unprecedented political step of advising the American government that the newly developed atom bomb should not be used against Japan. Its advice was rejected. This rejection, which subsequently became public knowledge, dramatized in the minds of many scientists the fact that, although scientists had created a device to annihilate entire populations, they were powerless to control its uses. Not that all wartime scientists concurred in the Franck report. As a matter of fact, several very eminent men of science sat on the interim committee that advised President Truman to use the bomb. But whether agreeing with or opposing the Franck report, large numbers of scientists were suddenly brought to the realization that they must re-examine their relations to the policy-makers. The scientific community was, from then on, involved in questions of politics and policy that it had been able more or less to ignore in the past.

The new sense of anxiety or at least unease led many scientists to band together in collective effort to come to grips with the new problems the splitting of the atom had brought to the fore. The Federation of Atomic Scientists (later amalgamated with the Federation of American Scientists) was officially organized in December, 1945, in order, according to the preamble to its constitution, "to meet the increasingly apparent responsibility of scientists in promoting the welfare of mankind and the achievement of a stable world peace." The influential *Bulletin of the Atomic Scientists*, closely connected with the F.A.S., has become a major medium for the clarification of issues involving the social responsibility of science. Its comments and warnings, often authored by leaders in scientific thought, attempt to clarify for the scientific community and for a wider public the whole gamut of policy issues that arise not only in the field of atomic science but in other areas as well. Such issues as secrecy, government clearance, and other impediments to free inquiry, as well as such policy questions as the uses of atomic energy and the effects of atomic tests, have been widely debated in its volumes. In 1950, a relatively small number of scientists, taking a more radical stand than the F.A.S. and the *Bulletin*, organized the Society for Social Responsibility in Science to bring together scientists who had decided to abstain from military work altogether.

In the immediate postwar years, scientists played a significant role in influencing public policy. There was a "science lobby" in Washington, and it proved powerful enough to help prevent passage of the May-Johnson Bill, sponsored by the War Department, which would have given the military preponderant control over the development of atomic energy. The F.A.S. and a broader *ad hoc* organization led a highly successful campaign to mobilize public opinion in support of civilian control of atomic energy. The Atomic Energy Act, as it was finally passed, embodied the principle of civilian control and constituted an important victory for the scientists.

Lobbying was not the only activity of these aroused scientists. A spate of books and a vast number of articles by leaders of the scientific community or by authors endeavoring to speak for segments of this community helped to raise the level of self-consciousness among scientists and to enlarge public concern.

After the immediate postwar years, however, two impediments to continued public activity by scientists became apparent: The level of interest in the scientific community at large began to decline, and various factions and alignments among the scientists concerned with public issues prevented the re-emergence of the united scientific front that had crystallized during the fight over control of atomic energy. The F.A.S. had about 3000 members in its early days, but already by 1950 it had shrunk to 1500. Many of those who had been perturbed and outraged by the events of 1945 withdrew into indifference as the immediate impact of Hiroshima began to pale. Most scientists returned to their laboratories and lost interest in larger issues. Furthermore, as more and more scientific research began to be sponsored and financed by the federal government, many scientists considered it "dangerous" to take stands on public issues. This attitude was naturally especially prevalent during the period of McCarthy's witch hunts and the disgraceful Oppenheimer hearings, but it has continued to the present. The fact is that most scientists today are dependent on the military. The armed forces, together with two defense-related agencies—the Atomic Energy Commission and the National Aeronautic and Space Administration—provide most of the support for American science. *Fortune* estimated in February, 1961, that "some 80% of all U.S. funds for research and development" are now directly or indirectly provided by these agencies. Fully one-half of total business research is now financed by defense funds. The federal government also finances more than two-thirds of all research carried on by the universities. We need not take an unduly cynical view of men's motivations to conclude that this very considerable dependence on governmental funds has not been conducive to widespread involvement of scientists in public debate.

Not only have scientists tended, in the great majority, to withdraw again from public involvement, but even when they have become involved they have, in recent years, tended to split into factions instead of presenting a united front as in the days of the atomic energy bills. Sometimes, as in the recent debates between Linus Pauling and Edward Teller over the test ban, the ideological predispositions of the contenders have been the bases of their differing policy proposals. But perhaps more often, scientists have reflected in their pronouncements differing policies advanced by the different branches of the administration or the armed services to which they happened to be attached. "It is striking," according to Dupré and Lakoff, "that not any of the various new relations of scientists to the government resulting from the missile program, has involved scientists in the kind of policy differences that have appeared in connection with atomic energy. Each of the branches has 'its own' scientists and they develop attachments which sometimes lead to competitive rivalries . . ."[31] But too often, disagreements on policy questions among scientists turn out upon inspection to be based on differences between air force and army orientations, between the interests of the new and sprawling space-research bureaucracy and other governmental organizations claiming larger shares of fund allocations. The dream of a unified scientific response to matters of national policy that was born in 1945 has tended to dissolve under the impact of the clashing commitments among scientists to contending bureaucratic organizations.

Not all American scientists have become the domesticated retainers of their bureaucratic masters. Not only the continued activities of the F.A.S. (for example, the part it played in the recent partial test-ban treaty) and the creation, in the last few years, of a variety of *ad hoc* committees of scientists concerned with such issues as civil defense, disarmament, arms control, and the like testify to this point: In addition, the emergence of a new elite of scientific statesmen in Washington must be noted. In recent years, a number of top scientists has moved into advisory positions on the highest governmental levels. In 1957, President Eisenhower created the post of Special Assistant for Science and Technology and appointed James R. Killian as the first incumbent. The Special Assistant has a very broad mandate. He has access to the proceedings of the Cabinet and the National Security Council, and he can convey his recommendations directly to the President. He is also the chairman of a broad President's Science Advisory Committee composed of leading nongovernment scientists. In addition, such other top scientists as the Director of the National Science Foundation have access to the highest levels of executive decision-making. There are now many ways of direct access to the executive for scientists who prefer not to become attached to particular governmental agencies. These top positions have allowed scientists of broad vision and uncommon reflectiveness to immerse themselves in the whole gamut of policy decisions that touch upon the relationship between science and policy. Men like Jerome Wiesner and his predecessors are neither garden-variety bureaucrats nor habitual "yes men."

The broadening of the scientist's role is not limited to top-level scientists who have gained the ears of policy-makers through advisory positions. Outside government, different groups of scientists have continued to exercise pressure. The Pugwash conferences, initiated by Bertrand Russell and attended by scientists from both sides of the Iron Curtain, have attempted to bypass official power politics and to discuss freely such issues as nuclear disarmament, inspection, and control. In 1957, more than 2000 American scientists, responding to a call by Linus Pauling, signed an appeal for an international test-ban agreement. Others have appealed for an end to the arms race and for a change in the prevailing strategic doctrine of preponderant atomic power. Many have been active in such organizations as SANE. Although the scientific community as a whole may have lost some of the *élan* that it showed in the immediate postwar period, many of its members show continued concern with national and international policy issues in a variety of ways and on a variety of levels. Such activities and concerns have been important counterweights to the bureaucratic pressures toward turning the scientist into a highly skilled yet powerless and voiceless expert.

Many scientists who had initially been aroused by the effects of Hiroshima have long since returned to their laboratories and withdrawn from issues raised by the new impact of science on society. Many others have by now accepted the subtle constraints involved in dependence on government funds and defense contracts. Many have become expert technicians defending the differing positions of their employing agencies. Yet many others, whether through involvement in top-level political decision-making or through participation in movements criticizing political decision-makers, have developed a sensitivity to public issues that was rather infrequent before the war. Among them there has been a remarkable broadening of intellectual horizons. Even though some may upon occasion have been induced to make rather naive pronouncements and to underestimate the complexity of political action, many have moved a long way from specialized competence in narrow areas to broad-gauged concern with the central issues and the very core values of our culture.

THE PROSPECT FOR SCIENTIFIC INTELLECTUALS

During the Scientific Revolution, a very high proportion of all those engaged in science consisted of generalizers with broad involvement in all fields of knowledge and ideas. This generalism is clearly no longer existent. Science has become a professionalized activity carried out by highly specialized personnel in bureaucratic settings. The great majority of these men are not intellectuals, nor do they aspire to be such. Only a small proportion of the huge number of practicing scientists still embodies in its style of work earlier generalizing tendencies—although in absolute numbers there may be more such men today than earlier. Specialization and programed research now dominate almost all branches of science, and they exercise pressures against broader involvement that are hard to resist.

Recently, greater financial support has been given to pure, as distinct from applied, research, and within the applied field there has been a tendency to let scientists have a leeway in their investigations that was not customarily granted earlier. These signs are hopeful ones. The continued existence of a number of scientific hybrids is also encouraging. It remains true, nevertheless, that for the vast majority of scientists today professional tasks in themselves seem to preclude wider scientific concerns. But the new social roles that many scientists have assumed in the postwar years have been somewhat effective counterweights to exclusive absorption in specialized activities. To be sure, the familiar type of middle-aged or aging scientists who, believing that he can no longer contribute to his field, spends much of his time making after-dinner speeches on topics of general concern has not moved any nearer to intellectual status. Most of these excursions into foreign territory yield only platitudinous pronouncements or pious generalities; they can hardly be taken as serious contributions to the world of ideas. But the postwar period has witnessed the emergence on many levels of scientists who, through sustained and far from amateurish involvement with the central issues of our age, have cultivated uncommon sensitivity to the values of our culture and the fate of our society.

They are true scientific intellectuals. There are good reasons to believe that a breed that has produced Robert J. Oppenheimer, Linus Pauling, and James Conant is nowhere near extinction.

NOTES

1. Norbert Wiener, *Cybernetics* (New York: John Wiley & Sons, Inc., 1948), p. 8.
2. Fritz Machlup, *The Production and Distribution of Knowledge in the United States* (Princeton: Princeton University Press, 1962), p. 157.
3. *Ibid.*, p. 152.
4. *Ibid.*, p. 193.
5. *Ibid.*, p. 194.
6. *Ibid.*, p. 161.
7. John K. Galbraith, *American Capitalism: The Concept of Countervailing Power* (Boston: Houghton Mifflin Company, 1952), p. 91.
8. James B. Conant, *Science and Common Sense* (New Haven: Yale University Press, 1951), pp. 303, 305.
9. Jean Thibaud, "The Implications of State-Financed Research," *Science and Freedom* (Report of the Hamburg Conference of the Congress for Cultural Freedom) (Boston: Beacon Press, 1955), p. 93.
10. Richard L. Meier, "The Origins of the Scientific Species," *Bulletin of the Atomic Scientists*, VII (June, 1951), No. 6, 169–73.
11. Conant, *op. cit.*, p. 317.
12. *Ibid.*
13. *Ibid.*, p. 319.
14. Percy W. Bridgman, *Reflections of a Physicist* (New York: Philosophical Library, Inc., 1950), pp. 294–6.
15. *Ibid.*, pp. 297–8.
16. *Ibid.*, pp. 299–300.
17. John Jewkes, *et al.*, *The Sources of Invention* (New York: St Martin's Press, Inc., 1958).
18. *The New York Times*, October 20, 1963. These figures differ somewhat from those in Machlup, *op. cit.*
19. For other aspects of the negative image of science and scientists among high-school students, see Margaret Mead and Rhoda Métraux, "The Image of the Scientist," *Science*, 126 (August 20, 1957), No. 3270.
20. Robert K. Merton, *Social Theory and Social Structure* (Rev. ed.; New York: The Free Press, 1957), p. 212.
21. Cf. Simon Marcson, *The Scientist in American Industry* (Princeton: Princeton University Press, 1960); William Kornhauser, *Scientists in Industry* (Berkeley: University of California Press, 1962); and John J. Beer and W. David Lewis, "Aspects of the Professionalization of Science," *Daedalus* (Fall, 1963), pp. 764–84.

22. *Cf.* Barney G. Glaser, "The Local-Cosmopolitan Scientist," *American Journal of Sociology*, LXIX (November, 1963), No. 3, 249–59.

23. *The Wall Street Journal*, April 16, 1959.

24. Quoted in Jewkes, *op. cit.*, p. 138.

25. Conant, *op. cit.*, p. 320.

26. George W. Gray, "What Scientists Win Nobel Prizes," Bernard Barber and Walter Hirsch, eds., *The Sociology of Science* (New York: The Free Press, 1962), p. 560.

27. Conant, *op. cit.*, p. 321.

28. Quoted in J. Stefan Dupré and Sanford A. Lakoff, *Science and the Nation* (Englewood Cliffs, N. J.: Prentice-Hall, Inc., 1962), p. 105. I have relied heavily on this fine book in the section that follows. Bernard Barber's *Science and the Social Order* (Rev. ed.; New York: Collier Books, Inc., 1962) has also helped me considerably throughout this chapter; it is indispensable for anyone interested in the social functions and consequences of modern science.

29. Meier, *op. cit.*

30. A survey conducted by *Time* in 1947 reported similar findings. Sixty per cent of the scientists in the sample voted Democratic, while 80% of those who listed themselves as engineers voted Republican. See Ernest Haveman and Patricia West, *They Went To College* (New York: Harcourt, Brace & World, Inc., 1952).

31. Dupré and Lakoff, *op. cit.*, p. 160.

Chapter 23

INTELLECTUALS IN
WASHINGTON

THE ASSESSMENT OF THE ROLE AND STATUS OF
intellectuals in the federal government requires a distinction between two dissimilar types of Washington intellectuals: those who
have become career officials and those who are *ad hoc* bureaucrats
who have joined the administration during periods of national
emergency or of unusual political change. The first type tends to
identify careers with service in the federal bureaucracy and therefore to be highly dependent on it. The intellectuals of the second
type are less likely to be constrained by bureaucratic pressures, for
they do not affiliate permanently with public administration and
have ready alternatives in private life or academic positions.[1]

THE INTELLECTUAL AS A CIVIL SERVANT

Intellectuals who have become career officials perform staff
functions in helping to formulate or implement policies within a
public bureaucracy. Such functioning within a bureaucratic context requires specialized performances within a hierarchically ordered organization. It requires, in addition, recognition that the
policy-makers for whom staff functions are performed are in posi-

315

tions to specify the problems to which the staff intellectual is to address himself.

The structural position occupied by professionals in public bureaucracy already indicates the inherent tensions and role conflicts that characterize the careers of such men. They have typically been recruited from the academy or one of the professions and, prior to their entries into bureaucratic careers, have been accustomed to consider their professional or academic colleagues as their main reference groups. In other words, they have previously measured their worth and performance against the judgment of their peers. But once they have entered a public bureaucracy, matters change. Policy-makers or hierarchical superiors become a reference group, the salient definers of standards of performance.

Depending on their positions in the administrative hierarchy, these men have two possible modes of adaptation. They may attempt a series of compromises between the bureaucratic requirements of their positions and their professional goals and intellectual concerns. (This mode of adaptation is available only to those who have attained high ranks on the administrative ladder.) Or they may alternatively conceive their roles as merely to implement policies defined by the policy-makers. (This adaptation is typical of lower-ranking members of the bureaucracy.) In the second case, they have become mere technicians by abdicating concern with policy goals and limiting their activities to the application of technically efficient means to preselected ends. In Merton's words, "The occupational code of the technician constrains him to accept a dependency-relation to the executive. This sense of dependency, which is hedged about with sentiment, is expressed in the formula: the policy-maker supplies the goals (ends, objectives), and we technicians, on the basis of expert knowledge, indicate alternative means for reaching these ends."[2] Technicians are characterized by heteronomy, whereas intellectuals are relatively autonomous. Technicians cannot be intellectuals and need therefore concern us no further. Matters are different, however, for those government professionals who, while striving to live up to the requirements of their bureaucratic positions, also attempt to maintain a voice in the goals of policy and to satisfy the standards prevailing in the wider professional and intellectual community. Such men may continue to reside in the house of intellect, even though they are likely to suffer from much role conflict owing to their dual allegiance.

The root of the strain under which the bureaucratic intellectual inevitably suffers is the fact that his client is not the public, remotely or directly, but his hierarchical superior or a policy-maker concerned with translating general purposes into concrete programs of action. While the unattached intellectual defines his own problems, the attached intellectual finds himself in a situation in which the goals of action are largely defined for him. In spite of this limitation, however, the degree of restriction of his freedom depends on the rigor with which the goals are specified. The bureaucratic intellectual may retain a certain degree of freedom when the goals of the policy-maker lack specificity and merely indicate broad areas in which some action is to be taken at some later point in time. When the demands are highly specific (for example, for an estimate of the impact of population trends in the Soviet Union on military policy), only a technician's role is possible. When they are more general, however (perhaps for an elaboration of alternative courses of action open to the United States in relation to the Common Market), the bureaucratic intellectual acquires a certain amount of leeway. To be sure, any policy directive inevitably constitutes a delimitation of the field of inquiry and thus limits the bureaucratic intellectual's scope, yet it may still allow him more than a technician's role and encourage him to adumbrate alternative policy proposals.

The specificity or broadness of the policy-maker's demands on the bureaucratic intellectual seems determined largely by the point in the policy problem at which the intellectual is consulted. "The earlier in the continuum of decision that the bureaucratic intellectual operates, the greater his potential influence in guiding the decision. When the area of inquiry is vaguely indicated by the policy-maker, the intellectual's research can, within limits, focus attention on certain alternatives of action by ascribing greater weight to certain types of evidence."[3] Such seems to have been the case with the elaboration of Wilson's Fourteen Points and with many early New Deal programs. In those instances, intellectuals were in positions to propose new lines of policy. More recently, certain military intellectuals have been influential in the choice between rival strategic doctrines in atomic warfare. In such instances, intellectuals have sometimes succeeded in initiating policy "from below."

In the more typical situation, however, the bureaucratic intellectual is consulted only after a general line of action has been chosen, and he is requested only to provide information for policies that have already been determined. Then his scope is severely limited. He can no longer explore alternative lines of action and can consider only those aspects of the total situation directly related to the proposed policy. This severe limitation upon his perspective constrains him to pay attention only to that order of data that may be helpful in the implementation of the policy-maker's purposes. Such limitations serve, naturally, a conservative function insofar as they lead to the neglect of alternative policies. "The bureaucratic intellectual who must permit the policy-maker to define the scope of his research problem is implicitly lending his skills and knowledge to the preservation of a particular institutional arrangement."[4]

Whether or not the bureaucratic intellectual is allowed to deal with problems of a general scope does not depend on his good intentions or his private motives, nor does it depend on the happenstance of a goal being defined broadly. Problems are defined in more general terms at early points in the decision-making process. It follows that only men in the higher brackets of the administrative hierarchy are allowed access to problems at those points. At later points, when men lower in the hierarchy become involved, it is almost inevitable that only technical expertise will be required.

There is another type of pressure that operates to force bureaucratic intellectuals to depart from modes and procedures to which they had previously been accustomed in the academy or in a professional *milieu*. Work in bureaucracies is usually tied to action; it is "practical" rather than "theoretical," "concrete" rather than "abstract." While the unattached intellectual is free to pose a problem on any level of abstraction he deems desirable, the bureaucratic intellectual is tied to concrete facts. There are strong constraints upon him to think in technical and instrumental terms and to consider only those variables likely to be relevant to the implementation of policy within a given situation and immediately useful in operation. The policy-maker is not concerned with gathering data that do not bear directly on the policy at hand. The intellectual must therefore accept criteria of significance different from those that guided his conduct before he joined the bureaucracy. He must work on problems that may be theoretically trivial though practically significant, and he is prevented from working on problems that are theoretically significant though of trivial practical importance. Again, it is likely that those placed high in the administrative hierarchy have better chances to work on problems not closely tied to practical implementation, while those lower down are of necessity fully absorbed in practical work.

Additional frustrations for the intellectual arise from another facet of the policy-makers' orientation to action. In contrast to the academy, which institutionalizes the opportunity to consider a problem at leisure, action-oriented policy usually operates under time pressure. Intellectuals thus come into conflict with policy-makers in terms of their differing time perspectives. The policy-maker who must act *now* is impatient with intellectuals who want first to explore all the evidence, all the foreseeable consequences of given courses of action. Intellectuals in their turn resent actions taken on the basis of what they consider flimsy evidence. Hence the "deadline neurosis" of bureaucratic intellectuals, which is induced by their belief that the problems raised cannot possibly be solved within the allotted time. Again, time pressure is more constraining on the lower levels.

Still other problems arise from a structurally induced clogging of the lines of communication between policy-makers and staff intellectuals: Research findings on the way to the policy-maker may be distorted by intermediary personnel, and the administrative processing of material may so simplify the original results as to emasculate them. Findings may never reach the policy-maker at all; they may remain buried in the files of intermediaries and thus may fail to influence any action. Finally, findings, even when they reach their intended destination, may not be used by those for whom they were intended. In all these instances, the staff intellectual is likely to develop a sense of uselessness. Such frustration is likely to be more pronounced in the lower ranks of the hierarchy. The smaller the social distance between policy-maker and staff intellectual, the less the chance of blocked communication.

To sum up, pressures to abandon the intellectuals' role and to become specialized technicians instead operate throughout the bureaucratic structure of any public administration. The chances to resist such pressures increase, however, the higher the hierarchical position of the bureaucratic intellectual. In top echelons, it is possible to participate in the establishment of alternative courses of action, to consider goals as well as means, and to influence policy decisions. In the lower ranks of the hierarchy, only technical roles can be successfully enacted, and intellectuals in such positions must give up their prior orientations and commitments if they are to operate with any measure of success.

"The honeymoon of intellectuals and policy-makers," writes Merton, "is often nasty, brutish and short."[5] It has led to a relatively stable and enduring union, we may add, only on the top levels of the administrative hierarchy. And even there, we presume, the divorce rate is high.

THE INTELLECTUAL AS AN *AD HOC* BUREAUCRAT

In contrast to the regular civil servant, the *ad hoc* bureaucrat does not anticipate a permanent governmental career. He joins the government during times of political upheaval or national emergency. The move of New Deal intellectuals from the academy to Washington, which was discussed in some detail in Chapter 14, is a case in point. A similar migration of previously unattached intellectuals to Washington occurred during World War I and World War II and again with the inauguration of the New Frontier. Though ideological motives may have varied considerably, in all these instances, intellectuals, from a sense of emergency or in response to the challenge that a new climate or reform seemed to provide, left positions in the academy or in various professions to join the administration. These men typically joined the government at fairly high levels in the hierarchy, so that they were in positions to concern themselves with questions of broad policy rather than with detailed implementation. Furthermore, the fact that they were defined and defined themselves as on only temporary duty in Washington gave them additional leverage in resisting pressures to confine themselves to technicians' roles. Nevertheless, one gains the strong impression that, except for a few individuals who attained policy-making ranks in or near the White House, the exigencies of their positions soon led to considerable restriction in the scope of their actions and the impact of their ideas. To be sure, in the very early days of an emergency, such intellectuals often seem to upset the sluggish routines of the various administrative branches to which they become temporarily attached. Not being bound by departmental traditions, they seem capable of transcending routines and of infusing their offices with new purpose. Yet, once this initial period is over—and it usually is over relatively soon —the bureaucratic apparatus absorbs these new men, slowly bending them to its procedures, habits, and styles. Much as biological organisms are capable of enveloping and neutralizing foreign bodies, so a bureaucracy is capable of bending the *ad hoc* bureaucrat to its own uses.

This process is understandable in light of the relationships between the policy-makers and the intellectuals who serve them in advisory capacities. The *ad hoc* bureaucrat, when he makes the move to Washington, thinks that he will be able to make a contribution to definition of the administration's policies and that his personal judgment will be sought by the decision-makers with whom he is to serve. But he typically finds that most of the time what is sought is his capacity to provide factual information rather than his considered judgment. He thinks that he will be on top, but he usually is only on tap. "The low valuation of personal views," says Henry A. Kissinger, "produces a greater concern with the collection of facts than with an interpretation of their significance; therefore the myth in our government that intelligence does not advise, it only reports."[6] Decision-makers are themselves in most cases not much given to reflection. Their work load is likely to be very high, and sheer lack of time inhibits the capacity to reflect upon larger perspectives. In addition, the requirements of rapid action, together with the general propensity of Americans to think in instrumental and pragmatic terms, leads decision-makers to move from decision to decision in rapid succession. That is why they tend to demand of their advisers not long-range answers based on thoughtful assessments of trends but factual information in tune with short-range requirements. "The smooth functioning of the administrative apparatus absorbs more energies than the definition of the criteria on which decision is to be based."[7]

The very scale and complexity of the questions that have to be decided by modern policy-makers, often upon fairly short notice, have led to proliferation of advisory staffs. Whenever a new difficulty arises, panels are set up to advise the policy-makers. Each problem becomes a special case to be discussed by a special set of advisers. Typically, each problem is studied separately in an *ad hoc* fashion, and the absence of clear-cut over-all goals leads to fragmentation of policy, which makes it difficult for the intellectual to introduce a general perspective. He is usually called upon in his capacity as a "specialist" in ideas. His advice is then combined with that of others from different fields, on the assumption "that the policy-maker is able to choose the correct amalgam between 'theoretical' and 'practical' advice. And even in this capacity the intellectual is not a free agent. It is the executive who determines in the first place whether he needs advice. He and the bureaucracy frame the questions to be answered. The policy-maker determines the standards of relevance. He decides who is to be consulted and thereby the definition of 'expertness' . . . The contribution of the intellectual to policy is therefore in terms of criteria that he has played a minor role in establishing . . . He is asked to solve problems, not to contribute to the definition of goals."[8]

Nor need we always assume that when the decision-maker calls in advisers he really wants or needs advice. If the adviser has an outstanding reputation, his name may be sought simply to legitimize a policy decision that has in fact already been made. In this case, "what the policy-maker wants from the intellectual is not ideas but endorsement."[9] In still other cases, the adviser may in fact become a sacrificial lamb. "If the solution proves unsatisfactory (as it certainly will to some), it is the expert who carries away the collective tribal guilt and permits the enemies to restore peace once more."[10]

This discussion highlights the paradox that a modern administration calls in many more intellectuals in advisory capacities than was the case earlier but that these intellectuals operate in environments that do not allow them to make the contributions for which they may best be suited. Every administrator has his panel of experts and intellectuals. Policy-planning bodies multiply, and study groups mushroom. Yet it is difficult "for the intellectual to introduce a general perspective even from the vantage point of his own calling."[11] *Ad hoc* intellectual bureaucrats, together with outside consultants and civil-service intellectuals, do indeed participate in the preparation of policy-making to an unprecedented degree. But their participation amounts mainly to the gathering of data rather than to contributions to judgments, whether long-range or short-range, on which policy must ultimately depend. Furthermore, even when the policy-maker requires judgment in preference to facts, he is likely to call in a variety of advisers with differing opinions. "These are then expected to adjust their differences by analogy with the committee procedure of the bureaucracy. Not surprisingly, the result is more often a common denominator than a well-rounded point of view."[12]

The demand for intellectuals in Washington arose, presumably, at least partially, because it was felt that, in a revolutionary period, intellectuals would be most able to initiate innovations. But "the administrative approach to intellectual effort tends to destroy the environment from which innovation grows. Its insistence on 'results' discourages the intellectual climate that might produce important ideas whether or not the bureaucracy feels it needs them."[13]

These are some of the reasons why the majority of intellectuals who initially move to Washington out of a sense of mission and devotion are likely to be disillusioned fairly soon. They may then return to their previous positions, or they may adjust to the administrative realities by toning down their expectations and accepting advisory roles that make few demands on their intellectual capacities. Or, they may attempt to move from advisory to policy-making tasks. But once they decide to make such moves, they must divest themselves of one of the key qualities of intellectuals: their disinterestedness.

Earlier parts of this book have explored in some detail the incompatibility between power and intellect. Intellectuals, it turns out, have rarely managed to acquire power while remaining intellectuals. This point is as true in the present as it was in the past. The judgment of Walter Lippmann, one of the few intellectuals who have, over a long period of time, acquired intimate knowledge of the ways of the men of power, remains valid. At the very height of the New Deal, Lippmann wrote of college professors who had become "entangled in the making of policy and the administration of government": "It is only knowledge freely acquired that is disinterested. When, therefore, men whose profession is to teach and to investigate become the makers of policy, become members of an administration in power, become politicians and leaders of causes, they are committed. Nothing they can say can be relied upon as disinterested. Nothing they can teach can be trusted as scientific. It is impossible to mix the pursuit of knowledge and the exercise of political power and those who have tried it turn out to be very bad politicians or they cease to be scholars."[14] There seems no reason to revise this judgment in view of what has happened in the almost thirty years since these lines were written.[15]

NOTES

1. Robert K. Merton, "Role of the Intellectual in Public Bureaucracy," *Social Theory and Social Structure* (Rev. ed.; New York: The Free Press, 1957), p. 214. I am greatly indebted to this essay. In fact, major

portions of this section are little more than restatements of Merton's analysis.

2. *Ibid.*, p. 213.

3. *Ibid.*, p. 216.

4. *Ibid.*, p. 218.

5. *Ibid.*, p. 222.

6. Henry A. Kissinger, "The Policymaker and the Intellectual," *The Reporter*, XX (March 5, 1959), No. 5, 30. I have drawn heavily on the insights in this essay.

7. *Ibid.*

8. *Ibid.*, p. 33.

9. *Ibid.*

10. Wilbert Moore, *The Conduct of the Corporation* (New York: Random House, Inc., 1962), p. 250. Moore writes of the role of experts in private administration, but most of his findings also apply to public administration.

11. Kissinger, *op. cit.*, p. 33.

12. *Ibid.*, p. 33.

13. *Ibid.*

14. Walter Lippmann, "The Deepest Issues of Our Time," *Vital Speeches*, July 1, 1936. Quoted in Arthur Schlesinger, Jr., *The Politics of Hope* (Boston: Houghton Mifflin Company, 1963), p. 147.

15. It has often been claimed that the Kennedy administration had a peculiarly intellectual character that distinguished it from previous regimes. I cannot accept this interpretation. Intelligence, taste, cultivation, and academic titles do not yet establish intellectual character. Intellectuals are characterized by, among other things, a critical stance toward existing institutions and habits of thought, and their politics aims at transforming reality in tune with a set of ideas. These characteristics seemed largely missing among the men in President Kennedy's entourage. They were specialists in power or of administration, of warfare or of rocket techniques. They were mainly highly skilled managerial experts, not intellectuals. Those intellectuals who, beside *knowing* something, also retained the will to *do* something new were soon shifted to peripheral positions in the administration—Chester Bowles became a kind of roving ambassador in Africa and later ambassador to India; Kenneth Galbraith preceded him in India and then returned to Harvard; George Kennan also became an ambassador (to Yugoslavia) and later returned to the Institute of Advanced Studies; W. W. Rostow became a sort of trouble shooter for the State Department; and Arthur Schlesinger wrote speeches—and movie reviews. *Cf.* Henry Pachter, "Wie Kennedy Regiert," *Die Neue Gesellschaft*, X (Maerz-April, 1963), No. 2.

Chapter 24

INTELLECTUALS IN THE
MASS-CULTURE INDUSTRIES

THE INDUSTRIES ENGAGED IN THE PRODUCTION OF MASS culture share basic characteristics with other mass-production industries. In both, the process of production involves a highly developed division of labor and the hierarchical co-ordination of many specialized activities. In these industries, no worker, no matter how highly placed in the organizational structure, has individual control over a particular product. The product emerges from the co-ordinated efforts of the whole production team, and it is therefore difficult for an individual producer to specify clearly his particular contribution.

Critics of the industrial mode of production since its inception have stressed its alienating and frustrating consequences for the producers. They have emphasized the loss of a sense of individual purpose and of individual achievement, the loss of a sense of autonomy and identity brought in its wake. They have especially stressed that work, which in earlier modes of production served to give meaning to man's life by furnishing him a sense of his own creativity, has become a meaningless routine in industrial production. The product of a man's labor is no longer the embodiment of his creative urges but an alien power in which he can no longer recognize himself.

Whatever may be true of other participants in the work process of mass industries, it stands to reason that, for intellectuals, mass-production methods are peculiarly unsuitable. Nothing is as important to the intellectual as the work he creates. Through this work, he affirms his calling, and his creation strengthens his identity. This characteristic commitment of the intellectual to his work is the root of the tensions and frustrations he experiences when he accepts employment within the framework of the mass-culture industries. In these industries, in radio, television, the movies, and most mass-circulation magazines, the end product is the result of the combined efforts of a great many people and can only in the rarest circumstances carry the imprint of any single personality. Furthermore, the mass-culture industry, by the very fact that it is an industry, must be concerned above all with salability. The products must be marketed, and in the normal course of events sales appeal takes primacy over all other considerations. The producers of mass-culture goods may privately care as much for aesthetic values or human truth as do other men, but, in their roles as producers, they must be primarily concerned with commercial returns.

The inherent contradiction between the goals and aims of the men in charge of the mass-culture industries and those of the intellectuals who have consented to become part of their apparatuses expresses itself in the contempt these intellectuals frequently show for their work. The products of their labor, far from being embodiments of their own thoughts, are experienced as alien. The French sociologist Edgar Morin has observed this phenomenon with great acuteness: "One notices the multiplication of authors within the cultural industries who are not only contemptuous of their work, but deny that their work is their work. The author can no longer identify himself with his work. An extraordinary repulsion has been created between it and him. Hence the greatest satisfaction of the artist which is that of identifying himself with his work, that is to justify himself through his work, to build on it his own transcendence, disappears. This is a type of alienation which is not without analogy with that of the industrial worker, but it takes place under peculiar subjective and objective conditions, and with that essential difference: the author is *over*-paid."[1]

The vast majority of those employed in the mass-culture industries can, by no stretch of the imagination, be called intellectuals. They may be first-rate craftsmen, men of talent commanding much expert knowledge, but they do not dwell in the house of intellect. Yet there are among them certain marginal men who must be considered here. The majority of these marginal men have entered the mass-culture industries only after achieving independent careers elsewhere. They have not risen through the ranks of the industry, slowly absorbing the requisite occupational norms in the process. Instead, they have begun as independent writers, reviewers, novelists, playwrights, or musicians, and only at later stages in their lives have they decided to shift careers. Others in this general category, although they entered the mass-culture industries earlier, came only after exposure to the standards of high culture during their university education. It is among these two types that we find the kinds of frustration suggested. They suffer from a clash of expectations, in the sense that they are unable to reconcile standards of excellence internalized in earlier parts of their life cycles with the standards and demands governing them once they have accepted work within the mass-culture industries.

THE MOVIE INDUSTRY

The movie industry furnishes prime examples of the clash between the standards of previously unattached intellectuals and of mass-culture production. A journeyman producer in Hollywood need not be troubled by discrepancies between his role and his self-image; men like F. Scott Fitzgerald in his script-writing years must be. Such a man finds it hard to reconcile himself to the idea that his work is only an interchangeable part of a larger product or process in which many have parts. A Hollywood script, for example, is never the product of a single writer; it is rewritten, restructured, changed, and adapted by a whole line of writers and producers. The authority of the hierarchical superior to revise script is a key symbol of the change of role and status the intellectual undergoes once he leaves his unattached position to join a mass-production team.

That the writing of movie scripts follows assembly-line techniques is by now a cliché. But one major difference between assembly-line production in a factory and movie production has usually been overlooked: Whereas industrial production proceeds according to rationally and efficiently planned principles, movie production is usually a highly irrational affair. Engineers and technologists may not all be led, as Thorstein Veblen believed, to replace magical and traditional thought-ways by matter-of-fact and rational thinking. But the industrial machine undoubtedly requires calculated and precise behavior from its tenders. In movies, however, the production process is characterized by whim, caprice, fickleness, and vanity. Men dominated by these traits wield their power capriciously and unpredictably over those engaged in the production process. The ordeal of producing ideas that are subsequently distorted, changed, or torn from their contexts is thus intensified by inability to explain these changes rationally.

The "parcelling out of the soul" that Max Weber considered a major characteristic of bureaucracy is reflected and symbolized in Hollywood's parceling out of credits. They often run: Screenplay by ——; From the book by ——; Adaptation by ——; Additional dialogue by ——; Additional scenes by ——. Seventeen writers worked on *Gone With the Wind*, and *Foreign Correspondent* used the services of nine writers, among whom were such well known names as Ben Hecht, Budd Schulberg, and Robert Benchley.[2] Not all films have so many collaborators working on the stories, but "team writing" is the rule. In contrast to typical bureaucratic procedures, however, such writing is not the result of careful planning but depends largely on the changes in mood of the producer or director as he goes along or on power struggles and intrigues in the front office. Writer number one may be asked to outline the story, and writer number two to fill in details. Later writer number three may be assigned to rewrite the dialogue or to change the plot. Objections by the director or even by a star may lead the producer, before shooting the film, to assign still another writer to correct the script. If the producer decides that the script needs more humor, a gag writer is put to work. There are writers specializing in romantic dialogue, tightening plots, or polishing dialogue. Although he may have had a part in writing the script, the screenwriter is rarely its author.

The basic cause of disaffection among Hollywood screenwriters who are not simply journeymen technicians is that, in Leo Rosten's words, they are "not writing prose or producing literature." They are "feeding an enormous machine that converts words, faces, sounds and images into some nine thousand feet of celluloid."[3] A few among those men may eventually succeed in becoming independent director-producers, so that they can be sure that their own scripts will not be mangled in the production process. But they are very few, and even they, one feels, are caught most of the time in the system and are therefore subject to compulsions over which they lack control. Lillian Ross, in her natural history of the making of the film *The Red Badge of Courage*,[4] shows why it is almost inevitable that box-office considerations will eventually defeat most high-minded efforts to produce works of artistic integrity. Miss Ross describes the various pushes and pulls between the writer-director John Huston, the producer Gottfried Reinhardt, and Doré Schary, the studio production head. She describes how the movie went through a number of successive transformations after various previews had shown that the mass audience was not likely to take to the original version. At the end of the process, Reinhardt described resignedly the new version: ". . . The picture has lost some of its complexities and colors. It was now a straighter, simpler picture. The consensus was, you can follow it now, you can understand it . . . It is probably a very fine picture. Everybody tells me it is. But I would lie if I said it was the picture I had hoped for . . ."[5] The alienative effect of Hollywood production methods seems almost impossible to avoid.

I know of few more poignant expressions of an intellectual's despair at sudden recognition of the discrepancy between the standards of Hollywood and those he previously adhered to than a letter from Fitzgerald to the producer Joseph Mankiewicz. Fitzgerald had come to screenwriting largely in order to recoup his fortunes. It was a period in his life during which he was tortured by self-doubts and craved reassurance and acceptance. Here is what he wrote in rage and anguish to Mankiewicz, after the latter had rewritten his script for *Three Comrades*: "To say I am disillusioned is putting it mildly. . . . For nineteen years . . . I've written best selling entertainment, and my dialogue is supposedly right up at the top. But I learn from the script that you've suddenly decided that it isn't good dialogue and you can take a few hours off and do much better . . . Oh, Joe, can't producers ever be wrong? I am a good writer—honest. I thought you were going to play fair."[6]

On the way to see the movie supposedly based on his script, Fitzgerald said to his companion, "at least they have kept my beginning." When it was over, he growled, "They have changed even that."[7] Fitzgerald is certainly among the few great stylists America has produced during this century, and that is why his "I am a good writer—honest" is so utterly pitiful. At the beginning of his Hollywood career, he was not yet aware that the standards of writing required in Hollywood had little relation to those prevailing in the literary world in which he had moved. He was to learn better—witness his unfinished Hollywood novel, *The Last Tycoon*. He continued to work in Hollywood, but his loathing for the kind of work he was doing, as well as his self-loathing, continued to increase. Nor was his despair simply a matter of his personal problems. One encounters such self-loathing among many other screenwriters, most of whom come to the industry after first working on their own. Leo Rosten sent a questionnaire to Hollywood script writers, which contained this request: "Comment on American movies today." The responses of 141 writers, who made a total of 169 remarks about movie content, include no fewer than 133 entirely unfavorable comments. (There were twenty-five entirely favorable comments and eleven comments that were neither favorable nor unfavorable.)[8]

In her anthropological study of Hollywood, Hortense Powdermaker states succinctly the reasons for the frustrations of the screenwriters: "The occupational satisfactions, traditionally a part of the writer's craft, are lacking. Even though the script writer's name may be among the list of credits for a movie, it is rare . . . for him honestly to feel that he has communicated anything of his own to an audience. He has ceased to be a writer in the real sense of the word. Instead, he takes dictation. For many who have known the satisfactions of creation out of their own experiences and imagination, this must inevitably cause frustration."[9] A certain number of writers manages to adjust to Hollywood careers, but they are not usually men who have previously known the satisfactions of creation. Those who find it easiest to accept the system are either men who have served as writer-employees before coming to Hollywood (newspapermen, advertising writers, publicists) or writers who have written only for the screen.[10] Those, on the other hand, who come to Hollywood from independent intellectual or creative careers, although they may relish its affluent life styles, almost invariably live "lives of quiet desperation."

One evidence of this desperation is the frequency of self-depreciative and self-hating comments made by screenwriters. I doubt that there are many occupations, except advertising, in which one finds practitioners who refer so obsessively to their having "sold out" or in which they compare themselves to kept women in New York's Park Avenue penthouses.[11] While in most occupations ability to command high salaries increases the self-esteem and confidence of the recipient, the contrary often seems the case among screenwriters. The fact that they are highly paid, because it suggests the discrepancy between the returns of "real writers" and their own, increases their lack of self-esteem.

Another indication of the estrangement and self-hatred so pervasive among Hollywood writers is the high proportion that was attracted to Stalinism in the Thirties and Forties. As the appeal of Stalinism proved strongest among those sections of the working class that were or felt themselves to be socially dispossessed, so it was most successful among those intellectuals suffering acutely from a sense of alienation. Independent intellectuals were also attracted to Stalinism, but for most of them their flirtations were only passing interludes, temporary reactions to the sense of dislocation that pervaded the country during the Depression. In Hollywood, by contrast, the lure of Stalinism proved more enduring and lasted till after the War. Few intellectuals in possession of their craft and able to employ it with some independence and creativity proved vulnerable to Stalinism for any length of time, but those lacking the possibility or capacity for serious work, especially those working in the mass-culture industries, found in Stalinism an outlet for their frustrations and self-hatred, their general *ressentiment*.[12] Hence the ironic fact that the Hollywood chapters of the Communist Party and its numerous satellites had many more members during the Thirties and early Forties than had chapters in highly industrialized areas.

THE WEEKLY MASS-CIRCULATION MAGAZINES

The frustrations and tensions of intellectuals in all the mass-culture industries stem from the structures of these industries. Despite their concrete differences in product, working conditions are similar in all of them. It is the nature of mass production for the market, rather than the peculiarities of each particular industry, that is decisive. That is why Hollywood and the weekly mass-circulation magazines partake of the same characteristics.

Like Hollywood screenwriters, most journalists and other newspapermen who work for these magazines are not intellectuals and lay no claim to intellectual standing. Again, as in Hollywood, we find a number of men who, after earlier careers as writers, book reviewers for elite magazines, novelists, and the like, have joined these weeklies. These men suffer the same frustrations as do their counterparts in the movies.

T. S. Matthews, who worked for twenty-four years at *Time* and was at one time its managing editor, is an especially valuable witness in his autobiography *Name and Address*.[13] After graduation from Princeton, Matthews "never intended to be a journalist, [but] meant to be a great writer."[14] When he needed a job in order to get married, he joined the staff of *The New Republic* as a book reviewer. Four years later, when a new editor took over, Matthews resigned and took a position with *Time*, again, at first, as a book reviewer. Here is how he describes the environment in which he worked: "On the *New Republic* I had grown accustomed to expressing myself as I pleased and then seeing my copy printed just as I had written it, without so much as a comma changed; on the *New Republic* I don't think I was ever 'cut for space.' Now my copy was hacked about, rewritten, cut to ribbons, rude questions and jeering comments scribbled in the margin; sometimes it disappeared altogether, and I learned later that it had been thrown out as hopeless, 'no story.' "[15]

The novelist John Brooks, who also worked for a while at *Time*, describes a similar experience in his novel *The Big Wheel*:[16] "As soon as I saw the appearance of the typescript I had a sick feeling. He had edited the text so much that it looked as if a hen had been walking on the paper with inky feet. I read it and tossed it back on his desk, then composed myself in a chair and waited for the blow to fall. 'Well, nice piece, Dick, nice piece.' I think my jaw dropped. 'You saw my editing. Just sharpening up. No essential changes. Nice idea you had.' . . . 'That's not rewriting. You ought to see a *Present Day* story after it's really rewritten. This is no learned journal. Nobody's words are sacred, everybody goes under the pencil, Dick. I'll tell you why. We have to have things a certain way. You know what I mean, Dick. *A certain way*.' "

The conditions of work described here seem not dissimilar to those faced by screenwriters. On these magazines, staff men are expected to put out products that conform to certain patterns that are the trademarks of the magazines. Marked individual departures are not permitted.

Dwight Macdonald's comment that "the specifications for an editorship at *Time*, Inc., are those for a good radio set: maximum receptivity and minimum static (read: individual thought)."[17] This de-emphasis on individual thought is symbolized in the anonymity of the product. *Time* articles are never signed. The writer's only public existence is on the masthead. Macdonald writes sardonically, "As nuns sacrifice their hair, so Luce's writers are shorn of their name."[18] Other news magazines may carry a few signed columns, but in all of them the bulk of the product is anonymous. There can therefore be no interplay between the writer and his audience. Although the news magazine story may not pass through as many hands as does the typical movie script, it does go through a series of rewrites so that the end product may bear little resemblance to the initial manuscript. Brooks describes the feeling of a man assigned to such rewriting: "I was making certain small changes which would completely change the import of something another man had written in Europe. Why? For myself? Of course not, absurd. For the ultimate reader? . . . What the reader was going to think meant nothing to me. On the other hand, what Burnside [the editor] was going to think meant a great deal to me. He was the man who held the buggy whip."[19]

Professional newspapermen, accustomed to heavy editing, are not likely to object to it. They take it in their stride, even though they may grumble about it. But writers from other environments and accustomed to considering a man's work his individual creation for which he alone is responsible are likely to experience feelings ranging from cynical dissatisfaction to acute frustration. Here is Mr. Matthews's testimony: "I couldn't take *Time* seriously . . . I didn't like *Time*. On every piece of copy I typed I could have written the truth, 'I don't like my work.' "[20]

During his seven years as a book reviewer at *Time*, Matthews read eight books a week, reviewing the five that interested him most, always dreading the moment when he had to sit down at the typewriter to turn out his 1500 to 2500 words, fully aware that the lead paragraph, over which he worked hardest, would be disfigured most in the editing. He nevertheless decided to enter the regular *Time* hierarchy and eventually made his way to the top. Even there, as he soon realized, he did not enjoy the freedom to change the operation of the magazine: "I soon discovered that it was all I could do to keep it plying back and forth on schedule, on its regular run."[21] He finally quit over a cover story on Adlai Stevenson: "The distortions, suppressions and slanting of its political 'news' seemed to me to pass the bounds of politics and to commit an offense against the ethics of journalism."[22] Yet he had spent half a lifetime on *Time*, and one of the reviewers of his autobiography seems justified in calling it "a commentary on the achievement of success and the simultaneous loss of identity."[23]

Not all intellectuals who worked at *Time* had Mr. Matthews's stamina or persistence. He tells the story of his friend Robert Cantwell: ". . . It was a bad day for him when he walked into the *Time* office. He had published two novels . . . and was obviously on his way to becoming a writer of some distinction . . . He was as out of place on *Time* as a canary in a coal mine . . . Cantwell's sensitive talent on occasion was invaluable to *Time*. But he never published another novel, and his career on *Time* ended in a breakdown."[24] Dwight Macdonald feels the same about his friend, the gifted writer James Agee, who, throughout most of his adult life, worked for *Time* and its sister publications.[25] Neither Macdonald nor anybody, I suppose, can *prove* that Agee failed fully to develop his talents because of his ties to these magazines, but the presumption is very strong. In his early days on *Fortune*, Agee was assigned to write on such topics as rare wines, famous orchid collections, and the world's ten most precious jewels. Later, according to Macdonald, "[Luce] thought it somehow immoral that a writer should do only what he was best at—there was a lot of the Puritan in Luce. So he assigned to Agee as occupational therapy an article on the Price of Steel Rails . . ." Still later, Agee was permitted to write on movies, a topic at which he *was* best. Comparison between these reviews and those he wrote for *The Nation*, however, strongly suggests the constraints that continued to operate on him.

I have attempted to show that the major frustrations from which the intellectual suffers in the mass-culture industries stem from his lack of control over his work and his absorption into an anonymous production process in which he loses his autonomy. It follows that, in magazines that to some extent depart from the "ideal type" of mass-circulation magazine and in which these characteristics are less pronounced, intellectuals are likely to find more congenial environments for their work. Magazines like *The New Yorker* that, while stressing particular editorial formulas, still shun mass-produced uniformity, leave leeway to individual contributors. Such magazines have been traditionally somewhat hospitable to intellectuals, and those who have worked for them, while they may have suffered all sorts of individual disappointments, seem not to have encountered systematized frustrations.

The chances for intellectuals in the mass-culture industries must be rated low. While they may upon occasion work within these settings in marginal employments—one thinks of William Faulkner's work in Hollywood—regular employment usually leads to systematic alienation and frustration. In fact, the mass-culture industries seem so inimical to intellect that they can fully absorb only those who have chosen to sacrifice it.

NOTES

1. Edgar Morin, *L'esprit du temps* (Paris: Grasset, 1962), p. 38.
2. Leo Rosten, *Hollywood* (New York: Harcourt, Brace & World, Inc., 1941), p. 311. I have profited much from this excellent study.
3. *Ibid.*, p. 308.
4. Lillian Ross, *Picture* (New York: Harcourt, Brace & World, Inc., 1952).
5. *Ibid.*, p. 222.
6. Quoted in Arthur Mizener, *The Far Side of Paradise* (Boston: Houghton Mifflin Company, 1951), p. 278.
7. *Cf.* Sheila Graham and Gerold Frank, *Beloved Infidel* (New York: Holt, Rinehart & Winston, Inc., 1958), p. 232.
8. Rosten, *op. cit.*, p. 326.
9. Hortense Powdermaker, *Hollywood, The Dream Factory* (Boston: Little, Brown & Co., 1950), p. 148. I have relied heavily on this major anthropological study.
10. Roston, *op. cit.*, p. 310.
11. Powdermaker, *op. cit.*, p. 149.
12. *Cf.* Irving Howe and Lewis A. Coser, *The American Communist Party, a Critical History* (Rev. ed.; New York: Praeger Paperbacks, 1962), p. 525. I have reproduced a few passages from this study.
13. T. S. Matthews, *Name and Address* (New York: Simon and Schuster, Inc., 1960).
14. *Ibid.*, p. 186.
15. *Ibid.*, p. 219.
16. John Brooks, *The Big Wheel* (New York: Pocket Books, Inc., 1951), pp. 40–1.
17. Dwight Macdonald, "Time, Life, Fortune," *The Nation* (May 22, 1937), pp. 583–6.
18. *Ibid.*
19. Brooks, *op. cit.*, p. 113.
20. Matthews, *op. cit.*, pp. 221–2.
21. *Ibid.*, pp. 260–1.
22. *Ibid.*, p. 271.
23. Gertrude Himmelfarb, "Anonymity, 'Time', and Success," *Commentary* (July, 1960), pp. 83–6.
24. Matthews, *op. cit.*, pp. 228–9.
25. Dwight Macdonald, "James Agee," *Against the American Grain* (New York: Random House, Inc., 1962), pp. 143–66.

Chapter 25

FOUNDATIONS AS GATEKEEPERS
OF CONTEMPORARY
INTELLECTUAL LIFE

THE LIFE AND WORK OF INTELLECTUALS ARE POWER-
fully influenced not only by their social and organizational settings but also by a variety of institutions that operate as brokers
of ideas and as cultural transmission belts. Such institutions play a
major part in the social process of reward and punishment through
which intellectual products are selected and received within the
culture at large. Only one such institution, the foundation, can be
considered here.

Irving Howe recently began a discussion of modern fiction with
a picture of what might have happened to a feverish, hungry, de-
spondent Raskolnikov, if, just before he resolved to kill the old
pawnbroker, the doorbell had rung, and he had received this letter:
"Dear Sir, It is my pleasure to inform you, on behalf of the Guggenheim Foundation, that you have been awarded a fellowship for
the study of color imagery in Pushkin's poetry and its relation to
the myths of the ancient Muscovites. If you will be kind enough
to visit our office . . . arrangements can be made for commencing
your stipend immediately." The terrible deed he had contemplated
could then be forgotten, and "gliding from fellowship to fellowship, Raskolnikov may now end his life as a sober Professor of
Literature."[1]

Whimsical though this passage may be, Howe highlights the

337

importance foundations have acquired in American life. They are a peculiarly modern and a peculiarly American institution. Few of them antedate the turn of the century, and there are practically no European equivalents. The foundation, an instrument for contributing private wealth to public purposes, may be defined formally as "a nongovernmental, nonprofit organization having a principal fund of its own, managed by its own trustees or directors, and established to maintain or aid . . . activities servicing the common welfare."[2] Or it may be defined alternatively as "a large body of money completely surrounded by people who want some."[3] However defined, the foundation has become one of the major determinants of intellectual life in America. "Very few important cultural projects of any size are consummated in this country without having experienced either the direct or indirect impact of foundation philosophy and influence."[4]

The foundations dispose of huge sums of money, which give them very considerable leverage in the cultural life of the country. Total expenditures of seventy-seven larger foundations in 1953 amounted to more than $160 million.[5] The Ford Foundation alone has an annual income of $100 million.[6] In the fiscal year 1957, the Ford Foundation reported, "a total of $345,200,897 was paid out on grants made within the year or carried over from prior years."[7]

The foundation is an institution exercising vital authority over men of knowledge, if for no other reason than that it controls funds that they require in the exercise of their tasks. Democratic political thought generally agrees that, where there is authority, there ought to be accountability to those over whom authority is exercised. But the foundation is not held accountable to its grantees or to the public at large. Its grantees are simply a group of claimants, and foundation officials have no obligation to account to them for their decisions. Similarly, the public at large exercises no control over the foundations' decisions—beyond some very general legal regulations connected mainly with their tax exemptions. Foundation officials are in situations similar to those of the managers of modern corporations. They make their decisions in a "responsible manner," but they are in fact responsible to no one outside the foundations.[8]

A foundation's organizational structure consists of salaried executives, usually with academic backgrounds, who run the day-to-day affairs of the organizations, and a board of trustees to whom they are accountable. The trustees then have the ultimate decision-making powers over what grants are to be made or withheld. Their general orientations are thus the major determinants of the foundation's policies and its impact on the cultural scene. That is, they are important gatekeepers of ideas. With the power of the purse, they are in positions to foster certain ideas or lines of inquiry while neglecting or de-emphasizing others.

A composite profile of foundation trustees shows them to be recruited disproportionately from elite schools on the Eastern Seaboard and to be engaged in occupations of prestige, among which law and business predominate. A study of trustees in twenty large foundations discloses that most come from a fairly narrow segment of the population. Almost half hold undergraduate degrees from Harvard, Yale, and Princeton Universities, another third was educated in other private colleges, and only 18% were graduated from state universities. In terms of occupational background, 37% come from business, 19% from law, and only 14% from education and research. Business, financial management, the law, and education together account for the backgrounds of 70% of these trustees.[9] Foundation trustees are an elite group representative of certain "establishment" values and traditions. It is to be noted, in addition, that top foundation officials frequently have close ties with Washington policy-makers and that there is a fairly constant interchange between top-level positions in the foundations and the federal government. Three recent secretaries of state, John Foster Dulles, Dean Acheson, and Dean Rusk previously held positions with major foundations.

A few years ago, the so-called Reece Committee of the House of Representatives investigated the foundations, charging them with attempts to undermine the "free enterprise system." In contrast, William H. Whyte, Jr.,[10] is of the opinion that "the problem is not that the foundations are boldly upsetting the *status quo*. It is quite the opposite. The problem is that the foundations may become a major influence in reinforcing the *status quo*."[11] Whyte may be correct about most major foundations, yet whether or not the backgrounds of top foundation trustees and executives conservatively influence their decisions on who will receive funds and for what purposes depends on the goals of the foundations and their organizational structures.

There are several types of foundation. Some give financial support to projects originated by outsiders, while others set up their own projects and take final responsibility both for originating and for administrating programs. The Carnegie Foundation may be taken as a typical example of the granting foundation; the Russell Sage Foundation, on the other hand, is a typical operating foundation. Other foundations may pursue both tasks concurrently.[12]

In the operating foundation, proposals within its general areas of interest are made by the staff or the trustees, although outside agencies or individuals may be consulted. If an appropriation is approved by the trustees, a project director is engaged; he may then either rely on the foundation's permanent staff or recruit his own. The results of his investigation are finally published as books or pamphlets, either by the foundation's own department of publications or through commercial channels.[13] Such operating foundations are essentially similar to other types of nonprofit research institute.

Granting foundations are of much greater importance in intellectual life. Two subtypes must be distinguished, however, not only because of differences in their organizational structures, but also because of their dissimilar impacts on the cultural scene. The first type is relatively small, has little bureaucratic apparatus, and selects worthy applicants for grants or fellowships without attempting to influence the directions of inquiry of potential grantees. The Guggenheim Foundation is an example of this type. A person applying for a Guggenheim grant proposes a project *he* wants to do, and the Foundation limits itself to selecting those applicants whose projects it considers to have the greatest potentialities. It stands to reason that, in such foundations, the trustees play fairly passive roles; they ratify the decisions of the executives normally without interfering in day-to-day operations. Matters are very different in the major foundations with large administrative staffs. These foundations define the areas of research or other cultural activities in which they are interested and help to stimulate and structure the requests for grants that they receive.[14] This approach means, of course, that the administrative staff has much greater powers over potential grantees and that the trustees have final say not only over general orientations but over specific grants as well.

There are three major reasons why the flow of funds from the major foundations differs from that of the minor ones. These reasons determine the distinctive impact of the major foundations on intellectual life: The major foundations tend to favor organizations rather than individual recipients for their grants; the funds they grant flow mainly to specific areas of interest rather than to all intellectually appealing projects; and they tend to favor those projects that center upon "problem-solving."

The big foundations—Ford, Rockefeller, Carnegie—tend to make most of their grants to institutions and large-scale projects, rather than to individuals. Of the roughly $11,500,000 a year (1953–54 average) given to the social sciences, for example, only $2,800,000 went to individual projects and fellowships.[15] "The majority of social scientists," writes William H. Whyte, Jr., "believe that the [major] foundations wish to support a) large projects, b) mapped in great detail, c) tailored to foundation interests."[16] Even if this image is somewhat distorted, "it summons up its own reality" by the very fact that it is given credence. In any case, the major foundations frankly admit that they are not equipped to handle too many individual requests. One of the Ford Foundation's earlier presidents, Rowan Gaither, Jr., said some years ago, "We plead guilty. We do try to take care of the individual but it's hard in a foundation of this size. It's very hard to support individuals without a staff of about one thousand so we prefer to rely upon other institutions to provide this service for us."[17] The Rockefeller and Carnegie executives make the same point, claiming that it often takes as much work to grant $5000 to an individual as to grant $500,000 to a university. In other words, most officials in the big foundations believe that, if their organizations were to deal mainly with individuals, they would have to enlarge their scales of bureaucratic organization beyond the administratively tolerable. It is true that the Guggenheim Foundation divides $1 million a year among 200 to 250 people with an apparatus consisting of the president, two assistants, nine office girls, and a group of volunteer advisers,[18] but such results are possible only because this foundation has a very simple structure. Once an organization has a complex bureaucratic apparatus, it needs a very large staff to take care of individual requests. Such organizations therefore find it more expedient to deal with other bureaucratic organizations or large-scale bureaucratically organized team projects.

The major foundations tend to define their areas of interest and to channel most of their funds into these areas. Once a decision has been made that substantial sums of money will be made available for mental-health research or international affairs, for example, applications unrelated to that field of interest are rejected because they "do not fit into the foundation's program." In such foundations, unsolicited appeals for funds prove acceptable only in a very small percentage of cases. Appeals to the Ford Foundation averaged about 300 a month during 1954 (exclusive of fellowship applications from graduate students, which often run to 100 a day). Yet in making grants of 60 million in 1953, the Foundation supported only about 168 projects (an average of fourteen a month), and many of them were continuations of previous projects or projects developed by the Foundation's staff or were payments to subcontracting organizations that the Foundation had previously set up. The Rockefeller Foundation reported the rejection of 3577 appeals for 1952.[19] Obviously, a great number of these appeals came from incompetents or even crackpots, but many others were rejected presumably because of their failure to fit into the current programs of the Foundation.

Finally, large foundations are likely to sympathize with projects that are clearly addressed to the solution of "practical problems" and tend to distrust applications for wide-ranging explorations that lack practical focus. Says one foundation official of trustees, "They are not too patient with the unknown. They feel relieved when they can vote for a good 'solid' problem, such as what to do about juvenile delinquency and things like that."[20] Another foundation official stated in an interview, "When it comes to social science: I got a letter from [a prominent official from another foundation] . . . He said, 'I've kept my foundation out of that. It's too full of crackpots and I can't tell them apart.' My criticism of social science is that . . . [it] is not enough interested in social engineering. In imitating the hard sciences the descriptive approach won't hold water . . . [I mean the attitude that] 'Well, if my next-door neighbor over here can spend the rest of his life describing the protein molecule, I'll do the same thing of society.' But society won't let you do that. You have to be willing to do something. The shelves are full of descriptive studies nobody reads."[21]

The typical large fund-granting organization is a bureaucratic enterprise, headed by elite men of affairs reflecting dominant American values and run by officials who act as middlemen between university administrators or heads of large-scale research projects and foundation trustees. This structure largely determines the major foundations' functions. It channels support for those scholarly or artistic enterprises that are most in tune with its structure and orientation, while deflecting support from others that do not fit them. Such selectivity is not always intended or recognized by the executives. Occasionally, a high foundation executive may warn potential recipients not to overstep the bounds of propriety. (A few years ago, Charles Dollard of the Carnegie Foundation warned sociologists that, "In their sometimes ruthless and cynical criticism of other elements in our culture, social scientists have often failed to reflect the anthropologist's discovery that a society, like a shirt, can split at the seams if it is handled too roughly; nor have they always factored out their own deep aggressions in analyzing and reporting their data on social and economic problems."[22]) Occasionally, a minor foundation may ask in its outline for filing applications, "Is the proposal diplomatically expedient? i.e., Will it be likely to arouse antagonisms, controversies or create splits and schisms?"[23] But, in the majority of cases, such manifest pressures to conform to prevailing orthodoxy are rare. Instead, more subtle pressures stemming from the backgrounds of key executives and trustees, as well as from the requirements of bureaucratic organizations, may help to shape the fund-granting policies of foundations and hence the impact of these foundations on intellectual life.

Although large foundations have upon occasion supported "unpopular" research—one thinks of the Ford Foundation in the years when it was headed by Robert M. Hutchins—they have, in the main, preferred the "safe" over the intellectually or politically venturesome. A foundation official said to William H. Whyte, Jr., of his trustees, "When you ask them to gamble on a relatively unknown man and a new idea, they may do so as a vote of confidence in you as an officer. But they'll do it only so many times. What you need is a vote of conviction in the *idea* of such ventures."[24]

Anyone scanning the yearly reports of the major foundations will become aware that their main support goes to projects unlikely to endanger the establishment consensus. Certain types of applicant are thus discouraged in advance. A social scientist who might be interested in studying the general impact of the military-industrial complex on the political orientations of Americans or a psychiatrist wishing to compare brainwashing techniques in China and the United States Marine Corps can hardly be blamed for deciding that it will not be worth his while to apply for grants from the major foundations. Occasionally, trustees of foundations have claimed that they would gladly support more venturesome, unorthodox, and intellectually exciting projects, but that such projects are simply not forthcoming. Such complaints seem beside the point. The major fund-granting foundations have projected an image within the academic community and among unattached intellectuals that frequently deters men of bold vision or unorthodox views from applying to them.

Trustees' decisions on what areas or fields of inquiry deserve support are naturally shaped by their perceptions of what appears problematic at any given time. These perceptions in turn are largely conditioned by the backgrounds and current positions of the perceivers. Trustees certainly tend to be men of good will animated by great public spirit, and they would be appalled at being accused of bias. But the sociologist is nevertheless impelled to note that their way of looking at the world and its problems is necessarily different from that of the man of knowledge. Social position influences perspectives. Trustees may therefore select areas for support that seem in their eyes to possess urgency, while intellectuals may assign those areas much lower priorities and may seek support instead for projects they consider more fundamental. Foundations, to be sure, have in the past supported "controversial" types of research, such as the work of Gunnar Myrdal on the American Negro and Alfred Kinsey on sexual behavior in America. But we should note that these problems were recognized within the establishment's enlightened elite, from which foundation trustees typically come. The study of other, and perhaps more fundamental, "problems," however, has not been undertaken, perhaps because elite opinion has not yet recognized them. As Everett C. Hughes has pointed out to me, the foundations seem prepared to support further studies on prejudice, but they are resistant to backing research on ways in which Negroes might break discrimination in housing and real estate.

Yet another reason for the relative timidity and conservatism of foundations when it comes to definitions of problem areas comes from their responsiveness to official governmental views of what is problematical. Given the backgrounds of trustees and their close relations with Washington policy-makers, this responsiveness is by no means surprising, but it further increases the tendency to make problem choices in terms of criteria other than those required by the sheer quest for knowledge. A few years ago, considerable funds were channeled into Russian studies; more recently Chinese and African studies have come in for heavy support. One ventures the guess that a proposed study of the Australian blackfellows is not likely to be greeted with the same enthusiasm as would a study of Laotian tribesmen.

A built-in tendency among large foundations to back the "practical" and "safe," in preference to the controversial, may stem in large part from the general orientations of its trustees, but these orientations do not account for tendencies to prefer large-scale projects over smaller-scale or individual ones. Here we must turn to the characteristics of foundation executives rather than to those of trustees.

Trustees do not have much contact with applicants for grants. Potential grantees are screened by executives, that is, by full-time professional foundation administrators. These men are usually recruited from the academy rather than from the world of affairs, and they are therefore less likely to share the trustees' inclinations toward backing the practical and the safe. But, apart from the fact that they are by and large unlikely to support applications they do not expect the trustees to accept, they are also influenced in their decisions by the positions they hold. Being themselves executives within bureaucratic structures, they tend to think in bureaucratic terms. A kind of elective affinity seems to have developed between foundation officials and large-scale research entrepreneurs in the academy. They speak the same language and have the same backgrounds. They have occasions for frequent contact of a formal and informal nature, and they therefore tend to evolve a high degree of consensus about what constitutes a project worthy of support. Research directors who have mastered the art of grantsmanship know the best ways to present problems to their opposites in the foundations. They know that a problem had best be stated without ambiguity or uncertainty, that the allocation of funds to various parts of the project had best be specified in detail, that manpower, man hours, and the necessary apparatus had best be worked out with maximum care. In other words, the chances of a proposal's being seriously considered by foundation officials are increased if it is presented so that it can easily be processed by the foundation executives to whom it is submitted. Furthermore, large-scale research organizations or teams within universities can often adjust their work to the problems currently emphasized by the foundations.

It is impossible to go into all the various activities that foundations support, nor is it possible to specify all the channels through which foundation funds flow. In view of the great variety, it would clearly be unjust to claim that individual intellectuals and scholars receive no support from the big foundations. Not only have individuals from time to time received "free grants" for general support of their work rather than for particular projects, but also a certain number of foundation grants to organizations like the Social Science Research Council and the American Council of Learned Societies or to universities is ultimately disbursed to particular individuals as personal grants or fellowships. It seems nevertheless that, because of the very structural requirements under which officials of large foundations operate, projects submitted by individuals have less chance for support than do those submitted by research organizations and teams. Similarly, projects that are sharply focused on clearly specified problems are likely to fare better than exploratory or wide-ranging work that lacks such concrete focus.

Intellectuals are usually not men who take easily to teamwork or organized and programed research. They therefore do not fare so well with the large foundations as they do with the latter's smaller and less bureaucratic counterparts. By and large it seems that large foundations have greatly helped experts and problem-oriented specialists, but they have been less successful in stimulating independent creativity and wide-ranging explorations. To the extent that they have contributed to the bureaucratization of the intellect, they have been instrumental in channeling into narrower pathways men capable of making broader intellectual contributions.

In contrast, the impact of smaller and less bureaucratic foundations and of such organizations as the Social Science Research Council and the American Council of Learned Societies, which give direct grants to individuals in their areas of interest, has been most positive for the country's intellectual life. Grants to unusually gifted individuals to enable them to study, travel, or accomplish creative work of their own have played a major part in enriching American culture. Even an informal perusal of the early works of novelists, poets, and scholars of various kinds discloses that a high proportion of them has benefited from the support of foundations like Guggenheim or Bollingen. One ventures to think that the greater cosmopolitan sophistication apparent in the younger generation of American intellectuals is, to a large extent, the result of opportunities provided for them by foundations to travel and study abroad. Foundation support of this kind performs functions similar to those once performed by individual patrons; it allows the recipients to escape at least temporarily from the pressures of the market place. And, unlike earlier patrons, foundations do not typically attempt to influence the fruits of the leisure thus gained.

It is sometimes claimed that the availability of foundation support has "softened" creative individuals and made them less hardy and venturesome than their forebears. I cannot find any evidence for this claim. Such reactions seem to stem from romantic nostalgia. There is little evidence that intellectuals of a past age who had to engage in desperate struggles for survival on Grub Street, on the fringes of the academy, or in Bohemia were therefore more creative and productive than are their modern descendants. The challenge of desperate circumstances may upon occasion bring forth a heightened creative response, but it may also, perhaps more often, lead to a stunting of creative potentialities. And would it not have been better, after all, if Raskolnikov, instead of murdering the old pawnbroker, had become a professor of Russian literature?

NOTES

1. Irving Howe, "Mass Society and Post-Modern Fiction," *A World More Attractive* (New York: Horizon Press, Inc., 1963), p. 77.

2. F. Emerson Andrews, *Philanthropic Foundations* (New York: Russell Sage Foundation, 1956), p. 11. This book is the standard work in the field.

3. Dwight Macdonald, *The Ford Foundation* (New York: Reynal & Company, Inc., 1956), p. 3.

4. E. C. Lindeman, *Wealth and Culture* (New York: Harcourt, Brace & World, Inc., 1936), p. 20.

5. Andrews, *op. cit.*, p. 263.

6. The Ford Foundation, *Annual Report, 1957*, p. 13.

7. *Ibid.*, p. 14.

8. *Cf.* the discussion of management legitimacy in an industrial setting in Peter F. Drucker, *The New Society* (New York: Harper & Row, Publishers, 1950), especially pp. 99ff.

9. Andrews, *op. cit.*, pp. 71–3.

10. The best discussion of foundations is to be found in two articles by William H. Whyte, Jr., in the October and November, 1955, issues of *Fortune*. In subsequent notes, they are referred to as Whyte I and Whyte II respectively.

11. Whyte I, p. 111.

12. Andrews, *op. cit.*, pp. 164–5.

13. *Ibid.*, p. 157.

14. *Ibid.*, p. 165.

15. Whyte II, p. 212.

16. *Ibid.*

17. *Ibid.*, p. 216.

18. *Ibid.*

19. Andrews, *op. cit.*, p. 171.

20. Whyte I, p. 260.

21. Quoted in Richard Colvard, "Risk Capital Philanthropy: The Ideological Defense of Innovation," in George K. Zollschan and Walter Hirsch, eds., *Explorations in Social Change* (Boston: Houghton Mifflin Company, 1964), p. 737.

22. Charles Dollard, "A Middleman Looks at Social Science," *American Sociological Review*, XV (February, 1950), No. 1, 18.

23. From the Louis W. and Maud Hill Family Foundation application form, reproduced in Andrews, *op. cit.*, p. 183.

24. Whyte I, p. 260.

Chapter 26

SUMMING UP

CULTURAL LIFE GENERALLY AND INTELLECTUAL LIFE in particular are characterized in America by an apparently contradictory process. They show a high degree of fragmentation and diversification concurrently with a tendency toward the integration of most cultural activities within a co-ordinated cultural establishment. These two tendencies will be discussed in sequence.

FRAGMENTATION AND DIVERSIFICATION

The fragmentation of American cultural and intellectual life seems to have two main interlocking determinants: geographical dispersion and functional diversification. Most high cultures of the past were located in geographical and spiritual centers. Whether the location was an agora, a piazza, or a coffeehouse district in the capital, it provided one vital center in which cultural producers and consumers could meet on equal footing and in which intellectuals had a chance to exchange ideas with their peers. Little of this opportunity exists in contemporary America. During the middle of the nineteenth century, Boston temporarily assumed a kind of cultural ascendancy over the rest of the country; before and after the First World War, Greenwich Village was the center of modernist

culture. But even then, these locations attracted only special types
of intellectual and special types of public, which were not representative of the whole. Currently, even those centers have declined.
At the present time, political life is centered in Washington, the
world of publishing and editing is in New York, Los Angeles remains the movie capital, the musical and art world is located in New
York, and the world of scholarship is dispersed throughout such
major university centers as Cambridge, Berkeley, and New Haven.[1]

The geographical fragmentation of cultural life is not conducive
to the emergence of a sense of cohesion among the intellectuals,
nor does it encourage the rise of a cohesive public for them. The
professors, scholars, and scientists gathered in a vast university center like Cambridge may have only minimal contact or even acquaintance with the New York intellectual *milieu* or with the cultured
minority audience that sustains it. One often encounters highly
cultivated Harvard or M.I.T. professors who are wholly ignorant
of the latest developments among New York intellectuals and who
have not heard the names of writers who are the latest vogue in
New York. To such men, the publication of a work by a Harvard
colleague may be more important than the emergence of a new star
in the New York literary firmament.[2] Similarly, the political elite
gravitating to Washington may have only the most tenuous connections with the world of New York intellectuals—the efforts of
the Kennedy administration to breach this gap were none too successful, and they are not likely to be continued under President
Johnson. Professionals and staff intellectuals, when they move to
Washington, tend to become ensconced in a world of their own and
to loosen their connections with the academic *milieux* from which
they originally came. Nor do Washington political decision-makers
typically constitute an appreciative audience for intellectuals. To be
sure, a Congressman nowadays is likely to meet many more staff
intellectuals in Washington than in the past, and he may have occasion to meet a few high-level editors and elite journalists, but he is
not tied to a cohesive intellectual community like those in Paris or
London.

The greater cohesiveness of French or English intellectual life
springs in part from the absence of geographical dispersion in these
countries. All the major cultural institutions of France and England
are located in or near the capital cities. London, for example, is
the center of radio and television as it is of publishing and is the
heart of the art and music worlds; political life is conducted almost

wholly in London, and high-level research and scholarship are centered in nearby Oxbridge. As a consequence, English intellectuals, whether they teach at Oxbridge or write for the BBC, whether they work for magazines or publishing houses or are unattached, have frequent occasion to meet one another. And such frequent interchange encourages the development of certain common assumptions and shared views that transcend institutional affiliations. Furthermore, the London intellectual community includes, in addition to creative intellectuals, a broad gamut of cultivated businessmen, lawyers, publishers, and members of Parliament, the majority of whom have common backgrounds as products of Oxbridge and elite "public schools."

Geographical dispersion shades into or overlaps with functional differentiation. In England, Richard Crossman, a former Oxford don and now a member of Parliament, moves freely among his former university associates, contributes to the dailies and weeklies, and is a well known commentator on TV. But such bridging of the boundaries between intellectual worlds is so uncommon in America that, when it occurs, it calls for special comment. When the prominent American historian Arthur Schlesinger, Jr., left Harvard for the White House, his move was widely discussed. But when, in addition, he began to write movie reviews for a New York magazine, the result was complete amazement. Similarly, the ability of a man like Max Lerner to move back and forth between the worlds of scholarship and journalism gives rise to a great deal of comment here, whereas it is taken for granted in England; nobody finds it strange that Denis W. Brogan makes distinguished contributions to both Oxbridge scholarship and London journalism.

One reason for the greater fragmentation of intellectual life in America, as compared to England, is that intellectual specialization has not yet progressed quite as far in England as here. There the ideal of the "scholar and gentleman" still lingers and constitutes a counterweight to a trend toward specialization that is nevertheless advancing rapidly. Countervailing forces to such specialization seem to be absent in America. For this reason, according to Talcott Parsons, "there are many different *kinds* of intellectuals. Therefore the 'intellectual community' tends to lose its solidarity in the sense that 'everyone knows everyone else.' Not only do fewer intellectuals know fewer nonintellectuals, like political figures, business people, etc., but they tend to know those intellectuals whose interests are relatively close to their own."[3] In other words, not only is there a minimum of intercourse between university intellectuals, for example, and inhabitants of the world of magazine editing, but also within the university itself there is little intercourse among scholars in different branches of study. Sociologists, for example, may have personal acquaintance with a high proportion of fellow sociologists distributed all over the United States, but they may hardly know many of their colleagues in other disciplines within their own universities and may be wholly unacquainted with New York intellectuals.

As we have seen earlier, there are relatively few unattached intellectuals in America today. Most now operate within the contexts of particular institutions—universities, research institutes, and the like. This attachment means, however, that, given the geographical dispersion of such institutions and the high degree of specialization and professionalization, the intellectuals functioning within them are separated from one another by geographical and social, as well as by departmental, barriers. Young people may begin with similar intellectual orientations and interests through exposure to the culture of the elite colleges. Yet, in the course of professionalization or in the course of becoming attached to various institutions, they separate, so that people who once read and discussed the same books and magazines may find themselves in the same university yet see one another rarely because they are in different departments.

There are, to be sure, certain countertrends to the fragmentation of intellectual life. Professionalization, for example, may not only separate intellectuals from one another; it may also help to overcome initial differences in ethnic and class backgrounds through common involvement in professional cultures. American intellectuals come from a wider variety of backgrounds than is the case in England. A high proportion of British intellectuals in the past were recruited from the descendants of merchant families, county parsons, dissenting ministers, and prosperous artisans. There was, in addition, a high rate of intermarriage among their offspring, so that it has been claimed, although with some exaggeration, that all British intellectuals are cousins.[4] In any case, by the early twentieth century, historians could point to a number of lineages that, over several generations, had produced leading intellectuals.[5] Exposure to "professional cultures" has, in contrast, been a leveling and de-differentiating factor in American society. Those who have moved up from ethnic ghettos and those born into the semipatrician cultures of Boston and Philadelphia typically relinquish much that is distinctive of their background and life styles when they become involved in a common professional culture. Professionalization, therefore, although it draws intellectuals apart, also helps to overcome initial ascribed differences.

As mentioned earlier, involvement with such broader public issues as those raised by the peace movements have helped to counteract tendencies toward specialization within the scientific community. The same may be said of the intellectual community in general. To the extent that the peace movement and the movement for racial equality have mobilized the political energies of intellectuals in recent years, they have broken down institutional and professional barriers. These movements have provided opportunities for the meeting of intellectuals, from diverse backgrounds and with otherwise diverse interests, who share concerns with political issues.

Finally, a word must be said about the role of "high-brow" magazines in bridging the gaps among various compartmentalized intellectual *milieux*. Here again comparison with England is instructive. At the risk of some exaggeration, we may argue that the British intellectual magazine expresses the interests of a relatively integrated intellectual community, whereas the American "high brow" magazine helps only to bridge the gaps among various fragments of the intellectual world. In England, *The Times Literary Supplement* is read by "everybody who is anybody," and it publishes every week general articles and reviews matched in the United States only by little magazines. Despite its wide circulation, it still manages to serve as a kind of family journal, expressing the fairly cohesive judgments of the members of the literary and scholarly establishments. It is interesting to note that, although its reviews and articles are unsigned, who wrote what is easily recognized in Oxbridge common rooms and London clubs.[6] In addition to the *T.L.S.*, a high proportion of British intellectuals is likely to read *The Listener, The Spectator, The New Statesman* and the Sunday literary columns of *The Observer* and *The Sunday Times*.

In contrast, the audience for magazines with intellectual pretensions is more fragmented in America, as the low circulation figures of high-level magazines show. A major *avant garde* literary magazine like *Partisan Review* prints only about 10,000 copies of each issue; *Commentary*, the leading monthly organ of New York liberalism, prints 35,000 copies; the circulation of *The New Republic* has recently risen considerably, but it still sells only around 100,000 copies. Even literary men in California usually do not read *Partisan*

Review, which appears to them too "New Yorkish." Few Harvard professors read *Commentary*. *The Yale Review* is hardly read beyond the Eastern Seaboard, and *The Chicago Review* has an almost exclusively local audience. Despite these restrictions in circulation, the "high brow" magazines still serve to overcome intellectual fragmentation to some extent. Professors who may not have much in common in terms of their professional involvements may still find a common topic of conversation in an article in *Commentary* or in a review in *The New York Review of Books*. Although none of these "high brow" media reaches more than a fraction of the total intellectual community, together they nevertheless serve to crisscross this community and therefore to help bind together men who would otherwise tend to withdraw into absorption with the specialized problems of their disciplines and professions. As the exchange of women from different kinship groups through marriage serves to bind a community closer together, so the exchange of ideas in unspecialized "high brow" magazines serves at least partially to counteract "incestuous" tendencies within fields of specialization.[7]

CONCENTRATION AND ABSORPTION

These tendencies toward fragmentation in the intellectual life of the United States are real enough, yet our picture would be very one-sided were we to overlook the concomitant strong tendencies toward both leveling and concentration of intellectual activities. Although these tendencies may be part of the process of differentiation itself, some constitute independent countervailing forces against the fragmentation that has been described.

We noted earlier the geographical dispersion of intellectuals, in terms of the spread of academic men to a number of university centers in different regions of the country. This dispersion has, as one consequence, the prevention of significant regional differences. Hence the decline in the pronounced regionalism in cultural and literary life that prevailed till about a generation ago. Half a century ago, for example, Chicago was the scene of the so-called Chicago renaissance. It was the birthplace of Margaret Anderson's *Little Review*, the home ground of such poets as Vachel Lindsay and Carl Sandburg and of a whole array of noteworthy novelists, journalists, social critics, and artists who endeavored to express in their work the characteristic qualities of the raw-boned life styles of the midwestern metropolis. Today there is no indigenous Chicago intellectual movement, and those intellectuals who remain there are found mainly at the University of Chicago, where they work on themes that are no different from those that preoccupy their fellow intellectuals at Berkeley and Harvard. The writers that the Midwest now produces are sucked into the New York megalopolis, or they are dispersed in universities throughout the rest of the country. Regional diversity has given way to the uniform concerns of a common cultural life. In similar ways, Boston, once the center of a distinctive New England culture, has become little more than an appendage of the New York cultural world. It still boasts a few distinguished publishing houses, but they seem little different in orientation and output from their New York counterparts. Boston no longer has its own literary community; the few literary figures still living there are either connected with the major universities and thus contribute to national rather than to regional culture, or they are New York "commuters," who happen to live in Boston or Cambridge. The prognosis for a distinctively southern intellectual community is similar. Even though there are still southern writers who attempt to wrestle with characteristically southern themes and problems, many in fact live in the North. The southern traditionalists who attempted to produce in the Thirties a coherent platform in favor of southern agrarianism and traditionalism have long since been dispersed; many of them now teach at Yale and other northern universities. And despite rumblings about the imminent appearance of a major San Francisco renaissance, the performance so far has hardly matched the promise. On the whole, we may venture to say that regional literary and artistic cultures have seen their day. Intellectuals are indeed dispersed over the whole expanse of the United States; they work mainly with national rather than with regional themes, and the variety of regional cultural centers that once existed has given way to the dominance of New York City in publishing, music, the theater, and the visual arts. For the first time in its history, the United States is developing a literary and artistic culture that is truly national and transcends regional settings.

In other types of intellectual activity, there are similar tendencies. At one time, for example, certain university centers cultivated characteristic approaches in the social sciences. In sociology, the so-called Chicago School, represented by men like Robert Park, George Herbert Mead, and Ellsworth Faris represented a distinct tendency in American sociology. Much of it centered around the idea that Chicago could be used as a kind of "sociological laboratory." Today the sociology department at the University of Chicago is staffed mainly by men trained elsewhere, whose interests are not specifically centered on Chicago problems. The last major figure of the Chicago School now teaches at Brandeis University in Massachusetts. And the same thing has happened in all parts of the academic world. The academic labor market is now a truly national market.

The decline in regional diversity of cultural life seems to be one of the consequences of increasing trends toward cultural centralization. In recent years, the haphazard and unco-ordinated growth of cultural life has been giving way to a measure of planning. More particularly, there now exists a much closer meshing between the wheels of government and those of academic centers. Much of it is determined by the rise of the United States to a position of world leadership and by the shift from uncontrolled free enterprise to a mixed economy in which the federal government has assumed a major part. Washington has assumed a political and economic importance in the life of the nation that it never possessed until the 1930s. It has become an enormous hub from which power radiates in all directions, a center of command from which major decisions, affecting all aspects of the social and economic life of the nation, flow continuously. In our days, wage levels are determined at least as much by decisions in Washington as by bargaining on a local basis. Economic trends are powerfully influenced by decisions of neo-Keynesian planners who prepare the budgets and decide the levels of interest rates. The flow of investment in industry responds to decisions by civilian planners and Pentagon experts. Examples could be multiplied. In any case, the American economy is now marked by a great deal of co-ordination and planning—haphazard and sporadic though it may be. Nor can private enterprise dispense with a degree of self-conscious planning and co-ordination. Industrial complexes like General Motors and United States Steel can no longer ignore the impact of their major decisions on their branches of industry as well as on the total economy. As a result, the huge bureaucracies, both public and private, need large numbers of planning and co-ordinating experts, economists, technicians, and engineers, not only to take care of their immediate problems but also to help fit their requirements and demands into the whole industrial-economic process. They need technical manpower of high quality for the sophisticated requirements of the modern economy.

When highly complicated machinery must be tended, there is need for a continuous flow of new recruits into the industrial economy. Hence the importance of education. The expansion in recent decades of educational opportunities is a response to the vastly increased needs for highly skilled manpower in American society. Not only is the university expected to provide new skilled manpower; its professors are also expected to lend their own skills. There is now an intimate interplay between the university and public, as well as private, bureaucracies, a continuous reciprocal flow and interchange between the universities and Washington, between private industry and the academy. Consultants, advisers, trouble shooters and committeemen now shuttle between Washington and Cambridge, between Berkeley and the Pentagon. Defense policy can no longer be the exclusive reserve of military men, Pentagon bureaucrats, and politicians. Academic advisers are being consulted about every phase of policy. Similarly, foreign policy can no longer be left to professional diplomats; a whole host of social scientists and other specialized advisers is now being consulted. This trend is visible in many other spheres. Experts of all varieties are needed at all nodal points of decision-making, and many are recruited from the academy. There has thus arisen a much closer co-ordination between the university and the locales of administrative decision-making than would have been conceivable earlier. While culturally Washington and Cambridge may not have much in common, in expertise they are dependent on each other—an interdependence that somewhat counteracts the intellectual segregation described earlier.

Nor is it only economists, scientists, and technologists who are now called upon by Washington decision-makers. Planning is not restricted to the economy and the polity. Mass communications, the arts, the whole of the nation's cultural life are affected. The federal government can no longer remain indifferent to a lack of foreign-language specialists—and it now subsidizes a great deal of foreign-language instruction. International competition in the arts is almost as important as competition in technology—and the State Department underwrites foreign tours for theater troupes, art exhibits, and the like. Increasingly, the powers that be are discovering that the arts are national assets that must be preserved and fostered as are other national resources.

These trends, which can be sketched here in only the briefest manner, have led to new types of co-ordination among institutions previously hardly connected and to continued exchange of top personnel among them. University administrators may now sit on top government advisory groups; professors may serve as consultants; foundation officials are called to fill policy-making positions in Washington, to do stints abroad for the diplomatic service and even the Central Intelligence Agency, or to serve in top advisory capacities. All three may eventually return to academic positions. Top lawyers from the elite law schools of the East and the major Wall Street corporation-law offices are now in high demand in Washington. They may serve sometimes on advisory or regulatory commissions and at other times in foreign posts, only to return finally to practicing law.

Some years ago T. S. Eliot revived the term "clerisy," originally coined by Coleridge. He had in mind a kind of grouping of scholars and artists who, far from being alienated like the *avant-garde*, would in fact be integrated into society and would assume certain directing functions within it. Coleridge saw in this clerisy a "third estate" of the realm, the members of which "were to be distributed throughout the country, so as not to leave even the smallest integral part or division without a resident guide, guardian and instructor . . ."[8] No such clerisy exists, of course, in the contemporary United States. Yet it may not be too fanciful to suggest that the lineaments of such a development become visible when one contemplates the gradual growth of a cultural establishment made up of elite lawyers, academicians, top-level government officials, technologists, and scientists who, through continual interchange, have begun to develop a common orientation and a common outlook. These developments then, to one degree or another, have begun to counteract the tendencies toward fragmentation discussed earlier. They will lead, should they eventually prevail, to the emergence of an official establishment culture that will inevitably be dominated by experts of various kinds but in which a few broad-gauged intellectuals may also find considerable scope for action.

ABSORPTION, ALIENATION, OR DETACHED CONCERN?

The trends sketched seem to point above all to an increasing absorption of intellectuals into various parts of the "establishment." If this process were to reach its logical conclusion, it would spell the end of intellectuals as recent history has known them. Intel-

lectuals have lived since the seventeenth century "in a permanent
tension between earthly power and the ideal."[9] This tension has
been, as a matter of fact, one of their major defining characteristics.
If the open world of the last few centuries gives way to a new
form of bureaucratic closure and integration and if the intellectuals
become fully absorbed within it, this will spell their progressive
obsolescence. It is precisely the fear of such a fate that animates
many younger intellectuals today. As Richard Hofstadter has written, "Many of the most spirited younger intellectuals are disturbed
above all by the fear that, as they are increasingly recognized,
incorporated, and used, they will begin merely to conform, and
will cease to be creative and critical and truly useful."[10] It is indeed
one of the paradoxes of recent developments that intellectuals, who
suffered in the past from the rejection by official society, now must
fear too ready acceptance.

It is questionable that the full integration of intellectuals is in
the best interests of American society. I should like to take my lead
from a memorable phrase coined by David Riesman, "Were not
intellectuals of more use to this country when they had less use for
it?"[11] I understand Mr. Riesman to mean that only those intellectuals who preserve a certain distance from their society can be of
maximum use to it. Only if intellectuals preserve critical intelligence, maintain some remoteness from day-to-day tasks, and cultivate concern with ultimate rather than with proximate values can
they serve society fully. Social arrangements that have become
habitual and totally patterned are subject to the blight of ritualism.
If attention is focused exclusively on habitual clues and if the customary is taken for granted, a social system is likely to ossify. A
system that is no longer challenged is no longer capable of creative
response. It may subsist, wedded to precedent and routine, but it is
no longer capable of renewal.[12] That is why there is continued need
for criticism and for men who have a peculiar vested interest in
detached and critical thought.

Were American society totally integrated and harmoniously
balanced, a call for the continued existence of critical intellectuals
would not amount to much more than a pious wish. But the fact
is that it is shot through with tensions and conflict and full of
internal contradictions. The tendencies toward closure are real
enough, but they are only tendencies. The United States remains a
pluralistic society in which contentions between interest groups,
classes, strata, and ethnic communities have by no means ceased,

although they may at times be more muted than they were in the past. It is precisely these pluralistic contentions that have fed the vitality of American democracy. As long as our society remains open and pluralistic, we may confidently predict that intellectuals still have vital roles to play. Full absorption into some future cultural establishment would emasculate intellectuals and turn them into glorified technicians. Yet the total alienation of America's intellectuals does not seem so desirable as has been claimed by some of the younger writers and artists.

Some of those who indulge in the loose talk about alienation that we often hear today appear to have forgotten, if they ever knew, that, for Hegel and Marx, alienation was a tragic condition and not a desirable state of affairs. Although certain romantic strains in nineteenth-century cultural history did indeed glorify retreat from the concerns of "*bourgeois* society," those who discussed alienation meant to describe a deeply unhappy state of affairs that they wished to see overcome.

A certain measure of alienation seems to be the perennial lot of the intellectual; he can never be "like other men." Criticism and detachment will always mark him, so that he will always be *in* the society without fully being *of* it. A certain degree of estrangement is the very precondition for playing the intellectual's role.[13] Yet this detachment may at the same time be based on a deeply felt commitment to the ideals and central values on which the society rests. We are likely to be especially critical of the things we love. Those with whom we are most deeply involved, our children for example, will also be most sharply criticized precisely because we expect so very much from them. Similarly, intellectuals may be highly critical of their society *because* they are intensely devoted to its main aspirations. And they will criticize its current performance in the light of these aspirations. They may attack what "is" in the name of an "ought" derived from the very value premises to which the society professes to adhere. In this sense, intellectuals may indeed be detached while they are at the same time deeply concerned. Such an attitude permits them to transcend both affective neutrality and blind involvement through *detached concern* with the fate of one's society and one's fellow men.[14]

Intellectuals of the future may indeed still play a major role in the United States—if they manage to avoid the twin temptations of total withdrawal and total integration. Such men in their devotion to the central values of the culture and to the critical functions that are their birthright will continue to be the "antennae of the race."

NOTES

1. The above paragraph owes much to Daniel Bell's fine "Les formes de l'expérience culturelle," *Communications* (Paris), No. 2, pp. 1–22.

2. "Intellectual circles in New York," writes Dwight Macdonald, "are neither concentric nor interlocking, and one knows 'personally' (the very expression suggests the American lack of contact) only a small proportion of the authors whose books and articles one reads . . . [in London] most literary parties of any size produce an M.P. or two, but in New York one could write about politics for years without seeing a Congressman except in the movies." See "Amateur Journalism," *Against the American Grain* (New York: Random House, Inc., 1962), pp. 350–1. Another commentator wrote recently in a similar vein, "If Socrates had lived in Scarsdale he'd probably never have known Aristophanes or Xenophon or Plato because the crowd of writers and intellectuals all lived in Greenwich Village and he wouldn't have known Pericles and Aphasia and that government bunch because they all lived in Washington." John Crosby in *The New York Herald Tribune*, November 18, 1960.

3. Talcott Parsons, "Comments on American Intellectuals," *Daedalus* (Summer, 1959), p. 494.

4. "What has astonished me, and what astonishes any American," wrote the American writer, Irving Kristol, after he had spent some time in England as an editor of *Encounter*, "is the extent to which almost *all* British intellectuals are cousins . . . In America it is otherwise, to put it mildly . . . It is by no means impossible that the senior editors of the *New Yorker* should never have met the senior editors of *Time*." Quoted in Dwight Macdonald, *op. cit.*, p. 350.

5. *Cf.* N. H. Annan, "The Intellectual Aristocracy," J. H. Plumb, ed., *Studies in Social History* (London: Longmans, Green & Co., Inc., 1955), pp. 243–87.

6. Macdonald, *op. cit.*, p. 351, writes, "*Time* writers don't sign their work because it isn't theirs; they are the middle workers on an assembly line . . . English anonymity doesn't imply collective fabrication; it is just that the family is so closely knit that 'everybody' knows who wrote last week's T. L. S. articles . . ."

7. It ought to be added that a number of middle-level mass-circulation magazines like *The New Yorker*, *The Atlantic*, and *Harper's* serve similar functions. Finally, *The New York Times Book Review*, which is read by "everybody" in American intellectual life, also mediates among various groups. Yet its lack of critical standards and the unevenness of its

reviews make it relatively insignificant as a medium for tying the intellectual community together.

8. *Cf.* Marcus Cunliffe, "The Intellectuals: The United States," *Encounter*, IV (May, 1955), No. 5, 23–33. The Coleridge quote is from his *Church and State*; see Raymond Williams, *Culture and Society* (New York: Columbia University Press, 1958), p. 64.

9. Edward Shils, "Ideology and Civility," *The Sewanee Review*, LXVI (1958), 459.

10. Richard Hofstadter, *Anti-intellectualism in American Life* (New York: Alfred A. Knopf, Inc., 1963), p. 393.

11. David Riesman, "Comments on American Intellectuals," *Daedalus* (Summer, 1959), p. 493.

12. *Cf.* Lewis A. Coser, "Social Conflict and the Theory of Social Change," *The British Journal of Sociology*, VIII (September, 1957), No. 3, 197–207.

13. *Cf.* Daniel Bell, "Comments on American Intellectuals," *Daedalus* (Summer, 1959), p. 497.

14. I have borrowed the term "detached concern" from Robert K. Merton and Renée Fox, who use it to characterize the physician's role. See Merton, *et al.*, *The Student Physician* (Cambridge, Mass.: Harvard University Press, 1957); and Merton and Elinor Barber, "Sociological Ambivalence," Edward Tiryakian, ed., *Sociological Theory, Values and Sociocultural Change* (New York: The Free Press, 1963), pp. 91–120.

Index

SUBJECT INDEX

NAME INDEX

Aaron, Daniel, 118n.
Abt, John, 182
Acheson, Dean, 339
Adams, John Quincy, 215
Addison, Joseph, 12, 21, 23, 39, 41
Agee, James, 334
Alembert Jean Le Rond d', 4, 13–5, 18n., 191, 228, 229, 231
Allen, Frederick Lewis, 243n.
Allen, Robert J., 25n.
Allen, Walter, 68, 68n.
Altick, Richard D., 49n.
Anderson, Margaret, 112, 114, 128–30, 132n., 354
Anderson, Sherwood, 112, 125, 129, 234
Andrews, F. Emerson, 347n., 348n.
Annan, R. H., 361n.
Aragon, Louis, 129
Arendt, Hannah, 270
Aristotle, 229
Arnold, Matthew, 254
Arnold, Thurman, 182
Aron, Raymond, 265
Asquith, Lord, 175
Astor, Lady, 237
Auden, W. H., 234, 235, 242n.

Bagehot, Walter, 77, 81n.
Bakunin, Mikhail, 159
Baldwin, James, 236, 270
Balfour, Arthur, 175
Ballantyne, James, 55
Ballantyne, John, 55
Balzac, Honoré de, 101
Barber, Bernard, 313n.
Barber, Elinor, 362n.
Barère, Bertrand de, 148
Barnes, Djuna, 125, 129
Barnes, Gilbert H., 225n.
Barrès, Maurice, 221
Barth, Hans, 204n.
Barzun, Jacques, 289, 293n.
Baudeau, Abbé, 227
Bauer, Alice, 262n.
Bauer, Raymond, 262n.

Bazard, Armand, 102, 103, 105, 106
Beer, John J., 312n.
Beljame, Alexandre, 25n., 48, 81n.
Bell, Daniel, 256, 258, 259, 262n., 265, 361n., 362n.
Belmont, Mrs. O. H. P., 126
Benchley, Robert, 328
Benda, Julien, vii, 218, 226n.
Benedict, Ruth, 270
Bennis, Warren, 287, 288, 293n.
Bentham, Jeremy, 74, 171, 173
Berelson, Bernard, 284, 285, 292n.
Berger, Bennett, 274n.
Berger, Peter L., 118n.
Bergson, Henri, 117, 129
Berkman, Alexander, 115
Berle, Adolf, 180
Bernal, J. D., 234, 238
Bertaut, Jules, 18
Bevan, Aneurin, 237
Bienkowski, Wladyslaw, 199, 202
Billaud-Varenne, Jacques-Nicolas, 148
Blanshard, Paul, 97n.
Blum, Léon, 135, 218, 219, 226n.
Bodenheim, Maxwell, 117
Bonald, Louis de, 220
Bonaparte, Napoleon, 101, 106, 136, 140–2, 189, 192, 194, 196
Boswell, James, 4
Bottomore, Thomas, 69n.
Boulanger, Georges Ernest, 217
Bourget, Paul, 221
Bourgin, Hubert, 226n.
Bourne, Randolph, 125
Bowring, John, 74, 80
Boyle, Robert, 28, 32
Brandeis, Louis D., 180, 181
Bridgman, Percy W., 299, 300, 312n.
Brinton, Crane, 154, 168n.
Brogan, Denis W., 351
Brombert, Victor, 222, 226n.
Brooks, John, 332, 335n.
Brooks, Van Wyck, 112
Brougham, Lord Henry Peter, 73
Broun, Heywood, 97n.

367